STINSON'S EARLY YEARS

1925 TO 1944

By John C. Swick

with

Elizabeth M. Flora-Swick

Wind Canyon Books
P.O. Box 7035
Stockton, CA 95267
702-503-7474

STINSON'S EARLY YEARS

1925 TO 1944

By John C. Swick

with

Elizabeth M. Flora-Swick

© Copyright 2022, John C. Swick

All rights reserved. No part of this book may be reproduced or transmitted in any form or by any means, electronic or mechanical, including photocopying, recording or by any information storage or retrieval system, except by a reviewer who may quote brief passages in a review to be printed in a magazine, newspaper or newsletter, without permission in writing from the publisher. The publisher takes no responsibility for use of materials in, nor for the factual accuracy of any portion of, this book.

ISBN: 978-1-891118-68-5

Published by
Wind Canyon Books
P.O. Box 7035
Stockton, California 95267
1-702-503-7474
e-mail: books@windcanyonbooks.com
www.windcanyonbooks.com

Editing and Layout by Steve Bogdan
Printed and manufactured in the United States of America by MK Printing, Inc., Santa Ana, California.

Cover Design: Wind Canyon Books © 2022

The title font is Rockwell, a slab serif typeface designed in 1934. In the late 1930s, the Stinson Aircraft Corporation used this font in aviation magazines to advertise their house publication *Stinson Plane News* (see page 74).

The cover colors mimic the aircraft paint scheme of the pictured 1935 Stinson SR-5E, NC14585, s/n 9322-A, owned by David Jackson. During both the 2020 and the 2022 Antique Airplane Association Inc. Blakesburg Fly-in, the author, John C. Swick, had the opportunity to fly this aircraft as pilot in command.

Cover photo and photo © Copyright 2022 by Sparky Barnes.

Dedication

To Toni Jaquith,
the First Lady of publishing,
for her patience and commitment.

Contents

About the Authors vi
Foreword vii
Introduction viii
Chapter 1 - 1919 to 1926: A Strong Beginning 1
Chapter 2 - The First Monoplane 9
Chapter 3 - 1928-1929: The Involvement of E. L. Cord 11
Chapter 4 - 1930: Creating an Airliner 18
Chapter 5 - 1931: A New Factory and a New Model 28
Chapter 6 - 1932: Death of a Salesman 34
Chapter 7 - 1933: The GB Braintrust Joins Stinson 39
Chapter 8 - 1934: Reliant - The Aircraft Standard of the World 48
Chapter 9 - 1935: The Talk of the Town 54
Chapter 10 - 1936: The Mighty Gull-Wing Has Arrived 62
Chapter 11 - 1937: Art and Engineering 71
Chapter 12 - 1938: The Rugged and Reliable SR-10 79
Chapter 13 - 1939: A Small-But-Mighty Aircraft 87
Chapter 14 - 1940-1943: The Last of the Giants 99
Chapter 15 - Production Numbers 1925-1945 109
Chapter 16 - Type Certificate Numbers 121
Chapter 17 - The Stinson *Greyhound* 142
Chapter 18 - The Early Airplanes 150

Chapter 19 - Edward Stinson: More Than a Pilot 156
Chapter 20 - Estelle: The Aviator's Wife 164
Chapter 21 - The 1928 Ford Reliability Tour 174
Chapter 22 - Record Attempts 180
Chapter 23 - The V-77 (AT-19) 191
Chapter 24 - Airmail Stinsons 197
Chapter 25 - Northwest Airlines' Stinsons 201
Chapter 26 - Diesel-Powered Stinsons 203
Chapter 27 - Albert H. Schramm: Pioneer Aviator and Stinson Test Pilot 208
Chapter 28 - Stinson Personnel 216
Chapter 29 - W. A. Wylam Technical Drawings 219
Bibliography 251
Index 253
Cover Captions and Credits 255

About the Authors

John C. Swick

John C. Swick is a published author and a foremost authority on Stinson history. John is an avid historian and has published four books: two books covering Luscombe Model 8 aircraft and two books covering Stinson 108 aircraft. Aviation books are not self-generating. John committed many hours of study, talent, grit, perseverance, creativity, investment, risk, and untold hours of work to bring this book to print.

Before retiring, John was a successful businessman, served on the Colorado Association of Commerce and Industry Blueprint for Colorado committee and received a gubernatorial appointment to the Colorado Commission on Higher Education. Currently, John serves as an elected representative on the Board of Directors for a regional hospital. John restores and drives vintage Ford F-150 pickup trucks. Flying has been his lifelong adventure. John soloed in a 1941 Aeronca Chief and at age 89, he is flying a 1946 BC12-D Taylorcraft.

Elizabeth M. Flora-Swick

Elizabeth M. Flora-Swick is an author-entrepreneur who loves antique aircraft. She earned a bachelor's degree in Child and Family Studies from John Brown University and a Master of Social Work from the University of Illinois at Urbana-Champaign.

Elizabeth currently studies theology at Global Awakening Theological Seminary where she plans to complete her doctorate. Much of her writing focuses on creating space for people with disabilities in theological discourse, but her passion for flying made *Stinson's Early Years* a natural opportunity for collaboration. While writing gives her wings in one capacity, she is happiest flying in a tail-dragger.

Foreword

Stinson...a name known throughout the annals of aviation history.

My long interest in the marque starts with a favorite memory from childhood. As a boy of nine I distinctly remember playing in the woods behind our home with my friends when a large black & red monoplane appeared overhead then circled our house before heading towards the Ottumwa airport. It was my father arriving home from the Hartford, CT area with the Air Power Museum's (APM) first aircraft, a 1931 Stinson Model S Junior. The airplane had been purchased from the original owner by APM co-founder J.G. "Jack" Lowe. As I recall my father saying, the purchase price was the princely sum of around $3500 1965 dollars.

Later that day when I got to see the airplane firsthand, the Model S Junior towered over the Curtiss Robin in the hangar next to it. Once Dad allowed me in the cockpit, it quickly replaced the Robin as my favorite. Instead of a control stick were control wheels that made it appear very ship-like, roll down windows and a cabin that could seat at least four, with a fold down arm rest in the bench rear seat...what luxury.

That initial encounter fired an interest in Stinson aircraft that extends to this day. Later in life I spent hours in the left seat of that Model S Junior hauling many rides here at Antique Airfield and taking the aircraft to various AAA Fly-ins throughout the Midwest. It still remains one of my all-time favorite aircraft, but especially my favorite Stinson.

With the experience of flying and working on straight-wings, gull-wings, tri-motors, 10s, L-5s, and 108s through the years, plus reading many of the volumes of what had been previously printed about Stinsons, I thought I knew a lot about them. That is until this volume you hold in your hands came along.

In reading through the twenty-nine total chapters of this volume, I have learned so much more I didn't know. I have especially enjoyed reading about the Stinson family's early days, the chapter on Eddie Stinson's wife Estelle, seeing test pilot Al Schramm's story come to light, as well as the stories of the various designs, record flights, and airmail Stinsons contained within.

But Wait !!...there's more as they say. There is a whole chapter devoted to the various model descriptions and production numbers, one devoted to the Stinson *Greyhound*, and another containing all the various W. A. Wylam drawings of Stinsons. Plus, the amount of newly come to light photos John has gathered together for this volume greatly enhances the story itself.

John, with the help of his co-author and granddaughter Elizabeth, have done a tremendous job in researching and gathering together what is a definitive history of Stinson.

As I pen this foreward on Father's Day 2022, I'm reminded of the interest in aviation history my father motivated in me, and obviously John has similarly done with his granddaughter. I hope a well-researched, documented, and well written book such as this will be used to help interest future generations in preserving the history, the legacy and the aircraft produced by Stinson, and keep them flying long into the future.

Brent L, Taylor
President Antique Airplane Association
Chairman Air Power Museum Inc.

Introduction

Writing this book on the early years of the Stinson Aircraft Company has been a labor of love and discovery. I conducted interviews and collected data and photographs as I revisited the historical events that shaped the United States from 1925 to 1944. I assembled that information into what I consider to be an accurate historical account. Preparing this book has been a wonderful and delightful experience. I hope that the reader will feel it was an informative trip into Stinson history.

After I wrote the manuscript, I persuaded my granddaughter, Elizabeth Marie Flora-Swick, to assist in editing the book. As she became familiar with the material, we collaborated on what direction and style the manuscript should take. She edited, rearranged, and sometimes rewrote sections. I thank Elizabeth for her scholarly contributions and compliment her superb editorial and writing skills. She is listed on the cover as co-author.

I am profoundly grateful to Robert L. Taylor, founder of the Antique Airplane Association (AAA) for his continuing support and advice during the years I attended the AAA/APM (Airpower Power Museum) invitational fly-in at the Antique Air Field in Blakesburg, Iowa.

AAA President, Brent Taylor, allowed me unfettered access to the hangers, flight lines, and aircrews at the Blakesburg fly-in. Following in his father's footsteps (who wrote the foreword for *Stinson's Golden Age*), Brent graciously agreed to write the foreword for this new book. Thank you, Brent—your cooperation has contributed to the quality of this work.

Sparky Barnes, aviation author, photographer, and pilot, photographed David Jackson's SR-5 Stinson that appears on the cover. Thank you, Sparky.

I thank Alan Abel and his late mother, Drina Welch Abel, for loaning me many Stinson photographs from their aviation photograph archives.

Passive inquiries during the writing of the book led me to many people whose information and contributions I would like to recognize:

Jody Jones, President of the International Stinson Club; Bruce Kitt, President of the Northwest Airlines Historical Center; Jerry Bergen, President of the American Aviation Historical Society; Carl Shemwell, a giant in the land of Stinson; Tammy Hendrickson, curator Custer County Historical Society; The Wayne Michigan Historical Society; Jim Hammond; Andy Heins; John Swander; John Collett; Ron James; Sharon Tinkler; Rosemary Duckworth; Dennis Parks; David Allen; William Byers; Mike Sellers; Raylene Canada; Lisa Droham; John Cilio; Stephen Black; Steve Sevier; Terry Wallace; Edward Martin; Harry Flint; Ron Shank; Madeline Marie Espinoza; Donna Witzel; Harry W. Smith; Chuck Doyle; Rick Rezabek; Kelly Swick; Mike Gretz; and Randy Phillips, who provided in-depth knowledge of the Reliant series.

Thanks to everyone else who shared his or her experiences with me. The book would not be as complete without your input. Apologizes to anyone I have forgotten.

My publisher, Wind Canyon Books, retained Steven P. Bogdan for the final editing, book layout, and graphic design. Steven Bogdan also has excellent research skills and was able to locate new documents related to Edward and Estelle Stinson and their aircraft, which had been released since the first draft of the manuscript. At my request, he rewrote chapters 17-19 to include the new material.

This book simply would not have been possible without the early support of George Jaquith, founder of Wind Canyon Books, and the support continued by his wife, Toni, after his death in 2019.

Flying has been a lifelong adventure for me. I soloed in a 1941 Aeronca Chief and have flown 24 different aircraft, including a 1931 Stinson Model S and a 1935 SR-5. I am currently flying a 1946 6BC-D Taylorcraft. In my opinion, there are only two kinds of historical aviation enthusiasts: those who own a Stinson and those who wish they did.

Throughout my career, I have been involved in some interesting entrepreneurial occupations. While in high school, I ran a shoeshine stand in a men's barbershop. Later, I was employed by a Jaguar Porsche dealership. A lifelong entrepreneur, at one time I owned a Ben Franklin department store and a Ben Franklin craft store. In 1963, I owned a half interest in a brothel located in Cheyenne, Wyoming. While this book worked its way through graphic design, I restored a 1965 Triumph Spitfire and was elected to a four-year term to our county hospital Board of Directors.

We make no representation or guarantee regarding the engineering accuracy of the data reflected and shown in the plans, specifications and drawings reproduced and presented in this history. I believe this history is true and complete to the best to my knowledge and ability, but we assume no liability for the use of this information, data, or specific details from this volume.

John C. Swick
Burlington, Colorado
2022

ERRATA

On the following pages the name Grangeville should read Granville:
Chapter 7, page 39 (twice)
Chapter 11, page 72
Chapter 16, page 129
Chapter 20, page 171
Chapter 28, page 216 (twice)

On the following pages the initials GB should read GeeBee:
Table of Contents, page iv
Chapter 7, page 39 (twice - chapter title and first paragraph)
Chapter 11, page 72
Chapter 20, page 171
Chapter 28, page 216 (twice)

Chapter 1
1919-1926: A Strong Beginning

The Stinson Detroiter prototype at Ford Airport in Dearborn, Michigan

Edward Stinson's dream was to manufacture aircraft, and in mid-1919 he perceived an opportunity in Dayton, Ohio to begin its fulfillment. An offer for consistent employment as a flight instructor, charter pilot and stunt pilot, plus the availability of a small hangar as a workshop was exactly what Stinson needed. That fall he formed the Stinson Aeroplane Company (then, and now, often mistakenly referred to as the Stinson Airplane Company). After marrying Estelle Judy on October 1, 1919, the Stinson family, which included Eddie's adopted son Raymond Judy, moved to Dayton.

After flying the new Lincoln Standard H. S. biplane, Stinson knew he could build a better aircraft. He immediately began to design and build what he considered to be the ideal airplane. In the Dayton area, there was a surplus of wrecked Curtiss Jenny parts available for minimal prices, including hinges, pulleys, control cables, bracing, instruments and wooden pieces. Stinson's new aircraft, the *Greyhound*, was made from these Curtiss Jenny parts. However, none of the airframe parts used in the *Greyhound* were interchangeable with the Jenny. Stinson participated in every stage of the *Greyhound's* development, but history does not tell us who else assisted in its construction other than his brother Jack.

Stinson flew the *Greyhound* to the New York Aeronautical Exposition in March 1920. The aircraft generated little attention because it did not offer substantial aeronautical or structural innovations. On the return flight to Dayton, the control stick broke off close to its attached point. But using the rudder and throttle, Stinson maintained some control over the aircraft and made what is best described as a controlled crash. He was not hurt, but from that time on, quality control in aircraft construction was very important to him. In later years, as a result of this experience, a sign hung in the Stinson factory stating "The pilot depends upon you." Stinson clearly had his priorities straight.

[The *Greyhound* biplane which Stinson flew from Dayton, Ohio to Mineola, New York is described further in the Stinson *Greyhound* chapter.]

In the spring of 1921, Stinson purchased a Junkers-Larsen JL-6 (a German Junkers F.13) which was sold as surplus property by the Air Mail Service. For the remainder of 1921 and into early 1922, Stinson's primary activities were flying his aircraft as a charter pilot, and testing experimental aircraft for other manufacturers. He made several extensive flights as pilot-in-command of a corporate executive aircraft. After flying many charters to and from Detroit, Stinson decided that an ideal base for his charter operations would be Packard Field in Detroit. So, in the summer of 1922, Stinson moved his family and his aircraft to Detroit and established the headquarters for his charter business. The business was successful and Stinson flew his aircraft and others to many points in the United States. He often flew charters for the *Detroit News*, delivering photos and stories, which enabled the *News* to print stories hours, and sometimes days, before the other Detroit newspapers. Through his charter business, Stinson developed friendships with many of Detroit's wealthy businessmen. One of these, William (Bill) A. Mara, would prove to be a vital connection for the development of Stinson's company.

Upon discharge from the U.S. Army, First Lieutenant Mara returned to his home in St. Louis and surveyed the central United States for the city with the best employment opportunities. In early 1919, he moved to Detroit, which had a much more aggressive business community than St. Louis. Mara was a handsome man with an excellent résumé, and he was quickly hired by the Detroit Board of Commerce. As a business promotion organizer, Mara had the opportunity to meet many of the influential men in Detroit's business community. Within the year, Harvey Campbell, Vice President of the Detroit Board of Commerce, invited Mara to be assistant secretary of the board and agreed to sponsor him as a member in the Detroit Athletic Club. Membership in the prestigious club would offer access to the leading business and political leaders of the city.

In early 1922 Mara arranged a charter flight out of Detroit to Buffalo, New York. At Packard Field he had his first opportunity to meet Eddie Stinson. Stinson, a flamboyant aviator, was dressed in the traditional pilot's apparel, while Mara, a polished businessman, wore a three-piece suit. They seemed to be complete opposites, but their business association would grow into a lifelong friendship. In mid-1922, Mara was appointed editor of the Board of Commerce's *Detroiter Magazine*. Stinson's Junkers-Larsen JL-6 was the only aircraft at the time that could fly a group of five businessmen and a pilot to points as far away as New York City, so Stinson's business was fre-

Northwest Airways Serial Number 1 with conventional landing gear. The Stinson-Detroiters were the first planes owned by Northwest and were first flown into Chicago in the fall of 1926.

quented by Mara and his associates. Mara wrote numerous stories on the safety of flying and featured Stinson's aircraft in many of the articles. After being featured in such a prestigious magazine, Stinson's charter business became quite successful.

In 1925, in an effort to promote aviation, four members of the Detroit Board of Commerce—Harvey Campbell, Bill Metzger, Lee Barnett and Bill Mara—decided to develop an airplane tour, which would depart from Detroit and visit 13 cities. Mara was selected to put the project together and, as expected, Eddie Stinson would fly the lead aircraft. The tour, with its 17 entries, departed Ford Airport September 28, 1925, and was given considerable attention in major newspapers throughout the eastern United States. After successfully visiting all 13 cities, the 17 aircraft returned to Detroit on Sunday, October 4. Mara was not a pilot, but flying to the 13 cities in advance of the tour and traveling with the tour itself opened his eyes to the tremendous opportunity of developing aviation activities in the United States.

A few weeks after the air tour, Eddie Stinson made an appointment to meet Bill Mara at his Detroit Board of Commerce office. For several months Stinson had been designing an aircraft using his kitchen table as a drafting board. Stinson presented a proposal to design and manufacture the most advanced four-place aircraft available at that time, which he had drawn on brown wrapping paper. Based on a biplane airframe, the Stinson design would include a fully-enclosed cabin, cabin heater, brakes, an electrical system, and an engine starter.

Stinson was confident that he could build a prototype aircraft for $25,000. Immediately recognizing the potential in Stinson's proposal, Mara asked permission from his boss, Harvey Campbell, to approach members of the Detroit Athletic Club and the Detroit Board of Commerce in an effort to raise the $25,000 needed for the aircraft. With this permission, Mara began the process of selling the opportunity to invest in this new type of aircraft. Several members of the Detroit Athletic Club and other businessman met with Mara and Stinson to organize the Stinson Airplane Syndicate with a capitalization of $25,000. Stinson was named President and Bill Mara, secretary-treasurer. Stinson convinced the group he could build his aircraft in three months' time.

Stinson was an accomplished pilot with a bold plan for the new aircraft, but had very limited engineering experience. So the first order of business was to establish an engineering department. After reviewing the proposed airplane's general layout, Professor Peter Altman of the University of Detroit Aeronautics Department understood the advanced design, and was hired as the chief engineer. On Altman's recommendation, a young engineer, William C. Naylor, was hired to complete the engineering team. As engineering work progressed and production drawings were produced, construction personnel were hired. The mechanic maintaining the Junkers, Ben B. Jacobson, was hired as shop superintendent. Two welders, several aircraft mechanics, and craftsmen filled out the manufacturing team.

The aircraft was completed well before the three-month target. The Stinson Detroiter was first flown Monday, January 25, 1926 from Selfridge Field with Eddie Stinson at the controls. The Detroiter's performance exceeded all expectations on cruise performance, rate of climb and landing qualities. This proved that the aircraft Stinson designed on his kitchen table was everything he projected. On Sunday, February 6, Stinson and Mara demonstrated the aircraft to a crowd of 500 people, including many of the investors. They were offered an opportunity to ride in the Detroiter, and everyone was impressed with the cabin heater and the landing brakes. During this demonstration however, an amusing event happened—the Detroiter accidentally taxied into a hot dog stand. It was after this incident, supposedly, that all Stinson aircraft were equipped with parking brakes. The Stinson Detroiter prototype Number 1 was essentially a handmade aircraft.

A meeting of the Stinson Airplane Syndicate investors was called for on Wednesday, May 5, 1926. Mara proposed to the investors to increase capitalization to $150,000. The capitalization goal was achieved that very night, and the name of the concern was changed to the Stinson Aircraft Corporation. After that, Mara immediately resigned his position with the Detroit Board of Commerce and devoted his management skills, time, and energy to develop the new corporation.

The Stinson Aircraft Corporation continued to thrive. With over $125,000 in the bank, the engineering team started to reengineer the Detroiter into a production aircraft. Stinson continued to fly charters in his Junkers and to demonstrate the Detroiter, while Mara handled sales and began the search for a manufacturing facility.

A member of the Detroit Athletic Club contacted Mara, wishing to sell a two-story, 50'x194' building in Northfield, Michigan. Although the internal structure of the building would not allow final assembly, the price was right, and Mara leased the building on a month-to-month basis. The decision was made to name the production aircraft the

SB-1 Detroiter with "SB" identifying it as Stinson's first production biplane.

Through June and July the Northfield warehouse was cleaned and the engineering department set up shop. A 200-hp Wright J4B aircraft engine was delivered and supplies of aircraft-grade wood, steel tubing, fabric, and dope were purchased. The production aircraft was completely redesigned with a wingspan increase of 2 feet, and the wing chord increased the length of the fuselage by over 10 inches. It was designed to carry four passengers and was equipped with an exhaust manifold-type cabin heater, electric engine starter, and parking brakes. It had a cruising speed of 100 mph.

In August 1926, the assembly of aircraft Number 1 began. It was built with production tooling. Mara leased a landing site near Northfield and constructed a small hangar for final assembly. Aircraft two, three, and four were nearly completed before the first flight on September 4. Starting with Serial Number 2, all aircraft were powered by a 9-cylinder 220-hp Wright J5C radial engine. Ten of these aircraft were delivered in 1926 with a total production run of 26 aircraft in 1926-1927. As the SB-1 was designed and manufactured prior to the Aeronautics Branch of the Department of Commerce establishing type certificate requirements, Approved Type Certificate Number 24 was granted retroactively after the end of production in January 1928. The formal description of Stinson's first aircraft was SB-1 Detroiter 4PCL ATC 24.

Mara soon realized there was an opportunity to sell aircraft to startup passenger and mail-carrier airlines. He sold three SB-1 Detroiters to Northwest Airlines, two to Wayco Air Service, two to Patrician Airways Limited in Canada, two to Alaska Airways, three to Florida Airways, and one to Purple Label Airways. Mara priced the aircraft to airlines purchasing two or more at $11,000, and individual aircraft at $11,500-$12,000 depending on the customer's requirements. Of the 26 SB-1 aircraft produced, 12 were purchased by startup airlines.

Seven years after Eddie's move to Dayton, the Stinson aircraft were selling well. Eddie's dream of manufacturing aircraft had become reality: Stinson had taken flight.

1935 photo of Eddie Stinson's Junkers-Larsen JL-6 (German Junkers F.13) used for his charter air service, powered by a 185-hp BMW IIIa engine. On December 29-30, 1921 Stinson and Lloyd Bertroud used this aircraft to break the world's endurance record by staying aloft for 26 hours, 19 minutes and 35 seconds.

CHAPTER 1

The San Diego Air & Space Museum Collection

National Stinson Club

NWA History Center Collection

Top and middle:

The Stinson Detroiter prototype first flew on Monday, January 25, 1926 from Selfridge Field with Eddie Stinson at the controls. It was powered by a Wright J-4 Whirlwind, 9-cylinder, 215-hp engine.

Bottom:

With changes, the prototype led to Stinson's first production aircraft: the SB-1. This ski-fitted example is Serial Number 1 - CAA license number C872, in Northwest Airways Inc. livery.

SB-1 prototype artwork from 1946 Stinson advertisements in aviation magazines. The top one illustrates the factory motto while the bottom one commemorates the incident that led to parking brakes.

The product of fifteen years' experience

EDWARD A. STINSON

THE unusual performance of the Stinson-Detroiter and the leadership it has achieved in airplane design are directly traceable to the fact that its design and construction are the result of 15 years' practical flying and designing experience.

Edward A. Stinson, the designer, has spent more time in the air than any aviator in the world. He first flew in 1911, in the early Wright planes. He also has the distinction of having taught more men to fly than any other flyer and for 10 years served as a test pilot, flying and testing all types of aircraft.

In producing the Stinson-Detroiter, Stinson had two ideas in mind: First, to build an airplane that was safer and easier to fly than any that had ever been built and, second, to build a machine that afforded its passengers complete comfort. In both features Stinson has succeeded. In fact the success of the Detroiter has been so marked that other manufacturers are now equipping their planes with brakes and other features proved practical in the Stinson-Detroiter. The Stinson-Detroiter plane is built by an organization that is financially sound—an organization that insists on building a strictly quality product that will stand up under continuous service and which will have a resale value.

Distinctive Features of the Stinson-Detroiter

1. Inherent stability is such that the Detroiter will fly itself. It will not spin or slip off on the wing even when the motor is throttled, the plane is placed in a stall, and both hands and feet are removed from controls.

2. The Detroiter has made a flight of 180 miles with pilot's hands off the controls.

3. Motor is equipped with a self-starter.

4. Individual brakes on the wheels make it possible to bring the Detroiter to a complete stop within 150 feet.

5. Ability, because of its brakes, to land in very short fields.

6. Combination of self-starter and brakes eliminate carrying a mechanic for starting and warming-up purposes.

7. Individual brakes permit easy handling on ground. The Detroiter will turn in its own length and taxi in a cross wind.

8. Luxurious enclosed cabin, heated in winter, carries four persons in comfort in most severe weather. Space is also provided for 300 pounds of mail or freight. Conversation may be carried on without effort while in flight.

9. Goggles and heavy fur-lined flying clothes are unnecessary in even the coldest weather.

10. Modern Wright "Whirlwind" radial air-cooled motor. Use of air-cooled motor eliminates 50 per cent of the forced landings due to frozen radiators, leaky water jackets and other plumbing troubles in water-cooled motors.

11. Large "pay load" carried makes the Detroiter an ideal machine for commercial operation.

12. Quick take-off from small fields.

13. Adjustable stabilizer.

14. Vertical fin set in line with propeller blast eliminates necessity of holding "right rudder."

15. Welded steel tube construction and metal ribs in wings.

16. Training plane factor of safety.

17. Designed in accordance with American Aeronautic Safety Code.

18. Unusual visibility.

19. Balanced rudder.

20. Light wing and horsepower loading.

21. Gravity feed gasoline system.

22. Seats may be removed if plane is used as a cargo carrier. Cabin contains 4.5 cubic yards of cargo space.

Specifications - Design and Performance

Type: *Four-passenger, enclosed cabin, heated.*

Length Overall: *28 feet, 10 inches.*

Height Overall: *10 feet, 7 inches.*

Chord: *(Both Wings) 63 inches.*

Stagger: *None.*

Airfoil: *Clark "Y."*

Angle of Incidence: *Upper wing, no degrees; Lower wings, no degrees.*

Sweepback: *None.*

Dihedral: *Upper wing, none; lower wing, 4 degrees.*

Angle of Ship when Resting on Ground: *14 degrees.*

Span: *35 feet, 10 inches.*

Span of Tail Plane: *12 feet.*

Area of Main Wings: *350 sq. feet, including ailerons.*

Weight: *(Empty) 1700 pounds.*

Useful Load: *1200 pounds.*

Total Load: *2900 pounds.*

Wing Loading: *8.28 lbs. per square foot.*

Power Loading: *14.5 lbs. per square foot.*

Fuel Capacity: *70 gallons.*

Flying Range: *500 miles.*

Speed: *Maximum, 125 m. p. h.; Cruising, 105 m. p. h.; Landing, 45 m. p. h.*

Rate of Climb: *(Initial) 800 feet per minute.*

Service Ceiling: *13,500 feet.*

Dimensions Inside of Cabin: *42 x 50 x 100 inches.*

Propeller: *Metal.*

Motor: *Wright "Whirlwind," 200 h. p., equipped with self-starter.*

PRINTED IN U.S.A. BY
EVANS-WINTER-HEBB, DETROIT

The Stinson-Detroiter for four passengers and baggage

Closed car comfort in the air

The Detroiter, with an enclosed cabin that resembles the interior of a fine coupe, is the last word in comfort. It is luxuriously upholstered and furnished with safe, luxuriant seats. The Detroiter carries four passengers comfortably and conveniently and in addition provides space for 300 pounds of baggage, mail or freight. The cabin is heated for winter flying, which means that it is never necessary for passengers to wear goggles or special flying suits. In the ordinary airplane passengers must communicate by written messages or by the sign language. In the Detroiter conversation may be carried on easily at all times. The cabin has such appointments as electric cigar lighter and ash receiver.

THE Stinson-Detroiter is a modern plane which carries four passengers, mail or freight, with the maximum degree of safety and speed at the minimum cost per mile.

It is designed for the every day use of individual owners, banks, trust companies, railroads, newspapers, air lines, air taxi lines, aerial photographers, and other commercial organizations.

The Detroiter is a fool-proof airplane. It actually flies itself. After flying the Detroiter recently, Major-General Sir Sefton Brancker, former Commander of the Royal Flying Corps and at present Director of Civil Aviation for the British Air Ministry, said: "The Detroiter is the most remarkable ship I have ever seen or flown. Brakes on the wheels, a self-starter, an enclosed and heated cabin and an inherent stability that is little short of marvelous. Really, the thing flies itself."

So perfectly is the Detroiter balanced that it has been flown from Cleveland to Detroit, a distance of 180 miles, with the pilot's hands completely free of the controls and merely with his feet on the rudder-bar. It can be placed in a stall with the motor throttled and while in this position hands and feet can be safely removed from the controls. The Detroiter will not go into a tail spin, or slip off on a wing. It immediately assumes a perfect gliding angle, no matter how rough the air, and descends in this gliding angle without attention from the pilot.

The Detroiter is built to endure and to render practical, dependable service. It has a training plane factor of safety, is of welded steel tube construction and uses metal ribs in the wings. Metal carries the load throughout. The plane is equipped with a modern 200-horsepower Wright "Whirlwind" motor which gives it a high speed of 125 miles per hour or a cruising speed of 105 miles per hour. And yet its landing speed is only 45 miles per hour.

And finally, the Stinson-Detroiter is equipped with individual brakes on each wheel, which permit it to be landed conveniently in very small fields—with brakes set and wheels sliding, if desired. Because of its running gear design, it cannot nose over on landing and tests have shown that it can be brought to a complete stop within 150 feet. The brakes, which operate in conjunction with a conventional type rudder-bar, also enable the pilot to steer the plane on the ground as easily as an automobile is handled. And the combination of brakes and self-starter make it unnecessary to carry an extra pilot or mechanic. There is no longer need to turn the propeller by hand. Just use the self-starter! No need to put blocks under the wheels while the motor is warming up. The pilot can hold the Detroiter with the brakes until he is ready to take off.

Convenient controls and full equipment

The Detroiter is equipped with dual control, making it ideal for instruction purposes and for pilot relief on long flights. Ample leg room and unusual comfort are provided for both pilot and forward passenger. The rear compartment is equally spacious. The lever at the left operates the adjustable stabilizer and may be thrown from "full on" to "full off," or set in any position instantly. Individual brakes are standard equipment. The attractive instrument board is fully equipped. The throttle and spark are in the center, close to either pilot. Note the rugged construction, dash light, cigar lighter, ash receiver, thermometer, and the individual brake pedals on the conventional type rudder-bar.

Advertising brochure for the SB-1 Stinson-Detroiter. The Detroiter boasted comfortable seating for up to four passengers, space for 300 pounds of luggage, and a quiet and heated cabin that featured such amenities as cigar lighters and ash trays.

The John C. Swick Collection

Chapter 2
The First Monoplane

SM-1 Detroiter in North American Airways livery, powered by a 220-hp Wright J-5C engine

Bellanca, Fairchild, and Ryan aircraft companies were building five- and six-place, high-wing biplanes when Mara realized that the era of the biplane had passed. In November 1926, Stinson, Mara, and the engineering team established the requirements for the next Stinson aircraft. The Stinson engineering team consisted of Professor Peter Altman and a bright young engineer, William C. Naylor. This new aircraft would be a high-wing monoplane powered by a 9-cylinder 220-hp Wright J-5C radial engine with a passenger compartment that could accommodate the pilot and four to five passengers. Using an Altman-designed airfoil, the wing would have a chord of 84", a wingspan of 45' 10" with a total wing area of 292 sq. ft. This would give the new aircraft exceptional payload capacity, which Mara knew would make it attractive to the small airlines and individual operators.

Responding to the prevalence of air commerce, Congress passed the Air Commerce Act of 1926. This act established the Aeronautics Branch of the Department of Commerce, which would regulate the aircraft industry. The first regulations were published in December 1926. All aircraft used for commercial purposes were to be registered and assigned an identification number by the Aeronautics Branch, and all pilots involved in interstate commerce were required to obtain a license. In January 1927, responding to Altman's request, the Aeronautics Branch sent the 45-page publication covering aeronautical regulations to the Stinson company. These rules set the standards for design, flight testing, and manufacturing from that time forward.

The flight testing standards required testing at design gross loads. To fulfill the first requirement, each aircraft had to complete a half-hour flight test at full-load capacity to determine aircraft stability. Requirement number two included a flight with a full load around two pylons 1,500 feet apart, making five successful figure eights at 1,000 feet without varying more than 200 feet in height. In the Structural Strength Requirements for Airworthiness, Stinson fell under Class II with over 2,500 to 4,500 Pounds. Fixed and movable control services were to be designed to withstand at least the following loads: ailerons and horizontal tail services would have to support 25 pounds per square foot, and vertical tail services would have to support 75% of the load required for horizontal tail services. The landing gear would be designed to carry a side load of 1.5 times the weight of the airplane, acting in either direction and applied to one wheel at its axle. The landing gear also had to withstand a fall of the fully loaded airplane with its thrust line horizontal, from a height drop of 22 inches. Closed-cabin airplanes, carrying passengers for hire or reward, could not have fewer than two exits affording maximum ease of operation, and were required to have a reserve fuel supply tank or a reliable apparatus for indicating to the pilot a depletion of the fuel supply. Propellers had to be balanced, without open glue joints, and have a ground clearance of at least 6 inches when the plane was in the horizontal position.

With the regulations in hand, the engineering and drafting department laid out the design of the new aircraft. Altman applied for an experimental registration number and was issued NX1524. At Altman's request, the Aeronautics Branch personnel visited the Stinson plant in March 1927 and gave temporary approval for production to start, giving formal approval at a later date. Production began in April with Stinson's first Approved Type Certificate (ATC) Number 16 issued in November 1927. The formal designation for this aircraft was SM-1 Detroiter 6PCLM. The SM-1, which could carry six people, was Stinson's first monoplane. 31 aircraft were delivered in 1927, 53 in 1928, and 26 of a 300-hp version in 1929, with a total production run of 110 aircraft. The factory price for the SM-1 Detroiter powered by a 220-hp Wright J-5C engine was $12,000-$12,500, and the 300-hp Wright J-6 version was $13,500. There were 13 individual ATC numbers assigned to the SM-1 Detroiter and they are described in detail in the type certificate section, Chapter 16.

There were over 20 attempts to set records flying the SM series Stinson Detroiter. With the exception of the *Pilot Radio* and SM-4 *Sally Sovereign*, which used a 300-hp Wright Whirlwind engine, all other aircraft were powered by a 9-cylinder 220-hp Wright Whirlwind J-5 engine. Of the over 20 attempts, six were abandoned because of engine failure. These are described in detail in the Record Attempts section, Chapter 22.

Soon after the production of the SM-1 Detroiter, Altman asked to leave Stinson as a nearly full-time engineer and continue on in a consulting capacity. Kenneth M. Roman was hired as chief engineer and William C. Naylor continued with him in the department. Randolph Page, a former airmail pilot, was placed in charge of flight testing and development.

The Stinson Aircraft Corporation was profitable, but sales were limited to the ability of its two salesmen, Stinson and Mara. At that time, other successful aviation companies were developing nationwide dealer organizations. Mara examined production cost numbers and determined that if production could be increased, Stinson could offer its dealers a 20% discount and still remain profitable. The dealer organization would start with the introduction of the SM-2 Junior in 1928. With a motivated dealer organization, the production potential was almost unlimited.

The opportunity to become a Stinson dealer was welcomed enthusiastically by businesses involved in air commerce, and in 1928, Mara began setting up the company's nation-wide dealer organization. Some were direct factory dealers, while others wished to be distributors who would establish their own sub-dealerships and cover a wider territory.

The Stinson SM-2 Junior received ATC number 48 in August 1928. Occasionally described as the Detroiter Junior, it was the first aircraft to use the new, 7-cylinder 110-hp Warner Scarab engine. This was also Stinson's first use of out-rigger landing gear using oleo struts. Stinson delivered 53 SM-1 Detroiters and 42 SM-2 Junior aircraft in 1928.

The SM-1 Detroiter continued in production powered by the 9-cylinder 300-hp Wright J6 engine. 26 of this model were built with an advertised price of $13,500. Eight different models of the SM-2 were manufactured in 1929. These aircraft were powered by Wright J-5 and J-6 engines, and Kinner K-5 and K-6 engines. There was a total production run of 98 SM-2 aircraft with an advertised price of $8,500-$13,500 depending on the type of engine used. Aircraft production was increasing each year, with 10 in 1926, 50 in 1927, 63 in 1928, and 128 in 1929. Simultaneous with increasing production, the Stinson Aircraft Corporation was receiving far more attention from the American business world. This attention would prove pivotal for the company's future.

Stinson SM-1 Detroiter flown by Orin Welch (right) of Portland, Indiana

Chapter 3
1928-1929: The Involvement of E. L. Cord

SM-2 AB Junior with 165-hp Wright J-6

In 1926, Bill Mara recognized the potential of selling Stinson aircraft to fledgling airline companies, so he directed his energy and aggressive sales techniques toward that end. Serving both as a corporate officer and a commission salesman, Mara's goal was to pick up an aircraft fresh off the assembly line and deliver it to a customer before the next one was completed. Mara developed his prospect list from the prominent businessmen in the automotive and financial world, and in April 1927, he delivered a SM-1 Detroiter to Errett Lobbman Cord. E. L. Cord was in the early stages of building his business empire, and he realized there was an opportunity to move into the aircraft manufacturing and airline businesses. Mara shared with Cord that there was immense opportunity in aircraft manufacturing, but Stinson did not have the capitalization or manufacturing facilities to develop into a major player in the industry. Cord suggested they meet in 30 days and he would share his thoughts concerning a Stinson expansion plan.

In their next meeting, Cord proposed a plan that would allow Stinson to mature as a manufacturer and provide an opportunity for the Cord Corporation to expand into the aircraft industry. There were four parts to his plan:

1. Stinson, under Mara's direction, would find a new location and build a factory large enough to assemble airline transportation aircraft.
2. Lycoming would soon come under Cord ownership. It had the capabilities of developing an aircraft engine suitable for the Stinson line of aircraft.
3. Stinson would develop a competitive airliner aircraft.
4. Once these goals were completed, the Cord Corporation would make an offer to purchase Stinson stock at a very attractive price.

Upon returning to Detroit, Mara convened a meeting of the Stinson Aircraft Corporation stockholders at the Detroit Athletic Club. Mara knew that the Detroit Wayne Industrial Airport was under development and convinced the stockholders that the opportunity to grow the Stinson Company was almost unlimited and the need for expansion imminent. The Stinson stockholders represented a vast cross-section of the business, financial, and political leadership in the Detroit area. Thus, an executive committee was formed to utilize their many interests. Under Mara's leadership, the stockholders would develop a financing plan, secure a site for the factory, hire an architect, and retain the services of a general contractor.

In July 1928, with excellent leadership from the executive committee, a site at the Detroit Wayne Industrial Airport was purchased. Adequate financing for construction had been secured and an architect to design the new factory was hired. The groundbreaking ceremony was held on November 7, 1928. The 380 ft. long, 180 ft. wide, 68,400 sq. ft. factory was completed in March 1929 and all manufacturing facilities were transferred from Northfield by the end of April.

In his travels selling the big 6-place Stinson SM-1, Eddie Stinson realized there was a great opportunity for a smaller aircraft designed for the owner pilot. Eddie sat down with Stinson engineer William Naylor and laid out his ideas for the design of a smaller 3 to 4 place aircraft. Naylor had some concern about the availability of a small power plant. Eddie was aware that an experimental "Travel Air" biplane was flying with a 7-cylinder "Warner Scarab" engine with a 110-hp rating.

Eddie further suggested they change the landing gear to the out-rigger type. This was the first Stinson to use this type of landing gear and it was quickly adapted to the larger Detroiter. The SM-2, following the basic Detroiter design, became known as the Stinson "Junior." The SM-2 received ATC Number 48 in August 1928. Powered by the 110-hp Warner Scarab engine, it retailed for $6,950.

After moving into the new, larger factory and increasing the engineering staff, an experimental department was developed to expand the Stinson model line. With the proliferation of models, Stinson began the numbers game. The SM-3, SM-4, and SM-5 were one-of-a-kind experimental aircraft (described in the type certificate section, Chapter 16). The SM-6 Detroiter, an 8-place 450-hp Pratt & Whitney powered aircraft was designed for the small airline and for flying freight into remote areas. 13 were manufactured in 1929 with a price of $18,000 each.

On a monthly basis, Cord was briefed on Stinson developments and in June 1928, Mara became an employee of the Cord Corporation, but still retained his employment with Stinson. Stin-

Texaco #3 was a SM-2 AC Junior powered by a 225-hp Wright J6-7 engine.

CHAPTER 3

Corman 3000 tri-motor ATC 2-140 powered by three 220-hp Wright J-5 engines

son's goal was to develop a small airliner that could be manufactured in the new facility. Additionally, Mara was instructed to develop an experimental aircraft program totally separate from Stinson. Given essentially a blank check, Mara hired an experienced aircraft engineer and designer, Horace E. Weihmiller, and leased a hangar in Dayton, Ohio that included facilities for the engineering and construction of large aircraft. Mara was aware that the new Lycoming engines were quite small, and in order to develop a 10-place airliner, the airframe needed to be constructed around three engines. The experimental department was launched in July 1928. As the design developed, the project became an eight-passenger transport. Prototype number one was used for structural testing, and the certification process began in January 1929. In August, prototype number two was nearing flight status, and Cord decided to form an aircraft corporation.

In late June of 1929 Eddie announced that he had agreed to sell to Bendix Aviation his patents for the Stinson brake control system. Ever since the Bendix Corporation was formed in 1924, they had been aggressively pursuing and purchasing patents for automotive and aviation brakes and braking systems. By the time Bendix Aviation was created in 1929, they held every major patent in the field except for the most significant one. The Stinson method was unique in the industry in that the brake and rudder control system allowed for the use of either the rudder or brake alone, or for the operation of one brake independent of the other. Bendix insistently lobbied Stinson to acquire his patent rights, and Eddie finally sold them outright for cash; a license to continue to manufacture the brake control himself; and the right to incorporate other Bendix patents into the Stinson design.

The Corman Aircraft Corporation was formed in August 1929. The name "Corman" was developed from the first three letters from Cord and the first three letters from Manning. Lou Manning had participated with Cord in earlier acquisitions, and was funding the Dayton, Ohio operation. Horace E. Weihmiller was elected president, a Mr. Rivers (first name unknown) was elected vice president, and Bill Mara was appointed chief operating officer. Prototype number two was completed in August and flight testing started immediately. Named the Corman 3000, this aircraft was powered by three 220-hp Wright J-5 engines as the Lycoming engines were not yet available.

During flight testing with a full capacity weight aboard equaling ten people, pilot Jack Kelly had maintained an altitude of over 15,000 for 30 minutes. The aircraft would fly considerably over 120 miles-per-hour on three engines, over 100 on two engines, and could maintain 80 miles-per-hour on just one engine, while maneuvering without losing altitude. Flying with just one of the side engines operating, the Corman 3000 could be trimmed to keep a straight and level course under full load without any input from the controls. The ability the tri-motor had to maintain an altitude indefinitely on just one its engines was said to be an aviation first. This design was granted ATC 2-140 tri-motor as a 7PCLM on October 9, 1929

The first public showing of the airliner was at

the 1929 National Air Tour for the Edsel Ford Trophy, the event Eddie Stinson won in 1927 in his SM-1. The latest Tour attracted a variety of aircraft from a diminutive 1,650-pound gross weight, 60-hp Gypsy Moth (flown by Frances Harrell, one of three women competing), to the behemoth 16,300-pound gross weight Curtiss Condor 18 featuring a pair of geared 600-hp Curtiss Conqueror V-12 engines. The Condor was the only twin-engined aircraft competing in the Tour, while the fabric covered Corman would join two metal-clad Ford tri-motors.

While no Stinsons were entered in the 1929 race, the Corman was entered as an official competitor by the Corman Aircraft Corporation. The company announced that they were negotiating with the U.S. Army Air Service to see if Lieutenant Alfred F. Hegenberger could be released from duty from October 5th through the 21st to fly the aircraft in the Tour. Lt. Hegenberger, along with Lt. Lester J. Maitland, won the Mackay Trophy for making the first non-stop flight from San Francisco to Honolulu June 28 - 29, 1927 in the *Bird of Paradise*, an Atlantic-Fokker C-2.

The news accounts of the day carried the Corman on the flight roster right up the starting date, and some speculated that it was the dark horse in the race. Unfortunately, the deadline for the participating aircraft to obtain a Department of Commerce Approved Type Certificate was the first day of October, and the Corman did not receive one until the 9th of October. For 1929 the Tour officials were strictly enforcing the rule that competing aircraft must have an ATC before the start of the race – a rule that they had been lax about imposing in the past. Therefore, the Corman 3000 was one of five entered aircraft that were ruled ineligible when the deadline expired. Four more entered aircraft, including three autogyros entered by the Pitcairn-Cierva Autogiro Company, had already been withdrawn when it was apparent that they would not receive their ATCs in time. However, with Jack Kelly in the pilot's seat, the Corman 3000 still flew the entire Tour course as a "non-contesting official plane" by carrying Thomas Harold "Doc" Kincade, the long-time engine expert for the Wright Aeronautical Corporation. At least 10 other "non-contesting official planes" (including 3 more Ford tri-motors), along with over a dozen "non-contesting unofficial planes" accompanied the National Air Tour.

Consolidating his many assets, Cord formed

SM-2 AB Junior powered by a 165-hp Wright J-6, showing out-rigger style landing gear

CHAPTER 3

the Cord Holding Company on September 4, 1929. This gave him an immense source of new investment capital. In mid-September, he approached the Stinson board and proposed purchasing 60% of Stinson stock. One week later, he presented his offer to a meeting of Stinson stockholders. They listened to the proposal, but were reluctant to accept Cord's offer, and asked him to revise his offer to make it more attractive.

Nevertheless, Cord knew the Stinson acquisition was imminent, and in a meeting with Mara and Manning, the decision was made to close the Dayton, Ohio plant in preparation for moving the entire operation to the Wayne, Michigan factory. On October 19, 1929, Mara flew to Dayton and summarily discharged all employees and locked up the manufacturing facility.

The Cord Corporation now included the Auburn Automobile Company, Duesenberg, Inc., Limousine Body Company, Lycoming Manufacturing Company, Columbia Axle Company, Spencer Heater Company, Expando Body Company, Auto-Prime Pump Company, L. G. S. Manufacturing, Saf-T-Cab Company, Central Manufacturing Company, and the not yet divested Corman Aircraft Corporation.

In press release dated October 22 the man in charge of Auburn operations at Connersville, Ellis W. Ryan, a vice-president and director of Auburn and a director of Corman, announced the addition of Stinson to the Cord empire. He further revealed that "Doc" Kincade had left the Wright company to take "charge of all experiment and construction work of the new Lycoming motor." In an expanded article *The Waterloo Press* on that date noted that the Auburn Automobile Company, in addition to the non-flying Corman prototype, had a fleet of five aircraft including "a tri-motor Corman; a six-place Stinson Detroiter, with a Wright J-5 motor; two Stinson Juniors, one of which has a Lycoming power plant; and a Travel Air biplane which also is equipped with a Cord-built Lycoming motor." The paper also sought out an interview with Jack Kelly, who they described as the chief pilot of the "Auburn aviation organization." The article noted that Kelly "refused to a statement about the Corman Airliner, except to say that 'she's a great ship.'" Kelly did speak at length about the Lycoming engines, noting that he flew the "Travel Air biplane on an 18-hour test flight into Canada, and over Pennsylvania and New York, using one of the new power plants, and the performance gained on the trip was unusual."

On October 29, 1929, on what is known as Black Tuesday, the stock market crashed. Although 1929 had been an excellent year for Stinson, the mood of the stockholders changed drastically. Cord was invited back to Detroit and made what appeared to the stockholders to be a very reasonable offer. This offer was "to purchase 60% of Stinson stock (on record as of November 1, 1929) at $17.50 per share on a cash basis, or two shares of Cord Corporation stock for one share of Stinson stock." By November 11, however, the Cord Corporation held 99% of the Stinson stock. All assets were transferred to the Wayne, Michigan factory in December. E. L. Cord visited the factory Wednesday, November 15. His first order of business was to reorganize the Board of Directors and approve other management personnel.

The new Stinson Aircraft Corporation Board of Directors was as follows:

> E. L. Cord, Chairman, Board of Directors
> Edward A. Stinson, President
> Harvey J. Campbell, Vice President
> William A. Mara, Secretary
> Kenneth M. Roman, Chief Engineer
> William C. Naylor, Engineer
> Bruce A. Raun, Factory Superintendent

Cord could now provide Stinson with the capital and equipment needed for the company to become a key player in the aircraft industry. Through the organization of the Cord Corporation and the purchase of Auburn Automobile Company stock, Cord had acquired 100% control of Lycoming Manufacturing Company. Immediately Lycoming was commissioned to develop an aircraft engine in the 220 to 250-hp range. These engines were to be certified and move into limited production for aircraft use by 1931.

As the year 1929 drew to a close, a small article buried on page 13 of the Saturday, December 21 issue of *The Dayton Herald* stated "Test flight of the third Corman tri-motor airplane, constructed under the direction of H. E. Weihmiller on Stewart street by Auburn automobile interests, was made Friday at the Dayton airport." No other periodical published a similar story. In reality the now-closed factory had produced just one flying example of the Corman 3000 airliner, and it was headed to Florida for more testing in better weather. Soon a decision on its fate would be made and a new Stinson would emerge. A connection with Cord that had started through the ingenuity of Mara's sales strategies ended with a Stinson Aircraft Corporation that now had the potential to soar.

THE NEW STINSON-DETROITER JUNIOR

FOUR PASSENGER CABIN MONOPLANE

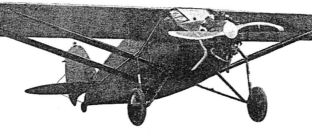

A MODERATELY priced, good airplane, roomy, fully equipped, powered by the Warner Scarab 120 h.p. engine.

The Stinson Junior, received with unbounded enthusiasm at the All-American Aircraft Show, has the same high standards of design and construction which give Stinson ships such a high degree of efficiency and performance.

The Stinson Junior Monoplane is ideal for business concerns and for private and commercial operators. Flying schools should investigate the Junior.

We are prepared to furnish operating costs and surveys to individuals or organizations who desire to purchase aircraft for personal or commercial uses.

Complete Information Sent on Request

STINSON AIRCRAFT CORPORATION - NORTHVILLE, MICHIGAN

Say you saw it in AERO DIGEST

Top: Corman 3000 tri-motor ATC 2-140 powered by three 220-hp Wright J-5 engines in flight
Bottom: SM-1 Detroiter powered by a 220-hp Wright J-5C engine

CHAPTER 4
1930: Creating an Airliner

Stinson SM-6000-B NC11175 (c/n 5025) in the livery of its second owner Chicago & Southern Air Lines

E. L. Cord and his entourage arrived at the factory Wednesday, January 8. The first order of business was to again reorganize the Board of Directors and approve other management personnel. With E. L. Cord holding 99% of the Stinson Corporation stock, the organizational meeting went very smoothly.

The January 1930 Stinson Corporation management team:

- E. L. Cord, Chairman, Board of Directors
- E. A. Stinson, President and Director
- W. A. Mara, Vice President and Director
- R. S. Pruitt, Secretary and Director
- W. R. Deerfield, Treasurer
- Kenneth M. Roman, Chief Engineer
- William C. Naylor, Engineer
- Professor Peter Altman, Consulting Engineer
- Randolph Page, Chief Test Pilot
- Bruce A. Raun, Factory Superintendent
- Estelle Stinson, Office Manager

The next item of business was deciding what to do about the Corman-3000. The aircraft E. L. Cord envisioned was one that could be marketed to the airlines; one that carried 10-passengers in addition to the pilot. Cord felt that the concept of a three-engine airliner using Lycoming engines had great potential. The Board of Directors had put together a list, which they shared with prospective clients and the press, that identified existing trimotor airliners, whether currently available, or in prototype form, including their own potential offerings. The list included aircraft model; engines used; passenger seating capacity; and price.

Existing, Prototype, and Proposed Trimotor Airliners for 1930

Plane	Motors	Seats	Price
Partrician	Cyclones	22	$85,000
Junkers G-24	Junkers	12	79,000
Boeing 80-A	Hornets	20	75,000
Fokker F-10	Wasps	14	67,500
Ford	Wasps	16	55,000
Pathfinder	Wasps	12	52,000
Ford	Whirlwinds	14	42,000
Emsco	Challengers	8	30,000
Corman	Whirlwinds	10	27,500
Corman	Lycomings	8	20,000
Kreutzer	LeBlond 90s	6	17,950

Ultimately, the production 10-passenger Stinson trimotor would sell for $18,000, fifty dollars less than the 4-passenger Kreutzer K-2 Air Coach. By now however, Stinson's engineering team

CHAPTER 4

Tampa Daily Times *photo of the Corman 3000 at the Tampa Airport*

had had an opportunity to examine the 7-passenger Corman and found it inadequate in many ways. To manufacture a 10-passenger airliner powered by three Lycomings, this aircraft would have to be totally redesigned in order to be marketable. Cord directed a management and engineering group to immediately start the redesign process. The new aircraft would be designated the Stinson Airliner SM-6000, with the goal of obtaining ATC approval and entering production in July 1930. The Corman 3000 was declared surplus.

The Fate of the Corman 3000

Even as that decision was being made in Wayne, the airplane itself was at the new Grand Central Airport on Weedon's Island near Tampa being prepped by Jack Kelly for a demonstration to local aviation officials. Accompanying him as mechanic was W. L. "Jack" Fortune of Stout Air Services. Alexis B. McMullen, who the year before had built the 5-passenger MAC Airliner, would assist in the testing.

The MAC, the first airplane built in Tampa, had been financed by E. L. Cord and L. B. Manning. They intended to use it as a test bed for their engines. It was designed by Alfred Corte, an Austrian who learned his craft at the Rumpler Aircraft Factories in Germany during the Great War. It utilized welded steel tubing for the wings and fuselage rather than the conventional wood construction. Both the Corman 3000 and the Stinson SM-6000 would employ the same type of welded steel tubing in their production. The aircraft was powered by a 400-hp Liberty V-12 and was delivered to Manning & Company in mid-April, 1929. By then however, Cord had decided on the Lycoming air-cooled radial engines, and did not need a test bed that was built around a water-cooled straight engine. McMullen flew the airliner back to Tampa and used in his own business until a hangar fire destroyed it and 12 other planes in December.

The tests that Kelly, Fortune, and McMullen were running replicated those performed for the Corman's ATC. The 60-foot wingspan airliner would be made to take off fully loaded with only two engines running and repeating with a different engine off each takeoff; go through an altitude test; be looped; thrown into tight spirals and side slips to see if it could keep out of a tailspin; and flown slow to show its stall speed. Two "hands off" control tests were made, the first under full power to check balance, and the second in a glide with all engines off to test the aircraft's inherent stability. Finally, upon landing, it had to stop within a certain distance. All this while carrying sandbags weighing the equivalent of 10 people and their baggage.

Loading sandbags equivalent to weight of 10 passengers onboard. Tampa Daily Times *photo*

The final resting place of the Corman 3000 near South Bend.
Photo by The South Bend Tribune

By January 16 Kelly and Fortune were headed back to Auburn, with stopovers in Atlanta and Dayton. After arriving in Auburn, Kelly flew the airliner up to the Stinson factory, where a buyer for the Corman was waiting. Kelly then took a Lycoming powered Stinson Junior back to Tampa for more demonstrations.

The buyer of the Corman was Harold C. Hannay, who claimed to be a real estate broker but in reality was a bootlegger. He had been arrested in 1925 when caught smuggling using his 65-foot cabin cruiser. The craft was seized and auctioned off by the government in April 1926, only to be seized again in August when the new owner used it to smuggle 144 half-barrels of beer. Hannay, who did not have a pilot's license, was arrested again in August 1929 after he landed near Utica, Michigan with 15 cases of Canadian liquor in a new airplane worth $6,500. While he was released on a technicality, the plane was impounded and in December turned over to the Customs Border Patrol for use to combat the ever-growing smuggling by aircraft, two years before an official air division was created in 1932.

At the end of January Hannay bought the surplus Corman 3000 for what he claimed was $50,000 and had it delivered to Thompson Aeronautical Corporation's servicing and repair hanger at the Pontiac Municipal Airport for two weeks' worth of refurbishing. At noon on Friday, February 14, the Corman took off headed to St. Louis with Charles Cameron as pilot and Harold Hannay as passenger. Cameron was another bootlegger who had been arrested and his car impounded in 1926. Three hours later, just as they were passing over South Bend, the airliner apparently developed engine trouble. The pilot circled several times trying to find a safe place to land before finally setting down on Michael Ciesielski's farm eight miles to the west of the city, and one mile south of Highway 20.

The plane bounced over the broken up and frozen ground, ripping off the landing gear and skidding hundreds of feet, then catching fire before crashing into a fence. Hannay and Cameron jumped out unharmed but made no attempt to put the fire out. In fact, they warned gathering spectators not to go near the burning craft. The interior and fabric on the wings and fuselage became an inferno, and soon all that was left was the steel frame and severely damaged engines. Hannay and Cameron then fled the scene and got Arthur Jain, a nearby farmer, to give them a ride to South Bend. Without revealing either of their names, Hannay told Jain that the airliner was new, and was being ferried from St. Louis to Detroit. They indicated that they would take a bus to Detroit. Once in the city they promptly disappeared. Jain thought they may have been drinking.

The next day a Cadillac with Michigan license plates passed through South Bend and headed straight for the crash site. That afternoon Hannay and another man appeared at Rowe Auto Supply and Garage in South Bend and arranged for the employees there to send a truck and salvage the three Wright J-5 Whirlwind engines and ship them to Detroit. Hannay acted as if he had not been on the airplane and refused to name the pilot or other presumed passenger. He told an employee that his pilot had taken several passengers to Chicago and was returning to Detroit when the accident happened. When the employee asked the pilot's name Hannay snapped "You're looking for too much damned information." Hannay left town that night.

St. Joseph County Sheriff Thomas A. Goodrick investigated after learning of the inconsistencies in Hannay's story. Inquiries from reporters found that no aircraft of the Corman's description had flown out of any St. Louis airport. A report came in that the plane had been stolen from a C. H. Nahey, who was supposedly the president of the Corman Aircraft Company in Detroit, but newsmen could not find any such person or company. Based on the shipping address for the salvaged engines, the Thompson Aeronautical Corporation was contacted, and the Sheriff learned of the original flight plan and of the owner. Once it was known that Hannay was a bootlegger, federal prohibition agents were contacted, but a search of the wreckage failed to uncover any trace of liquor. Instead the agents noted that the interior had still been in an airliner configuration when the plane burned, rendering it incapable of serving as a cargo plane. With that information the investigation ended, and news of the crash faded away, as did any further mention of Harold C. Hannay. The Corman 3000 was gone and now it was time for Stinson to focus their attention on a new airliner.

With the 210-hp Lycoming R-680 engine entering production, Cord told Stinson management that he could offer his power plant to Stinson at a very reasonable price. Utilizing volume production, the Stinson management team discussed the lowest price a Junior could be offered to the public and still realize a minimal amount of profit. They proposed a retail price of $5,775. To achieve this, the dealer discount would be reduced from 20% to 18%, as many stamped parts as possible would be used, and the production line would be realigned for more efficient assembly. Cord was ecstatic. In his opinion, this gave Stinson the opportunity for national headlines by offering the least expensive four-place plane in 1930.

Even though the new factory was only eight months old, it was quite obvious it was not designed to handle SM-6000 production. Management decided to hire the original architect to design a 100,000 square-foot addition to the factory. Every effort would be made to complete the factory in the fourth quarter of 1930. The company had received an infusion of funds sufficient to ramp-up production and begin the development of new models. Funding for the addition to the factory was promised later. At this time, management decided SM-7 and SM-8 were to be the 1930 model numbers. Cord had a high level of confidence in the Stinson management and at the end of a two-day visit, he instructed them to carry on.

The next day newspapers were reporting that the "greatest expansion program yet undertaken in the aviation industry" was being launched by the Stinson Aircraft Corporation. While already said to be producing more cabin airplanes that any other manufacturer in the world, Stinson's 1930 growth projection was calling for minimum of a 300 percent increase in production. To this end, two days later Lycoming announced that Stinson had ordered 500 airplane engines—the largest single order for aircraft engines ever made. They were all to be the 210-hp Lycoming R-680, with production to begin in two weeks and final delivery by May 1. Two weeks later, on January 25 Bendix Aviation Corporation announced the largest sale of airplane parts and accessories in the history of the aviation industry. Stinson had ordered "500 Scintilla magnetos, 500 Stromberg carburetors, 500 Bendix aviation-type brake sets, 300 sets of Eclipse electric starters and 300 sets of Pioneer aviation instruments." The press noted that these record-making purchases would be used solely for a new model plane, said to be "similar to the famous Stinson Junior" that would be a four-place cabin aircraft in completely new price range for a quality plane of this type.

The engineering department took the basic 1929 SM-2 Junior and, without changing the fundamental design, sought to improve production efficiency. The engineering department worked

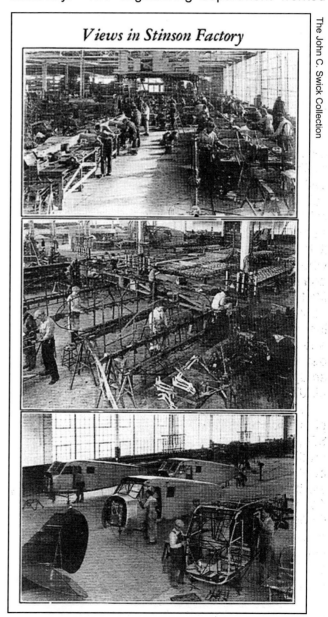

Factory views from Stinson brochure

The 10 passenger interior of the Stinson SM-6000

diligently, and the SM-8A Junior was approved February 11, 1930, powered by a 9-cylinder 210-hp Lycoming R-680 radial engine. With Stinson and Lycoming now controlled by the Cord Holding Company, Cord required Lycoming to offer aircraft engines to Stinson at the cost of production. In a drive to establish Stinson as the premier American aircraft manufacturer, the price of the SM-8A was set at $5,775 for aircraft accepted at the Wayne factory. This model was advertised as a $10,000 airplane for $5,775. 292 SM-8As were manufactured in 1930.

The Packard Car Company began developing a diesel aircraft engine in 1925 and received approval in late 1929. Stinson purchased two of the Packard engines and they were installed on the basic SM-8A Junior airframe. The new aircraft, SM-8D Junior, powered by a 225-hp DR-980 Packard diesel engine was approved April 8, 1930. There were two major objections to the Packard engine, however. First, excessive vibration frightened the passengers and annoyed the pilot. Second, with the use of kerosene as fuel, the engine developed an offensive smell.

The SM-6000 airliner, powered by three 215-hp Lycoming R-680 engines, was approved on July 10, 1930. Stinson's engineers had successfully redesigned the Corman 3000 into an airliner with room for 11 passengers plus the crew. It was a very comfortable coach style aircraft designed for short trips.

The Stinson SM-6000 was purchased by N. Y. Philadelphia and Washington Airline, Pennsylvania Airlines, American Airways, Trans American, Chicago and Southern, Eastern Air Transport, and Delta Air Lines. To fulfill airline orders, production ran through 1931.

Bill Mara became the lead salesman for the SM-6000. When Cord heard that Mara was making presentations to railroad executives and airlines, he asked if he could sit in on a presentation. Cord was so impressed with the possibilities, he decided to start his own airline using the SM-6000. Cord formed Century Airlines on a route from Cleveland to St. Louis with stops at Toledo, Detroit and Chicago. He then formed Century Pacific Airline serving a route from San Diego to San Francisco.

Several specialty aircraft were produced in 1930. The SM-8B Junior powered by a 225-hp Wright J-6 engine was offered to customers who preferred a Wright powered aircraft. The SM-7A Junior, powered by a 9-cylinder 300-hp Wright, J-6 engine, offered spectacular performance, and the SM-7AB Junior, powered by a 300-hp P&W Wasp Jr. engine, was offered to customers who preferred a P&W Wasp powered aircraft. One of the most interesting aircraft developed by Stinson in 1930 was the SM-9. It was a high-wing amphibian experimental aircraft powered by two 215-hp Wright J-5C engines. Unfortunately, the aircraft was abandoned because of no ATC approval. [The 1930 specialty aircraft are described in more detail in the type certificate section, Chapter 16.]

The SM-6000 two-seat cockpit

was contacted, and the Sheriff learned of the original flight plan and of the owner. Once it was known that Hannay was a bootlegger, federal prohibition agents were contacted, but a search of the wreckage failed to uncover any trace of liquor. Instead the agents noted that the interior had still been in an airliner configuration when the plane burned, rendering it incapable of serving as a cargo plane. With that information the investigation ended, and news of the crash faded away, as did any further mention of Harold C. Hannay. The Corman 3000 was gone and now it was time for Stinson to focus their attention on a new airliner.

With the 210-hp Lycoming R-680 engine entering production, Cord told Stinson management that he could offer his power plant to Stinson at a very reasonable price. Utilizing volume production, the Stinson management team discussed the lowest price a Junior could be offered to the public and still realize a minimal amount of profit. They proposed a retail price of $5,775. To achieve this, the dealer discount would be reduced from 20% to 18%, as many stamped parts as possible would be used, and the production line would be realigned for more efficient assembly. Cord was ecstatic. In his opinion, this gave Stinson the opportunity for national headlines by offering the least expensive four-place plane in 1930.

Even though the new factory was only eight months old, it was quite obvious it was not designed to handle SM-6000 production. Management decided to hire the original architect to design a 100,000 square-foot addition to the factory. Every effort would be made to complete the factory in the fourth quarter of 1930. The company had received an infusion of funds sufficient to ramp-up production and begin the development of new models. Funding for the addition to the factory was promised later. At this time, management decided SM-7 and SM-8 were to be the 1930 model numbers. Cord had a high level of confidence in the Stinson management and at the end of a two-day visit, he instructed them to carry on.

The next day newspapers were reporting that the "greatest expansion program yet undertaken in the aviation industry" was being launched by the Stinson Aircraft Corporation. While already said to be producing more cabin airplanes that any other manufacturer in the world, Stinson's 1930 growth projection was calling for minimum of a 300 percent increase in production. To this end, two days later Lycoming announced that Stinson had ordered 500 airplane engines—the largest single order for aircraft engines ever made. They were all to be the 210-hp Lycoming R-680, with production to begin in two weeks and final delivery by May 1. Two weeks later, on January 25 Bendix Aviation Corporation announced the largest sale of airplane parts and accessories in the history of the aviation industry. Stinson had ordered "500 Scintilla magnetos, 500 Stromberg carburetors, 500 Bendix aviation-type brake sets, 300 sets of Eclipse electric starters and 300 sets of Pioneer aviation instruments." The press noted that these record-making purchases would be used solely for a new model plane, said to be "similar to the famous Stinson Junior" that would be a four-place cabin aircraft in completely new price range for a quality plane of this type.

The engineering department took the basic 1929 SM-2 Junior and, without changing the fundamental design, sought to improve production efficiency. The engineering department worked

Factory views from Stinson brochure

The 10 passenger interior of the Stinson SM-6000

diligently, and the SM-8A Junior was approved February 11, 1930, powered by a 9-cylinder 210-hp Lycoming R-680 radial engine. With Stinson and Lycoming now controlled by the Cord Holding Company, Cord required Lycoming to offer aircraft engines to Stinson at the cost of production. In a drive to establish Stinson as the premier American aircraft manufacturer, the price of the SM-8A was set at $5,775 for aircraft accepted at the Wayne factory. This model was advertised as a $10,000 airplane for $5,775. 292 SM-8As were manufactured in 1930.

The Packard Car Company began developing a diesel aircraft engine in 1925 and received approval in late 1929. Stinson purchased two of the Packard engines and they were installed on the basic SM-8A Junior airframe. The new aircraft, SM-8D Junior, powered by a 225-hp DR-980 Packard diesel engine was approved April 8, 1930. There were two major objections to the Packard engine, however. First, excessive vibration frightened the passengers and annoyed the pilot. Second, with the use of kerosene as fuel, the engine developed an offensive smell.

The SM-6000 airliner, powered by three 215-hp Lycoming R-680 engines, was approved on July 10, 1930. Stinson's engineers had successfully redesigned the Corman 3000 into an airliner with room for 11 passengers plus the crew. It was a very comfortable coach style aircraft designed for short trips.

The Stinson SM-6000 was purchased by N. Y. Philadelphia and Washington Airline, Pennsylvania Airlines, American Airways, Trans American, Chicago and Southern, Eastern Air Transport, and Delta Air Lines. To fulfill airline orders, production ran through 1931.

Bill Mara became the lead salesman for the SM-6000. When Cord heard that Mara was making presentations to railroad executives and airlines, he asked if he could sit in on a presentation. Cord was so impressed with the possibilities, he decided to start his own airline using the SM-6000. Cord formed Century Airlines on a route from Cleveland to St. Louis with stops at Toledo, Detroit and Chicago. He then formed Century Pacific Airline serving a route from San Diego to San Francisco.

Several specialty aircraft were produced in 1930. The SM-8B Junior powered by a 225-hp Wright J-6 engine was offered to customers who preferred a Wright powered aircraft. The SM-7A Junior, powered by a 9-cylinder 300-hp Wright, J-6 engine, offered spectacular performance, and the SM-7AB Junior, powered by a 300-hp P&W Wasp Jr. engine, was offered to customers who preferred a P&W Wasp powered aircraft. One of the most interesting aircraft developed by Stinson in 1930 was the SM-9. It was a high-wing amphibian experimental aircraft powered by two 215-hp Wright J-5C engines. Unfortunately, the aircraft was abandoned because of no ATC approval. [The 1930 specialty aircraft are described in more detail in the type certificate section, Chapter 16.]

The SM-6000 two-seat cockpit

CHAPTER 4

The engineering, drafting, and business offices moved to a separate location through 1930 to make room for increased production and for the assembly jigs to certify the SM-6000. Starting in the Northfield factory, Stinson had utilized outside sources for all interior furnishings for the aircraft. This was continued in the new factory and, as production increased, it was necessary to rent a small warehouse to store raw materials before being processed into aircraft parts. Even though the stock market had dropped in October 1929, the economy was still strong, and automobile production was running at a pre-depression pace. So when the Stinson company began hiring personnel to ramp up production, it had to compete with the automobile industry for personnel.

By February 1930, Bill Mara and Eddie Stinson had established an active nationwide dealer network. Eddie developed a unique demonstration and sales program that he personally offered to the dealers. To participate, the dealer had to have one new Stinson in inventory and have at least five prospects willing to take a demonstration flight with Stinson. Eddie would then personally fly a new aircraft to the dealer's field. It always looked impressive for the prospective customer to view two new aircraft sitting side-by-side on the tarmac in front of the dealer's hangar. In doing this, Eddie's goal was to sell both aircraft and convince one of the new owners to ferry him back to the factory. He liked to brag that he had a 100% success in selling two aircraft and many times having a third customer place an order for future delivery.

The expansion to the factory was slow-going because funding for it was not approved by the Cord Holding Company until September. Construction was difficult in the Michigan winter and, as a result, the expansion was not completed until January 1931. This did not seem to impede Stinson's success. By the end of 1930, sales had reached an all-time high. The Stinson Aircraft Corporation sold 362 aircraft—352 single-engine aircraft and 10 tri-motor airliners. All in all, 1930 was an excellent year for Stinson.

1930 SM-8A Junior, NC415M (s/n 4006), powered by a Lycoming R-680 215-hp engine, priced at $5,775

1930 SM-8A Junior, NC911W (s/n 4085), powered by a Lycoming R-680 215-hp engine

The Able Collection

CHAPTER 4

Opposite page, top: SM-7A engaged in aerial mapping, powered by a 300-hp Wright R-975 engine, one of eight built

Opposite page, bottom: Detail of a SM-8A powered by the new 9-cylinder, 210-hp Lycoming engine

Left top: The 1930 Stinson SM-6000 airliner powered by three 215-hp Lycoming R-680 engines

Middle: NX11117 was an experimental twin-boomed amphibian (designated 'Model A' but not to be confused with the later Model A tri-motor airliner) and was powered by two 215-hp Lycoming R-680 engines. It was completed in January 1931 and shown at the Detroit Aircraft Show, then tested at Belleville Lake and later scrapped.

Bottom: SM-8A powered by a 215-hp R-680 Lycoming engine. 1 of 302 built, price $5,775

Col. Clarence M. Young, assistant secretary of Commerce in charge of aeronautics inspects the Detroit Wayne Industrial Airport at Wayne, Michigan. Photo shows (L to R) William A. Mara, vice president of the Stinson Aircraft Corporation, whose factory is located at the airport; Edward A. Stinson, president of the Stinson Corporation; Col. Young; Capt. John F. Donaldson; and A.P. Tappan.

SM-8A Junior at Floyd Bennett Field, Brooklyn, N.Y., 1930

NC415 M built in 1929 as SM-2AA with a 165-hp Wright J-6 engine, converted with a 215-hp Lycoming engine in 1930 to become the first SM-8A.

Chapter 5
1931:
A New Factory and a New Model

Stinson factory at Wayne, Michigan in 1931

The addition to the factory was completed in the third week of January, 1931. [All geographic locations are based on views from the back of the factory facing forward, and all dimensions are rounded to the nearest foot.] The first new structure was a two-story, 60x140 ft. brick addition added to the back of the factory facing the railroad tracks. This was designed so the railroad spur would run very close to the right side of the structure with the first floor the same level as a boxcar to facilitate offloading raw materials. The second floor of this addition was built with expansive continuous windows and would be used for manufacturing small items. When necessary, it also would be used as a meeting place for the drafting department.

The second structure built was the water tower located at the end of the two-story addition. A well, fire plugs, and other fire-suppression equipment were also strategically arranged near the factory building. The third step to the construction process was the completion of the 40x40 ft. boiler room and an 80x140 ft. storage facility running the full width of the factory, connecting the two-story addition to the existing factory structure.

On the right side of the complex facing west, a small 50x60 ft. hangar was constructed. It would be used for experimental aircraft. Next, a 70x140 ft. building known as the paint room was built, running nearly to the property line. At this time, a product called dope was used to shrink the fabric covering of aircraft, and the paint room was where the dope was applied. Dope was highly flammable, and many aircraft facilities burned down when dope came in contact with a heated surface. For safety, therefore, the paint room was attached to the main factory using fireproof doors that would close automatically if the temperature rose above a specified setting.

The original factory doors opened to the west, but a 125x180 ft. addition was added to the west end of the building with impressive aircraft hangar doors facing to the south. A 60x120 ft. engineering and office complex was then added to the west of this addition along with a covered walkway, which connected the factory's various buildings. Lastly, a 125x100 ft. service hangar was constructed at the edge of the property facing north. In sum, the original 68,400 sq. ft. factory had been enlarged by 99,800 sq. ft., bringing the total factory area to 168,200 sq. ft.

From a January 1931 perspective, the Stinson Aircraft Corporation was in a position to thrive. The factory was completed and ready for volume production. The company had an excellent engineering department and a strong dealer organization covering the United States and Canada. Although the economy seemed to be failing, there was still high demand for Stinson aircraft. With these facts in mind, Eddie Stinson called for a meeting of the corporate principals. Attending were E. L. Cord, Bill Mara, Kenneth Roman, William Naylor and Bruce Raun. Eddie suggested the company should aggressively pursue the development of new aircraft while SM-6000 and SM-6000-B production continued through the remainder of the year. He suggested the engineering department develop an upgrade for the SM-8 Junior, which would enter production in midyear, and begin the development of a totally new aircraft to replace the Junior with production to start in late 1931 or early 1932. Eddie also proposed that the company design a new tri-motor airliner for 1932. The Stinson marketing plan would follow the automobile company model of planned obsolescence—produce new aircraft quickly to stimulate the interest of the dealers and their customers.

Cord agreed with Eddie's proposals, and Stinson management began to make preparations to move forward with production. It appeared to management that the economy probably would continue to shrink and personal contact with the active dealers would be crucial. To make this possible, Chief Pilot John C. "Jack" Kelly (often spelled Kelley) was appointed Sales Manager. He was assigned a SM-8 Junior for demonstrations and for his personal transportation. If a customer or a dealer was in need of an aircraft, he would sell his immediately and ride the train back to the factory to pick up a new one. This helped facilitate quick sales.

The Stinson dealer organization at the time consisted of fixed-base operators as well as individuals with the resources to deal in Stinson air-

SM-8A Junior based at the Broken Bow, Nebraska Airport. Powered by a 215-hp R-680 Lycoming engine, it was 1 of 204 built in 1931.

craft while maintaining other business interests. When the factory design was laid down in 1930, provision was made to build a large service hangar. This facility was available to Stinson owners and all Stinson dealers to service and upgrade their aircraft. Over the years, this became a very profitable endeavor for the Stinson Company.

As SM-6000s were completed, Eddie Stinson would deliver the aircraft to the airlines and spend time with the airline pilots. He continued to spend a great deal of time in his favorite activity: giving demonstration flights and assisting in selling aircraft at a dealer's airport. For a great many years, pilots would reminisce about the quality time they had in the air when they flew with Eddie Stinson.

Mara approached Lycoming and other suppliers asking them to lower equipment prices so that Stinson could lower the price of its new model and stay competitive. Stinson management had decided, after some discussion, to name the new aircraft the Stinson Model S Junior. Most suppliers were receptive to Mara's request and the Model S entered production in May with a retail price of $4,995. Many upgrades were included in the new model. As a result, the aircraft was 111 pounds heavier than the SM-8.

To fill customer requests for a 300-hp Pratt & Whitney powered aircraft, Stinson produced five examples designated as the Model W. The plan was to present the Model W as a new aircraft. To do so, the engineering department started with the SM-7 design, enlarged the cabin area, both in length and height, and fitted it with a luxurious interior. This was the last redesign of the Junior aircraft, which had been in continuous production since 1928.

With Eddie's insistence, the design for 1932 was to be a completely new aircraft. Early on, Stinson management decided to name this aircraft the Stinson Model R. The fuselage would be much deeper, allowing for more head room and leg room, and the engine cowling would be blended into the fuselage to give a more pleasing line. The SM-8 landing gear would be replaced with a more modern design, and a stub wing would be added to the bottom of the forward fuselage. The stub wing was a unique design used only on the Model R aircraft. The Model R was designed with fixed landing gear, but the stub wing was built to fully enclose a retractable landing gear that would be developed in future models.

The R was the most deluxe aircraft Stinson had offered to the public. Its first flight was Tuesday, December 1, 1931, and the process of obtaining a type certificate began immediately. This was the first truly new Stinson design since the SM-2 Junior had been introduced in 1928. Eddie, who mothered the Model R's design through development, described this aircraft as the shape of things to come for the Stinson Aircraft Corporation.

Throughout 1931, Stinson sold 270 aircraft through their dealer organization and 48 tri-motor aircraft to the airlines, making a total sale of 318 aircraft. The future looked bright for the Stinson Company.

Red and black Stinson Junior SM-7B powered by a 300-hp P&W Wasp Jr. engine

Better Plane at Lower Price
STINSON $4995
F. O. F. WAYNE, MICH.

215 H. P. 4-Passenger Cabin Plane
Equipment other than standard extra

A complete revision in the salability of airplanes was caused about a year ago at the St. Louis Show, when for the first time in the history of this business, a cabin plane in the $11,000 price class was offered to the public for $5775. This radical departure was made possible only because of the Stinson Aircraft Corporation's affiliation with the Cord group under the management of E. L. Cord. At that time Stinson openly admitted that production did not warrant the new low price. It was their belief, however, that public acceptance would follow. This belief was vindicated, as evidenced by Stinson's leadership in the cabin plane field. Last year Stinson built more than 50% of all cabin planes built.

Again Stinson takes leadership! The 1931 Stinson program, with another new radically low price and an improved plane, is a continuation of the policy which made last year so successful. Again, the management says that the present volume does not warrant the new price of $4995. But by putting an even better plane at an even lower price within the reach of vastly more people, the Stinson management again believes volume will follow.

It is Stinson's policy always to make continual improvements but no radical changes in design that obsolete investments of Stinson owners. It is our belief that the basic design of the present Stinson plane will be continued for years to come.

OTHER STINSON PLANES- Four Passenger, 300 H. P. Wasp — $8,995 • Stinson Airliner Eleven Passenger Tri-Motored Transport — $25,900 • Eight Passenger, Tri-Motored Executives' Model, prices upon request. • All prices F. O. F. Wayne, Michigan. Equipment other than standard, extra. Prices subject to change without notice. Stinson Aircraft Corporation, Wayne, Michigan. • Division Cord Corporation.

Top: $4,995 Model S powered by a 215-hp R-680 Lycoming engine. 51 built. Photographed July 15, 1960 by Willian A. Oates, for The Indianapolis Star

Middle: SM-6000-B tri-motor powered by 3 215-hp R-680 Lycoming engines photographed March 1930 at United Airport - now Bob Hope Airport, a.k.a. Hollywood Burbank Airport.

Bottom: 1931 SM-8A cockpit

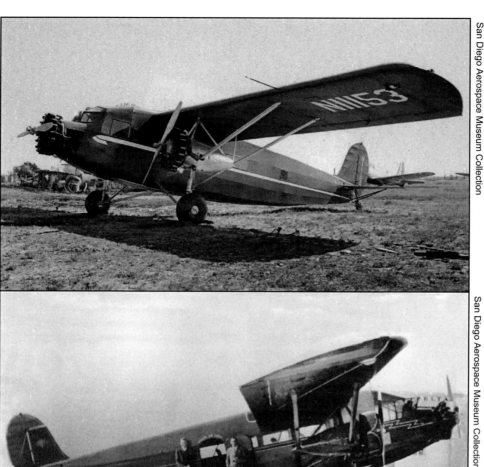

1931 Stinson SM-6000-B NC11153 s/n 5021 originally sold to Century Airlines, it went on to serve American Airways, Chicago and Southern Airlines, and Chesapeake Airways.
In 1955 the fabric on the wings and fuselage was removed and the replaced with replaced with aluminum. It has been restored and at this writing is kept in flyable condition at the Mid America Flight Museum in Mt. Pleasant, Texas.

One of 6 SM-600-B aircraft that Delta Air Lines acquired in 1934 from American Airways for $5,400 each. When began their first air mail service on July 4, 1934, the planes were, except for a name change on the fuselage, still in American Airway livery: dark navy blue with fire engine red cheat line and lighting bolt. These aircraft were sold out of the fleet by 1937.

1931 Stinson SM-6000-B NC11170 s/n 5023 originally sold to American Airways. The EAA was among the previous owners of this aircraft, which earned its keep by giving rides at the annual Oshkosh Airshow. At this writing is kept in flyable condition at the Fantasy of Flight Museum in Polk City, Florida.

Chapter 6
1932:
Death of a Salesman

Final Tribute - To Dean of U.S. Aviation Pilots

Detroit Jan. 30, 1932 - Firing a farewell salute over the grave of Edward A. Stinson, famous American flyer, who died when a plane he was testing in Chicago crashed in Jackson Park after colliding with a flagpole that the pilot failed to see in the dusk. Mr. Stinson, who was 38 years old, was the dean of American aviation pilots and Chief Civilian Instructor of Army pilots during the World War.

On January 25, Stinson flew the new Model R to Chicago's municipal airport to give demonstration flights with a local Stinson dealer. Flying out of Clark Field at dusk, Stinson neglected to refuel his aircraft, thinking he had sufficient fuel for one more demonstration flight. But as he flew over the Lake Michigan shoreline, the engine suddenly stopped from fuel starvation. Rather than landing on the beach, Stinson attempted to land on a golf course. He successfully landed the Model R on the Jackson Park golf Course, but soon after touchdown, the right wing struck a sturdy flagpole. A large male passenger riding in the back seat had neglected to secure his seat belt. When the aircraft struck the flagpole, he flew forward into the back of the pilot seat, crushing Eddie's chest into the control column. Sustaining some broken ribs and other injuries, Eddie was pulled from the aircraft and driven to Illinois Central Hospital, where he collapsed in the admitting room. He never regained consciousness and passed away early the next morning. By the time of his death at age 38, Eddie Stinson had more than 16,000 hours of flying time.

At the inquest two days later, Bill Mara informally testified before two Army aviation experts appointed as special deputy coroners. Mara revealed that this Model R had a new type of glass tube sight-gauge mounted to the end of the wing-tank inside the cabin. When the aircraft was in level flight, the correct amount of fuel was displayed, but when the plane was resting on its tail-wheel, the level shown would be inaccurate. Mara noted that Stinson was not fully acquainted with this new type of gauge and surmised that Stinson would have seen a low fuel indication, but would have believed he had more than enough, and so waved off a mechanic that had offered to refuel the airplane. This type of fuel gauge was never installed in another Stinson aircraft.

A few days after the funeral, Cord made a call on Estelle. He was concerned about her finances and asked about the money from the sale of their Stinson company stock. Estelle reported they had sold their first house and purchased a modest, more modern one along with some new furniture and a car. The remainder of the funds was invested in certificates of deposit or other secure investments. Cord assured Estelle her job was safe with the company and told her he would direct the treasurer to draw a check for Eddie's 1932 salary.

In late February, Cord, appointed Lou B. Manning president and director of Stinson. Manning had been a business associate of Cord, and in 1929 had funded the Corman Corporation that developed the Corman 3000 tri-motor aircraft. After the merger of the Corman Corporation with Stinson, Manning held a respectable piece of the Cord Holding Company stock.

One of Manning's first duties as president and director of Stinson was to appoint an executive committee to handle the day-to-day operations of the company. Manning reserved the right to participate in all major management decisions. The March 1932 Stinson Aircraft Corporation executive management team included William A. Mara, vice president and director, Kenneth M. Roman, chief engineer, and Bruce A. Raun, factory superintendent.

The depression had not yet bottomed out, and the Stinson dealer organization continued to sell aircraft well. By renegotiating prices with their suppliers, Stinson was able to offer the Model S, powered by a Lycoming engine, for the low price of $4,995. The Model R, on the other hand, was marketed to the wealthy owner and was furnished with an elegant interior. Stinson manufactured two more models based off of the Model R. The Model R-2 was designed for the feeder airline or charter service. The Model R-3 was fitted with retractable landing gear and priced at $6,497. Neither of these models sold well.

The Stinson Model U tri-motor entered production in June, and by years end, 19 were built. This aircraft was a much improved follow-up aircraft to the SM-6000. It fit the needs of the startup airlines and was priced at $32,900 FAF.

The Stinson Model M 4PCLM was an all-metal, low-wing, experimental aircraft powered by a 300-hp Wright R-760 engine. This aircraft had been in the planning stages for over a year and was an effort to penetrate the high-end, high-performance corporate market. The aircraft was assigned NR12123 and finished in polished aluminum. Stinson was excellent at producing steel tube fabric-covered aircraft at competitive prices, but an all-metal aircraft presented many new production problems. Engineering and management evaluated the cost of tooling up for the Model M's construction and decided the aircraft would be priced out of the market. The aircraft did not receive ATC approval, and the project was abandoned with only one experimental version built.

The Stinson Corporation finished 1932 with all accounts payable current, including both federal and state taxes paid. The year-end profit and loss balance showed Stinson operating at a net loss of less than $500. When the Cord Corporation assumed control of Stinson in 1929, there was no debt from building the first factory. The 1931 fac-

Original Associated Press photo of the Jackson Park Golf Course fatal crash site of Edward A. Stinson's Model R

tory expansion, however, was built with 100% financing, and after renegotiating with their lenders, the Stinson Corporation was able to service the debt with interest payments only.

Sales for 1932 were over $1,200,000. This total included the sale of aircraft through their dealer organization as well as the profit from the service department for Stinson dealers and customers. In addition to the newer models, seven SM-7 Junior aircraft were manufactured to fill a specific customer request. Despite a weakening economy and the tragic death of one of its founders, The Stinson Aircraft Corporation sold 94 aircraft through their dealer organization and 20 tri-motor aircraft to the airlines in 1932.

The completely redesigned Model R powered by a 9-cylinder Lycoming engine of 250-hp was approved for production 1/25/32, priced at $5,995. The landing gear was attached to a stub-wing built into the bottom of the fuselage that serviced attached points for the wing struts and landing gear. With C.A.A. approval imminent, Eddie Stinson began demonstration flights on the 24th.

1932 Stinson Model M NR12123, s/n 32000, experimental all-metal low-wing—one built

CHAPTER 6

Above: 1932 Stinson R NC12157 s/n 8510 in Mobiloil livery, showing lower landing gear stub wing. Sold 1933 to Belgium (OO-HVS), then United Kingdom (G-AFUW, X8522 RAF)

Left: Ex-American Airways 1934 Stinson U NC12118, s/n 9006 in Consolidated Airlines livery, showing lower landing gear and engine mounting stub wing

Below: 1934 Stinson U NC12121, s/n 9009 sold to American Airlines and then to Mayflower Airlines. In September 1938 a mysterious fire broke out on the unoccupied airliner, which was destroyed.

STINSON
Model R-3

*240 H.P. LYCOMING TRANSPORT MOTOR

Cruises 118-120 M.P.H.
Ceiling 14,000 feet
Gross 3,500 lbs.
Span 43' 3"
Price $6,495.00
F.O.F. Wayne, Mich.
Equipment other than standard extra.

This illustrates the Stinson Model R-3 in flight with landing gear down in locked position ready for landing. The wheels are retracted only when the ultimate cruising speed is desired.

The retractable mechanism is a simple worm and gear windlass and the wheels can be easily lifted in about thirty seconds, then released for landing in about TWO SECONDS by pulling a lever in handy reach of the pilot. The gear is locked down automatically for landings when released.

This illustrates the manner in which the wheels are retracted into the fuselage so as to reduce drag and increase speed. More than year of development work perfected this simple mechanical lift.

Note the clean streamlined appearance of this most practical of all cabin airplanes with retractable landing gear. This plane may be equipped with radio, landing lights and other accessories.

*80 Octane Ethyl Gasoline must be used.

Inside back cover ad from the December 1932 issue of Stinson Plane Talk, *showing 3 views of the Stinson Model R-3 in flight. Top photo shows landing gear down and locked, middle photo shows gear retracting and the bottom photo shows the landing gear fully retracted.*

Chapter 7
1933:
The GB Brain Trust Joins Stinson

The prototype Model O, NX13817, s/n 1000, an open-cockpit two-seat aircraft

In January, two talented engineers, Robert L. Hall and Robert W. Ayer, visited the Stinson factory. For several years, they had been employed by the Grangeville Brothers Aircraft Company in Springfield, Massachusetts and were responsible for designing the famous GB racers. In December, Manning had hired a talented artist and industrial stylist, Lloyd Skinner, giving Stinson a new, creative engineering team. With this team hired, Manning contacted Cord and requested to make a major management change.

The Feb. 1, 1933 Stinson Management Team:

E. L. Cord. Chairman, Board of Directors
L. B. Manning, President and Director
De Weese, Vice President and General Manager
W. A. Mara, Vice President and Director
R. S. Pruitt, Secretary and Director
C. R. Stocke, Treasurer;
Robert L. Hall, Chief Engineer
Robert W. Ayer, Transport Engineer
J. C. "Jack" Kelly Jr., Transport Engineer and Sales Manager
C. R. "Jack" Irvine, Engineer
Professor Peter Altman, Consulting Engineer
Lloyd Skinner, Artist and Industrial Stylist
Estelle Stinson, Office Manager

In planning the next Stinson aircraft, the engineering staff took ideas from the Model S and Model R, and created a unique design. This was the first time in Stinson history that a stylist participated in new aircraft design. Ayer's and Hall's experience designing aircraft for Grangeville Brothers, gave Stinson fresh ideas. In the spring of 1933, Lloyd Skinner, Robert Hall and Robert Ayer were sitting around a drafting table brainstorming on the external appearance of a new aircraft. Lloyd sketched pencil drawings as the engineers talked about the aircraft design. Lloyd added an updated, sleek paint trim. The old Stinson interiors were abandoned as Lloyd inserted contemporary automobile designs. Engineers Hall and Aye took Lloyd's drawings and designed a new aerodynamic aircraft that could be manufactured efficiently and meet Stinson's high standards. There is an old saying that if an aircraft looks good, it will fly good. The new aircraft not only flew well, it presented a stunning appearance on the tarmac. From a marketing standpoint, this bold aircraft required a bold name, and the name Reliant was chosen. Although a completely new design, the Model SR Reliant retained Stinson reliability, carrying capacity, passenger comfort, and that large Stinson presentation when sitting beside contemporary aircraft.

E. L. Cord visited the factory in February and requested a meeting with Manning, De Weese, and Mara. Cord desired Stinson to be number one in aircraft sales in the United States. One way to achieve this would be to reduce the price of the new aircraft to $3,995, and he challenged the management team to make it happen. As one of the divisions of the Cord Corporation, Lycoming would be instructed to reduce the price of their engines, but there were also many outside purchased parts needed for the Reliant, including steel tubing, fabric, instruments, wheels, and aircraft grade cable. Mara was given the responsibility to meet with Stinson's vendors and persuade them to give price reductions based on a production run of over 100 aircraft. When the Stinson Reliant, Model SR, received ATC 510 on July 29, 1933, the retail price was officially established at $3,995. There are accounts that the employees were asked to take a pay cut in 1934 to assist in lowering the price of the SR. However, the author was unable to establish that this was indeed a fact.

Special order aircraft became very profitable as they could be sold at a premium price. The numbers game began with the SR-1, SR-2, SR-3 and SR-4, which were sold with increased horsepower and higher gross weights. The Stinson Model U tri-motor continued in production and a special order for an SM-8A was filled. Looking toward export and military sales, a very unique aircraft was developed. ATC 520 was given to the Stinson Model O on November 9, 1933. The Model O was a parasol-wing tandem two-seat aircraft with an open cockpit. Many SR parts, including the landing gear and tail services, were used on the O. This aircraft was designed as a trainer, not a warplane, and was sold to the governments of China, Brazil and Honduras as training aircraft.

1933 was the start of many twists and turns in the Stinson Company's ownership. E. L. Cord's holding company, which Cord established in 1929, was created by inviting several entities to invest in the Cord Corporation. One of these investors, the Aviation Corporation, would eventually become the largest investor, holding more stock in the Cord Corporation than Cord held. In 1933, the Aero Digest magazine published an extensive account of the holdings of the Cord Corporation. Sections of the articles are reprinted here to give the reader a better perspective of aviation up to that time.

Aero Digest
November 1933
Aeronautical Activity of the
Cord Corporation

No story of the Cord Corporation can be told without including the story of the man behind it—a man whose meteoric rise in the industrial world was one of the most outstanding achievements in modern business history. After E. L. Cord tried his hand at automobile racing and various other endeavors, he turned out to make an exceptional automobile salesman. In 1919, he gained profit from selling Moon Cars in Chicago. His efforts were so impactful that his employer soon owned the largest automobile agency in the country. But in 1924, after he discovered that the car he represented was losing its appeal, Cord decided to enter the production end of the automobile business.

Cord spent time in the factory of the almost insolvent Auburn Car Company after being introduced to the Company's president. Cord returned to Chicago with many ideas and plans for a new model and, after dressing up and disposing of the previous models in the factory, he prepared to market his new car. Backed by definite notions of public demand, Cord introduced a car that featured snappy lines, advanced engineering refinements, and speed to match its appearance. He was made vice-president and general manager after proving to be largely instrumental for bringing more than a half million dollars in profit to the company within six months.

By 1925, Cord was president of Auburn, and by 1926 he was ready to enlarge his sphere of activities. Always a lover of speed, Cord assumed control of Duesenberg, Inc., a company with little financial return that principally manufactured racing automobiles. By

1927, he took over control of the Lycoming Manufacturing Company which had supplied engines to Auburn and had long been building automobile, marine and industrial engines.

At this point, Cord decided to consolidate his possessions, and in 1929 the Cord Corporation formed to be a holding and management company for the properties Cord and his associates controlled. This was Cord's doorway into the aeronautical field. When the Cord Corporation became concerned with its aviation department, inquiries came to its officials from many parts of the country through its connection with the Stinson Aircraft Corporation. Some people congratulated the company on their move; others were surprised that Cord would ever take aviation seriously. Cord explained that to him and his associates, aviation was merely a mean of transportation. Cord's personal experiences in the air (he had obtained a pilot's license) convinced him that this new factor for speed was worthy of investigation.

Cord began developing ideas that the cost of air-transportation must be lowered. He believed that since the public preferred to ride in cabin planes, flying must be made easy for the individual and that the purchase of a commercial airline plane ticket must be made affordable. Cord set out to accomplish ideas as he cut the prices of models which formerly sold for $11,000 down to $5,775. As he did this, he embarked on a campaign to educate the public about the advantages of flying.

Now content with manufacturing and selling airplanes, Cord and his Corporation decided to test-fly them. In March 1931, the company entered into the operations field with the establishment of Century Airlines and Century Pacific Airlines, Ltd., two transport companies which operated on a basis of reduced fares and frequent schedules.

Century Airlines operated between Chicago, Detroit, Toledo, Cleveland, and St. Louis over routes totaling 886 miles. Fourteen Lycoming-powered Stinson airliners were pressed into service to carry the 40,213 revenue pastors who flew during the first six months of operations. Century Pacific Airlines Ltd. began operations between San Diego, Los Angeles, Oakland, and San Francisco, but extended their routes to approximately 900 miles by opening Sacramento and Phoenix, Arizona terminals.

In early 1932, the Cord Corporation sold the holdings in its transport companies to The Aviation Corporation and American Airways. Mr. Cord occupied a place on the di-

Model U Tri-motor NC12192, s/n 9018, photographed at the Chicago Municipal Airport in 1934. Powered by three 240-hp R-680-AB Lycoming engines, carrying ten passengers and one pilot.

Model SR Reliant priced at $3,995 and powered by a 215-hp R-680 Lycoming engine

rectorate, and with his subsequent assumption of control of these companies, brought one of the largest transport units in the world under his scope.

The year 1933 had seen further expansion of the Cord Corporation. As an additional step to rounding out the company's manufacturing facilities for the building of various units of transportation, it acquired the New York Shipbuilding Corporation, one of the oldest builders of battleships and commercial ships in the country. Three weeks later, control of the Checker Cab Manufacturing Corporation passed into the hands of the Cord Corporation, giving it the ownership of one of the largest taxicab manufacturing companies in the country.

Now the Cord Corporation's activities entailed holdings in companies whose scopes included transportation on water, land, and in the air. Among its other properties are the Central Manufacturing Co., manufacturers of automobile bodies, Columbia Axel Co., auto and truck axle manufacturers, L. G. S. Devices Corp., freewheeling devices, Limousine Body Co., custom and convertible auto bodies, and the Spencer Heater Co., which manufactures boilers and heating units.

Aero Digest
November 1933
Aeronautical Activity of the Lycoming Manufacturing Company

The Lycoming Manufacturing Company was founded in 1908 as the Lycoming Foundry and Machine Company, which was formed to transact a general foundry of the machine manufacturing business. In 1927, the Lycoming Manufacturing Company became a subsidiary of the Auburn Automobile Company, when the latter acquired 62.5% of its existing capital stock. In 1929, following the organization of the Cord Corporation, the Lycoming Company acquired a large block of Auburn stock plus the remaining 37.5% of the common stock of Lycoming Company, which was then used to begin the development of its first aircraft engine. Known as model R–680, the engine attracted considerable attention because of its smoothness and silent operations. It was granted an approval certificate with a rating of 215hp at 2000 RPM. Its proven dependability and reliability made it an ideal engine for transport purposes; and it wasn't long before the Lycoming engine made its appearance in airliners flying over many parts of the country.

The production of the model R- 680 has been continued up until the present time, but during the latter part of 1931, the 240hp model R–680–BA was developed to meet the demand for increased speeds on transport lines. With a rating of 240hp at 2000 RPM, the R–680–BA engine was granted its 81st approval certificate on March 29, 1932. With an increased compression ratio on this engine, 80-octane fuel is required. The present executive personnel includes W. H. Beal as president and Mr. Cord as chairman of the board of directors.

Aero Digest
November 1933
Aeronautical Activity of the
Smith Engineering Company

The demand for better performance of aircraft through decreasing distance for landings and take-offs as speeds were increased brought aircraft engineers face-to-face with a new problem. Propellers, designed to be satisfactory for the high performance which aircraft rapidly obtained, caused exceedingly poor take-off characteristics. While experiments had been conducted for some time, it was not until late 1931 and early 1932 that a solution apparently had been reached in the results obtained by the use of controllable pitch propellers.

The mechanism of the Smith propeller described in the November 1932 issue of Aero Digest was simple and ingenious. It was controlled from the cockpit by a small push-pull lever connected with a non-rotating sleeve in the thrust bearing cover plate. On each sleeve was a worm thread. By means of this lever, the sleeve could be shifted forward to increase the pitch of the propeller or backward to decrease the pitch.

In 1933, the Cord Corporation purchased all of the capital stock of the Smith Engineering Company and arranged with the Lycoming Manufacturing Company to manufacture the Smith propeller. Subsequently, the plant was moved from Cleveland to Williamsport, Pennsylvania, home of the Lycoming Company, and the engine company prepared to transform the propellers into three-blade models.

Airplane Development Corporation

The Cord Corporation formed the Airplane Development Corporation to develop the Vultee, a low-wing, all-metal monoplane designed for transport use. The new plane, known as the V–1 Transport (described in the April, 1933 issue of Aero Digest) was engineered and constructed at the Grand Central Air Terminal in Glendale, California, and completed its first successful test on February 19, 1933, when it displayed outstanding performance in both top and cruising speeds. The president and general manager of the Airplane Development Corporation is Don P. Smith, and Gerald Vultee is vice president and chief engineer.

Aero Digest
November 1933
Aeronautical Activity of the
Aviation Corporation

Formed in 1929, the Aviation Corporation brought a great system of airlines under its control. As a holding company, it took over a great number of airlines, including Universal Aviation Corporation, Southern Air Transport, Colonial Air Transport, Canadian Colonial Airways, Colonial Western Airways, Embry-Riddle Aviation Corporation and Interstate Air Lines. The corporation continued to operate them as divisions. The current Executive Personnel of the Aviation Corporation consists of L. B. Manning, President; T. J. Dunnion, Treasure; R. S. Pruitt, Secretary, and Mr. Cord, Board Chairman.

Founded in 1930, American Airways, Inc., the operating branch of the Aviation Corporation, ranks among the top five greatest airlines in the United States by the virtue of its vast system. Its operations extend from "Canada to Mexico and from coast to coast!"

Aero Digest
November 1933
Aeronautical Activities of the
Stinson Aircraft Corporation

As you fly over the Stinson airport at Wayne, Michigan soon after passing the city of Detroit, you will see on one side of the spacious field a huge building displaying the name "STINSON AIRCRAFT" on its roof. Underneath their roof is one of the most modern aircraft factories in the country where line production methods are employed in the manufacturing of a complete line of cabin monoplanes.

The Stinson Company startled the aeronautical industry next by introducing a four-place cabin ship for sale for $5,775, as compared with a previous price of $11,000. The new price was based upon the belief that, as the public learned of the safety, comfort and ease of flying, the demand for a dependable ship would quickly justify the price. The Cord Corporation, through Mr. Cord, was beginning a campaign to educate the public in the advantages of transportation by air. Stinson always had held a place in the front rank as a builder of cabin airplanes, but the value of this particular airplane with its startling low price, gave it a dominating position in this field.

As early as 1926, Mr. Cord and L. B. Manning were planning to develop a transport plane which could be produced at a price that would permit fares to be lowered and thereby attract greatly increased public patronage. The first of these planes, known as the Corman, was completed in 1928 but was redesigned and retested again in 1929. With the purchase and the control of the Stinson Company, this plane that Mr. Cord and Mr. Manning had developed was produced in 1930 as the Model T Stinson Airliner. The ship, an eleven-passenger monoplane powered by three Lycoming engines, was the largest of its type ever produced by the company. Stinson had paved the way for a new era of airline transportation by offering a tri-motor plane for $25,000 as compared to the previous prices of tri-motored equipment ranging in price from $60,000 to $75,000.

Throughout 1930, Stinson continued the production of the Stinson Junior series of four-place cabin monoplanes powered by the Lycoming engine, also manufactured by a Cord subsidiary. In addition, the Stinson Detroiter, which accommodated six, and the SM-6B with room for eight was also produced.

Additional space became necessary in 1931. The construction of an addition to the factory and a service hangar adjacent to the original factory provided space for the engineering department, motor division and stock rooms and gave the company an additional 100,000 square feet of floor space. Production was concentrated on the Model T, which by this time was being used by Trans-American Airlines, Pennsylvania Airlines, Century Airlines, Century Pacific Airlines Ltd, and Ludington Airlines. How the Stinson tri-motor kept pace is best indicated by the fact that by 1931, one year after its introduction to the industry, more than 70% of all tri-motors sold in America were Stinsons, and the percentage grew from here.

In early 1932, a new Stinson tri-motor plane known as the model U was placed on the market. It combined all the experience gained in Model T operation, but offered at no additional cost. The aircraft featured faster cruising speeds, greater payloads, more power and lower maintenance and operating costs, as well as additional comfort for passengers and pilots. As a result, more than 90% of all American tri-motors delivered were Stinsons. Stinson also supplemented its Model S, a four-place cabin monoplane of the Junior series, with a new model known as the Model R. This plane was powered by a Lycoming engine of 215-hp. Variations of this aircraft were produced. The Model R2 had the 240-hp Lycoming and the Model R3 featured a retractable landing gear.

The outlook for the Corporation at the beginning of 1933 was better than any time during the two previous years. More people were employed and work was being pushed to facilitate delivery of the Model U transports. A large overhauling and rebuilding program was underway for operators of Stinson equipment. Officials were optimistic about the development of a considerable export business. Early in the year, the SR Reliant was placed on the market at a all-time low price of $3,995 based on a production run of 100 aircraft. It is a four-place, high-wing cabin monoplane powered with the improved Lycoming 215-hp engine. By year's end Stinson had produced 110 Reliants.

For the future, production was expected to start on a new ten-place airliner, known as the Model A, a deluxe high-speed tri-motor monoplane featuring club-car comfort and low initial and operating costs. Into this new plane would be incorporated all of the reliability and maintenance lessons learned in operating previous Stinson airliners more than 15,000,000 miles.

July 1933 Aero Digest *magazine advertisement for the first Stinson SR Reliant*

July 1933 Aero Digest *magazine advertisement for the first Stinson SR Reliant*

CHAPTER 7

Opposite page:

Top: 1931 Stinson Junior S NC443G, s/n 8069 in Northwest Airways livery. Note the wind generator mounted on the front left wing strut.

Bottom: View showing Northwest Airways logo; number '15' representing the 15th aircraft Northwest acquired; and the airmail contract number, A.M. 9 on the fuselage

This page:

Top: Stinson Junior S cockpit

Left: View from right-hand cockpit seat

Sold new to the Kansas Pipeline & Gas Company and registered as NC12162. 1943 resold in Colorado, then into North Dakota in 1948. In 1958 it was sold again, converted and until 1961 used for crop spraying. Restored back to original condition, but with the addition of a tow hook for towing gliders. In 1975 a Minneapolis area Northwest Airlines captain purchased the Model S and, with Northwest Airlines approval, restored it as NC443H, s/n 1088, an original Stinson SM-2AB that flew for Northwest Airways. However, registration number NC443H was already taken by a Cessna 320, so NC443G was chosen instead. Since restoration this Stinson has participated in Northwest Airlines anniversary celebrations and employee reunions. Today the aircraft is kept in flying condition in Minnesota by its latest owner, Chuck Doyle.

Chapter 8
1934: Reliant
The Aircraft Standard of the World

SR-5A Reliant sold to the US Coast Guard - USCG Model RQ-1 (tail number mismarked, later R3Q-1)

In an October 1933 meeting with D. B. De Weese, Bill Mara, and Robert Hall, Robert Ayer shared his design of a unique low-wing, three-engine transport. Model U1 production had stopped in 1933 after six were manufactured, and airlines were looking for new aircraft to fill the short haul market. If Stinson was to remain in the transport market, a new design needed to be developed immediately. Ayer was commissioned to start developing his design with the goal of making a public announcement in January.

In a meeting held January 8, 1934, Stinson management discussed a wide range of engineering and design options. All present were aware of the engineering progress in Robert Ayer's tri-motor transport design, and potential airline customers had been given advanced details of the design in November. Management decided the new aircraft would be known as the Model A, and a press release would soon be given to all aviation publications. To lower costs and save time, the prototype would be manufactured with production tooling. The transport department's engineering team was ready to begin building the tooling immediately, and Lloyd Skinner was asked to prepare sketches of both interior and exterior designs for management review. Once the sketches were approved, they would be used in presentations to potential airlines. A development timetable was established. The first flight of the prototype was set for late April, certification in September, and deliveries to the airlines to begin in November.

Since October of 1933, Jack Irvine had been working almost single-handedly on a new wing design for the 1934 SR-5 line. Up to this time, all Stinson aircraft used Clark Y airfoil with a chord of approximately 75 inches and a wingspan averaging 43 feet. Irvine's new wing would be shortened to 41 feet, the wing chord increased to 80 inches, and the wing thickness increased from 8 and 1/4 inches to 9 and 3/8 inches, using a modified Clark Y airfoil. The new wing would use what is known today as trailing edge flaps, but Irvine invented the term "speed arresters" for them. The speed arresters were located between the ailerons and the wing roots, permitting the pilot to choose steeper angles of approach without building up airspeed. They maintained lift during descent so that the aircraft could land and come to a complete stop in a shorter distance. The new wing design was to go into production immediately following CAA approval.

In conversations with Stinson's nationwide dealer organization, Mara found their inventory of new and used aircraft were at very low levels. Using creative marketing and the introduction of Stinson's new models, Mara scheduled a production run of 150 aircraft in 1934, compared to 106 in 1933.

A great emphasis was placed on an early completion of the first Model A. With the completion of production tooling, personnel were transferred from the Reliant production line. Model A NC14141, serial number 9100 was completed Friday, April 20, 1934. Taxi tests began the following Monday and the first flight was scheduled for Friday, April 27. Ralph DeVore of American Airlines was invited to be pilot in command of the first flight. To save time, the assembly line for the Model A was set up prior to receiving CAA certification. Stinson's development plan was a success. ATC 556 was granted on September 25, 1934, and four aircraft were delivered by years-end. In addition to the Model A, the SR-5A and SR-5E received CAA approval May 5, 1934 and went into immediate production. Equipped with Lycoming-Smith variable pitch-propellers and landing flaps, both models gained wide acceptance in the industry.

In August 1934, Aviation Corporation acquired the Stinson Aircraft Corporation from Cord and it became a subsidiary of the Aircraft Development Corporation. Stinson retained its management however, and continued to be a self-managing corporation.

In order to have a better understanding of the above-mentioned transaction, we must go back to 1929 and follow the funding mechanism that capitalized the Stinson Company. It all began when W. Averill Harriman and Robert Lehman formed Aviation Corporation (AVCO), as a Delaware Corporation in March 1929 with a capitalization of $35 million. The investors in the Aviation Corporation included Victor Emmanuel, Schroder Rockefeller, Henry Lockhart, and Tom Gridler, who were also the primary financing arms for

Originally ordered by William Randolph Hearst, the only V-1AD Special built is an eight passenger/two pilot deluxe executive variant of the V-1A (19 built including converted prototype), but powered by a 1,000-hp Wright Cyclone R-1820-G2 radial engine rather than the 650-hp version that powered six other V-1AD deluxe executive variants. Restored in 1971 by Harold Johnston as the Spirit of Pueblo *and shown here at the Tucson airport in 1973—the same year the author rode in it from Burlington, Colorado to Blakesburg, Iowa and back to attend the Antique Aircraft Association fly-in—it was later rechristened* Lady Peace II. *It is the sole surviving Vultee V-1A in the world and is now on display at the Shannon Air Museum in Fredericksburg, Virginia.*

SR-5 Reliant without trailing edge wing flaps, powered by a 225-hp R-680-4 Lycoming engine

Cord enterprises.

In 1929, the Cord Corporation was formed as a holding and management company for the properties Cord and his associates controlled. AVCO was the second largest investor in the Cord Corporation, bested only by Cord's personal investment. Even though it was named as part of the Cord Holding Company, AVCO retained its own corporate identity and board of directors. On November 12, 1929, Stinson announced a merger with the Cord Corporation, and in 1932, Cord and Gerald F. "Jerry " Vultee formed the Airplane Development Corporation to expand their holdings in the California aircraft manufacturing area. The majority of the financing for the California venture was furnished by AVCO. Stinson's merger with the Cord Corporation and the establishment of the Airplane Development Corporation paved the way for AVCO's acquisition of Stinson.

In the spring of 1934, AVCO investors were becoming concerned with Cord's involvement in so many activities, and decided it was time to protect their sizable investment in the Cord Corporation. In a stock and cash transaction, AVCO acquired the Airplane Development Corporation from Cord in July 1934 and renamed it the Aviation Manufacturing Corporation. In August 1934, AVCO acquired Stinson from Cord, and it became a subsidiary of the Aviation Manufacturing Corporation.

A blend of new and old management personnel came with the new ownership. Victor Emmanuel, Henry Lockhart and Tom Gridler became the directors of Stinson, and Mara became vice president and general manager. B. D. De Weese remained president of the company and the engineering staff remained the same.

Certification problems with the new wing held up production of the SR-5 series. The SR-5B RELIANT was approved April 5, 1934, the SR-5A RELIANT received ATC approval May 5, 1934. SR-5E RELIANT ATC 537 was approved May 5, 1934 using a 225-hp Lycoming R-680-4 engine. The SR-5E was structurally identical to the SR-5A and was offered with minimal optional equipment. The customer was allowed to custom order their aircraft. With a base price of $5775, most customers ordered optional equipment that pushed the price to near $9,000.

All SR-5 aircraft were fitted with a redesigned wing. The span decreased 2 feet and the chord increased to 80 inches, reducing the wing aspect ratio. All SR-5 aircraft were equipped with trailing edge flaps. The landing flaps were activated by a mechanically tuned torque tube and could be lowered to any desired setting from a control marked "Selective-Guide" in the cabin.

The fuselage was completely redesigned, starting with a NACA engine cowling. The flight instruments are mounted on the indirectly lighted instrument panel. The Lycoming engine was attached to engine mounts with improved rubber mounted fittings. Ground handling was improved with the use of hydraulic disc brakes and low-pressure air wheels.

Passenger comfort was improved with new cabin insulation, cabin heater, and ventilation system which permits passengers to regulate the amount of warm or cool air entering the cabin. The baggage compartment is of adequate size to hold bags and golf clubs. Stinson engineers developed a new and more aerodynamic windshield which provides wider vision, and a sun visor is standard equipment. Safety glass is used throughout the cabin. An armrest is provided, the dual control column is adjustable, and one control wheel is conveniently removable. Both pilot seats are adjustable.

Two 37.5 gallon wing tanks were standard and an optional 50-gallon tank was available. The wing span of the SR-5A was 41 feet, wing chord 80 inches, using a Clark Y airfoil with a total wing area 230 sq. ft. With a gross weight of 3475 pounds, a cruising speed of 120 mph, landing speed no flaps 58 mph, and landing speed with flaps 50 mph, the SR-5A offered to the flying public a remarkable aircraft.

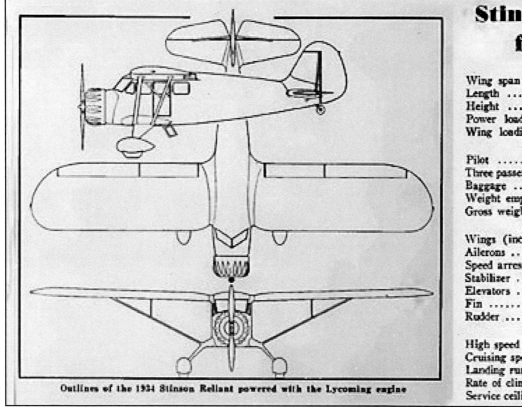

Stinson Reliant information from the February 1934 issue of Aero Digest *magazine*

SR-5C Special with trailing edge wing flags and powered by a 245-hp R-680-6 Lycoming engine. As new price was $6,595

SR-5A Special, approved for higher gross weight, and modified with a smaller tail group

1934 photograph of the Stinson factory in Wayne, Michigan

CHAPTER 8

Yellow with red trim 4-place SR-5E Reliant NC13863, s/n 9237-A, powered by a 225-hp R-680-4 Lycoming engine, equipped with trailing edge wing flags and priced at $5,775. Owned by Newark Air Service and photographed at the Newark Metropolitan Airport

1934 SR-5A Reliant NC14150, s/n 9247-A, equipped with trailing edge wing flaps

Chapter 9
1935:
The Talk of the Town

Artist rendering of American Airlines Stinson Model A tri-motor, NC14141, s/n 9100, eight passenger, two pilots and one stewardess, powered by three 260-hp R-680-5 Lycoming engines, price to airlines $37,500

Immediately following the approval of the SR-5 in May 1934, Jack Irvine realized the huge marketing potential for adapting the double-tapered wing design from the Model A to the Reliant line of aircraft. Irvine assembled the company's engineering team and industrial stylist, Lloyd Skinner, and challenged them to design the very best Stinson Reliant yet, using the Model A wing design. This aircraft would eventually become the SR-7, and its journey to production would last through 1935. Adding the new wing to the Stinson line would require extensive design, structural testing, and flight testing to receive approval. With this in mind, management set a goal to have the new wing approved and in production very early in 1936.

The SR-5 wing was redesigned using trailing edge flaps, and would be continued without engineering changes through 1935. The double-tapered wing was designed for a single-wing strut, but the new wing for the SR-6 would continue to use the double-wing strut arrangement. The fin and rudder were redesigned for the SR-6, giving the aircraft excellent in-flight control and a pleasing appearance. The engineering team also changed the horizontal tail assembly, and for the first time on a Stinson aircraft, put balance controls on the elevator.

The engineering team asked Lloyd Skinner to prepare several drawings of potential exterior and interior design for the SR-6. Skinner thought the square door design used on all Reliant aircraft was obsolete by 1935 standards. He suggested widening the door and using larger windows to give the aircraft a more modern appearance. He requested a nearby Packard automobile dealership to display one of their high-end models for the engineering team to observe. The SR-6 would use many of the Packard interior styling innovations. With the more efficient wings, Jack Irvine also suggested that the fuselage be widened, making the width of the rear seat at least 52 inches. Due to the availability of higher-horsepower engines, the SR-6 could be certified as a true five-place aircraft.

Displaying a new windshield design, redesigned instrument panel, and a much larger cabin area, the SR-6 was marketed as a new aircraft. To maintain the structural integrity of the fuselage, the wider door was given a stylized, tapered appearance. Once the SR-6 entered production, the engineering department focused exclusively on designing the new double-tapered wing destined for 1936 production.

Acceptance of the Model A exceeded Stinson's expectations, and with over 20 orders placed, the factory was a beehive of activity. Delta Airlines purchased three Model A airliners. SR-6 production did not start until late July with a total production run of 60 aircraft by years-end. Engineering, structural testing, and in-flight testing continued for the double-tapered wing that would also soon be in production in the coming year.

Aero Digest
March 1934
Stinson Model A: A Low-Wing Airliner

The Model A, a high-speed, low-wing, tri-motor airliner powered with Lycoming R–680BA engines is designed to fill a new place in scheduled air transportation. It is placed in production by the Stinson Aircraft Corporation in the spring.

When the first design was created in 1932, it was not the intention of the company to build a large transport for long-haul, transcontinental operations because all of their experience had been centered on smaller units for frequent, short-haul service. A survey of the situation at the time indicated the need for a fast tri-motor of good performance, which would sell for less additional cost than the larger transports, operating for less cost per passenger mile.

These planes were intended for bad weather flying and night flights, but were primarily used as high-speed parallel feeders for larger planes. This means that the Model A can handle the mail, passenger and express business from the intermediate cities now inadequately served by the

Stinson Model A cabin, seating for 8-passengers, 2 pilots, and 1 stewardess

large transports, due to the added costs for such stops and the reduced through speeds.

For example, high-speed service has been made available from coast to coast, but the transcontinental planes do not stop at important cities such as Albany, Rochester, Dayton and Cincinnati. To furnish the same superior service to these cities, the Stinson airliner will leave terminals an hour in advance of the transcontinental plane, stop at intermediate cities, collect passengers, and deliver them to a terminal at which the transcontinental plane makes regular stops, thus providing a service previously unavailable.

Stinson Model A right wing panel at the factory

The need for this type of airliner is obvious to the operators of all major airlines in this country, with the exception of those interested only in transcontinental routes. Some of the airlines also have routes which cannot support larger planes and require smaller planes to do the job economically.

The Model A is powered by three Lycoming nine-cylinder radial engines rated at 240hp each at 2000rpm. It has a low-wing design with the inner section of the wings "gulled" and braced to avoid the use of deep cantilever sections. The wheels retract into the nacelles and the "speed of arresters" (flaps) extend from nacelle to nacelle on the under surface of the wings. They are operated in unison or with retraction of the wheels if desired.

To complete this design, it was necessary to develop a new type of sequential cantilever wing, which was originally considered in 1931. With this wing an accomplished fact, the balance of the airplane does not deviate from standard construction practice as the entire structure is of chrome and molybdenum tubing, welded and heat treated in the same conventional manner as the other Stinson tri-motor airliners. The engines are covered with metal within the exhaust areas, this being several feet behind the cylinder heads and several feet out from the center line. The remainder of the structure is covered with fabric.

Special attention has been given to passenger comfort, vision, quietness, ventilation, heating, and other modern airliner prerequisites. The insulated cabin has adjustable, hammock-type chairs for eight people. Individual heating, ventilation, and lighting are all provided. The baggage compartment to the rear of the cabin is accessible from the inside, but is loaded from the outside. Additional mail space is provided in the nacelles, as well as a commissary furnished with a well-equipped laboratory located in the very back of the cabin.

The cockpit has space for a pilot and co-pilot (if a co-pilot is required on service of this type) and all controls are within handy reach and easy to operate. Vision is excellent. A hatch located over the cockpit is fitted with a large rear vision mirror for use primarily while taxiing. The Smith controllable pitch propellers operate in unison and are virtually automatic after takeoff if the pilot desires. This feature simplifies the synchronization of the engine revolutions.

Instruments and Equipment

Standard equipment also includes Sperry's horizon, Sperry's gyro, standard flight and engine instruments (all on dashboard), electrically operated landing gear, a 25amp generator, Pyrene fire extinguisher equipment, landing lights, air wheels, and hydraulic brakes. Extra equipment includes stewardess seating, two-way radio and mast, reversible chairs, cabin air cooling, an international standard 3-minute flare, and three 1½ minute flares. Goodrich de-icing equipment, dual controls, Lux fire extinguisher equipment, engine-driven vacuum pump, adjustable booster brake control, and heated airspeed pitot tube are also provided.

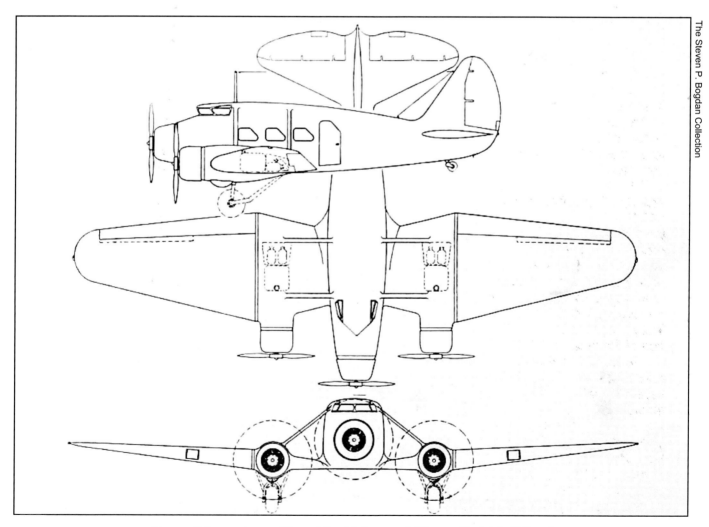

Above: "Three-view outline of the high-speed Stinson Model A Airliner"
Top: Front view of the Stinson Model A. Both drawings from the March, 1934 issue of Aero Digest

Loading mailbag into storage compartment in engine nacelle. Pittsburgh based Central Airlines purchased five of the Model A

The following is taken from a 13-page pamphlet handed out to both prospective and actual buyers of the Stinson Model A Airliner.

RECOMMENDATIONS
for the
OPERATION
of the
STINSON MODEL "A" AIRLINER

STINSON AIRCRAFT CORPORATION
WAYNE, MICHIGAN.

BETTER SERVICE FOR PASSENGERS
MORE REVENUE FOR AIRLINES
MORE JOBS FOR MORE PEOPLE

The Stinson Model "A" Airliner * was built to do three definite jobs which should produce more traffic and therefore, more work for a greater number of people.

1. For use as a "Parallel Feeder", meaning to feed traffic from intermediate cities on main Airlines to the large cities which have Transcontinental Terminals. Thus, people in the smaller towns still get improved service. This will produce more revenue and more jobs.

2. For use as an emergency plane in bad weather when the load available does not require the use of a larger plane. Instructors in 'blind' flying have pronounced the "A" as excellent even with one motor out. An additional safety factor in bad weather is the fact that the Model "A" may be landed very shortly and then has the ability to get out of small fields.

3. For use by Airlines having comparatively short hauls. Many lines must stop approximately every 100 miles. The through Transcontinental Planes cannot make those stops economically because they must fly at high altitudes to obtain their maximum speed and must make very few stops in order to speed up through schedules.

Because the Stinson Airliner can serve the intermediate towns with fast, comfortable service, it is destined to create more traffic for the main Lines and work for more Pilots, Mechanics and other personnel connected with flying.

Stinson engineers realizing that to make fast schedules with frequent stops a ship must have speed "on the ground" as well as in the air have designed into the "A" many features which, if used properly, will make for considerable economics in ground time. At the same time they have attempted to simplify many other operations and have created, we believe, an airplane which will appeal to the Pilot, the Passenger and the Operator.

*(The word 'Airliner' is copyrighted and has appeared on the fin of all Stinson Trimotors built since 1929).

Top: In 1935 Delta Air Lines purchased three of the Model A to begin their first night flight operations. These were Delta's first aircraft to include a co-pilot (called a "handyman"), and their first with reclining seats in sound-proofed cabins, and with retractable landing gear.

Bottom: Ex-American Airlines 1936 Stinson Model A in the livery of the Roscoe Turner Aeronautical Corporation, used for aerial sight-seeing tours above Indianapolis

SR-5A Reliant NC13853, s/n 9227-A, powered by a 245-hp, R-680-6 Lycoming, with trailing edge flaps - 76 built. Purchased new by oilman Deane Gill, NC13853 is now being restored in a Texas museum.

SR-6 Reliant, a five-place aircraft powered by a 245-hp R-680-6 Lycoming engine, priced at $5,995

CHAPTER 9

Lycoming-Smith Controllable Propeller

Chapter 10
1936:
The Mighty Gull-Wing Has Arrived

SR-7B NC3040, s/n 9654, a five-place aircraft powered by a 260-hp R-680-5 Lycoming engine

By mid-October 1935, the first pair of the double-tapered wings were complete and ready to be added to an aircraft fuselage. NC15139 was pulled from the production line, and the fuselage and wing strut attachment were modified to support a single strut. The uncovered wings were fitted to the fuselage to make sure there was adequate room for the fuel lines. The wings were then removed and covered, and the aircraft was prepared for flight testing. The aircraft was named SR-6X and was licensed as an experimental aircraft. Final inspection and taxi tests were completed the first week of November and the first gull-wing Stinson lifted into the air on Tuesday, November 12. A second set of wings were then built for structural testing to comply with certification rules.

Stinson management intended to announce to the world a brand-new SR-7 aircraft. The adaptation of the Model A wing using the double-tapered design gave the aircraft a completely new appearance. The new wing was not designed as, or marketed as, a gull-wing yet. Through the flight test portion of certification, many people had an opportunity to view the aircraft, and when a dealer arrived at the factory to pick up a new SR-6, he asked Jack Irvine to describe the wing. Irvine coined the word "gull-wing", and it stuck. From December forward, the new aircraft was known as the Gull-Wing Reliant. Anticipating ATC approval, production of the SR-7B began in late January, and several aircraft were ready for delivery when ATC 594 was granted February 13, 1936.

As the economy grew, the United States was experiencing a great amount of inflation, and it became obvious early on in the SR-7 production run that retail prices for Stinson aircraft must rise substantially.

Rather than increasing the price of the aircraft in the middle of the model run, a decision was made to slightly update the SR-7 and announce another new aircraft. The SR-8 Reliant was essentially a SR-7 with a redesigned interior. The standard version came with seats upholstered in leather, but was available on special order in a variety of fine fabrics. The SR-8A came with a 25-gallon fuel tank in each wing as standard equipment. The SR-8B had a 35-gallon tank in each wing and SR-8C had a 41-gallon fuel tank on each wing. The SR-8 ATC was approved May 28, 1936. Its retail price covered the increased costs of manufacturing the aircraft.

Another aircraft, the Model B, was also designed in 1936. This was Stinson's only attempt at building a twin-engine aircraft. A mockup of the Model B was completed and advertisements ran in trade magazines and airline presentations. The airlines were not interested, however, because the corporate aircraft market had not yet developed.

When the Aviation Corporation acquired Stinson from Cord in August 1934, Stinson lost its ties with Lycoming. Under Cord Ownership since 1931, Lycoming had been required to sell aircraft engines to Stinson at a substantially reduced price, sometimes below their manufacturing costs. After AVCO's acquisition, Lycoming immediately raised the price of their aircraft engines, and Stinson was given permission to purchase engines from other manufacturers. The SR-8D and E were approved for Wright engines, and Stinson purchased 46 Wright R-760E2 engines in 1936. Even with the increase in cost, Stinson did not experience price resistance and the SR-8 sold extremely well.

Aero Digest
March 1936
Standard in Long-Range:
The Stinson Reliant Models SR7-A and SR7-B

The 1936 Stinson Reliant, recently put into production by the Stinson Aircraft Corp., is an improved and faster version of the 1935 model. While it is somewhat similar in appearance to its predecessor, the new Reliant, which is available in special and standard models, is more economical to operate and incorporates vacuum-operated flaps with slots which enable slower and steeper landing glides with less run after the plane is landed.

The standard job, known as the SR7-A, and the special model, known as the SR7-B, are identical in appearance and construction, with the exception that the special model is equipped with a Lycoming controllable pitch propeller, an additional fuel tank, special leather upholstery with color

1936 SR-7C Reliant NC16113 s/n 9666 powered by a 245-hp R-680-6 Lycoming engine. 1 of 3 built.

options, and a more powerful engine.

The fuselage is made of welded steel tubing and is fabric covered. Seats are arranged in tandem, the rear seats being of the "form-fitting" type. Pilot seats are adjustable forward and backward and have a folding back. Armrests are provided for the pilot and the copilot, as well as the two passengers. All seats are upholstered in tan Spanish leather in the standard model, with four shades of special leather available for choice on the SR-7B. Cabin trim includes a recessed instrument panel, tope sidewalls, map pop pockets, ash receivers, assist cords, rear cabin sidelights and a carpeted floor.

Windows are operated with automobile-type regulators, and are made of safety glass. No-draft ventilation is provided in the rear windows. The windshield is the transport V-type, provided in the 1936 series, greater visibility because of its large size. Windshield glass is mounted in adhesive to eliminate drafts and moisture, and each front side quarter remains clear in wet weather. Baggage allowance and space have been increased, space being provided under the rear seats for full-size Gladstone bags. Additional baggage space is provided in another compartment, accessible from a door on the outside and equipped with lighting facilities.

Ventilation is controllable. Air used for heating or ventilation is taken from in front of the engine to eliminate all fumes and ensure pure air. The air is then forced through large ducts which carry it to the front and rear of the cabin. A heater tube has been placed in the exhaust, and this may be easily and quickly removed for inspection. When the plane is being operated in warm climates, this unit can be eliminated.

As in the 1935 models, Stinson engineers have eliminated the large control column on which the wheel was mounted. The appearance has been improved and more room provided by the use of auto-type dual controls, which protrude from the dash and remove all obstruction from the center of the cockpit. The unit on the right is removable. Instruments have been mounted in an indirectly lighted, rubber insulated panel, which is equipped with a Kollsman compass, airspeed indicator, tachometer, altimeter, and oil pressure and oil temperature gauges. Combined rudder and brake pedals are provided. The brakes are operated by depressing the heel on the pedal, while the rudder is controlled with

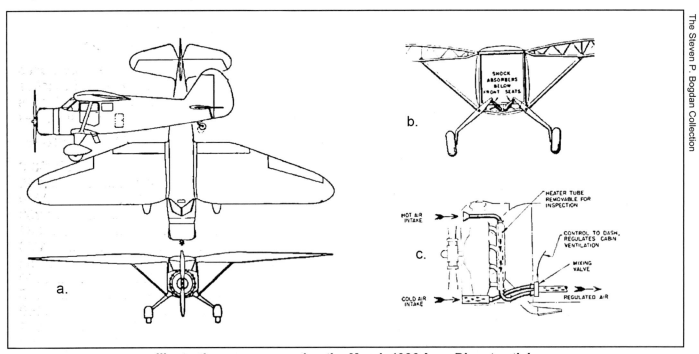

Illustrations accompanying the March 1936 Aero Digest article

a. 3-view drawing of the Stinson Reliant SR-7
b. Shock absorber mounting location below front seats
c. Upper hot air intake and lower cold air intake in front of engine

Illustrations accompanying the March 1936 Aero Digest *article*

d. Drawing showing tail wheel deflection upward and backward
e. Vacuum operated flap diagram
f. Cabin detail showing location of outer baggage door

the forward motion of either foot. The brakes are made of a series of copper and steel discs activated by hydraulic action. Entrance to the cabin is by a steel tube step on each side through two large doors. The wing structure is of the gull type and is made of metal with a fabric covering. The spars are made of welded chrome molybdenum steel tubing and the ribs are riveted, square sections of dural tubing with dural gussets. Flaps are the trailing edge type made of riveted dural and covered with fabric. The flaps are run by vacuum cylinders with a pressure tank to automatically ensure operation. A vacuum line leads from the engine, and a 200 cu.in. reserve tank provides an ample and constant source of power.

A wide-tread, cantilever-type landing gear with 8.50x10 low-pressure Goodyear tires is provided on the Reliant. The gear is hinged at the lower corners of the fuselage with the inner ends of the beams attached to Cleveland Pneumatic Aerial shock absorbers. Metal pants, or guards, are optional equipment.

The tail wheel is a double-action, fully-swiveling unit equipped with a 10"x5" streamlined Goodyear pneumatic tire and a long stroke shock absorber. The wheel is hinged so that shocks and landing loads are taken with a backward as well as an upward movement, which decreases shocks to the rear and improves comfortable taxing.

The standard model SR7-A is equipped with an adjustable pitch Hamilton Standard metal propeller driven by a 225-hp Lycoming R680-4 engine enclosed in a full NACA cowl. A 245-hp Lycoming R680-6 engine is used to power the SR7-B.

Standard equipment on both models includes Bauer and Black first aid kit, Eclipse direct drive starter and booster coil, cabin heater, Pyrene fire extinguisher, 35 amperage hour Exide storage battery, Grimes navigation lights, and Fafnir ball bearings for plane and cockpit controls. Color on this SR7-A is black for the fuselage with silver on the wings and the stripes set off with by a red pinstripe.

SR-7 specifications from the March 1936 *Aero Digest* article

Wing span	41 feet 7.25 inches
Overall length	26 feet 8.81 inches
Overall height	8 feet 6 inches
Wing area	256.5 square feet

	SR-7A	SR-7B
Engine Lycoming	R680-4	R680-6
Horse power	225	245
Empty weight (lbs.)	2260	2310
Useful load (lbs.)	1115	1290
Payload (lbs.)	615	662
Gross weight (lbs.)	3375	3600
Baggage (lbs.)	105	152
Fuel capacity (gals.)	50	70
Oil capacity (gals.)	4	5
Maximum speed (m.p.h.)	148	150
Cruising speed (m.p.h.)	138.5	141
Landing speed (with flaps)	48 (m.p.h.)	50
Landing speed (no flaps)	55 (m.p.h.)	57
Service ceiling (feet)	12,800	14,600
Rate of climb (ft./m.)	715	850
Cruising range (miles)	400	560

Stinson distributors and factory representatives attending the annual sales convention at the Stinson factory in mid-January 1936, posing in front of the SR-6X, NC15139 (s/n 9641)—the test mule that was taken off the production line and fitted with the wings that had been developed for the SR-7. The SR-6X took its maiden flight just two months before the sales convention.

Dealers meet For New Sales Campaign

Stanley C. "Jiggs" Huffman, an aviation businessman in Cincinnati, and the President of the National Air Cab Association, attended the January 1936 Stinson factory annual sales convention for distributors and factory representatives. There they were introduced to the new SR-7. On the 26th of that same month *The Enquirer* of Cincinnati quoted him saying:

"When fully loaded, the new Reliant will take off with the pilot's hands removed from the controls. It will fly indefinitely in the air with the hands off the controls. When stalled and with power shut off with hands removed from the controls it will not spin, but merely assumes a normal gliding angle. The plane is equipped with flaps, or air brakes, which allow it to descend even more slowly than a parachute, and on the ground hydraulic brakes bring the plane to a stop with a landing roll of only 250 feet."

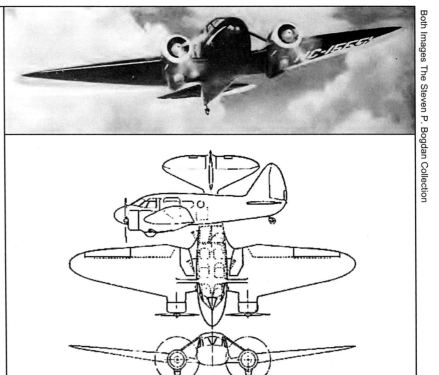

Model B Specifications	
Wing span	52' 6"
Overall height	31' 8"
Overall length	10' 6'
Wing area	357 sq. ft.
Wing loading	18.5 lbs./sq. ft.
Power loading	12.7 lbs./h.p.
Empty weight	4500 lbs.
Useful load	2100 lbs.
Payload	1150 lbs.
Gross weight	6600 lbs.
Estimated Performances	
Cruising speed (6000 ft.)	160 mph
Cruising speed (3000 ft.)	155 mph
Cruising speed (1000 ft.)	52 mph
Rate of climb	1150 fpm
Service ceiling	16,000 feet
Service ceiling (1 engine)	3800 feet
Cruising range (full load)	900 miles
Take-off run	650 feet

Left: The projected Specifications and Estimated Performances of the cancelled Model B project

Upper right: Artist rendition of the proposed Stinson Model B Bi-motor for corporate customers and as a feeder for small airlines. In reality this project did not go beyond the mockup stage.

Lower right: 3-view scale drawing of the proposed Model B

CHAPTER 10

SR-8C Reliant, four passenger, one pilot, and powered by a 260-hp R-680-5 Lycoming engine

SR-8E Reliant powered by a 320-hp Wright R-760-E2 engine, four passengers, one pilot, and priced at $12,000

Safety Developments Pioneered by STINSON

TAIL SPINS. To Edward A. Stinson, founder of this Company, goes the credit for having been first to discover how to come out of a Tail Spin. Most merciless Killer of the early days the Tail Spin had claimed scores of lives prior to Stinson's discovery. How many additional lives have been saved since that time would be impossible to estimate.

INHERENT STABILITY. To prevent the unintentional Tail Spin the first Stinson plane, in 1926, and all Stinsons since that time included the principle of Inherent Stability in their design. Not only has Inherent Stability made flying easier but it has also prevented untold scores of accidents.

WHEEL BRAKES. Brakes were first used by Stinson in the early exhibition days prior to the war. The first brakes on the wheels of a commercial production airplane were installed on the first Stinson in 1926. Without the ground control afforded by brakes the transport planes of today would not be possible. Impossible also is it to estimate the number of accidents which Stinson's brake discovery has prevented.

VACUUM FLAPS WITH SLOTS—HYDRAULIC BRAKES. No single feature in recent years has done more to increase the safety of flying than Vacuum Flaps with Slots which make possible more vertical descent, permit a plane to descend slower than a parachute and with the aid of Hydraulic Brakes to stop in a distance of 250 feet. Again Stinson was first to offer these features to the private flyer as standard equipment.

ELECTRIC STARTERS. The old method of pulling propellers through by hand claimed many lives—caused many injuries. To prevent these accidents Stinson was first to make electric starters standard equipment on its airplanes.

SAFETY GLASS. Again in 1926, in spite of its then great cost, Stinson pioneered Safety Glass which has been standard equipment since that time.

CONTROLLABLE PITCH PROPELLER. Because it makes possible quicker take off, more rapid climb and the carrying of greater loads the Controllable Propeller is playing an important role in the cause of safety. No longer is it necessary to clear obstructions on small airports by inches. Again Stinson has led by placing more Controllable Propellers in the hands of private flyers than any other commercial builder.

RUBBER MOTOR MOUNTINGS. To ward off vibration and metal fatigue; to lengthen airplane life and deaden noise, Stinson pioneered Rubber Motor Mountings in 1927 as standard equipment. This was prior to the time that the term "Floating Power" was coined and generally accepted in the Automobile Industry.

MARCH 1936

The keynote of the Stinson policy has always been SAFETY and RELIABILITY.

Apart from the desire to throw every safe-guard around human life good business has dictated this policy.

As a result, Stinson has never compromised SAFETY to meet passing fads.

Each year this policy has paid dividends in lives, in lower maintenance costs and in ever increasing public acceptance of Stinson planes as sound dependable transportation units both at home and abroad.

Private, or non-scheduled flying, was 100% safer in 1935 than in 1934, according to Department of Commerce statistics, with a fatality for approximately each million miles of flight.

During the same period the pilots and owners of Stinson planes, representing a sizable total of all airplanes in use in America, flew approximately 2,000,000 miles per fatal accident or about 100% safer than the average for all non-scheduled flying.

Believing that in the 1936 Stinson 'Reliant' we have developed an even safer and more reliable plane, we have asked the pilots and owners of Stinson planes whose good judgment and careful piloting made possible the 1935 safety record to join with us in a national campaign to further increase confidence in aviation by making 1936 the outstanding SAFETY year.

Stinson Aircraft Corp.

DIVISION OF AVIATION MANUFACTURING CORP.

Wayne, Mich., U. S. A.

In 1936 Beech sold 44 Staggerwing aircraft while Stinson sold 183 Reliants.

1936 Stinson Reliant SR-7B NC15166, s/n 9656 five-place aircraft, powered by a 245-hp Lycoming R-680-B6 radial piston engine. 47 built

The Able Collection

Chapter 11
1937:
Art and Engineering

The large sign in front of the SR-9C NC18415 reads "The 900th 4 & 5 Passenger Stinson Powered By Lycoming, Delivered By Stinson Aircraft Corp., Wayne, Mich." There are two more aircraft behind NC18415 and one to its left. The sign hanging from the ceiling above the right wingtip reads, as it has since 1926, The Pilot Depends On You.

Although the Model A tri-motor was very successful, Stinson management realized that airlines were converting to all-metal aircraft. They were purchasing the Douglas DC-3 and phasing out smaller aircraft. Stinson did not have the engineering or production ability to compete in the all-metal market, and Stinson suppliers, providing power plants, propellers, and steel tubing were experiencing the greatest inflation since 1932 and they were passing the increases on to the aircraft manufacturers. Stinson management was concerned that inflation would negatively affect the sale of aircraft. Therefore it was decided to introduce new models with increased horsepower in order to generate more interest in Stinson.

In a major departure from all previous windshield designs, which used flat glass panels, Stinson engineers developed a mold to produce a curved front windshield. The new design used large plastic panels from flat stock. These were heated in a mold to the correct shape and then trimmed to fit the aircraft. The windshield was supported by a structural member in the center and had an attractive, stylized curve on the right and left side of the fuselage.

Introduced as the improved Reliant for 1937, the SR-9B was well received by the dealer organization. Stinson offered three production versions of the SR-9. The SR-9C was offered with a ski fuselage designated by the letter S added to the serial number. A baggage compartment near the cabin was lengthened to accommodate several pairs of skis. The SR-9DM was offered as a multi-purpose aircraft designated by the letter M. The accessory options for the SR-9DM included an auxiliary door near the main door on the right side, large doorframes for the main and auxiliary doors, a removable back on the copilot's chair, a stretcher door in the back wall, a ski-type fuselage, provisions for an ambulance litter, and installation of a metal-lined cabin. The SR-9F could be ordered from the manufacturer with a special longer cabin providing a compartment near the baggage compartment with a 200 pound maximum weight limit. Because of this, the Model F differed structurally from the other models of the SR-9 series, and the SR-9FM was offered as another multipurpose aircraft.

Based on customer requests, Stinson departed from mainly manufacturing aircraft powered by Lycoming engines. These models commanded a much higher price point. The SR-9D, powered by a 285-hp Wright engine was priced at $12,000, the SR-9E, powered by a 320-hp Wright engine, was priced at $12,500, while the SR-9F, powered by a 400-hp P&W Wasp engine, was priced at $18,000. These three models represented 50 percent of 1937 production.

When mechanical engineers Francis A. Pratt and Amos Whitney left the Colt Firearms Company in 1860 to form Pratt & Whitney Engineering Company, an R-985 was not mentioned in their management plan. In their wildest dreams they could never have imagined that in 2022 the names Pratt & Whitney would be associated with the world's most prestigious aircraft engine company.

Robert L. Hall, Chief Engineer (former engineer for Grangeville Brothers Aircraft Company where he was responsible for designing the famous GB racers) proposed to management that he should design a SR-9 powered by a 450-hp Pratt & Whitney aircraft engine. The engineering department was aware that the current line of SR-9 aircraft would require structural changes for certification with the 450-hp engine. With management approval, the redesign was given a high priority.

Maintaining the same exterior dimensions of the lower horsepower aircraft the fuselage wings and tail services was strengthened to handle the increased horsepower. The SR-9F was a totally redesigned aircraft with very few components interchangeable with the other SR-9 aircraft in production at the time. From the firewall forward, it

Amateur period photo of Katherine Edward's Stinson Reliant SR-9FD NC18425 s/n 5715, repowered in 1951 with a 450-hp Single Stage Supercharged P&W R-985-AN-1 Wasp Jr Engine. In 1993 its Razorback Fiberglass fabric had deteriorated to a point that it rendered the aircraft unairworthy. The fabric was replaced with Randolph Dope and Ceconite fabric. Rick Rezabek has owned this aircraft since 2005.

was totally new and included an increase in cowl length to aerodynamically cover the larger power plant. The SR-9F, powered by a 450-hp P&W Wasp engine, was priced at $18,000. These three non-Lycoming powered models represented 50 percent of 1937 production.

Pittsburgh Press
September 11, 1932
Katherine Edwards Solos

The next society woman candidate for a private pilot's license is Miss Katherine May Edwards, 4801 Forbes St. Miss Edwards has completed the required number of hours of solo flying and will take her private pilot's examination within the next two weeks.

Miss Edwards is numbered among the pioneer aviation enthusiasts. She has two ships, a four passenger Stinson and a Monocoupe. She travels all over the country by air and usually takes a guest or two with her. Recently she returned from the air derby where she had two passengers as guests.

The two aircraft mentioned in the press release was a Monocoupe 110 and a Stinson SM-7B Junior powered by a 300-hp Pratt & Whitney Wasp Junior engine. Born in 1873 Edwards was 59 years old when she obtained her private pilot's license. Prior to obtaining a private pilot's license Edwards used the services of a professional pilot.

The air derby mentioned in the press release was the 1932 National Air Races held in Cleveland Ohio. Estelle Stinson attended the air races and is covered in Chapter 20. As a Stinson owner and a woman aviator Katherine Edwards received VIP status and had the opportunity to meet Estelle Stinson.

In 1937, as ordered some three months earlier, Edwards accepted a black with red trim SR-9FD Reliant, NC18425, s/n 5715. The bill of sale dated August 6, 1937, listed of the owner as Katherine May Edwards. The data plate shows August 10, 1937 as a manufacture date. The base price $18,000 for this aircraft delivered at the Wayne factory, compared to the $4,000 cost of an average home. With options this aircraft retailed for over $22,000. A comparable aircraft in 2022 would be the Piper M600/SLS powered by a Pratt & Whitney PT6A-42A 600-shp (shaft horsepower, derated from 800-shp) priced at $3.3 million.

Miss Katherine May Edwards, the first owner of the Stinson SR-9FD Reliant NC18425

The Stinson Reliant Model SR-9FD as ordered by Edwards

Weights

Gross weight: 4,500 pounds
Useful load: 1,565 pounds
Allowance for special equipment: 150 pounds
Fuel: 130 gallons
Oil: 8 gallons
People: 4 including pilot - 680 pounds
Empty weight: 2,935 pounds

Performance

Cruising speed at 9,600 feet: 178 mph
Cruising speed at 5,000 foot 169 mph
Takeoff run [calm air]: 545 feet
Landing run [calm air]: 375 feet
Climb rate at sea level: 1,510 ft/min
Surface ceiling: 22,600 feet
Range normal: 690 miles

Standard Equipment

Built in pressure fire extinguisher
Carburetor air temperature gauge
Rate of climb indicator
Sensitive altimeter
Landing lights
15 amp generator
Engine driven fuel pump
Manifold pressure gauge
Disk-type hydraulic brakes
Radio bonding and shielding

Special Equipment

Constant speed Hamilton-Standard propeller
Extra 24 gallon fuel tanks in wings
    [1050 mile range]
Sperry directional Gyro
Artificial horizon
Fuel analyzer
Radio receiver
Radio direction finder
Radio transmitter
Heated pilot head
Electric flares

During World War II nearly 50 Reliants were impressed into wartime service. Late in 1941 Miss Edwards was forced to sell NC18425 to the government, making her SR-9F one of four that received the military designation UC-81E. However, her aircraft did not serve with the military directly, but was sent to the newly created Civil Air Patrol (CAP), the civilian auxiliary of the United States Army Air Forces. Piecing the story together from original news accounts and Civil Air Patrol Bulletins, it appears that NC18425 was delivered to Group 217 in Western New York, specifically to the Squadron at Jamestown. Group 217 was commanded by John H. Wright, who owned several telephone companies in Pennsylvania, along with being president of the Jamestown Telephone Corporation, as well as the National Chautauqua County Bank of Jamestown. Wright's personal aircraft, which he used in the same manner as Miss Edwards to visit his businesses, had been impressed by the government before his appointment to the CAP. The government sent NC18425 to Jamestown to fill a gap they had inadvertently created. Wright, a seriously enthusiastic amateur motion picture maker, received the Stinson under the whimsical moniker "Wright's Motion Pictures" and put it into service as a trainer and patrol plane. In May 1942 Wright

Left: Ad in June 1937 issue of Aviation Magazine

personally bought and donated an Aeronca trainer, and Jamestown citizens gathered funds to buy another. NC18425 was then transferred to Republic Aircraft in East Farmingdale, New York.

Republic Aircraft used NC18425 as a corporate asset for nearly the rest of the war, mostly at their Evansville, Indiana plant where they manufactured P-47 Thunderbolts. It was used to check out new test pilots, and transport company personnel as needed. Although P-47 production would not end until October 1945, by August of that year Republic had no further need for NC18425 and sold it for $15,000 to Edward Warren, one of their company pilots.

Miss Edwards had replaced the Reliant with a Fairchild 24, only to find that the Fairchild just did not have the same performance and appeal. Warren had NC18425 barely a month before Miss Edwards, having found out the Stinson was no longer in government service, located the new owner of her old aircraft, only to be dismayed to discover that it wasn't for sale. On September 22, after some negotiation she managed to purchase it from Mr. Warren, at a reported twice his purchase price, plus the trade of the Fairchild 24 she had been flying as a replacement. She kept it until ill health led her to sell it in 1950.

After Miss Edwards parted with the Reliant, it went through a succession of owners with the sixth one being Jonesy Paul, the longtime president of the National Stinson Club. Under his stewardship (1966 – 1993), NC18425 became the subject aircraft for AMT's 1:48 scale model. The next owner (1993 – 2005), Dr. David Stark, began a seven year frame up restoration, bringing it to its current show winning condition, right down to the period correct color and rib stitching.

Rick Rezabek purchased N18425 in January 2005 and bases his SR-9FD near Los Angeles. Today the aircraft is black with red trim, with a new R-985-AN-1 450-hp P&W engine installed in 1957, state-of-the-art fabric covering, modern radios and a meticulous maintenance program. Rezabek's Stinson SR-9FD is a far superior aircraft today compared to when it rolled out the factory door in 1937. The R-985 easily reaches 2,300 RPM for takeoff and cruises at 150 mph indicated at 7,500 feet. Rezabek regularly commutes from McCall, Idaho, to Los Angeles and reports his Stinson has spectacular climb performance.

SR-9 advertisement from the October 1937 edition of Aviation Magazine

1937 Stinson Factory Photos

Top Left:

Stacked pre-made SR-9 wing sets - some will be fitted with wing tanks available as an option on some models.

Middle Left:

Fuselage under construction

Bottom Left:

Stinson factory fuselage assembly line where basic fuselages were built in batches and stored. When an order was received they could finish the aircraft to meet the customers needs.

CHAPTER 11

1937 Stinson Factory Photos

Top Right:

Stored fuselages with the window style that the factory only used in 1937

Middle Right:

All Stinson SR-9 aircraft bearing a NC184** were registered in 1937 except for SR-9F NC18483 s/n 5722, which received its CAA NC number in 1938 after the first 10 SR-10s had been registered.

Bottom Right:

SR-9 crated for delivery to Stinson's distributor in the United Kingdom

SR-9E Reliant with a 320-hp Wright R-760E-2 engine, four passengers, one pilot and priced at $12,500

Left photos

Top, left to right:

January 1936 SR-9 ad from Flight magazine

-

May 1937 Model A ad from Aeroplane magazine

-

May 1936 Flight magazine ad for the never-built Model B

Bottom right:

Receipt of another Reliant at Croydon Airport. Note the DH 85 Leopard Moth in the hangar

All photos The Steven P. Bogdan Collection

Brian Allen Aviation was the exclusive Stinson distributor in England. A former WWI pilot, he ran a motorcycle business for most of the 1920s where he sold numerous motorcycles to his occasional Croydon riding partner T. E. Lawrence of *Lawrence of Arabia* fame. He launched his aviation business in May 1935 at the Croydon Airport in South London.

In addition being the Stinson distributor, he was the exclusive distributor for the Belgian designed Tipsy and ran an aerial photography business. He advertised heavily in the British magazines *Aeroplane* and *Flight*. In 1937 he was offering the SR-9 for £2,000 with delivery promised in six to eight weeks.

During WWII Brian Seamer Allen and his wife Kathleen were killed by a German V-1 flying bomb. His company continued on until July 1953.

Chapter 12
1938:
The Rugged and Reliable SR-10

In June and July 1938, Bill Mara contacted several Stinson dealers for their thoughts concerning the expansion of the Stinson line. At the time, Stinson was only building large aircraft, which were expensive and inaccessible to much of the market. There was also high inflation, further increasing the price of Stinson's aircraft and lowering sales. Mara knew that Stinson needed to develop a small, less expensive aircraft that would continue Stinson's legacy of excellence at a price more customers could afford. He discussed these ideas with Stinson's dealers, and they agreed that this is what the civilian aircraft market was requiring.

[On June 23, 1938, the Civil Aeronautics Authority, CAA, replaced the Bureau of Air Commerce.]

Mara's solution was for Stinson to develop a three-place aircraft in the $3,000 range. He thought this might well be the means of providing the stimulus needed to raise sales for which the industry had waited so long. Mara suggested that between now and the next management meeting, the basic design philosophy should be developed. He also suggested that the president of Aviation Manufacturing Corporation, L. B. Manning, be invited to attend along with M. A. Mills, L. E. Reisner, and Professor Peter Altman of the University of Detroit.

A timetable for the new design was then established, beginning immediately and continuing until the start of production. Basic engineering was to be completed in September and October, with final acceptance of the design in November 1938. The first prototype assembly and structural testing was to be completed in December and January, and flight tests were to be conducted in February and March. All tooling was scheduled to be completed and ATC approval obtained in April 1939. Following this schedule, limited production could begin in March.

With some fine-tuning, primarily to increase the efficiency of production, the design was approved for the new aircraft in November. Altman recommended fixed wing slots for the aircraft. He explained that to obtain the desired flight characteristics without these slots, the design would need longer wings and there would have to be a decrease in cruising speed. Stinson management decided, however, that fixed wing slots were an added expense since they were not being used on the company's current production lines. Thus, they were not included on the first prototype.

Over the past several years, Stinson had invested a great amount of resources in updating the Reliant line of aircraft. With relatively low production runs, reengineering expenses had a negative effect on Stinson's profitability. As a result, management decided upon a major updating of gull-wing aircraft for 1938, the SR-10, planning a three-year production run for this aircraft with only minor changes.

On Monday, August 3, 1938 the Aviation Manufacturing Corporation purchased the Stinson Aircraft Corporation. This change, which involved the liquidation and dissolution of the Stinson Aircraft Corporation, was made primarily for corporate reasons. The Stinson company, now the Stinson Aircraft Division, became a subsidiary of the Aviation Manufacturing Corporation, but it continued to operate independently.

On August 23, 1938 the U.S. Army Air Corps issued a specification for a short range, three-seat liaison observation aircraft. Twelve manufacturers submitted proposals and by the end of February, 1939, Stinson was selected as one of three finalists. The Stinson Model 74, designed by A. P. Fontaine, followed the pattern of German engineer, Fieseler Storch. Full-span, Handley Page automatic slots were fitted to the leading edge of the wing along with pilot-operated slotted flaps on the trailing edge.

Aviation Magazine
March 1938

The industry lost one of its finest engineers and most admired personalities when Gerald and Sylvia Vultee, flying a Stinson SR-6, crashed in Arizona on January 29. They were returning from Washington D.C. to California. Flying in a blinding snow storm. They crashed between Sedona and Flagstaff, if the aircraft was 100 foot higher they would have cleared the ridge.

Aero Digest
May 1938

The Stinson SR-10 is a Five-Place Cabin Plane Showing Refinements of Design and Structure

Although basically similar to the models that preceded it, the new model SR-10 Stinson Reliant for 1938, shows refinements in design and improvements in construction details, which provide greater operational utility as well as easier and simplified maintenance and repair.

Four models are available for 1938: the SR-10B with the 245hp Lycoming R-680-D6, the SR-10C with the 260hp Lycoming R-680-D5, the SR-10ED with the 320hp Wright Whirlwind R-760-E2, and the SR-10FD with either the 450hp P&W Wasp Junior SB, or the 440hp TB. The first three are provided with electrically-operated Lycoming-Smith controllable pitch propellers and the latter with a hydraulically-operated Hamilton Standard constant speed propeller. The models 10B and 10C have tankage for 76 gallons of fuel and 5 gallons of oil; models 10ED and 10FD have tankage for 100 gallons of fuel and 8 quarts of oil.

Structurally, the fabric-covered, gull-type wings of the 1938 Reliant follow previous Stinson practice, having a girdered, chrome molybdenum steel front spar, chrome molybdenum compression struts, and dural rear spar ribs and leading-edge. Appearance, however, has been altered slightly by utilizing a flatter deck across the top of the fuselage and between the wings. The vacuum-operated trailing edge flaps, introduced by Stinson three years ago, have been retained. These flaps are activated by a vacuum-controlled valve on the instrument panel.

Fuselage construction of welded chrome molybdenum steel tubing, aluminum covered forward, and fabric covered aft has been retained. However, there is a noticeable evidence of additional streamlining, particularly in the contouring of the underside of the fuselage, which is rounded, and in the angle of the windshield. More baggage space is now available due to a larger compartment near the cabin, which has the capacity for 20 cu. ft. of baggage and is accessible through an outside baggage door measuring 17" x 26". A large opening near this compartment permits entry to the rear of the fuselage where flares and a reserve vacuum tank for flap operation are located. The battery also has been relocated, so that it is now in the rear baggage compartment where it can be more easily reached for servicing. Additional baggage space is in the cabin under the rear seat.

Further improvements are evident in the interior of the airplane. Entrance has been made easier by providing a wider door, two additional steps, and a more spacious aisle between the front and rear seats. The front seats have been redesigned, and there is more space between the two front seats to give an adequate entering aisle. Each is equipped with arm rests. Seats are adjustable forward and backward, and recline.

Rear seats are 52" wide, are posture-fitting, and accommodate three persons in comfort. Appearance is enhanced by the use of chrome hardware, assist cords, and moldings finished in grained hardwood. The moldings on the rear windows are curved to fit the shoulder. Comfort is aided by the installation of a heating and ventilation system, as well as by the use of fabrics which have sound proofing qualities.

Ventilation is achieved by drawing air into the cabin from the wings and expelling it downward from the forward part of the cockpit by a controllable suction ventilator. The plane is heated by warming fresh air through a heat-resisting intensifier tube in the exhaust stack.

A new instrument panel is used in the 1938 Reliant. The panel is mounted with rubber to decrease vibration and increase instrument life. It is arranged so that the flight panel is directly in the center where it is easily visible to the occupants in front. It is indirectly lighted and is hinged at the bottom so that it can be tilted forward to expose all instruments. The instruments are flush-mounted, and their appearance is further enhanced by the use of fared-in controls and inset panel wheels. Instruments formally mounted on the walls or ceiling are now grouped on a shelf below the main panel. Standard instrumental installation includes a compass, altimeter, tachometer, airspeed indicator, manifold pressure, carburetor air temperature, oil temperature and oil pressure gauges.

Visibility has been improved by the use of the new windshield, which provides better forward, upward and rear vision for the occupants in the front seats, and by large safety glass windows for the occupants of the rear seat. The window at the pilot side forward may be lowered.

Provision has been made for the installation of radio equipment. Both the engine and airplane are bonded and shielded, and an inbuilt metal radio compartment is located under the rear seat below the floor. All radio controls can be located on the instrument panel.

The aircraft is equipped with cantilever landing gear, which has a tread of 116" and is constructed of heat-treated chrome molybdenum steel. The shock absorbers are the long stroke Springdraulic type and have oil snubbers. The tail wheel unit is a twin-action pneumatic-type with a Springdraulic shock absorber and swings up and back when contacting an obstacle. The landing gear is also equipped with semi-low-pressure tires, Goodrich-Palmer hydraulic brakes with chrome-plated brake drums, and American Brake block linings that are automatically adjustable for wear. Brakes are heel-operated from the pilot's set of rudder pedals. Wheel pants are standard equipment as well, and are provided with baffles to prevent clogging with mud, ice or snow.

Engine accessories and engine mount are assembled as a unit and are attached to the fuselage by steel alloy bolts bushed in rubber to reduce noise and vibration. The engine is enclosed in a cowering, which is hinged on top so that it can be raised and lowered like the hood of an automobile. It is thus possible to inspect and service the engine without removing the cowling, making cowling removal necessary only when a major engine overhaul is undertaken. In addition, additional space has been made available in the engine compartment to facilitate inspection.

Baffled fuel tanks of heavy gauge aluminum are located in each wing, and there is an electric fuel gauge on the instrument panel. Oil tanks are located in the engine compartment. Fuel lines are aluminum tubing and all valves are cadmium-plated brass.

Texaco's SR-10E NC18478, s/n 5-5802 on static display while factory demonstrator SR-10C NC18477, s/n 3-5801 flies overhead

Presenting the New Stinson Reliant - - -

The 'Reliant' is a *fine* airplane because the *people* who own 'Reliants' demand its quality of *greatness* in everything they own. Owners of 'Reliants' represent a Blue Book of Leadership. They include partners of the House of Morgan. Presidents by the score of Internationally known Automobile and Industrial Concerns. The Leaders in the Oil Industry. Great stars of the Radio and Screen. The leading Airlines. Professional men whose names are bywords. Sportsmen and Sportswomen in all the great Nations of the World. And lastly, those professional flyers whose long experience has taught them to recognize and appreciate the priceless reliability that is a part of every Stinson.

Probably you do not look under the hood any oftener than most plane or automobile owners. There isn't much need for that these days. But airplane mechanics will tell you that the ability to raise the 'Reliant's' hood in a jiffy and to find all mechanical details accessible saves many dollars in maintenance costs each year.

The 'Reliant's rear seat is spacious enough for three or wide enough for one to comfortably relax. The deep upholsteries are so inviting that relaxation is almost obligatory.

The 'Reliant' has grace and verve. Its tapering gulled wings are quickly recognizable, for no other plane has its distinctive profile. In its new dress it is more shapely and streamlined than ever before. It appears to have the desire to go places and it will do exactly that. The experience of 15 years of going almost every place where there is air qualifies the 'Reliant' to take you any place with the maximum of comfort and the minimum of bother. No plane has a better safety record. No plane has earned a better right to carry the supreme accolade of the air "Dependability."

Left
Getting into a 'Reliant' is no problem. There is no lower wing to climb over. The doors are welcomingly wide. The double steps are convenient. The entrance assist handles are within easy reach.

Left Center
Special effort has been paid to detailed streamlining in the new 'Reliant'. Cabin entrance steps now retract smoothly into the fuselage. Here the steps are in the down position. See the large photo on Page 7 for a view of the steps retracted. Note too the new chrome seat backs and smart duo-toned paneling on the door.

Now More Desirable Than Ever Before

The 'Reliant's' new instrument panel is delightfully artistic—an entirely new note in dignified styling. Utility was the first objective in order to secure more forward visibility, more space for instruments, and to group all radio controls in plain view on the wide shelf beneath the center indirectly lighted panel. Color plays an important part in the decorative scheme: wheels and control button in Burgundy; grays for neutral backgrounds; Blond Harewood outlined in stainless steel, tastefully touched with tiny vermilion stripes to center the interest.

The 'Reliant's' spacious cabin has for years been the standard of comparison. Now it has been completely restyled with enticingly durable fabrics, new hardware, new window panelings in soft pastel colors.

New motor cowling improves streamlining and visibility. With new striping, Stinson name plate in stainless steel, new louvers of polished metal, and new streamlined exhaust stacks a definite feeling of speed and power has been achieved.

Particular attention has always been paid to creating properly designed seats. This is even more important in airplanes than in automobiles because one must be able to ride with ease for several hours. Note the shoulder supporting height of this rear seat. Front pilot's seats are adjustable and give equally scientific support to achieve the ultimate in comfort.

Right Center
Wheel pants, too, are better looking, more aerodynamically perfect. Polished metal bands along the center line and two upper sides add strength and beauty.

Right
As an indication of the size of the enlarged baggage compartment, we call your attention to the picture on the left. There is additional space for baggage in the cabin where it is carried beneath the rear seat. See the photo directly above. There is also a large shelf for cameras, purses, coats and smaller items directly above and behind the rear seat.

Left and opposite:

Inside pages of a 17 x 22.5" advertising brochure for the Stinson Reliant

Flip side advertised the Stinson 105

The STINSON RELIANT for 1938

New in the sense that a FINE DESIGN IS IMPROVED

New cowling reduces temperatures, improves streamlining . . . new windshield has racy appearance, may be cleaned in flight.

A new instrument panel mounts all instruments and radio before the pilot's eyes. Note the improved vision.

Instrument men will be delighted with the accessibility of the new instrument panel which simplifies inspection of instruments.

Practical radio men designed this inbuilt radio compartment located beneath the cabin floor board.

The New Reliant has a score of new features . . . better speed . . . slower landing speed . . . more vision . . . better brakes . . . softer shock absorbers and a number of other desirable improvements which make flying easier, more comfortable and reduce operating costs.

The New Reliant does improve a fine pattern so popular during the past few years that we have been able to say that Reliants are *America's First Choice* four—five passenger cabin planes . . . we say this because more people bought more Reliants than most all similar types of planes combined.

We hope you will like the New 1938 Reliant so much that *you will buy it* . . . we invite you to visit your Stinson Distributor . . . he will allow you to examine the Reliant as crtically as you please . . . then fly it enough to appreciate its superior points . . . it is our experience that the more carefully a Reliant is compared with other planes, and the more it is flown the surer are the probabilities that the Reliant will be the plane purchased . . . we can't talk quality into a Reliant but we do put it there where you can *see* and *feel* and *fly* it . . . ask for a demonstration.

STINSON AIRCRAFT CORPORATION
(Division of Aviation Manufacturing Corporation) WAYNE (Detroit Suburb) MICHIGAN

AVIATION
May, 1938

Only the New Stinson "105" Offers All These Desireable Advantages, Combined With Automobile Economy

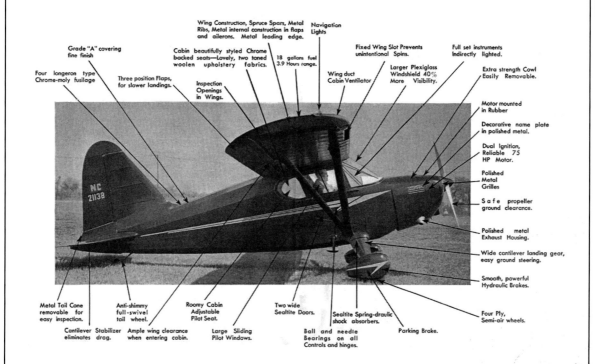

Stinson "105" Specifications, Weight and Performance Data

Engine, Propeller and Battery — Reliable Continental A-75, 75 HP Engine. Hydraulic Tappets. Dual Ignition. Mica Spark Plugs. Altitude Adjustment. Carburetor Heater. Oil Cooler. Automatic Valve Lubrication. Metal Tipped Wooden Propeller. 6 Volt, spill-proof Storage Battery.

Landing Gear, Brakes, Shock Absorbers, Parking Brake — Wide cantilever landing gear for easier landings or handling in cross winds. Goodrich-Hayes Expander Tube Hydraulic Brakes. Smooth and powerful in action but with non-grabbing and quick release features. Mechanical parking brake.* Stinson triple-sealed Spring-Hydraulic Shock Absorbers. Full swiveling, anti-shimmying solid rubber tire tail wheel.

Bearings — All controls and hinges are equipped with ball or needle bearings.

Flaps — New NACA balanced type Flap, mounted on trailing edge of wing between cabin and ailerons. Makes possible steeper glide angle and shorter, slower landings.

Slots — Fixed Type Slots guaranteeing greater lateral or aileron control at slow speeds and preventing unintentional spins.

Fuel and Oil Tanks — 18 Gallon Wing Tank with gasoline for 3.9 hours' cruising at 75% rated engine power. Maximum economical range 391 miles in still air. Electric Fuel Gauge located on instrument panel. One Gallon Oil Tank built integral with engine. No separate oil tank or oil lines required.

Motor Cowling — Heavy gauge metal, quickly and easily removable. Fully enclosed. Designed for pressure cooling. Polished metal grilles cover and decorate carburetor, engine air intakes and exhaust stacks.

Wings — Sitka Spruce Spars completely bushed at bolt holes. Metal ribs. Metal drag trusses and compression members. Metal leading edge. Covering is Grade "A" Standard Fabric.

Instruments — Compass, Air Speed Indicator, Altimeter, Tachometer with revolution counter, Oil Pressure and Temperature Gauges. Indirectly lighted Instrument Panel. Primer, Dual Ignition Switch, Navigation Light Switch, Electric Gas Gauges, Carburetor Heat Control.

Controls — Dual Phantom Wheel Control. Dual Rudder Controls with both right controls easily removable. Toe Hydraulic Brakes. Elevator Tab Control with micro-adjustment and position indicator. Three position lever for flap control within convenient reach of pilot or co-pilot.

Cabin Finish and Equipment — Two wide seal-tight doors with sliding windows. Form fitting seats with chromium finished sides and top. Deeply upholstered. Pilot's seat is adjustable. Cabin trimmed in rich, two toned Boucle Woolen Fabrics. Larger Plexiglass windshield with 40% greater vision. Folding opera seat in rear of cabin. Baggage Compartment. Ash Trays, Vanity Case and attractively designed hardware.

Ventilation and Heat — Wing Duct Ventilators bring fume-free air into cabin. Heater at slight extra cost.

Exterior Finish — Wings, Fuselage and Tail Surfaces Blue. Stripe in contrasting Red set off by pin stripe in Aluminum.

Other Equipment Details — Navigation Lights, Hand Fire Extinguisher, Log Books, First Aid Kit, Improved Double Grip, quickly adjustable Safety Belts.

* At slightly extra cost.

Weight Specifications

Empty Weight	900 Lbs.
Useful Load	
3 Persons at 170 Lbs. 510	
18 Gallons Gasoline 108	
1 Gallon Oil 7½	
Baggage and Special Equipment 54½	680
Gross Weight	1580 Lbs.

Performance Specifications
Fully Loaded

Cruising Speed	105 MPH
Landing Speed, flaps down	43 MPH
Landing Roll	150 Feet
Maximum Economical Range	391 Miles
Ceiling	10,000 Feet
Rate of Climb, Sea Level	452 F.P.M.

The Loveliest Lady or Wealthiest Man Can Be Proud to Own the New "105"

The new Stinson "105" has so many desirable qualities which make it outstanding. Beauty and styling unavailable before at any price. Comfortable seats for three persons. Automobile economy of 25 miles to the gallon plus a range of nearly 4 hours at 105 MPH. A combination of safety devices never before offered the private owner. Slots which retard stalls and spins. Flaps which simplify landings. Hydraulic Brakes which eliminate "grabbing" and make landings practical in incredibly small places. A worthy companion of the popular Stinson 'Reliant', the new "105" carries the prestige of the Stinson name with the reputation for quality which it denotes.

The "105" has the sleek racy lines of a thoroughbred. It gives a smooth ride in rough air and can be landed easily in high ground winds. The wide cantilever landing gear is better for cross wind landings.

Wing slots which retard stalls and spins are located in the leading edge of the wings. Engine is completely cowled. Attractive grilles, Stinson name plate and exhaust covers in bright metal add a decorative note.

The stabilizer is full cantilever. The tail cone is neatly streamlined. Flaps with three adjustable positions simplify landings.

A folding opera seat accommodates a third passenger comfortably. There is ample luggage space. Note wide windows, chromed seat backs and two toned upholstery treatment with decorative bands which encircle the cabin.

Illustrating the roominess of the "105". Pilot's seat is adjustable. The Co-pilot's seat back folds forward.

There are good reasons for the pleased expressions of the passengers. They are nice people who appreciate a fine plane and they helped to create the "105" because they are members of the Stinson Organization

Here's a delightful new style note: First Aid Kit and Vanity Case are made a part of the interior design. Knobs are of fawn plastics. The vertical band is aluminum with two tiny vermilion stripes.

The "Jewel Case" indirectly lighted panel harmonizes stainless steel and fine wood finishes with control wheels and knobs in fawn colored plastics. The large Plexiglas windshield has 40% more visibility. Controls wheels are of distinctive design. Ash trays are conveniently located on the top deck of the instrument panel. Wide doors, assist handles and high wing design make entrance easy.

Chapter 13
1939: A Small-But-Mighty Aircraft

SR-10J3 Reliant N2308, s/n 5924 powered by a 390-hp R-860-E3 Lycoming engine, priced at $12,585

In January 1939, Stinson was offering four models of Reliant aircraft and production was running at a slow but steady pace. The four gull-wing Reliant models priced between $10,995 and $19,000 were the SR-10C, priced at $10,995, the SR-10E, priced at $14,350, the SR-10F, priced at $18,000, and the SR-10K, priced at $19,000. Stinson had never produced the $3,000 aircraft, and there was concern among the Stinson management team about whether or not a profitable production run could be obtained with the limitations of the present factory.

Assembled in Stinson's experimental hanger, the first small aircraft in the company's history, Model HW-75, was assigned NX21121. This would later become the Model 105. The aircraft was designed as a three-place with the pilot and passenger facing forward seated side-by-side. To stay within the center of gravity limits, a third seat was mounted sideways. In keeping with the earlier management decision, leading edge slots were not built into the wings. Stinson was very secretive concerning the 105 because management wanted to take the world by surprise. Management also wanted to avoid bad press if it could not be developed successfully, or there were delays receiving the ATC. Moreover, with a military bid in progress, any engineering problems with any aircraft could negatively affect the possibility of Stinson receiving a contract for the Model 74.

Peter Altman had been correct about the wing slots. It took only three test flights to determine that the slow flight characteristics of the aircraft were not satisfactory. A new pair of wings was assembled using built-in slots forward of the ailerons. After this installation, flight characteristics were greatly improved and built-in wing slots would be incorporated in the wings of all future three- and four-place Stinson aircraft.

A syndicate consisting of Victor Emanuel, Schroder Rockefeller, Henry Lockhart and Tom Girdler decided to take advantage of a financial opportunity and establish a large aircraft company in California—Vultee Aircraft, Inc. Vultee was created on November 14, 1939, as a Delaware Corporation. Its assets included the 133,000 sq. ft. Downey, California plant, and all operating capital, machinery, production equipment, and aircraft designs. Richard W. Millar, a private pilot and previous investment banker with Universal Studios, was installed as president. Millar assumed management responsibilities for the Stinson division of the Aviation Manufacturing Corporation as well.

The division would soon have two facilities: the 80,000 sq. ft. plant in Wayne, Michigan and an 180,000 sq. ft. plant in Nashville, Tennessee. The contract to build the Nashville plant was fully funded, although no allowance had yet been made for equipment or start-up expenses.

Arriving in Wayne on Wednesday, December 20, Millar planned to spend three days becoming acquainted with his Stinson division. Stinson was not going to reach a production breakeven point for the 105 until October, and Millar wished to identify and correct the problems. Stinson management contended that the Aviation Corporation decision not to expand the Wayne factory and their indecision in moving to Nashville contributed to the low production numbers. They also explained that Continental had been slow in delivering engines early in the production run, thus further contributing to lower production.

Before Millar departed for Downey on Friday, a 1940 management plan was established for the Wayne division. According to the plan, Stinson would develop an improved model of the 105 to be put into production at the earliest possible time, and the 105 production line would be moved to the Nashville plant, which was scheduled to be completed in June. The Reliant and Stinson Model 74 production lines would continue, but would also be manufactured in Nashville. Lastly, all Stinson parts, manuals, brochures, and advertising would continue to use the title "Stinson Division of the Aviation Manufacturing Corporation." Millar gave Stinson management a great deal of freedom in implementing the plan. His final instructions were to make it happen and make it profitable.

The Special Ks of the New York City Police Department

The record of the aeronautical arm of the New York City Police Department would not normally fall within the scope of this work, but as that history includes Stinsons, a brief recounting of the narrative is in order.

Today the New York City Police Department Aviation Unit, which is managed within the Special Operations Bureau, predominately operates helicopters. They do, however, have a long and storied relationship with fixed-wing aircraft dating back to 1914. And while their official record claims September 26, 1929 as the day that the original Air Service Division (ASD) was established, there were earlier incarnations that played significant roles in their history. In fact, there are four separate incar-

SR-10J Reliant powered by a 390-hp R-680-E3 Lycoming engine, 1 of 11 built in 1939, price $12,585

nations of police aviation service, and Stinson–both the man and the machine–played important roles in two of those manifestations. Those roles are worthy of our consideration; therefore we take a few pages here to tell the story of the NYPD aviation units and relate the part that Stinson the Man played in helping establish the very first police aviation unit, and the part that Stinson the Machine, Howard Hughes, and surprisingly enough, bad gas played in establishing the current modern unit.

The Man

In June 1914 New York City Police Officer Charles "Mile-a-Minute" Murphy, a former champion bicycle racer, demonstrated that an airplane could keep pace with a fleeing vehicle by chasing a car nine times around a race track while flying a parasol monoplane. When the Police Reserve was formed four years later, an Aviation Section was included with well-known aviator Colonel Jefferson De Mont Thompson heading the unit. By the time the wartime restriction on flying was lifted in 1919, the Section had a cadre of 20 experienced pilots, all veterans who had flown in the war. In early April 1919 Colonel Thompson had been asked to supervise the work of creating an aerial police station for the upcoming Second Annual Pan-American Aeronautical Convention to be held at Atlantic City. May 6 was to be "Police Day" at the convention, when police officials from across the country would be in attendance, and Thompson realized this was an opportunity to showcase New York's new aerial unit. This could be no ordinary fly by however, Thompson needed something to impress both the novice and old-time flyers. He needed an extraordinary something that, in today's language, had a wow factor. He decided that he needed Eddie Stinson.

Stinson already had a very heavy schedule for the month-long convention where he was representing the Curtiss Aeroplane Company. He started the day with his well-known stunt performance, which began when his airplane appeared in the sky above the grandstands. As the aircraft moved slowly past the crowd, they realized that he was flying upside down and they could read the name STINSON painted in large bold letters on the top of the upper wing. After his performance was over, he would land and offer to take anyone from the audience up for rides and test their capacity for thrill-seeking. One 80-year old widow named Ida C. Wilcox told him "I want you to go as high as you can and do all of the stunts I have seen you do with others." Stinson took Mrs. Wilcox up to 3,000 feet where they performed ten loop-the-loops and finished that maneuver with an Immelmann turn. Eddie next took Mrs. Wilcox into a nosedive, then a tailspin, and ended with a new stunt just invented at the Aeronautical Convention, the "Aeroplane Shimmy" which made the plane appear as though it was skipping through the air. Upon landing Mrs. Wilcox declared "It was simply wonderful. Now I can really say that I have lived."

Stinson's other daily performance consisted of a parachute show which consisted of three separate demonstrations. Assisted by French Army officer Lieutenant Jean Ors, Stinson would approach the airfield and at intervals, Lt. Ors would toss out mailbags (filled with sand to simulate the weight of a fully loaded bag) connected to parachutes. They would land softly, showing the feasibility of delivering airmail to remote locals that did not have landing fields. The second part of the demonstration featured a bit of levity as, while Stinson turned around for another run, it was announced to the crowd that the next drop was going to be a crate of rotten eggs. This caused a bit of consternation in the stands as the audience had seen the wind push some of the mailbags out-of-line. As Stinson once again passed in front of the grandstands now at 700 feet and 70 mph, Lt. Ors dropped the egg crate overboard. The attached parachute lowered the eggs slowly, and just as the crate was about to touch the ground, the parachute released automatically and the crate would gently set down.

It turned out that the eggs where fresh, and not rotten as advertised. They were sold as souvenirs for twenty-five cents apiece. The last portion of the demonstration had the aircraft returning over the field at 500 feet and at 80 mph, whereupon the good Lt. Ors jumped out with his parachute.

Despite his heavy workload, Stinson agreed to work with Colonel Thompson. Expanding on the aerial pursuit theme used by "Mile-a-Minute" Murphy five years earlier, it was decided that they would show the ease at which an automobile-bound thief would be tracked from the air. While Stinson was dropping Lt. Ors overboard, Atlantic County Sheriff Alfred J. Perkins parked his car near the end of the grandstand, in full view of the audience. After Stinson landed and was getting out of his plane, the sheriff wandered over and started chatting with him. A New York City Police plane flown by Captain Horace Keane began circling the field. Suddenly a car thief (played by Police Detective Richard Black of the Atlantic City vice squad) jumped into the sheriff's car and sped off past the stands. As the car thief headed towards Pleasantville on the mainland, Stinson once again climbed into his plane, while the sheriff bent down and grabbed a parachute from one of the mailbags, then jumped in after him. As the "stolen" car made it onto the road, Deputy Chief (and Reserve Major) S. Herbert Mapes announced to the crowd that he recognized the culprit as "a notorious New York motor bandit. Major Mapes acting from headquarters, used a radiotelephone to contact the police plane and ordered to give pursuit.

Rather the having to circle a racetrack nine times as "Mile-a-Minute" Murphy had, the road to Pleasantville was straight and flat for five miles, and in plain view of the grandstands. As Captain Keane flashed overhead, Stinson was just lifting off. He caught up to Black, and then they both caught up to the stolen car. While Captain Keane stuck with vehicle, Stinson and Sheriff Perkins flew on ahead to where a policeman was directing traffic on Meadow Boulevard (now North Albany Avenue), the only road off the island. Circling overhead, the sheriff dropped a note to the officer below, using the parachute that he had grabbed from a mailbag. The officer spotted the miscreant and stopped all vehicle movement, effectively trapping the stolen car in traffic. Stinson landed in a clearing nearby and the sheriff moved to arrest. Captain Keane also quickly landed and placed a retainer on the car thief. Eleven minutes after the car was stolen, the thief was handcuffed to a detective and being paraded in front of the grandstands.

This was the end Stinson's involvement for the demonstration, but not with the Aviation Section. The event was such a success that Colonel Thompson asked Eddie to be an instructor at the aviation school. Having agreed, Eddie Stinson soon showed up and was sworn in as a lieutenant colonel in the New York City Police Reserve Aviation Section. Shortly, working under the unit commander Colonel Fiorello H. La Guardia, Stinson was instructing and advising as his schedule permitted and the next six years saw rapid growth of the unit. However, by the time the Aviation Section was disbanded by a new administration in City Hall in January 1926, Eddie was test-flying his new Stinson Detroiter.

The Machines

In late 1929, City Hall changed its mind again and started a new aviation unit, but this time within the regular Police Department rather than the Reserves. By the beginning of 1930, the unit was fully staffed and equipped. In April 1937, the World's Fair Corporation announced that Howard Hughes had been appointed Aeronautical Advisor to the New York World's Fair of 1939. The main part of the job would be to induce famous pilots from all over the world to visit the fair during its run. Noting that Hughes was only 31, the announcement noted that the choice was not made because of the flyer's achievements, but rather because he "represented the younger element in aviation." But of course, Hughes' achievements were notable, since just two months before he set a new non-stop transcontinental record. Rather than just being a young face, as the technical advisor Hughes would be helping create the air transportation and aeronautical exhibits and developing an aviation program for the fair. The problem facing the NYPD Air Service Division was that, after seven years of constant duty, their fleet was worn out.

Meanwhile, in addition to his World's Fair duties, Hughes spent much of 1937 and 1938 preparing for a record-breaking around-the-world flight attempt, for which he ultimately chose a twin-engine Lockheed Super Electra Model 14-N2 (NX18973). The story of Howard Hughes' mystery plane and the around the world attempt was reported on April 18, 1938.

1934 SR-5E (NS14177, s/n 9281-A) of the Nassau County Police Department, powered by a 225-hp Lycoming R-680-4 engine

The very next day it was announced that police department's last two planes had been condemned and turned over to the Board of Education for use in trade schools, and that no request for replacements had been made.

Hughes had worked out that if he started from Floyd Bennett Field, he could shave off a third of the time it took Lindbergh to fly from New York to Paris. After landing in France, he would decide whether to continue on and break Wiley Post's around-the-world record. In the meantime, acting in his official World's Fair capacity, he could tie the flight—and the resulting publicity—to the Fair itself. While Hangar No. 7 at Floyd Bennett Field was being made ready, the aircraft left Burbank on July 3, and flew to Wichita for an overnight stay. The next afternoon it departed Wichita and landed in New York in the evening of the Fourth of July.

Already cleared to land at Le Bourget Airport in Paris, the crew began a few final tests before the 5:00 p.m. take off on Saturday, July 10. However, during fuel consumption tests on the day before takeoff, it was discovered that the lead content in high-test fuel that was used for earlier experimental runs on the West Coast had scarred or pitted the cylinder walls of the starboard engine. The only fix was to demount the two engines and replace all eighteen cylinders.

Hughes quickly arranged for the parts to be delivered, and gathered a team of eight aircraft engine mechanics, which included some of the former mechanics from the demobilized Police Air Service Division. The mechanics removed and tore down the large Wright Cyclone engines. In the morning they were relieved by another team. Just after midnight, making it now Sunday July 10, the engines were successfully ground-tested. Just before 7:00 p.m. Hughes taxied to the front of the Administration Building where the aircraft was christened *New York World's Fair 1939*. The new aerial emissary of the Fair (already adorned with an appropriate logo on its nose) then took a forty-seven second roll before lifting off at 7:20 p.m., to the delight of 6,000 spectators.

The *New York World's Fair 1939* returned to Floyd Bennett Field three days, nineteen hours, and fourteen minutes later, having flown around-the-world in record time. The Herculean efforts by the mechanics, police and otherwise, had made it possible and Hughes was grateful. As Aeronautical Advisor to the Fair, he was responsible for the planning of air safety and patrol. It was understood that the New York City Police Department Air Service Division needed to get

1937 Stinson SR-9EM (NS3640, c/n 5269) powered by a 350-hp Wright R760E-2 engine, that replaced the Nassau County Police Department's 1934 SR-5E. This was the aircraft that inspired the New York City Police SR-10Ks. Daily News *photo*

back in the air as soon as possible. The question was, 'Get back in the air in what?' The answer came in less than a week.

After the record flight, the crew was celebrated throughout New York City. Eventually one had to report back to the Army for active duty, but the rest were invited to be the honorary starters for the third annual Nassau County Police Department auto races. Three of them immediately agreed, and it was offered to Hughes, now in Washington D.C, that the Nassau County police plane be dispatched to bring him to the race.

That aircraft was a 1937 Stinson SR-9EM (NS3640, s/n 5269) powered by a 350-hp Wright R760E-2 engine. It had been built for the Nassau County Police as a one-off cargo version of the SR-9E. During World War II the plane would be impressed by the Army as a UC-81M (42-94134), but for now it was the specially equipped police plane that was being examined. In its first year of service, the aircraft had totaled 27,955 miles. NS3640 was the replacement for an earlier, but equally remarkable Stinson, a 1934 SR-5E (NS14177, s/n 9281-A) powered by a 225-hp Lycoming R-680-4 engine, said by the *New York Daily News* to be "the first plane ever built specifically for police work." According to the department's description, that unique Stinson carried "smoke and tear gas canisters, a two-way radio, and a .30 caliber machine gun that synchronized firing through the propeller."

The Stinson Model SR was proving to be popular for police departments. The Michigan State Police had a 1937 SR-9C (NC81Y, s/n 5353) with a 260-hp Lycoming R-680-B5 engine. With 65 built, the C was the most popular version of the SR-9.

The Michigan Department of Aeronautics had used the registration number NC81Y on two previous SR models.

The Pennsylvania State Police used a 1938 SR-10C (NC2330, s/n 3-5838) with a 260-hp Lycoming R-680-D5 engine. It was later upgraded to a SR-10G with a 290-hp Lycoming R-680-E1. NC2330 survives and at this writing is on display at the Commemorative Air Force-Arizona Wing, at Mesa-Falcon Field in Mesa, Arizona. It is now powered by a 225-hp Lycoming R-680-4P-B4 engine, an engine type originally considered for power on the ultimately unbuilt SR-9A.

Given the popularity of the Reliant and given Stinson's ability to build police-specific aircraft, it was easy for Howard Hughes to propose two custom-ordered Stinson Reliants for the New York City Police Department. Each would be a 1939 Stinson SR-10K (NC21147, s/n 5905 and NC21148, s/n 5906) with 450-hp Wright R-975-E3 Whirlwind engines powering Hamilton Standard constant-speed propellers. NC21147—costing $19,000 and delivered as a floatplane with twin Edo floats—had a top speed of 180 mph and a cruising speed of 155 mph. NC21148—delivered as a land plane costing $14,641—had a top speed of 200 mph and cruised at 176 mph. Each SR-10K was set up for instrument flying and had two-way radios that could communicate with not only headquarters, but also with the four radio patrol cars and the three radio-equipped boats of the Harbor Squad. Each Reliant also carried first aid medical supplies, a collapsible life raft for marine emergencies, and a gurney style stretcher that would enable them to instantly become an aerial ambulance. They were painted in the livery style of the patrol cars—green fuselage with white wings.

The aviation unit, which started with thirty-six men in 1929, was reinstituted with just twelve (six pilots and six ground crew who also acted as the observers on aerial patrol), and officially renamed the Aviation Bureau, under the Emergency Service Division of the Police Department. All pilots and mechanics recruited were from the regular Police Department. Of the six pilots, three had commercial licenses and three had private licenses. These men also held licenses as commercial radio operators. The twelve Aviation Bureau members went to the Stinson factory in Wayne, Michigan—the ground crew to learn the details of the aircraft as they were being built—the pilots to familiarize themselves with flying the SR-10. The ground crew next went to the Wright factory in Paterson, New Jersey for training on their particular engine, then the instrument factories, and then on to the radio company for more instruction. The installation of the radios would take place at Port Washington, Long Island for the floatplane, and Roosevelt Field, Long Island for the land plane.

The announcement that the dormant air unit was to be reactivated came on June 2, 1939. The aircraft were delivered to the city on July 2 and acceptance testing began. On July 12 the Stinson SR-10Ks were dedicated in a ceremony

1937 SR-9C (NC81Y, s/n 5353) with 260-hp Lycoming R-680-B5 engine in Michigan State Police service, posing with a 1940 Ford Tudor sedan, and 1940 Harley-Davidson

at Floyd Bennett Field led by the former Commander of the Police Reserve Aviation Section, and now New York City Mayor, Fiorello H. LaGuardia.

In his remarks the Mayor thank Howard Hughes for helping reestablish the Aviation Bureau. Then, with the Police Band playing 'Come, Josephine, in My Flying Machine,' Mayor LaGuardia, Police Commissioner Lewis Valentine, and New York Yankee pitcher Lefty Gomez—with Acting Sergeant Forsythe piloting—took the first official flight. The New York Police Department was back in the air. However, the New York World's Fair had already been open for two months.

Ex-Pennsylvania State Police 1938 SR-10C, later upgraded to a SR-10G, NC2330 survives on display with the Commemorative Air Force-Arizona Wing.

The New York Times reported that the SR-10Ks of the Aviation Bureau were tasked to "protect life and property, enforce aircraft regulations over the city, patrol the harbor and furnish aerial photographs of city areas under local investigation." The most important immediate task of course, was to enforce the ban on planes flying over the fairgrounds, that the Department of Commerce had put into place before the Fair opened on April 30. There already were numerous complaints concerning nuisance aircraft over the fairgrounds. It was intended that the offending pilots would be ordered to land at the nearest airport where a summons would be issued. Formal patrols started on July 16, and it was expected that the aircraft would be working around the clock.

From the summer of 1939 up to the start of World War II, the SR-10Ks served in every capacity possible, including both land and air traffic monitoring, crime monitoring, search and rescue, and prisoner transport. However, the war saw restrictions placed on civilian aircraft, including the police planes, and consequently the Stinsons were relatively inactive at LaGuardia Field for the duration. The Police Re-

Pilots and mechanics of the NYPD Aviation Bureau at dedication ceremony for the Stinson SR-10Ks on July 12, 1939 at Floyd Bennett Field

1939 Stinson SR-10K NC21148, s/n 5906 powered by a 450-hp Wright R-975-E3 Whirlwind engine displaying NYCPD aircraft No. 1, although it was the second SR-10K built. Both of the airplanes and four 1939 Plymouth patrol cars were radio-equipped. The NYCPD livery was green and white.

serve Aviation Section had been similarly affected during the last war. At 8:00 a.m. on February 8, 1946, the police planes were allowed back in the air and at 11:00 a.m. NC21148 returned to service by flying two burglary detectives to Philadelphia to testify in a trial there, returning late that afternoon. The huge flow of returning soldiers made train travel difficult, so in addition to resuming their normal duties, the police planes were also to be used as convenient transportation until railroad accommodations returned to normal.

NC21147 and NC21148 would eventually return to Floyd Bennett Field, but for now, they were back on patrol duty and chasing down and issuing summons to low or errant fliers. Sometime during the summer of 1946, a hard landing damaged the land plane, and on February 19, 1947 the Civil registration, N21148, was cancelled. The floatplane, NC21147, was then converted to a land plane. In theory, the converted floatplane now should have the land plane capabilities, that is, a top speed of 200 mph and a cruise speed of 176 mph. In reality, the much-used airplane now had a top speed of only 140 mph. In December 1946, the Police Department acquired a war surplus twin-engine Grumman Widgeon amphibian with a top speed of 150 mph to augment the converted Stinson floatplane. This acquisition was quickly followed by the purchase of a Grumman Goose.

With the newer and faster amphibians in the fleet, the remaining SR-10K was removed from patrol and relegated to transport and whatever extra duties that were assigned. One

1939 Stinson SR-10K NC21147, s/n 5905 with twin Edo floats, delivered as a floatplane at $19,000 was $4,359 more expensive than the land plane.

of those extra duties had actually begun on September 12, 1947 for the Health Department when a special device was attached to the aircraft. A hopper was installed in the cabin with a nozzle protruding through the bottom of the fuselage. This was used to dust Staten Island with DDT as part of a massive mosquito extermination program. Four-hundred pound of DDT and talc mixture could be carried on each trip. In 1948 750 acres of marshland in Queens was treated, while Idlewild Airport was treated twice with a total of six tons of the insecticide.

In mid-August 1951 the residents of Howard Beach in Queens asked once again for the police plane to spray the salt marshes, only to be told that the specially equipped Stinson SR-10K had been sold within the last month. The dusting equipment could not be attached to the amphibians, nor would it work with the new float-equipped helicopters. The mosquitoes had to be eradicated by hand on

NC21147 working with Police launch No. 4, one of the three radio-equipped NYPD boats

the ground. The next year the outbreak was affecting Queens again, along with Brooklyn, and the Health Department was still lamenting the loss of the Stinson.

With twelve years of duty, NC21147 remains the longest serving straight-wing aircraft in the Police Department's history. After its retirement it was sold into Canada and in 1952 was registered as CF-FBB. Over the years it acquired a 450-hp Pratt & Whitney engine, and in 1981 was purchased by Advance Energy Ltd Calgary, Alberta, which still owns it as of this writing. The corporation had been in talks with the New York Police Department Museum for the return of the erstwhile floatplane, but when Hurricane Sandy devastated the museum, those talks were put on hold.

Top Right: NC21147 used as a aerial photography platform in December 1946. Daily News photo
Top Left: NC21147, converted to land plane, spraying DDT for the Department of Health
Bottom: Ex-NC21147 now bearing Canadian registration. Photo by George Trussell

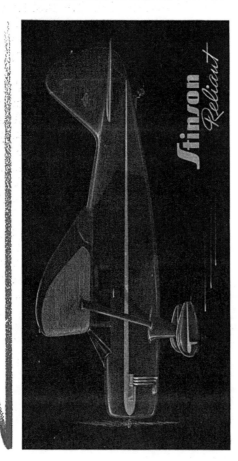

1939 Stinson double-page advertisement

Chapter 14
1940-1943:
The Last of the Giants

Stinson Factory Nashville, Tennessee 1940

1940

After some debate, Stinson management decided to name the aircraft the "New 105" and to use this slogan in all advertising. The tooling and flight testing of the aircraft was completed the first week of April. New nose grills, new nameplate, and new striping graced the 105 along with many other refinements including increased cabin width. Stinson received ATC approval number A-709 on April 22, 1940, and production started with serial number 7501. The New 105 for 1940 was powered with a Continental A-80-6 engine rated at 80-hp at 2,700 rpm. It was priced at $3,370 at the factory field. In many respects, the 1940 aircraft was a great improvement on the 1939 model. Stinson assigned Model 10 to the New 105 in order to differentiate the two aircraft, but did not use the name, Model 10, in any of the print advertising.

By May 1940, the Stinson aircraft division had nearly completed its move to the new larger factory in Nashville. The factory was air-conditioned and designed for in-line production using three separate production lines. Throughout May, machine tools arrived and were organized on the production floor with the final delivery of equipment from the Wayne plant arriving in Nashville on June 18th. In order to announce that the Nashville plant was operational, two New 105s were hurriedly completed by June 28th. The first New 105 built in Nashville was assigned NC26411. Because of a shortage of production personnel, the Reliant production was not scheduled to begin until August 26th.

Richard Millar arrived in Nashville Monday, August 5th and announced he had good news and bad news. The good news was the 750,000 sq. ft. expansion of the Nashville plant had been approved, bringing its total area to 930,000 sq. ft. The bad news, however, was that the Stinson assembly lines would be moved back to the Wayne, Michigan plant and production would be suspended at the end of August. Vultee wanted to take advantage of the potential export and Army Air Force purchases of the A-31 Vengeance dive bombers, but the Vultee Downey plant was committed to only BT-13 production and had no room for future expansion. The logical place for future large-scale production was the Stinson plant in Nashville, and purchases of the dive bombers far outweighed the Stinson income potential in the Nashville plant. The Model 74, Army 0-49 production line would stay in Nashville, and to accommodate Stinson's needs, the Wayne plant would be expanded by 78,000 square feet. Stinson's employees were upset about the move back to Wayne and most took a financial loss.

At that time, France was being threatened by

Germany, and the French army purchased 33 Model 105 aircraft from Stinson that were produced near the end of Stinson's production run in 1939. Aviation enthusiast, Hillis W. Cunliffe, witnessed the May 1940 arrival of the aircraft at the Houlton, Maine airport. Below are the only known photographs of the aircraft after they departed New York City, and they show the first U.S. pilots to fly airplanes across the border into Canada since World War II began. These pilots were recruited to deliver the 33 Stinsons to Halifax, Nova Scotia for observation use by the French army. In the photos, a storm had just passed through the field, and the two runways were drenched. Upon arrival in Maine in preparation for their flight into Canada, each aircraft was fitted with temporary radio insulation and the pilots were instructed how to put on fittings for radio antennas. The United States "NC" letters were painted out, but numerical license numbers remained visible on the aircraft. Once the painting was completed, the pilots gave the airworthiness certificates to the Stinson representative who was coordinating the deal for the French. After a 36 hour layover, the aircraft continued on into Canada. The French military was poorly equipped and unprepared to resist the German attack. They surrendered before the Stinsons could reach France. The complete account of the disposition of the 33 aircraft is covered in detail in Volume One of *Stinson's Golden Age*.

In October 1940, Stinson announced the sale of six Reliants to three airlines: four to Pan Am, one to American Airlines and one to the Boeing school. Garnet newspapers purchased its fifth Stinson, and six Stinson 105s were shipped to distributors in Brazil. The new Stinson 105 was exhibited at four automobile shows: Detroit, Erie, St. Louis and Boston.

1941

Aero Digest
March 1941

STINSON "VOYAGER"

A New Three-place Monoplane for the Private Pilot, Fixed Base Operator and Flight Training

Resembling its predecessor, the Model 105, only in internal construction, Stinson's three-place high-wing monoplane, the Voyager, is a refined and improved version of the airplane that made its debut two years ago and today boasts wide acceptance among private pilots, many fixed base operators, and innumerable flight training centers.

The only known photographs of the Stinson 105s bound for France at an overnight stay at Houlton, Maine on their way to Halifax, Nova Scotia. They were taken by Hillis W. Cunliffe's father, a Houlton native

CHAPTER 14

Painting of a 1943 Stinson AT-19 (V-77)

Retaining the structural and aerodynamic features that characterized the Model 105, the Voyager has additional horsepower, greater luxury in its interior, and numerous other refinements intended to enhance performance and passenger comfort.

The fuselage is a fabric-covered, wood-flared, truss structure made of welded chrome molybdenum steel tubing. It has two individual form-fitting chairs in the front and another seat behind on the port side. Following modern automobile color style trends, the Voyager carries a two-tone paint treatment throughout.

Outwardly, appearance is similar to the 1940 models, except that the cowl has been completely redesigned to provide greater visibility for the pilot seats, and the single, bayonet exhaust stack has been placed on the starboard side of the cowl. The contour of the windshield has been changed to minimize deflection. The two cabin doors can be locked and have been further insulated for greater cabin quietness. The doors swing forward and open behind the wing struts. They are equipped with a spring-steel, leather-covered stop, which holds the door just short of the strut. Access to the cabin is simplified by use of convenient entrance steps and assist handles.

As before, the interior of the new Stinson reflects extensive attention to luxurious detail. The new walnut-finished instrument panel has a glove compartment on the right side, and at the corresponding space on the left is a removable door, which permits the easy installation of radio equipment. Control buttons and switches have been rearranged for greater efficiency, and instruments have been flight grouped. A new heavy-duty master switch is now in the center below the panel for easy operation from either pilot seat. Accessories include a recessed ashtray, two-tone broadcloth contrasted on the seats, and side panels with rust leather trim. Seats are now more deeply padded with the bolster rolls, and further comfort is achieved by the use of cabin ventilators and soundproofing throughout. Working in conjunction with the ventilators, a controllable cabin heater increases the flow of circulating air so that a comfortable temperature is maintained throughout the cabin. Cooling air is brought in through screened openings in the leading edges at the root of the wing on each side and distributed in the cabin through adjustable ventilators. Windows are adjustable are provided with catch locks, which not only assure tightness but also reduce vibration.

A more accessible battery box, with easily operated latches, is located directly behind the pilot's seat instead of under it. Sufficient space is available behind the starboard seat for baggage, and there are baggage tie-down straps attached to the flooring on both sides of the cabin.

Instruments are indirectly lighted and include an Airpath compass, an Aeromarine airspeed indicator, an altimeter, AC tachometer, oil pressure and oil temperature gauges, King-Seeley ammeter, and an electric field gauge. Provision is made in the panel to accommodate additional instruments such as a turn and bank indicator, a rate of climb indicator, and a clock. The aircraft is equipped with spokeless wheel controls inset in the panel, and the stabilizer control is in the ceiling directly over the front seats where either occupant can easily reach it.

Following Stinson design, the wings are of the semi-cantilever type braced by streamlined V-struts. The straight leading edge is cut away at the point where the wing attaches to the fuselage. Wing structure is fabric-covered, and is built of solid spruce spars, pressed aluminum ribs, and an aluminum alloy leading in trailing edge. The ailerons are built of steel torque tube and aluminum alloy ribs, and the airfoil is part of the NAAC 4412 series.

Demonstrated in service and operation as a real advance in safety and control, the wing slots and the three-position flaps familiarly associated with the Model 105 have been retained in the Voyager. The flaps are of the NAAC balanced type, and are manually operated, fabric-covered steel tube structures extending inboard from the inner edge of the ailerons to the cabin. Slots are of the fixed inset type and extend to over 50 percent of the aileron span at the leading edge of the wing.

Stinson L-1A in late 1942

CHAPTER 14

The ex-Royal Navy AT-19 FK887 (s/n 74), which later carried U.S. number 42-46713, then civilian number NC69996, seen here after its award winning restoration (see Chapter 23 V-77 AT-19)

Tail surfaces are full cantilever, and the fin, rudder and elevators are built of steel tube spars and pressed steel ribs. They are fabric covered. The stabilizer employs spruce spars and ribs and is covered with phenolic, glued plywood. The leading edge of the elevators is continuous and a trimming tab is provided on the port elevator. All movable services are provided with ball and needle bearings.

The landing gear is full cantilever and has replaceable bronze bushings and Springdraulic shock absorber structures made of heat-treated chrome molybdenum steel. Hydraulic brakes are standard equipment as are wheel pants and a full-swiveling tail wheel.

Power is supplied by a dual ignition Franklin 4AC-199-E3 engine which develops 90-hp at 2500rpm. The engine compartment is now six inches shorter than before, which has permitted lowering the angle of the cowl and thus has increased forward visibility. The cowl is redesigned into a three-piece unit with a fixed center-piece and a hinged outer piece on each side, which opens up in automobile fashion. Dzus fasteners keep the cowl in place, and new chevron grills impart a modern, functional design.

Tankage is provided for 20 gallons of fuel and one gallon of oil. The fuel tank is carried in the starboard panel from which the fuel is gravity-fed to the carburetor. If an additional tank is desired, this can be provided in the port panel. This tank would also hold 20 gallons. Equipment includes a metal-tipped, wood propeller, and other standard equipment on the deluxe model includes radio bonding, parking brake, battery, Grimes navigation lights, Autolite electric starter and generator.

1942

Based on the Stinson SR-10 series, the V-77 [Vultee sequence number V-77] was modified as a navigational trainer for the Army Air Force. An order for 250 aircraft was placed with Stinson with the first prototype flying in July 1942. Later, however, the Air Force reported that there was no longer a need for this type of trainer, and the order was cancelled. Also during this time in the war, the AT-19 was offered to England under the Lend-Lease program, and 500 aircraft were accepted by the Royal Navy's "Fleet Air Arm."

1943

The merger of Consolidated Aircraft Corporation and Vultee Aircraft Inc. was completed in March of 1943, and the name of the new company became Consolidated Vultee Aircraft Corporation. This was now the world's largest aircraft company. It's board of directors included Tom M. Gidler, chairman, Harry Woodhead, president and another director of interest, Victor Emanuel, president of Aviation Corporation.

The new company consisted of eleven plant divisions: Consolidated plants in San Diego, CA and Fort Worth, TX, a new plant in New Orleans, LA, modification centers in Tucson, AZ and Elizabeth, NJ, Vultee plants in Vultee Field, California and Nashville, TN, the Stinson division in Wayne Michigan, a new plant in Arlington, PA, a modification center in Louisville, KY, and International Aircraft Corporation, a subsidiary of Vultee, in Miami, FL. Consolidated also had the Stout Research Division in Dearborn, MI.

It was very prestigious to be part of the world's largest aircraft company. Stinson was one of the smallest in size and dollar value of the eleven factories, and Stinson factory management was well aware of their low status in the company.

[As a sidenote related to Stinson, throughout World War II, 28 Stinson employees become POWs: 11 held by Germany and 17 held by Japan. All of the Stinson employees held in the European theater returned to work in 1945 and 1946. None of the Stinson employees held by the Japanese were physically able to return to their former Stinson factory jobs, and most were permanently disabled. Whether these physical difficulties were the result of injuries before capture or treatment while prisoners, or some of both, is not known.]

Throughout the 18 years between 1925 and 1943, the story behind all the numbers shows that the American free enterprise system was alive and well. From the Stinson employees' perspective, their profitable company offered steady employment, good working conditions and an above-average salary even during the Depression years. During this time, the Beechcraft, Luscombe, Stinson, and Waco companies refined their manufacturing techniques and remained profitable.

The history of the Stinson Aircraft Company from 1938 through 1950 is presented as part of Wind Canyon Books Golden Age of Aviation series. *Stinson's Golden Age* is published in a two-volume set. Volume 1 is *The Voyager – The Story of the Classic Model 108 - Stinson Aircraft - 1938-1947,* and Volume 2 is *The Voyager – The Story of the Classic Model 108 - Stinson Aircraft - 1948-1950 and Beyond.*

Stinson L-1A in the Panama Canal Zone 1944

The new Stinson Voyager de luxe

- GREATER POWER
- MORE SPEED
- FASTER TAKE-OFF
- FASTER CLIMB
- STARTER & GENERATOR
- SPARKLING NEW BEAUTY
- UNEQUALED SAFETY RECORD
- SLOTS & FLAPS
- HYDRAULIC BRAKES

For the business executive and salesman, for the sportsman and the socialite, for those requiring a modern three-place plane for school and commercial purposes, and for the inexperienced person planning to do his own flying for the first time ... the new Stinson Voyager is indisputably the ideal plane.

John C. Swick Collection

CHAPTER 14

1941 Model 10As at the factory

Chapter 15
Production Numbers 1925-1945

This chapter is presented to give the total aircraft production of the Stinson Aircraft Co. from 1925-1945. Each Stinson aircraft is identified by model number, approved type certificate number [ATC], production run, engine horsepower and the retail price when produced. The ATC number represented a commitment by the factory that each aircraft would be built in conformity as approved by the Civil Aeronautics Administration [CAA] for that particular model.

Readers will find Group 2 ATC numbers throughout the chapter. The Group 2 approval process was developed for aircraft that would be built in small numbers. Group 2 approvals were used primarily for modifications of ATC approved aircraft including special order aircraft, a different engine installation, increased or decreased seating arrangement, major interior changes, and increased fuel capacity.

To simplify the identification of individual Stinson models in most years, the total production is recorded in that calendar year. Stinson did not start each new model in January for a specific model year, and the previous year's production would continue until the replacement model received its ATC number and entered production.

To present a broader perspective, the production of three automobile companies and five aircraft companies are shown. Automobile sales are based on the model year production run. Much more attention is paid to WACO Aircraft Co. production than the others because from 1931-1941 Stinson and WACO dominated the high-performance, closed-cabin aircraft market. WACO was organized in 1919, but did not produce aircraft in volume until 1925. In 1931, WACO introduced their first enclosed cabin aircraft to compete directly with Stinson. Through the years, WACO produced competitively priced 4 to 5-place cabin-biplanes, offering excellent workmanship and superior performance. WACO was also very prolific in obtaining ATC approval, and many aircraft were produced in small numbers.

Selected historical facts are also included throughout the chapter to present a broader understanding of the times. History has to be taken into context to better grasp the mentality of the time.

1920

August 26 the 19th amendment to the United States Constitution becomes law, and women can vote in the fall elections, including the presidential election.
The aircraft carrier Langley (CV-1) is commissioned.

1925

By the end of October, Eddie Stinson and Bill Mara raise $25,000 and the Stinson-Mara Syndicate is formed.

Col. William "Billy" Mitchell found guilty of insubordination on October 28th.

Ford Automobile Production: 1,669,847
Studebaker Automobile Production: 133,104
Chrysler Automobile Production: 132,474

Employment rate: 96.8%
Unemployment rate: 3.2%

1926

Eddie Stinson flies the experimental Detroiter on its maiden flight on January 25, 1926.
In May 1926, the Stinson-Mara Syndicate becomes the Stinson Aircraft Corporation and is capitalized in the amount of $150,000.

From May to December, Stinson deliver 10 SB-1 Detroiters priced at $11,000 FAF. The factory is located at Northville, Michigan.

Ford automobile production: 1,426,612
Chevrolet automobile production: 547,724
Chrysler automobile production: 162,242

Employment rate: 96.8%
Unemployment rate: 3.2%

Marilyn Monroe born June 1st.

1927

Stinson SB-1 Detroiter ATC 24, 16 built powered by a 220-hp Wright J-5 engine.
Stinson SM-1 Detroiter ATC 16, 36 built, powered

by a 220-hp Wright J-5C engine.
Price: $12,000
The last Ford Model T was produced.
The aircraft carriers, Lexington (CV-2) and Saratoga (CV-3), are commissioned.
On May 20, Charles Lindbergh departs New York for Paris.

Chevrolet automobile production: 1,001,820
Hudson automobile production: 276,404
Chrysler automobile production: 182,195

Employment rate: 97.6%
Unemployment rate: 3.3%

1928

Stinson SM-1 Detroiter ATC 16, 23 built, powered by a 220-hp Wright J-5C engine.
Stinson SM-1B Detroiter ATC 2-24, 3 built, powered by a 220-hp Wright J-5C engine, approved for higher gross weight.
Stinson SM-2 Junior ATC 48, 29 built, powered by an 110-hp Warner Scarab engine.
Price: $6,950
Stinson SM-1DA Detroiter ATC 74, 5 built, powered by a 220-hp Wright Whirlwind J-5C engine.
Stinson SM-1DB Detroiter ATC 76, 1 built, powered by a 220-hp Wright Whirlwind J-5C engine.
Price: $12,500
Stinson SM-1DC Detroiter ATC 77, 1 built, powered by a 220-hp Wright Whirlwind J-5C engine, approved for higher gross weight.
Stinson SM-1DD Detroiter ATC 78, 1 built, a 2-place aircraft designed to haul freight powered by a 220-hp Wright Whirlwind J-5C engine.

The antibiotic, penicillin, is discovered.
Ford Model A production begins.
On June 17, Amelia Earhart becomes the first woman to fly nonstop across the Atlantic Ocean.

The Lycoming Company begins the development of its first aircraft engine.

Chevrolet automobile production: 1,193,212
Hudson automobile production: 282,203
Chrysler automobile production: 160,670

Employment rate: 95.8%
Unemployment rate: 4.2%

1929

Stinson SM-1D Detroiter ATC 2-60, 4 built, powered by a 300-hp Wright J-6-9-300 engine, approved for higher gross weight.
Stinson SM-1D Detroiter Special ATC 2-142, 1 built, powered by a 225-hp Wright J-5 engine.
Stinson SM-1F Detroiter ATC 136, 22 built, powered by a 300-hp Wright J-6-9-300 engine.
Stinson SM-1FS Detroiter ATC 212, 6 built, a six-place aircraft offered with Edo floats powered by a 300-hp Wright J-6-9-300 engine.
Price: $13,500
Stinson SM-6B Detroiter ATC 217, 13 built, an 8-place aircraft powered by a 450-hp P&W Wasp C-1 engine. Price: $18,500
Stinson SM-6B Detroiter ATC 2-89, 2 built, a 7-place aircraft powered by a 450-hp P&W engine.
Stinson SM-2AA Junior ATC 145, 22 built, powered by a 165-hp Wright J-6 engine.
Price: $8,500
Stinson SM-2AA Junior ATC 2-73, 1 built, powered by a 165-hp Wright R-540 engine.
Stinson SM-2AB Junior ATC 161, 32 built, powered by a 165-hp Wright J-6 engine.
Price: $10,500
Stinson SM-2AC Junior ATC 194, 22 built, powered by a 225-hp Wright J-6 engine.
Price: $11,000
When mounted on Fairchild floats, the price was $13,500
Stinson SM-2AC Junior ATC 2-143, 1 built, powered by a 225-hp Wright R-760 J-6 engine.
Stinson SM-2K Junior ATC 2-136, 3 built, a 3-place aircraft powered by a 100-hp Kinner K-5 engine.
Stinson SM-3A a low-wing, experimental aircraft with retractable landing gear, project abandoned.
Stinson SM-4 *Sally Sovereign*, lost in an ill-fated record attempt.
Stinson SM-5A an experimental, high-wing aircraft powered by a Wright engine, project abandoned.
Corman 3000 tri-motor ATC 2-140, 1 built, a 7-place, experimental high-wing aircraft.

The move to the enlarged factory at Wayne, Michigan is completed in April.
On March 1, Aviation Corporation (AVCO) is established.
The Corman Corporation is established in August, and on September 4, the Cord Holding Company is created.

On October 29, the stock market crashes. This becomes known as Black Tuesday, and is considered the start of the Great Depression.

From October 1929 to July 1932, the stock market loses 89% of its value. Throughout the years of the Depression, Stinson, WACO and Beechcraft remained profitable.

Stinson announces the merger with the Cord Corporation on November 1, 1929. Stinson retains its identity as the Stinson Aircraft Corporation.

Ford automobile production: 1,507,123
Chevrolet automobile production: 1,328,605
Chrysler automobile production: 92,592

1930

Stinson SM-1 Special ATC 2-174, 7 built, powered by a 225-hp Wright J-6 engine.
Stinson SM-1B Special ATC 2-224, 1 built, powered by a 220-hp Wright J-5 engine.
Stinson SM-2ABS Junior ATC 2-267, 2 built, powered by a 220-hp Wright J-5 engine and mounted on twin Edo floats.
Stinson SM-7A Junior ATC 298, 8 built, powered by a 300-hp Wright R-975 engine. Price: $10,695
Stinson SM-7A Junior ATC 2-313, 1 built, powered by a 300-hp Wright R-975 engine mounted on Edo Q floats.
Stinson SM-7B Junior ATC 329, 8 built, powered by a 300-hp P&W Wasp Jr. engine. Price: $10,695
Stinson SM-8A Junior ATC 295, 302 built, powered by a 215-hp R-680 Lycoming engine. Price: $5,775
Stinson SM-8A Junior ATC 2-30, 11 built, powered by a 215-hp R-680 Lycoming engine, approved for higher gross weight. Lycoming engines were standard equipment on the SM-8A. Price: $5,775
Stinson SM-8B Junior ATC 294, 5 built, powered by a 225-hp Wright J-6 engine. Price: $10,500
Stinson SM-8D Junior ATC 312, 2 built, powered by a 225-hp Packard DR-980 diesel engine. Price: $8,995
Stinson SM-1DX Detroiter ATC 2-228, serial number 303, 1 built, powered by a 225-hp Packard DR-980 diesel engine.
Stinson SM-9 experimental amphibian, 1 built, project abandoned.
Stinson SM-6000 tri-motor ATC 335, 10 built, powered by three 215-hp R-680 Lycoming engines. It carried 10 passengers and 1 pilot. Standard Price: $23,900/price to airlines: $18,000
Stinson SM-6000-A tri-motor ATC 367, carried 10 passengers and 1 pilot. This is a modification/remanufacturing of all SM-6000 aircraft. The SM-6000-A and later versions are referred to as the Model T until the Model U is introduced.

On January 31, the 3M Company begins marketing program for Scotch Tape.
On May 15, the first flight attendant is employed by a U.S. airline.

Ford automobile production: 1,140,710
Studebaker automobile production: 123,215
Chrysler automobile production: 77,881

Employment rate: 91.9%
Unemployment rate: 8.1%
The GNP falls 9.4%.

1931

Stinson SM-8A Junior ATC 295, 204 built, powered by a 215-hp R-680 Lycoming engine. Price: $4,995 (Lycoming engines were standard equipment on all SM-8s priced at $4,995.)
Stinson Model S Junior ATC 423, 51 built, powered by a 215-hp R-680 Lycoming engine. Price: $4,995/Seaplane price: $6,995
Stinson Model W ATC 435, 5 built, the same as the SM-7 with minor changes powered by a 300-hp P&W Wasp Jr. engine. Price: $8,995
Stinson SM-7B Junior ATC 329, 10 built, powered by a 254-hp R-680-6 Lycoming engine. Price: $8,995
Stinson SM-6000-B tri-motor ATC 420, 24 built, powered by three 215-hp R-680 Lycoming engines. It carried 10 passengers and 1 pilot. Standard Price: $25,900/price to airlines: $19,500
Stinson SM-6000-B1 tri-motor ATC 420, 10 built. It carried 10 passengers and 1 pilot.
Stinson SM-6000-B2 tri-motor ATC 420, 14 built, powered by three 215-hp R-680 Lycoming engines. It carried 8-9 passengers plus mail, and 1 pilot. Price to Airlines: $19,500
Stinson SB-1 Detroiter ATC 2-330, for serial numbers 1, 3, and 90. Converted to a 3-place aircraft powered by a 200-hp Wright J-4 engine.

On January 9, the Stinson factory at Wayne Michigan completes its expansion by 99, 800 sq. ft., making the total area 168, 200 sq. ft.

WACO produces its first closed-cabin aircraft. All previous production had been open cockpit biplanes.
WACO Model QDC ATC 412, 37 produced in 1931 and 1932, a 4-place cabin-biplane powered by a 165-hp Continental A-70-2 engine.

Price: $5,985.

The Empire State Building was completed.
In Las Vegas, a small local community made the decision to legalize gambling.

Ford automobile production: 615,455
Studebaker automobile production: 96,173
Chrysler automobile production: 65,819

Employment rate: 83.7%
Unemployment rate: 16.3%
GNP falls 8.5%.

1932

Stinson Model S Junior ATC 423, 1932-1933: 56 built powered by a 215-hp R-680 Lycoming engine. Standard price: $4,595/Seaplane Price: $6,995.
Stinson R ATC 457, 31 built powered by a 215-hp R-680 Lycoming engine. Price: $5,995.
Stinson R-2 ATC 489, 3 built powered by a 240-hp R-680-AB Lycoming engine. Price: $6,497
Stinson R-3 ATC 493, 3 built, retractable landing gear, powered by a 240-hp R-680-AB Lycoming engine. Price: $6,995.
Stinson Model M, 1 built, an experimental all-metal, low-wing aircraft, project abandoned.
Stinson Model U tri-motor ATC 484, 19 built powered by three 240-hp R-680-AB Lycoming engines. It carried 10 passengers and 1 pilot. Price: $32,900
Stinson Model U1 tri-motor ATC 2-413, 1 built, carried 10-11 passengers and 1 pilot, powered by three 240-hp R-680-AB Lycoming engines. Price: $32,900
Stinson SM-2K Junior ATC 2-414, 1 built, a 3-place aircraft powered by a 125-hp Kinner K-5 engine.

WACO Model UEC ATC 467, 45 produced, a 4-5 place cabin-biplane powered by a 210-hp Continental R-670.

Jimmy Doolittle in Cleveland, Ohio becomes the first person to fly over 300 mph.
In February, the Aircraft Development Corporation (Vultee-Cord), a California Corporation, is established.

The Beech Aircraft Company is founded in April.

Eddie Stinson dies January 26th. Because of fuel starvation, he makes an emergency landing on a golf course near Detroit, crashing the Model R into a flagpole. Edward Anderson Stinson, Jr.: July 11, 1894 - January 26, 1932.

Ford automobile production:
   4-cylinder: 118,225
   V8 Production: 275,947
   Total production: 394,182
(The new Flathead V-8 was priced approximately $10 more than the four-cylinder model.)
Chevrolet automobile production: 313,404
Chrysler automobile production: 25,291

Employment rate: 75.9%
Unemployment rate: 24.1%
GNP falls 13.4%.

1933

Stinson Model SR Reliant ATC 510, 99 built, powered by a 215-hp R-680 Lycoming engine. Price: $3,995
Stinson SR-1 Special ATC 513, 2 built, powered by a 240-hp R-680-7 Lycoming engine.
Stinson SR-2 Special ATC 510, 1 built, the same as the SR-1 with minor changes.
Stinson SR-3 Special ATC 513, 2 built, the same as the SR-1 with minor changes.
Stinson SR-4 ATC 519, 2 built, the same as the SR-1, but powered by a 250-hp Wright engine.
Stinson SM-8A Special ATC 2-461, 1 built, powered by a 220-hp Wright engine, approved for higher gross weight.
Stinson Model U tri-motor ATC 484, 5 built, carried 10 passengers and 1 pilot, powered by three 240-hp R-680-AB Lycoming engines. Price: $32,900
Stinson Model U1 tri-motor ATC 2-437, 1 built, powered by three 285-hp Wright R-760-E1 engines.
Stinson Model O ATC 520, 2 built, an open-cockpit aircraft powered by a 240-hp R-680-2 Lycoming engine. Price: $5,995

WACO Model UIC ATC 499, 84 produced, a 4-place cabin biplane powered by a 210-hp Continental W-670 engine. Price: $5,985

Beech Aircraft Company sells 1 Staggerwing aircraft.
Vultee sells 2 V-1 aircraft.
The Luscombe Aircraft Company is founded in the spring.

Congress authorizes the Tennessee Valley Authority.

On December 5th, the 21st Amendment to the Constitution is ratified, repealing the 18th

Amendment and bringing an end to the national prohibition of alcohol in America.

Ford automobile production: 334,969 (The standard Ford four-door sold for $560.)
Studebaker automobile production: 43,024
Chrysler automobile production: 30,220

Employment rate: 74.8%
Unemployment rate: 25.2%
GNP falls 2.1%.

1934

Stinson Model O ATC 520, 9 built, powered by a 240-hp R-680-2 Lycoming engine. Price: $5,995.
Stinson R-3-S Model R-3 ATC 539, a conversion for a Lycoming-Smith variable-pitch propeller.
Stinson Model A tri-motor ATC 556, 4 built, carried 8 passengers, 2 pilots, and 1 stewardess, powered by three 260-hp R-680-5 Lycoming engines. Price to airlines: $37,500.
Stinson SR-1 Reliant Special ATC 2-471, 1 built, powered by a 240-hp Lycoming R680-BA engine.
Stinson SR-1 Reliant Special ATC 2-496, 1 built, powered by a 225-hp Lycoming R680-B4 engine.
Stinson SR-5 Reliant ATC 530, 14 built, powered by a 225-hp R-680-4 Lycoming engine. Price: $5,775 without trailing edge wing flaps.
Stinson SR-5 Reliant Special ATC 2-492, 1 built, powered by a 225-hp R-680-4 Lycoming engine equipped with trailing edge wing flaps and a smaller tail group.
Stinson SR-5 Reliant Special ATC 2-494, 3 built, powered by a 245-hp R-680-6 Lycoming engine, approved for higher gross weight and modified with a smaller tail group.
All Stinson aircraft beginning with the SR-5A are equipped with trailing edge wing flaps, and 225-hp R-680-4 Lycoming engines are standard equipment on the SR-5s priced at $5,995.
Stinson SR-5A Reliant ATC 536, 76 built, equipped with trailing edge wing flaps.
Stinson SR-5A Reliant ACT 2-491, 1 built, powered by a 245-hp R-680-6 Lycoming engine mounted on twin Edo floats.
Stinson SR-5B Reliant ATC 530, 1 built, powered by a 240-hp R-680-2 Lycoming engine.
Stinson SR-5C Reliant ATC 530, 6 built, powered by a 260-hp R-680-5 Lycoming engine. Price: $6,595
Stinson SR-5D Reliant ATC 531, 1 built, powered by a 215-hp R-680 Lycoming engine.
Stinson SR-5D Reliant ATC 2-493, 1 built, powered by a 215-hp R-680 Lycoming engine and modified with a smaller tail group.
Stinson SR-5E Reliant ATC 537, 54 built, equipped with trailing edge wing flaps. 225-hp R-680-4 Lycoming engines are standard equipment on the SR-5E priced at $5,775.
Stinson SR-5F Reliant ATC 530, 2 built, same as the SR-5E, but powered by a 250-hp Wright engine. Price: $6,995
Stinson SR-5F Reliant ATC 550, 2 built, powered by a 285-hp Wright R-760-E1 engine.
Stinson SR-5X, 1 built, prototype for the SR-6.
Stinson Model L, a low-wing replacement for the SR-5, project abandoned.
WACO Model YKC ATC 533, 55 produced, a 4-place cabin-biplane powered by a 225-hp Jacobs L-4 engine. Price: $6,450
WACO Model UKC ATC 528, 44 produced, a 4-place cabin-biplane powered by a 210-hp Continental R-670-A engine. Price: $6,285
WACO Model CJC ATC 538, 37 produced in 1934 and 1935, a 4-5-place cabin-biplane powered by a 250-hp Wright R-760-E engine. Price: $8,165
Beech Aircraft Company sold 19 Staggerwing aircraft in their first full year of production. Price: $8,550
Luscombe Aircraft Company sold 4 Phantom aircraft.
Vultee sold 12 V1-A aircraft. It is designed for 8 passengers and 2 crew members and is powered by a 650-hp Wright Cyclone engine.

In August, Aviation Corporation (AVCO) acquires Airplane Development Corporation (Vultee) from Cord, which is renamed Aviation Manufacturing Corporation.

Also in August, Aviation Manufacturing Corporation acquires Stinson from Cord. Stinson retaines its management, however, and continued to be a self-managing corporation.

May 14, 1934 is the first delivery of an 18-passenger Douglas DC-2 to TWA.

The aircraft carrier Ranger (CV-4), is commissioned.

On May 23rd, Bonnie Parker and Clyde Barrow were killed.

Ford automobile production: 563,921
Chevrolet automobile production: 551,191
Chrysler automobile production: 36,929

The big news in the automobile industry is the revolutionary airflow design introduced by Chrysler, which uses all of the most modern concepts from automotive and aviation design.

Employment rate: 78.0%
Unemployment rate: 22.0%
GNP rises 7.7%. The long road to recovery begins.

1935

Stinson Model A tri-motor ATC 556, 18 built, carried 8 passengers, 2 pilots, and 1 stewardess, powered by three 260-hp R-680-5 Lycoming engines. Price to airlines: $37,500
Stinson SR Reliant ATC 2-499, 1 built, powered by a 215-hp R-680 Lycoming engine.
Stinson SR-5A Reliant Special ATC 2-511, 1 built, powered by a 245-hp R-680-6 Lycoming engine, approved for higher gross weight.
Stinson SR-6 Reliant ATC 580, 51 built, powered by a 245-hp R-680-6 Lycoming engine. Price: $5,995-$9,000 with all optional equipment. All SR-6 aircraft are equipped with trailing edge wing flaps.
Stinson SR-6A Reliant ATC 580, 3 built, powered by a 225-hp R-680-4 Lycoming engine.
Stinson SR-6B Reliant ATC 580, 3 built, powered by a 260-hp R-680-5 Lycoming engine. Price: $6,995
Stinson SR-6C Reliant ATC 580, 1 built, powered by a 240-hp R-680-2 Lycoming engine.
Stinson SR-6X, 1 built experimental gull-wing aircraft.

WACO Model YKC-5 ATC 533, 22 produced, a 4 to 5-place cabin biplane powered by a 225-hp Jacobs L-4 engine. Price: $5,490
WACO Model YOC ATC 569, 50 produced, a 4 to 5-place cabin biplane powered by a 225-hp Jacobs L-4 engine. Price: $6,895.
WACO Model YOC, 13 produced, powered by a 285-hp Jacobs L-5 at $7995.
WACO Model CUC and ATC 575, 13 produced, a 4-5-place cabin-biplane powered by a 250-hp Wright R-760-E engine. Price: $8,400
WACO Model CUC-1, 12 produced, powered by a 285-hp Wright R-760-E1 engine.

Beech Aircraft Company sells 44 Staggerwing aircraft.
Luscombe Aircraft Company sells 10 Phantom aircraft. Price: $5,995
Vultee sells 10 V1-A aircraft.

DuPont creates nylon, the first completely synthetic fiber.
Aircraft-detecting radar is developed in England.
In January, Jimmy Doolittle flies a Vultee V1-A across the United States in 11 hours and 59 minutes.

Ford automobile production: 820,253
Chevrolet automobile production: 548,215
Chrysler automobile production: 50,010

Employment Rate: 79.9%
Unemployment Rate: 20.1%
GNP grows 8.1%.

1936

Stinson SR-7 Reliant ATC 594, 3 built, a 4-place aircraft powered by a 225-hp R-680-4 Lycoming engine. The SR-7 is the first gull-wing Reliant.
Stinson SR-7A ATC 594, 5 built with 225-hp Lycoming.
Stinson SR-7B Reliant gull-wing ATC 594, 52 built, a 5-place aircraft powered by a 245-hp R-680-6 Lycoming engine. Price: $6,485
Stinson SR-7C gull-wing Reliant ATC 594, 3 built, a 5-place aircraft powered by a 260-hp R-680-5 Lycoming engine. Price: $6,995
Stinson SR-8A Reliant gull-wing ATC 608, 2 built, a 4-place powered by a 225-hp R-680-4 Lycoming engine. Price: $6,500
Stinson SR-8B Reliant gull-wing ATC 608, 57 built, carried 4 passengers and 1 pilot, powered by a 245-hp R-680-6 Lycoming engine. Price: $7,500
Stinson SR-8C Reliant gull-wing ATC 608, 20 built, carried 4 passengers and 1 pilot, powered by a 260-hp R-680-5 Lycoming engine. Price: $9,995
Stinson SR-8D Reliant gull-wing ATC 609, 11 built, powered by a 285-hp Wright R-760-E2 engine. Price: $10,500
Stinson SR-8E Reliant gull-wing ATC 609, 35 built, powered by a 320-hp Wright R-760-E2 engine. Price: $12,000
Stinson Model A tri-motor ATC 556, 12 built, carried 8 passengers, 2 pilots and 1 stewardess, powered by three 260-hp R-680-5 Lycoming engines. Price to airlines: $37,500
Stinson Model B, a twin-engine executive based on the Model A, mock-up only.
Stinson Model PT, 1 built, an experimental low-wing aircraft with retractable landing gear designed as a military trainer. No sales - project abandoned.

WACO Model YKS-6 ATC 533, 65 produced in

1936 and 1937, a 4-place cabin-biplane powered by a 225-hp Jacobs L-4 engine. Price: $4,995

WACO Model DQC-6 ATC 597, 11 produced, a 4-5-place cabin-biplane powered by a 285-hp Wright R-760-E1 engine at: $8975.

WACO Model EQC-6 18 produced, 350-hp Wright R-760-E2 engine at: $9,650

WACO Model ZQC-6 ATC 598, 66 produced from 1936 to 1938, a 4 to 5-place cabin-biplane powered by a 285-hp Jacobs L-5 engine. Price: $7,835.

WACO Model ZKS-6 6 produced, 285-hp Jacobs L-5 engine.

WACO Model YQC-6 ATC 598, 14 produced from 1936 to1937, a 4-place cabin-biplane powered by a 225-hp Jacobs L-4 engine. Price range: $7,295.

WACO Model AQC-6 ATC 598, 11 produced from 1936 to 1939, a 4-place cabin-biplane powered by a 330-hp Jacobs L-6 engine. Price: $8,975

Beech Aircraft Company sells 44 Staggerwing aircraft.

Luscombe Aircraft Company sells 9 Phantom aircraft.

Spartan Aircraft Company sells 3 Executive aircraft. Base price: $23,500

Vultee sells 3 V1-A aircraft designed for 2 crew members and 8 passengers and powered by a 650-hp Wright Cyclone engine.

Beech is offering the Model C-17R powered by a nine-cylinder, 420-hp Wright R-975-E2 engine priced at $14,500, and the C-17L Special powered by a 225-hp Jacobs engine priced at $7,495.

On April 29, the first 28-passenger Douglas DC-3 is delivered to American Airlines.

Ford automobile production: 930,778 (Ford prices ranged from $510-$780.)

Chevrolet automobile production: 918,278

Chrysler automobile production: 71,295

Employment Rate: 83.1%
Unemployment Rate: 16.9%
GNP grows 14.1%.

1937

Stinson Model A tri-motor ATC 556, 2 built, carried 8 passengers, 2 pilots and 1 stewardess, powered by three 260-hp R-680-5 Lycoming engines. Price to airlines: $37,500

Stinson SR-9A One built with 225-hp Lycoming R-680-B4 engine.

Stinson SR-9B Reliant gull-wing ATC 621, 35 built, carried 4 passengers and 1 pilot, powered by a 245-hp R-680-B6 Lycoming engine. Price: $9,385

Stinson SR-9C Reliant gull-wing ATC 621, 65 built, carried 4 passengers and 1 pilot, powered by a 260-hp R-680-B5 Lycoming engine. Price: $9,995

Stinson SR-9D Reliant gull-wing ATC 625, 18 built, powered by a 285-hp Wright R-760-E2 engine. Price: $12,000

Stinson SR-9E Reliant gull-wing ATC 625, 43 built, powered by a 320-hp Wright R-760-E2 engine. Price: $12,500

Stinson SR-9F Reliant gull-wing ATC 640, 34 built, powered by a 400-hp P&W Wasp engine. Price: $18,000

WACO Model YKS-7 ATC 626, 66 produced from 1937 to 1940, a 4-place cabin-biplane powered by a 225-hp Jacobs L-4 engine. Price: $6,995.

WACO Model VKS-7 ATC 648, 19 produced from 1937 to1941, a 4 to 5-place cabin-biplane powered by a 240-hp Continental R-670-M engine. Price: 7,770

WACO Model ZGC-7 ATC 627, 29 produced from 1937 to1938, a 5-place cabin biplane powered by a 285-hp Jacobs L-5 engine. Price: $8,935.

WACO Model ZKS-7 ATC 626, 21 produced from 1937 to 1941, a 4 to 5-place cabin biplane powered by a 285-hp Jacobs L-5 engine. Price: $6,435.

WACO Model EGC-7 ATC 639, 40 produced from 1937 to 1939, a 5-place cabin-biplane powered by a 350-hp Wright R-760-E2 engine. Price: $11,125.

Spartan Aircraft Company sells 10 executive aircraft. Base price: $23,500

Beech Aircraft Company sells 67 Staggerwing aircraft.

Luscombe Aircraft Company sells 8 Phantom aircraft. Price: $6,000

The aircraft carrier Yorktown (CV-5) is commissioned.

Japan invades China, beginning eight years of occupation.

On February 27, Joan Marie Hyatt is born.

On May 20, Amelia Earhart departs Oakland, California on her around-the-world flight.

On August 11, E. L. Cord sells his interest in the Cord Corporation to the Aviation Corporation (AVCO) for $2,000,000.

Ford automobile production: 942,015 (Ford offers a smaller 60-hp V-8 engine to complement the 85-hp V-8.)
Chevrolet automobile production: 815,375
Chrysler automobile production: 107,872

Employment Rate: 85.7%
Unemployment Rate: 14.3%
GNP rises 5.0

1938

Stinson SR-10 gull-wing Reliant 1938 to 1941, 123 built. Price range: $9,995 to $19,000 depending upon the type of engine installed on each aircraft.
Stinson SR-10B gull-wing Reliant ATC 678, 2 built, carried 4 passengers and 1 pilot, powered by a 245-hp R-680-6 Lycoming engine. Price: $9,995
Stinson SR-10C gull-wing Reliant ATC 678, 37 built, carried 4 passengers and 1 pilot, powered by a 260-hp R-680-5 Lycoming engine. Price: $10,995
Stinson SR-10G and SR-10G3 gull-wing Reliant ATC 678, 12 built, carried 4 passengers and 1 pilot, powered by a 290-hp R-680-E1 Lycoming engine. Price: $12,585
Stinson SR-10H not built
Stinson SR-10E gull-wing Reliant ATC 679, 8 built, powered by a 320-hp Wright R-760-E2 engine. Price: $14,350
Stinson SR-10K gull-wing Reliant ATC 679, 2 built, powered by a 420-hp Wright R-975-E3 engine. Price: $19,000
Stinson SR-10F gull-wing Reliant ATC 685, 10 built, powered by a 450-hp P&W Wasp engine. Price: $19,000

WACO Model AGC-8 ATC 664, 15 produced in 1938 and 1939, a 4 to 5-place cabin biplane powered by 330-hp Jacobs L-6 engine. Price: $10,495
WACO Model AVN-8 ATC 677, 16 produced, a 4 to 5-place cabin biplane powered by a 330-hp Jacobs L-6 engine. Price: $11,375. Model ZVN-8, 5 produced, powered by a 285-hp Jacobs L-5 at $10,695.
WACO Model ZGC-8 ATC 664, 6 produced, a 4 to 5-place cabin biplane powered by a 285-hp Jacobs L-5 engine. Price: $9,895.

Beech Aircraft Company sells 53 Staggerwing aircraft.
Luscombe Aircraft Company sells 71 of the Model 8 ATC 694, an all-metal, 2-place aircraft.
Spartan Aircraft Company sells 3 executive aircraft. Base price: $23,500

On August 3, the Stinson Aircraft Corporation is dissolved and becomes the Stinson Division of Aviation Manufacturing Corporation.

The aircraft carrier Enterprise (CV-6) is commissioned.

Chevrolet automobile production: 465,158
Ford automobile production: 410,263
Chrysler automobile production: 41,946

Employment Rate: 81.0 %
Unemployment Rate: 19.0%
GNP falls 4.5%.

1939

Stinson HW-75 ATC 709, advertised as the Model 105, 233 built, powered by a 75-hp Continental engine. Price: $2,995
Stinson SR-10C gull-wing Reliant ATC 678, 10 built, carried 4 passengers and 1 pilot, powered by a 260-hp R-680-D5 Lycoming engine. Price: $10,995
Stinson SR-10J and SR-10J3 gull-wing Reliant ATC 678, 11 built, carried 4 passengers and 1 pilot, powered by a 390-hp R-680-E3 Lycoming engine. Price: $12,585
Stinson SR-10D gull-wing Reliant ATC 679, 3 built, powered by a 300-hp Wright R-760-E1 engine. Price: $14,000
Stinson SR-10E gull-wing Reliant ATC 679, 9 built, powered by a 320-hp Wright R-760-E2 engine. Price: $14,350
Stinson SR-10F gull-wing Reliant ATC 685, 2 built, powered by a 450-hp P&W Wasp engine. Price: $19,000.

WACO Model ARE, 6 produced, from 1939 to 1941 a 4-5-place cabin biplane powered by a 330-hp Jacobs L-6 engine. Price: $14,900

Beech Aircraft Company sells 75 Staggerwing aircraft.
Luscombe Aircraft Company sells 256 Model 8 and Model 8A aircraft.
Spartan Aircraft Company sells 9 executive aircraft. Base price: $23,500

Vultee Aircraft Division of Aviation Corporation (AVCO) is reorganized as an independent company. Vultee Aircraft Inc. is established on November 14, 1939 as a Delaware corporation.

The movies "The Wizard of Oz," "Gone with the Wind," and "Mr. Smith Goes to Washington" are released.

Betty Grable purchases a Stinson SR-10C painted pink, probably NC18485.

On September 1, the Second World War began when the German Luftwaffe begin their attack on Polish airfields.

Ford automobile production: 487,031
Chevrolet automobile production: 577,278
Chrysler automobile production: 67,749

Employment Rate: 82.8%
Unemployment Rate: 17.2%

1940

Stinson Model 105 ATC 709, 42 built, powered by a 75-hp C-75 Continental engine. Price: $2,995

Stinson Model 10 ATC 709, 176 built, powered by an 80-hp C-80 Continental engine. Price: $3,370

Stinson Model 10B, 1 built, powered by a 75-hp GO-145 Lycoming engine, experimental.

Stinson SR-10C gull-wing Reliant ATC 678, 3 built, carried 4 passengers and 1 pilot, powered by a 260-hp R-680-D5 Lycoming engine. Price: $10,995

Stinson SR-10E gull-wing Reliant ATC 679, 3 built, powered by a 320-hp Wright R-760-E2 engine. Price: $14,350

Stinson Model O-49 LTC-26-2, later re-designated the L-1, built 142. Price: $10,565

On July 12, Vultee Aircraft Corporation takes possession of the Stinson Division of Aviation Manufacturing Corporation in exchange for 302,168 shares of Vultee stock.

In May, Stinson moves production to Nashville and manufactures 138 Model 10 aircraft there. However, they return to Wayne in September because Vultee wants to build dive bombers in the Nashville plant.

The Stinson factory at Wayne is expanded by 62,900 sq. ft. making it 231, 100 sq. ft.

WACO Model SRE, 20 produced 1940 and 1941, a 5-place cabin-biplane powered by a 450-hp P&W Wasp SB3 engine. Price: $18,900.

WACO Model HRE 4 produced, a 5-place cabin-biplane powered by a 300-hp Lycoming R-680-E3 engine. Price: $14,175

Luscombe Aircraft Company sells 497 Model 8A and Model 8C aircraft. The Model 8A is priced at $1,975, and the Model 8C priced at $2,795.

Spartan Aircraft Company sells 9 executive aircraft. Base price: $23,500

Howard Aircraft Company sells 44 DGA-15 aircraft powered by a 400-hp P&W engine. Price: $19,885

Fairchild Airplane & Engine Corp. sells 97 Fairchild model 24 aircraft.

The aircraft carrier *Wasp* (CV-7) is commissioned.

Ford automobile production: 541,896
Chevrolet automobile production: 764,616
Chrysler automobile production: 115,824

Employment rate: 85.4%
Unemployment rate: 14.6%

1941

Stinson Model 10 ATC 709, 84 built, powered by an 80-hp C-80 Continental engine. Price: $3,370

Stinson Model 10A ATC 738, 466 built, powered by a 90-hp 4AC-199-E3 Franklin engine. Price: $3,655

Stinson SR-10C gull-wing Reliant ATC 678, 3 built, carried 4 passengers and 1 pilot, powered by a 260-hp R-680-D5 Lycoming engine. Price: $10,995

Stinson SR-10E gull-wing Reliant ATC 679, 1 built, powered by a 320-hp Wright R-760-E2 engine. Price: $14,350

Stinson SR-10F gull-wing Reliant ATC 685, 6 built, powered by a 450-hp P&W Wasp engine. Price: $19,000

Stinson Model O-49 LTC-26-2, later re-designated the L-1, 182 built. These aircraft manufactured under the Stinson name in Nashville. Price: $10,565

On December 20, Vultee Aircraft, Inc. purchases 440,000 shares, or 34%, of Consolidated Aircraft common stock.

WACO Model VKS-7F 21 produced, 1940 and 1941 a 5-place cabin biplane powered by a 240-hp Continental W670-M engine.

Price: $12,500.
Luscombe Aircraft Company sells 275 Model 8A, Model 8C, and Model 8D aircraft combined.
Howard Aircraft Company sells 21 DGA-15 aircraft powered by a 400-hp P&W engine.
Price: $19,885

The aircraft carrier *Hornet* (CV-8) is commissioned.

On December 7, 1941, Japanese carrier aircraft attack the US Pacific Fleet based at Pearl Harbor. 2,403 Americans die in the attack and 1,178 are wounded. 188 planes were destroyed, and 19 ships were damaged or sunk.

Ford automobile production: 691,544
Chevrolet automobile production: 1,008,976
Chrysler automobile production: 161,704

Employment Rate: 90.1%
Unemployment Rate: 9.9%

1942

Stinson Aircraft Division build 34 Model 10A aircraft.
Stinson Aircraft Division build 10 Model L-5 aircraft.

As a subcontractor, the Stinson factory supports the Vultee A-31 dive bomber production. Stinson manufactures 1,531 pairs of outer wing panels for this aircraft with production running from late 1941 into 1943. Wing sections are completed in Wayne and shipped to the factory in Nashville.

Luscombe Aircraft Company sells 19 Model 8C and Model 8D aircraft.

17 B-25 bombers fly off the *USS Hornet* April, 18 1942 led by Lt. Col. Jimmy Doolittle.

The Battle of Midway ends June 6, 1942. Aircraft carriers *Yorktown*, *Enterprise*, and *Hornet* participate in the battle.

In May, the Stinson division is awarded the U. S. Treasury Department's Minuteman flag when all its employees subscribe to the payroll deduction plan for the purchase of war bonds.

The aircraft carrier *Essex* (CV-9) is commissioned.

Ford Automobile Production: 160,432
Chevrolet Automobile Production: 254,885
Chrysler Automobile Production: 36,586

Following the Japanese attack on Pearl Harbor and the U.S. Declaration of War, production of vehicles for civilian markets is halted to devote all factories to the manufacturing of war materials. The deadline calls for the last passenger car to be manufactured on February 9, 1942 and trucks to stop production March 3rd. Civilian production of automobiles will not resume until 1946.

Employment Rate: 95.3%
Unemployment Rate: 4.7%

1943

Stinson Aircraft Division Model AT-19 ATC 774, 250 built, powered by a 285-hp R-680-3BL Lycoming engine. These aircraft are sold to the British Royal Navy Fleet Air Arm.
Stinson Aircraft Division Model L-5 ATC 764, built 1,116 built, powered by an 185-hp O-435-A Lycoming engine. Price: $10,165

The merger of Consolidated Aircraft Corporation and Vultee Aircraft Inc. is completed in March, and Stinson becomes a division of Consolidated Vultee Aircraft Corporation.

Employment Rate: 98.1%
Unemployment Rate: 1.9%

1944

Stinson Aircraft Division sells 250 Model AT-19 aircraft ATC 774 powered by a 285-hp R-680-3B Lycoming engine priced at $22,496. Lend-Lease to the British Royal Navy Fleet Air Arm.
Stinson Aircraft Division sells 1,361 Model L-5 aircraft ATC 764 powered by a 185-hp O-435-A Lycoming engine. 1944 contract price $9,704

Employment Rate: 98.8 %
Unemployment Rate: 1.2 %

1945

Stinson Model L-5 ATC 764, 988 built, powered by a 185-hp O-435-A Lycoming engine.
Price: $8,023
Stinson Model L-5G ATC 764, 115 built, powered by a 190-hp Lycoming engine.
Stinson Model XL-13 ATC AR-10, 2 built in Michigan. 298 L-13A and L-13B are later manufactured by Consolidated Vultee in San Diego.
Stinson Model 108 Voyager ATC 767, 10 built in Nashville, powered by a 150-hp 6A4-150-B3 Franklin engine.

CHAPTER 15

Employment Rate: 98.1%
Unemployment Rate: 1.9%

The activities of the Stinson Aircraft Company from 1938 - 1950 and beyond are presented in a comprehensive two-volume set *"Stinson's Golden Age"* published by Wind Canyon Books.

1946 through 1948 production figures are also presented here to offer the reader an opportunity to view the Stinson's company production from 1925 through 1948.

Stinson Model 108 ATC 767, 742 built, powered by a 150-hp Franklin engine. Price: $5,645
Stinson Model 108-1 ATC 767, 1,507 built the same as 108 with minor changes. Price: $5,745
Stinson Model 108-2 ATC 767, 1,249 built, powered by a 165-hp Franklin engine, the same as 108-1 with minor changes. Price: $5,745
Stinson Model 108-3 ATC 767, 1,749 built a redesigned aircraft with a large tail, powered by a 165-hp Franklin engine. Price: $6,289
Stinson Model 108-4, 1 built, an experimental 1949 model powered by a 180-hp Franklin engine.
Stinson Model 108-5, 1 built, powered by a 180-hp Franklin engine.
Stinson Model 106, 1 built, an experimental all-metal, low-wing pusher powered by a 230-hp Franklin engine, project abandoned.
Stinson Model 118, 1 built as an experimental flying car. The aircraft portion was powered by a 190-hp Lycoming engine and the car portion, which could detach from the aircraft, was powered by a 26-hp Crosley engine.

Total production of Model 108 Stinsons: 5,260
Total production of civilian 3 place aircraft: 1,035
Total production of tri-motor aircraft: 145
Total production of AT-19 (V-77) aircraft: 500
Total production of L-5 aircraft: 3,590
Total production of 0-49 aircraft: 324
Nonproduction experimental aircraft: 16
Production from 1926 to 1948: 12,389
Total ATC Numbers: 124

Production numbers 1920 - 1945

1920

One biplane aircraft
Total 1920 production: 1

1921 through 1925

No production

1926

10 biplane aircraft
One experimental aircraft
Total 1926 production: 11

1927

16 biplane aircraft
36 high wing aircraft
Total 1927 production: 52

1928

63 single-engine aircraft
Total 1928 production: 63

1929

130 single-engine aircraft
One tri-motor aircraft
Two experimental aircraft
Total 1929 production: 133

1930

352 single-engine aircraft
10 tri-motor aircraft
One experimental aircraft
Total 1930 production in 363

1931

270 single-engine aircraft
48 tri-motor aircraft
Total 1931 production: 318

1932

94 single-engine aircraft
20 tri-motor aircraft
One experimental aircraft
Total 1932 production: 115

1933

106 single-engine aircraft
Six tri-motor aircraft
Total 1933 production: 112

1934

173 single-engine aircraft
Four tri-motor aircraft
Two experimental aircraft
Total 1934 production: 179

1935

60 single-engine aircraft
18 tri motor aircraft
One experimental aircraft
Total 1935 production: 79

1936

188 single-engine aircraft
12 tri motor aircraft
Two experimental aircraft
Total 1936 production: 202

1937

196 single-engine aircraft
Two tri-motor aircraft
Total 1937 production: 198

1938

71 single-engine aircraft
Total 1938 production: 71

1939

35 single-engine Reliant aircraft
233 three-place aircraft
Total 1939 production: 268

1940

Seven single-engine Reliant aircraft
142 Model O-49 aircraft
218 three place aircraft
One experimental aircraft
Total 1940 production: 367

1941

10 single-engine Reliant aircraft
182 Model O49 aircraft
550 3-place aircraft
Total 1941 production: 742

1942

34 three place aircraft
10 L-5 aircraft
Total 1942 production: 44

1943

1,116 L-5 aircraft
250 AT-19 aircraft
Total 1943 production: 1,366

1944

1,361 L-5 aircraft
250 AT-19 aircraft
Total 1944 production: 1,611

1945

988 L-5 aircraft
115 L-5G aircraft
Ten 108 aircraft
Two experimental aircraft
Total 1945 production: 1,115

Production Numbers Summary by Type

SB Detroiter Biplane - 27
SM Detroiter Monoplane - 143
SM Junior - 423
SR Reliant - 431
Gullwing - 495

Chapter 16
Type Certificate Numbers

In 1926, Congress passed the Air Commerce Act, instructing the Secretary of Commerce to establish an Aeronautics Branch. The Aeronautics Branch established air commerce regulations—with the first rules published in December 1926. All aircraft used for commercial purposes now had to be registered and assigned an identification number.

The Aeronautics Branch established a numbering system which, with some modification, is still in use today. An aircraft company that had received an approved type certificate for a specific model would be granted a block of NC numbers such as NC22001 to NC25000. Depending upon aircraft sales, this block of numbers could be assigned to an individual manufacturer's aircraft over a several year period. When this block of numbers was exhausted, a new block would be issued. The Aeronautics Branch and later the Civil Aeronautics Administration (CAA) began assigning numbers in 1927. Initially the plan was to issue a new block of numbers each year, but the increased volume production in 1929 and 1930 required an exception to this rule. As production ramped up again from 1938-1941, the number system was expanded to cover the unexpected increase.

The CAA used other letters to designate special types of aircraft. NX was assigned on a single aircraft basis for experimental testing, leading to an approved type certificate. NR was assigned to special-purpose aircraft such as exhibition flying and spray planes, and NS was assigned to federal, state, and territorial possessions aircraft. The government entity was required to request the NS at the time of delivery from the original manufacturer. There were very few requests for the NS number, and the CAA discontinued its use in 1939.

When the first type certificate specifications were established in 1927, the procedure for approvals was relatively simple. The CAA, however, frequently rewrote the requirements for obtaining ATC approval from 1927-1941. In its early years, Stinson was prolific in obtaining ATC approvals, but as time went on and aircraft became more sophisticated, fewer aircraft were submitted to the CAA for approval.

Common terms in this chapter

ATC: approved type certificate
hp: horsepower
s/n: serial number
5PCL: five-place, closed, land plane
6PCLM: six-place, closed, land monoplane
2PCHWM: two-place, closed, high-wing monoplane

1927

SB-1 Detroiter 5PCL ATC 24 powered by a 220-hp Wright J5C 9-cylinder radial engine. This was Stinson's first production aircraft manufactured in the Northfield, Michigan plant. One prototype and 26 production aircraft were assembled in 1926-1927. The prototype was powered by a 200-hp Wright J4B engine. A major selling point of the Stinson SB-1 was its fully-enclosed, heated cabin. The production aircraft were equipped with an electric engine starter, parking brake, and an exhaust manifold type cabin heater. The SB-1 was designed and manufactured prior to CAA type certificate requirements, and ATC number one was not issued until March 1927. ATC Number 24 was granted to the SB-1 retroactively after the end of production in January 1928. The selling price averaged around $11,000. SB identified this aircraft as a Stinson biplane.

The SB-1 Detroiter data as furnished by Stinson in a 1927 brochure: Type: four passengers, enclosed cabin, heated. Length overall was 28'10". Height overall was 10'7". The wing chord on both wings was 63 inches. The wings used Clark Y airfoil. Stagger: none. Angle of in incidence: upper wing, no degrees; lower wing, no degrees. Sweepback: None. Dihedral: upper wing, none, lower wing: 4 degrees. Angle of ship when resting on the ground: 14 degrees. Span: 35 feet, 10 inches. Span of tail plane: 12 feet. Area of main wings: 350 sq. feet, including ailerons. Weight: (empty), 1700 pounds. Useful load: 1200 pounds. Total load: 2900 pounds. Wing loading: 8.28 pounds per square foot. Power loading: 14.5 pounds per square foot. Fuel capacity: 70 gallons. Flying range: 500 miles. Speed: maximum 125 mph, cruising 105 mph, landing 45 mph. Rate of climb: (initial) 800 feet per minute.

Service ceiling: 13,500 foot. Dimensions inside of cabin: 42x50x100 inches. Propeller: metal. Motor: Wright "Whirlwind" 200-hp equipped with self-starter.

The SB-1 became popular with early passenger and mail carrier airlines. One of the concessions Northwest Airways management negotiated in the purchase of production aircraft four, five, and six was that their aircraft would start with serial number 1. In order to close the sale, Bill Mara agreed and the numbering system of the SB-1 production run was altered.

For historical purposes, the 27 Stinson biplanes are listed in numerical order. The CAA assigned four-digit license numbers to aircraft manufactured in 1926 through 1929. The prototype completed in January 1926 was not given a serial number or a CAA license number. There is no record that it ever left the factory and was probably either salvaged for parts or destroyed in an accident. Production started with: license number C2762, serial number (s/n) 10, Wayco Air Services; C3597, s/n 20, Florida Airways; C881, s/n 30, Horace Dodge; C872, s/n 1, Northwest Airways; C873, s/n 2, Northwest Airways; C874, s/n 3, Northwest Airways; license number unknown, s/n 4, Wien Alaska Airways; NC5262, s/n 5, Wien Alaska Airways; NS-5 s/n 60, Department of Commerce; C-CAFW, s/n 70, Patricia Airways; NC36, s/n 80, Dodgeson Motor Co, Detroit; NC2707, s/n 90, Wise Birds Club, Detroit; NC3588, s/n 102, Continental Motor Co, Detroit; NC3707 (later changed to C-CAGF), s/n 103, Purple Label Airways; NC3708 (later changed to C-CAJC), s/n 104, Patricia Airways; NC3036, s/n 106, Midwest Aircraft, Indianapolis; NC2763, s/n 107, Wayco Air Services; NC2779, s/n 108, Boston Airport Corp; NC3795, s/n 111, Boston Airport Corp; NC1419, s/n 112, Vance Air Services, Great Falls, Montana; NC3123, s/n 113, Jones Flying Corp, Old Orchard Beach, Maine; C877, s/n 114, Alaskan Airways; NC1621, s/n 115, H H Linn Airplane Co, Morris, NY; NC1429, s/n 116, Harry S Hilliker, Buffalo, NY; NC1381, s/n 117, Westchester Airways Rye, NY; and NC3050, s/n 201-B, F H Taylor, Watertown, NY. None of the SB-1 aircraft survived into the 21st century.

While owning a beautifully restored Model S Stinson NC10886 for several years, Jim Hammond began a worldwide search for a re-buildable Stinson SB-1. There were rumors of a "basket case" in Canada, but a specific location was never ascertained. In 2011, Jim began a serious research project to find sufficient data and production drawings to construct a replica. N877 assigned to SB-1 serial number 114 in 1927 was available and in 2012 construction began of a replica of this aircraft. In 2014 correspondence with the author, Jim Hammond reported the tail, landing gear and controls were nearly finished. The top wing and center section is finished, and the bottom wings are going together. Jim decided to use a 225-hp Lycoming with 300 cylinders which gives appearance of a Wright J5. Although a photo could not be found, the author believes Pioneer Instruments purchased serial number 114, the 22nd SB-1 manufactured in 1927. NC877 was purchased in late 1931 or early 1932 by McGee Airways, the predecessor of Alaska Airlines.

SM-1 Detroiter 6PCLM ATC 16 was approved November 1927 and was powered by a 220-hp Wright J5C 9-cylinder radial engine. The first flight of prototype NX1524 was April 1927. One prototype and 74 production aircraft were built from 1927 through 1930. Early production used the split axle landing gear found on the SB-1; later production used the wide tread outrigger-type landing gear. Even though the ATC data shows a higher gross weight, the production aircraft seem to have been manufactured with an empty weight of 1,815 pounds and a gross weight of 3,280 pounds. The SM-1 was approved with an empty weight of 1970 pounds and a gross weight of 3485 pounds and its cruising speed was listed at 105 mph. It had a wingspan of 84 feet and a length of 32 feet. SM identified this series of aircraft as a Stinson monoplane. A representative sampling of registration numbers assigned to the SM-1 production line was NC4583, NC473H, NC857, NC5889, NC1524 and NC966. The standard fuel capacity was 70 gallons and optional 90-gallon capacity was available. Serial numbers, M-219, M-224 and M-234, were eligible with a 105-gallon tank capacity. The following placard had to be displayed in full view of the pilot: "Always check fuel flow at strainer drain before takeoff. Never fly on one tank when fuel is low." Delta airline purchased one SM-1 NC3350 s/n M-216.

Scenic Airways, the predecessor company to Grand Canyon Airlines, purchased a Stinson SM-1B Detroiter aircraft in 1928. N1517 ATC 2-22 was one of only three built powered by 220-hp Wright J-5C engine approved for higher gross weight than the standard capital SM-1 Detroiter. John Seybold of Bristol LTD purchased N1517 and began a total ground up restoration. John shared with the author progress in 2011 and a photo of the completed aircraft in 2014. N1517 has been restored as it appeared when it rolled out the factory door and the Rainbow Route Scenic Airways paint trim is displayed on the aircraft.

1928

SM-B1 ATC 2-24 approved October 24, 1928 as a 3PCLM aircraft at 3,485 pounds gross weight. This approval was for serial numbers 241, 253, and 254.

SM-1DA 6PCLM ATC 74 approved October 1928. The five aircraft manufactured are identified as NC5900, NC6762, NC9600, NC9601, and finally NX9617. Empty weight: 2,432 lbs., gross weight: 4,500 lbs. Wheel tread: 108 inches, gas capacity: 90 gallons, oil 6 gallons. The price at the Stinson factory field was $12,500 and it was powered by a 220-hp Wright J-5C.

SM-1DB ATC 76 approved October 1928. Only one aircraft NC6580 serial number M301–1DB was manufactured. This aircraft carried an empty weight 2,522, gross weight 4,500 pounds

SM-1DC ATC 77 approved October 1928. This aircraft was licensed as a single-place transport with a payload of some 1,300 pounds. NC9618 M30710C was approved for an empty weight of 2,514 pounds and a gross weight of 4,500 pounds.

SM-1DD ATC 78 approved October 1928. NC486H was licensed as a two place aircraft with the remainder of the cabin structured as cargo space. This one-of-a-kind aircraft with an empty weight of 2,280 pounds and a gross weight of 4,500 pounds gave the SM-1DD a 2,220-pound payload capacity.

SM-2 Junior 3/4PCLM ATC 48 approved August 1928. Powered by a Warner Scarab 7-cylinder 110-hp engine. The Junior was a totally new aircraft, essentially a scaled down version of the SM-2 Detroiter. Up to this time, Stinson had used Wright engines and this was the company's first experience with a new power plant. This was the first installation of the new 7-cylinder Warner Scarab engine on an aircraft with an ATC. Sometimes called the Detroiter Junior, this was Stinson's first entry into the light cabin airplane field as a personal aircraft for the private owner or the small businessman.

The Warner Scarab powered Junior had a wingspan of 41'5", a length of 26'3", an empty weight of 1,516 pounds, a 510 pound payload, and a gross weight of 2,500 pounds. The Stinson Junior had a top speed of 106 mph, a cruise speed of 90 mph, and a landing speed of 42 mph. This was the first Stinson aircraft to use the Clark Y airfoil. The SM-2 carried 40 gallons of fuel, 3 gallons of oil, and baggage capacity was listed as 10 pounds. Serial numbers 1 through 1041 were eligible under this type certificate. A representative sampling of registration numbers assigned to the SM-2 was NC2604 and NC5889. A placard had to be displayed in full view of the pilot: "Always check fuel flow at strainer drain before takeoff. Never fly on one tank when fuel is low."

1929

SM-1F Detroiter 6PCLM ATC 136 approved April 1929. Powered by a Wright Whirlwind J-6-9-300 9-cylinder radial engine rated at 300-hp. Total production reached at least 26, and there is reason to believe a few more SM-1F aircraft were manufactured. The SM-1F was licensed with a wingspan of 46'8", length 32'8", height 9'0", and wing chord 84 inches total. Wing area: 292 sq. ft. The airfoil was a modified M-6. The empty weight was 2,614 pounds, useful load 1,685 pounds, and the payload with 100 gallons of fuel was 874 pounds. The gross weight was 4,300 pounds. The cruising speed of the SM-1F was 113 mph, maximum speed 132 mph, and landing speed 56 mph. Rate of climb first minute at sea level was 850 feet. Fuel capacity was 100 gallons, and oil was 6 gallons. The fuel consumption at 15 gallon per hour gave a cruising range of 680 miles. As this list shows, the CAA assigned Stinson a wide variety of license numbers: NC9691, s/n 500; NC9698, s/n 503; NC445H s/n 516; NR487H, s/n 519; NC404M, s/n 519; NC413M, s/n 521; NC910W, s/n 522; NC966W, s/n 525. Serial numbers 500-525 were eligible under this type certificate.

SM-1FS ATC 212 approved August 24, 1929. Powered by a Wright Whirlwind 9-cylinder radial J-6-9-300 engine rated at 300-hp. The SM-1FS was the pontoon mounted version of the SM-1F Detroiter. Edo Model J or Model K floats were approved, starting with s/n 509. Equipped with Edo Model K metal pontoons, the SM-1FS was approved with an empty weight of 3,198 pounds, reducing the payload with 91 gallons of fuel to 730 pounds. Approval for an increase in gross was not approved, and it stayed at 4,700 pounds. Equipped with pontoons, the cruising speed was reduced to 100 mph.

SM-2AA 4PCLM ATC 145 approved May 1929. It was powered by a Wright J65, 5-cylinder 165-hp, engine. This aircraft was the first of 6 SM-2 aircraft approved in 1929. The gross weight was increased to 3,152 pounds with an empty weight of 1,972 pounds. The cruising speed was listed at 97 mph, and the fuel capacity was increased to 60 gallons. 22 aircraft were built in 1929, and this probably was the last aircraft manufactured in the Northfield factory. A representative sampling of registration numbers assigned to the SM-2AA is NC457H, NC400M, NC8435, and NC9695. The following placard had to be displayed in full view of the pilot: "Always check fuel flow at strainer drain before takeoff. Never fly on one tank when fuel is low."

SM-2AA 4PCLM ATC 2-73 approved May 31, 1929 was powered by a Wright R-540 engine. Production was limited to one special order aircraft.

SM-2AC 4PCLM ATC 194 approved August 1929. Powered by a Wright J6 7-cylinder 225-hp engine. The SM-2 airframe remained basically the same until the SR series was introduced in 1933. The major changes in production were power plants, floats and special order aircraft. With an empty weight of 2,091 pounds, useful load of 1,126 pounds, the payload was 510 pounds with the fuel tanks filled to their 70-gallon capacity. Cruising speed was advertised at 113 mph with the maximum gross weight of 3,217 pounds. The thick wing brace straps were of heavy gauge steel tubing that was enclosed with balsa wood fairings. These fairings were airfoil-shaped to create added lift. The wing spars were solid spruce and rooted into an I-beam section. The wing leading edges were covered with aluminum sheet as far back as the front spar. The advertised price at the Wayne factory was $11,000, and if the aircraft were equipped with Fairchild floats, $13,500. Stinson produced 20 SM-2AC aircraft. A representative sampling of registration numbers assigned to the SM-2AC was NC462H, NC474H, NC402M, and NC405M. Serial numbers, land plane 1056 to 1129 eligible. Approved as a seaplane, serial numbers 1062, 1063, 1091, 1092, 1094, and 1097 to 1129 eligible.

SM-1D Detroiter Special 4PCLM ATC 2-142 approved October 23, 1929 powered by a 225-hp Wright J-5 engine. Approval for all SM-1 for a gross weight increased to 4,500 pounds.

SM-2AC 4PCLM ATC 2-143 approved October 23, 1929. Powered by a Wright R-760 J6-7 cylinder 225-hp engine. A special order floatplane with a gross weight increased to 3,522 pounds. A second aircraft was approved as a floatplane with a 4,500 pounds gross weight.

SM-2K 3PCLM ATC 2-136 approved October 4, 1929. Powered by Kinner K5 100-hp engine. Four of this three-place model was produced with a 2,500 pounds gross weight.

SM-2AB 4PCLM ACT 161 Approved June 1929. Powered by a Wright J5 220-hp engine. With the J5 engine still in production, Stinson decided to offer an improved model. The cabin interior was lengthened for more leg room, and the landing gear was lengthened to increase clearance. To compensate for the higher performance, the landing gear was also strengthened. The fuselage was lengthened and the "Junior" became higher, longer and bulkier. The aircraft now had a length of 28'4" and the height of 8'4". The aircraft empty weight was listed at 2,169 pounds and a new gross weight of 3,229 pounds. Representative registration numbers assigned to the SM-2AB aircraft was NC442H, NC458H, NC8438,and NC9699. The following placard had to be displayed in full view of the pilot: "Always check fuel flow at strainer drain before takeoff. Never fly on one tank when fuel is low."

SM-1D 300 ATC 2-60 approved April 13, 1929 as 6PCLM equipped with a Wright R-975 J6-9-300 engine rated at 300-hp for serial numbers 300 through 307 at 4,300 pounds gross weight

Corman 3000 tri-motor 7PCLM ATC 2-140 approved November 9, 1929. Prototype for Stinson SM-6000 powered by three 220-hp Wright J-5 engines. The Corman 3000 was designed and built in Dayton, Ohio.

SM-3 4PCLWM Powered by a Wright J-5C 220-hp engine. A low wing, retractable experimental aircraft. The project was abandoned with no ATC approval.

SM-4 Junior 2PCHWM powered by a 300-hp Wright R-975 engine. The *Sally Sovereign* aircraft, no ATC approval.

SM-5 4PCLWM Powered by a Wright J-5C 220-hp engine. Redevelopment of the SM-3, project abandoned, no ATC approval.

SM-6B Detroiter 8PCLM ATC 217 approved August 29, 1929. Powered by a Pratt and Whitney C-1 450-hp Wasp engine. It was the largest aircraft the Stinson Company had manufactured up to this time. The SM-6B was approved with a useful load of 1,854 pounds, an empty weight of 3,496 pounds, a payload with 110 gallons of fuel at 954 pounds, and a gross weight of 5,350 pounds. The wing span was 52'8", wing chord 84 inches, and the total wing area was 334 sq. ft. Performance was listed as cruising speed 128 mph, maximum speed 148 mph, and landing speed of 60 mph. Burning 23 gallons per hour, the range was listed at 575 miles. This aircraft was designed for the smaller airline or to carry up to 954 pounds of cargo. Representative registration numbers assigned to the SM-6B Detroiter aircraft were NC219W, NC412M, NC460H, NC8426 and NC9697.

SM-6B Detroiter 7-8PCLM ATC 2-89 approved July 3, 1929. Powered by a 450-hp P&W Wasp C-1 engine. A very large eight place aircraft serial numbers 2000 and 2001 were certified with a 5,000-pound gross weight.

1930

SM-1B Special ATC 2-174 approved January 16, 1930, serial numbers M219, M224, M234, M249, M250, M251 and M255 at 3,485 pounds gross weight.

SM-1B Special ATC 2-224 approved June 13, 1930 as a 5PCLM with a 220-hp Wright J5 engine for s/n M212 at 3,597 pounds gross weight.

SM-8B Junior 4PCHWM ATC 294 approved February 1, 1930. Powered by a 225-hp Wright J-6 engine. An improved and deluxe version of the SM-2 Junior was offered to customers who preferred a Wright powered aircraft. Serial numbers 4001 to 4257 eligible.

SM-2ABS Junior 4PCL M ATC 2-267 approved September 5, 1930. Powered by a Wright J-5 220-hp engine. Fitted with twin Edo floats with a gross weight of 3,450 pounds. Serial numbers 1062 and 1094 were manufactured in September 1930.

SM-2AB 4PCLM ACT 2-267 approved September 6, 1930. Powered by a Wright J-5 220-hp engine. Two special order aircraft were fitted with Edo twin float gear with a gross weight of 3,450 pounds.

SM-8A Junior 4PCHWM ATC 295 approved February 11, 1930. Powered by a radial 210-hp 9-cylinder Lycoming R-680 engine. With Stinson and Lycoming now controlled by the Cord Holding Company, E. L. Cord required Lycoming to offer aircraft engines to Stinson below the cost of production. In a drive to establish Stinson as the premier American aircraft manufacturer, the price of the SM-8A was reduced to $5,775 for aircraft accepted at the Wayne factory. This model was advertised as a $10,000 airplane for $5,775. The SM-8A was offered with a soundproof cabin, shatterproof glass windows, cabin heater, cabin ventilation, electric engine starter, wheel brakes, and emergency brake for parking. Stinson listed the specifications as using a Clark Y airfoil, empty weight 2,161 pounds, useful load 1,134 pounds, 61 gallons of fuel, cruising speed 105 mph, landing speed 50 mph, and an absolute ceiling of 14,000 foot. Representative registration numbers assigned to the SM-7A Junior aircraft were NC208W, NC224W, NC416M and NC429M. Serial numbers for land planes, 4000 and up were eligible and seaplanes, s/n 4100 and up were eligible. The following placard had to be displayed in full view of the pilot: "Always check fuel flow at strainer drain before takeoff. Never fly on one tank when fuel is low."

SM-7A Junior 4PCHWM ATC 298 approved February 18, 1930. Powered by 9-cylinder 300-hp Wright J-6 engine. This aircraft offered spectacular performance. Specifications included an advertised cruising speed of 120 mph, 90-gallon fuel capacity, dual wheel controls, adjustable metal propeller, and an electric inertia-type engine starter. Available at extra cost included a battery, generator, skis, parachute flares, navigation and landing lights. Representative registration numbers assigned to the SM-7A Junior aircraft were NC216W, NC406Y and NC410M.

SM-8D Junior 4PCHWM ATC 312 approved April 8, 1930. Powered by a 225-hp DR-980 Packard diesel engine. Number one diesel as we know it today was not available in the 1930s and the RD-980 was designed to run on kerosene or the slightly cheaper distillate. Registration numbers assigned the SM-8D Junior aircraft were NC200W and NC227W.

SM-6000 Airliner 11PCLM ATC 335 approved July 10, 1930. Powered by three 215-hp Lycoming R-680 engines. After examining the Corman 3000, Stinson's engineers completely redesigned the aircraft into a true 11-passenger plus crew airliner. The Stinson airliner was a very comfortable coach style aircraft designed for shorter trips. The SM-6000 had an overall length of 42'10", a height of 12 feet, wingspan 60 feet, wing chord 105 inches, and total wing area 490 sq ft. The aircraft used Goettingen airfoil. With an empty weight of 5,625 pounds, a useful load of 2,875 pounds, payload with 120 gallons of fuel was 1,865 pounds, baggage 215 pounds, and a gross weight of 8,500 pounds. The SM-6000 Airliner listed a cruising speed of 115 mph, landing speed of 60 mph. The climb to 10,000 feet was 25 min and a ceiling of 14,500 feet. Soon after production started, low drag Townsend-ring fairings became available for the engines as well as large streamliners for the main gear. A representative sampling of registration numbers assigned to the SM-6000 Airliner were NC429Y, NC498Y, NC975W and NC979W. Serial numbers, 5005 to M5014 eligible. Standard weight could be increased to 8,800 pounds when the aircraft was reworked at the factory to conform to approved technical data.

SM-1DX 3PCLM ATC 2-228 approved June 20, 1930. NX7654 s/n M262 was powered with a 225-hp Packard DR-980 diesel engine. This aircraft was approved with a 4,245 pound gross weight.

SM-7B Junior 4PCHWM ATC 329 approved June 20, 1930. Powered by a 300-hp P&W Wasp Jr. engine. This version of the Junior was offered for those customers who wished for higher horsepower and better performance. The SM-7B was purchased by General Electric, the Auburn Automobile Company, A. Felix DuPont Jr. and others who appreciated a higher performance aircraft. Serial numbers eligible: M3003 and up.

SM-6000-A Airliner 11PCLM ATC 367 approved September 19, 1930. Powered by 3 Lycoming R-680 215-hp engines. All SM-6000s were returned to the factory to receive many structural, mechanical and interior updates and the resulting remanufactured aircraft were designated as SM-6000-A. The SM-6000-A, B, B1 and B2 were referred to as the Model T.

SM-8A Junior 4PCHWM ATC 2-301 approved November 15, 1930. Powered by a Lycoming R-680 215-hp engine. One aircraft manufactured, s/n 4201, with an increased gross weight to 3,195 pounds. Except for gross weight, this aircraft was identical to ATC 295.

SM-7AS Junior 4PCHWM ATC 2-313 approved December 26, 1930. Powered by a Wright J-6 300-hp engine. One aircraft manufactured, and fitted with Edo Q floats, s/n 3100.

SM-9 5PCMAM powered by a Wright J-5C 215-hp engine. Built in 1930 as a high-wing amphibian experimental aircraft, project abandoned, no ATC approval.

1931

SM-6000-B, also known as the Model T, ATC 420 approved April 23, 1931. Powered by three Lycoming R-680 215-hp engines. The B model was available with various seating arrangements from 6 to 10 passengers. The B was also available as an all-cargo carrier. As an executive aircraft, the B could be ordered with club interiors with seating for 6 to 8 passengers.

SM-6000-B1 ATC 420 approved April 23, 1931. Powered by 3 215-hp Lycoming R-680 engines. This model was the all-passenger vehicle version seating 10 passengers, allowing just 25 pounds of luggage per passenger.

SM-6000-B2 ATC 420 11PCLM approved April 23, 1931 Powered by three 215-hp Lycoming R-680 engines. This model was the mail passenger version with provisions for 8 to 9 passengers and up to 350 pounds of mail and baggage. The Model B was purchased by Century Pacifica Line, Pennsylvania, Airlines, America Airways, Trans-American, Chicago, and Southern, Eastern Air Transport, and Delta Airlines.

At least 48 Model B aircraft were manufactured. CAA note passenger type designation 11PCLM. Fuel 160 gallons maximum, installation consisting of two 60-gallon tanks and two 20-gallon tanks. Any combination was eligible. The number of passengers 10, maximum allowable baggage 227 pounds, and serial numbers 5016 and up were eligible.

Model S Junior ATC 423 4PCHWM approved May 12, 1931. Powered by a 215-hp Lycoming R-680 engine. The Model S was the improved and updated version of the 1930 SM-8. Priced at $4,995, this aircraft was a terrific value compared to other aircraft on the market. Data for the SR-8D is as follows: A wingspan of 42'1", length 28'11", height 8'9", wing chord 75 inches, and a wing area of 235 sq. ft. The S used a Clark Y airfoil. It had an empty weight of 2,172 pounds, useful load 1,085 pounds, and a payload with 50 gallons of fuel at 585 pounds. The new design speed ring cowing offered a cruising speed of 105 mph, landing speed of 48 mph, and a ceiling of 13,500 feet. At cruising speed, fuel consumption was 12.0 gallons per hour, giving a 440-mile range. A metal propeller, electric engine starter and navigation lights were standard equipment. Extra equipment included wheel pants, parachute flares, and a speed ring engine cowling. A sampling of registration numbers include NC8463, NC10886, NC11165 and NC12141, with serial numbers 8000 and up.

Model W ATC 435 4PCHWM approved July 14, 1931. Powered by a 300-hp P&W Wasp Jr. engine. The W was a limited production aircraft for the customer that wanted more performance. The fuselage was longer and a little taller with some weight gain. The aircraft was delivered with deluxe interior and deluxe equipment as standard. This was the last redesign of the Junior aircraft. Serial numbers 3080 and up were eligible. The following placard had to be displayed in full view of the pilot: "Always check fuel flow at strainer drain before takeoff. Never fly on one tank when fuel is low." A representative sampling of registration numbers assigned to the Model W were NC12144, NC12146 and NC12177.

SB-1 Detroiter ATC 2-330 approved March 4, 1931 for serial numbers 1, 3 and 90, converted to a 3-place aircraft powered by a 200-hp Wright J-4 engine. At a customer's request, Stinson applied for ATC 2-330.

1932

SM-2K 3PCLM ATC 2-414 approved June 11, 1932. Powered by Kinner B5 125-hp engine. A special order aircraft with a gross weight of 2,520 pounds.

Model R ATC 457 4PCLM approved January 25, 1932. Powered by a 9-cylinder Lycoming R-680 engine of 215-hp. The R was a totally new design from the futuristic nearly half-circle wingtip to the presentation of the landing gear, giving a totally new look. The wing ribs were spaced closer together, using 21 compared to the Model S using 19. The aileron was lengthened to nearly 3/4 of the wing and the only carryover from earlier aircraft was a use of the Clark Y airfoil. The landing gear was mounted on a very short highly-tapered steel tube structure that was covered with aircraft grade aluminum. The landing gear attach point and the wing strut attach point were at the outer end of what could be described as a stub wing. The forward fuselage was enlarged to fit smoothly behind the fully cowled engine. The cabin interior was fitted with the most luxurious presentation of any Stinson up to this time. A representative sampling of registration numbers assigned to the Model R was NC437M, NC479M and NC12147, NC12197. Serial numbers: 8501 and up.

Model U ATC 484 12PLCM approved May 12, 1932 Powered by three 9-cylinder Lycoming R-680-BA engines of 240-hp each. The Model U airliner was designed to replace the SM-6000. The Stinson engineering staff reengineered the Model U with many aerodynamic, mechanical and structural improvements. The most recognizable change was a short wing where the outboard motors, the landing gear, and the wing struts were attached. The short wing was designed to hold baggage and cargo in a position near the center of gravity. The new aircraft offered a slightly better cruising speed and a modest payload improvement over the SM-6000. The U was designed for 10 passengers and a crew of two. A fully loaded aircraft could maintain 7,000 feet with any two engines. The U carried 140 gallons of fuel and at a cruising speed of 123 mph, consumed 40 gallons an hour. Serial numbers 9001 and up were eligible. Serial numbers 9001 to 9006 maximum allowable baggage was 355 pounds in the lower stub wing, total allowable baggage 505 pounds. Serial numbers 9007 and up were eligible with forward sloping windshield. Serial numbers 9015 and up were eligible for standard weight of 9,400 pounds when remodeled at the factory. Serial number 9015 and up were eligible as an executive model with six passengers and crew of three. The maximum fuel could be increased to 200 gallons. It has been noted that this model was unstable longitudinally when loaded from the rear. Operators were advised to load passengers and cargo from the front to the rear.

Model U1 ATC 2-413 12PLCM approved July 8, 1932. Powered by three 9-cylinder Lycoming R-680-BA engines of 240-hp each. This was for one aircraft only: the prototype SM-6000 s/n 9000. ATC 484 was granted in May and by July this aircraft was brought up to 484 standards and sold as an approved aircraft.

Model R-2 ATC 489 4PCLM approved July 27, 1932. Powered by a 9-cylinder Lycoming R-680-AB engine of 240-hp. This aircraft was specifically designed for the air taxi or small airliner operation. The Standard Oil Company of Indiana purchased an R-2 and used it for the fast movement of equipment or personnel.

Model R-3 ATC 493 4PCLM approved September 1, 1932. Powered by a 9-cylinder Lycoming R-680-AB engine of 240-hp. When the design for the Model R was laid down in 1931, provisions were made in the design for a retractable landing gear version. The landing gear retracted inward from the tips of the short stub wing. It was a mechanical system operated by the pilot using a winding crank. Using a drum and cable arrangement, the pilot could determine whether the gear was retracted when he ran out slack in the cable. The gear could be locked in the up position. Gear retraction was very slow, depending upon the pilot's speed winding the landing gear crank. Gravity helped lower the gear, and there was a type of lock down device. A small amount of the gear could be seen from the pilot's window, and when this appeared, the pilot was reasonably sure the gear was in the down position. The R was designed as a small airliner and came equipped with night and foul weather equipment. With a listed cruising speed of 118 mph, the R-3 was only 6 mph faster than the 112 mph of the R-2.

Model M 4PCLM experimental all metal low-wing powered by a 240-hp Lycoming R-680-BA engine. No ATC approval, 1 built as a design and construction study. The Model M, NR12123 (s/n 32000) was used by Stinson as a test mule, and for establishing speed/distance records between Detroit and other cities. Repowered with a 220-hp Wright J-5. Sold to a private party in early 1934 and displayed at several air events. Later bought by investment broker and commodity trader William D. Gann to replace his 1933 Stinson SR (the first one off assembly line), used as a flying office while making crop surveys. Repowered again with a more powerful Wright Whirlwind engine and entered in the 1934 Cleveland National Air Races, but not allowed to compete due to lack of ATC. Sold and exported from Florida with registration canceled on September 13, 1937.

1933

Model U trimotor ATC 484, 10 passengers 1 pilot. 1933 production, 5 built, powered by three 240-hp R-680-AB Lycoming engines and priced at $32,900 FAF.

Model U-1 ATC 2-437 12PLCM approved February 7, 1933 powered by three Wright R-760-

E-1 engines of 285-hp each. This was for one aircraft only—a special order with Wright engines, NC12129, s/n 9014, Eastern Air Transport.

SR Reliant 4PCHWM ACT 510 approved June 29, 1933. Standard engine was the 215-hp Lycoming R-680. This was a totally new aircraft. The SR was a large aircraft with a wingspan of 43'3", length 27 ft, height 8'5", chord 75 inches, and a wing area of 235 sq. ft. The SR used a Clark Y airfoil. It had an empty weight of 2,070 pounds, useful load 1,085 pounds, and a payload with 50 gallons of fuel (575 pounds). The new design offered a cruising speed of 115 mph, landing speed 55 mph and a ceiling of 14,000 ft. At cruising speed, fuel consumption was 12.5 gallons per hour, giving a 460-mile range. The landing gear was totally redesigned, with this type of landing gear fitted to all Stinson Reliant aircraft throughout their production run. The gear consisted of one-piece cantilever legs that were attached to short extensions on either side of the fuselage to provide landing gear attachments. Each landing gear leg hinged on the short fuselage extension and attached to a shock adsorbing strut completely enclosed in the fuselage. Each gear operated independently and was designed to absorb landing loads and give the passengers a comfortable ride over uneven terrain. To provide the pilot with light control pressures, ball bearings were used throughout the control system. The first production aircraft was given NC12191, s/n 8700. Optional equipment available to Stinson SR aircraft: two 37-gallon fuel tanks with the maximum capacity of 74 gallons, larger engine ring cowl, radio bonding and shielding and wing, stabilizer fairings, Lear radio, five one-minute flares. leather trim, Ryan retractable landing lights, and wheel streamlines. A representative sampling of registration numbers assigned to the Model SR was NC12191, NC13800, NC13818, and NC13474. Serial number 8700 and up.

SR-2 Reliant Special 4PCHWM ACT 510 approved June 29, 1933, powered by a 240-hp Lycoming R-680-2 engine. 1 built. Except for a gross weight increase to accommodate the heavier engine, it was identical to the SR.

SR-1 Reliant Special 4PCHWM ACT 513 approved August 5, 1933, powered by a 240-hp Lycoming R-680-2 engine. 2 built. A new gross weight increased to 3323 pounds was offered to customers who preferred a Wright-powered aircraft. The two aircraft were given NC13485, s/n 8900, and NC13499, s/n 8901.

SR-3 Reliant Special 4PCHWM ACT 513 approved August 5, 1933, equipped with a 240-hp Lycoming R-680-2 engine. The horizontal tail services were redesigned with a gross weight of 3323 pounds. 2 built. The two aircraft were given s/n 8921 and s/n 8922.

SR-4 Reliant Special 4PCHWM ACT 519 approved October 23, 1933, powered by a 250-hp Wright R-760 engine offered to customers who preferred a Wright- powered aircraft. 2 built.

SM-8A Junior 4PCHWM ATC 2-461 approved November 8, 1933. One aircraft only, a special order with a 220-hp Wright J5 engine.

Model O 2POLM ATC 520 approved November 9, 1933. Powered by a 220-hp 9-cylinder Lycoming R-680-4 engine. The Model O was a parasol wing tandem two-seat aircraft and was designed primarily for the military and export market. Practical SR parts, including the landing gear and tail services were used on the Model O. With a wingspan of 39'11", wing area 215 sq ft, length 27'8", and empty weight of 1945 pounds, this aircraft was smaller than the SR. The prototype aircraft was assigned X13817, s/n 10000.

Starting in 1933, Lycoming standardized their engine numbering system. R-680-1 was assigned to experimental engines. The following is included to give the reader a better perspective of the Lycoming power plants used in Stinson aircraft.

R-680 215-hp 2,000 rpm, 5.3 compression ratio minimum octane 58

R-680-2 240-hp 2,000 rpm, 6.5 compression ratio minimum octane 80

R-680-3 200-hp 2,000 rpm, 5.2 compression ratio minimum octane 58

R-680-4 225-hp 2,100 rpm, 5.5 compression ratio minimum octane 58

R-680-5, -6, -7 to be fitted with Lycoming-Smith variable-pitch propeller

R-680-5 260-hp 2,300 rpm, 6.5 compression ratio minimum octane 80

R-680-6 254-hp 2,300 rpm, 5.5 compression ratio minimum octane 58

R-680-7 240h-p 2,300 rpm, 5.3 compression ratio minimum octane 58

1934

SR-5 Reliant Special 4PCHWM ACT 2-471 approved February 28, 1934. One aircraft only, a special order with a 240-hp Lycoming R-680-BA engine. Manufactured without trailing edge and landing flaps.

SR-5 Reliant 4PCHWM ATC 530 approved April 5, 1934. Standard equipment was a 225-hp Lycoming R-680-4 engine. Advertised as an economy model. Manufactured without trailing edge and landing flaps.

SR-5B Reliant 4PCHWM ACT 530 approved

April 5, 1934. One aircraft only, a special order with a 240-hp Lycoming R-680-5 engine and equipped with landing flaps.

SR-5C Reliant 4PCHWM ATC 530 approved April 5, 1934, using a 260-hp Lycoming R-680-5 engine. A limited production deluxe model equipped with landing flaps.

SR-5D Reliant 4PCHWM ATC 531 approved April 5, 1934. One aircraft only, a special order with a 215-hp Lycoming R-680 Engine. This aircraft was not equipped with landing flaps.

SR-5A Reliant 4PCHWM ATC 536 approved May 5, 1934, powered by a 245-hp R-680-6 engine. Standard equipment included the Lycoming-Smith variable-pitch propeller and landing flaps. This was a deluxe aircraft and options included radio, night flying equipment, and navigational aids. All SR-5 aircraft were fitted with a redesigned wing with a shorter span and a wider wing chord, reducing the aspect ratio. Except as noted, all SR-5 aircraft were equipped with trailing edge flaps. The landing flaps were activated by a mechanically tuned torque tube and could be lowered to any desired setting from a control marked "Selective-Guide" in the cabin. Starting with the SR-6, all Stinson landing flaps were vacuum operated. The fuselage was completely redesigned, starting with a NACA engine cowling and a new windshield. The Lycoming engine was attached to engine mounts with improved rubber-mounted fittings. Ground handling was improved with the use of hydraulic disc brakes. Passenger comfort was improved with new cabin insulation, cabin heater, and ventilation system. Two 37.5-gallon wing tanks were standard and an optional 50-gallon tank was available. The wing span of the SR-5A was 41 feet, wing chord 80 inches, using a Clark Y airfoil with a total wing area 230 sq. ft. With a gross weight of 3,475 pounds, a cruising speed of 120 mph, landing speed no flaps 58 mph, and landing speed with flaps 50 mph, the SR-5A offered to the flying public a remarkable aircraft. A representative sampling of registration numbers assigned to the Model SR-5A was NC13848, NC14172, NC14574, NC14585, and NC14595. Serial numbers 9207-A and up.

SR-5E Reliant 4PCHWM ATC 537 approved May 5, 1934 using a 225-hp Lycoming R-680-4 engine. The SR-5E was structurally identical to the SR-5A and was offered with minimal optional equipment. The customer was allowed to custom order their aircraft. With a base price of $5,775, most customers ordered optional equipment that pushed the price to near $9,000.

SR-3-S 4PCHWM ATC 539 approved May 17, 1934, powered by a 240-hp Lycoming R-680-5 engine. This was the approval to fit SR-3 with the Lycoming Smith, controllable propeller. No production.

SR-5F Reliant 4PCHWM ATC 550 approved August 10, 1934, a custom built SR-5E fitted with a 285-hp Wright R-760-E Cyclone engine.

Model A 10PCLM ATC 556 approved September 25, 1934. Powered by three 9-cylinder Lycoming R-680-5 engines of 260-hp each. In March of 1933, Robert W. Ayer examined Stinson's line of tri-motor transports and concluded there was an opportunity for something new to present to the airlines. For several months before leaving the Grangeville Brothers Aircraft's company and joining Stinson, he was developing a method of tapering the inboard section of a multiengine aircraft. By utilizing a thinner center section, it would free up space inside the fuselage. A heavy structural wing center section located on the bottom of the fuselage created a greater frontal area and a corresponding reduction in cruising speed. Ayer presented his unique design to the engineering department proposing a low-wing Lycoming powered trimotor utilizing retractable landing gear with provisions for two pilots and eight paying passengers and one stewardess. His plan was enthusiastically accepted by the engineering staff and immediately presented to management. E. L. Cord personally examined the proposal. He approved the design and assured Stinson management of adequate financial resources to place the new aircraft in production as soon as possible.

The transport division engineering staff was increased dramatically. A mockup of the wing-to-fuselage design was completed by May and the design was approved by management. Built from production tooling, the first flight of the Model A was April 27, 1934. A representative sampling of registration numbers assigned to the Model A was NC15153, NC15156, NC15159, and NC15165. Serial numbers 9100 and up.

SR-5A Reliant Special 4PCHWM ATC 2-491 approved October 4, 1934 and fitted with a 245-hp Lycoming R-680-6 engine.

SR-5D Reliant 4PCHWM ATC 2-493 approved October 4, 1934 powered by a 215-hp Lycoming R-680 engine. A special order aircraft with redesigned small tail controls.

SR-5 Reliant Special 4PCHWM ATC 2-494 approved October 4, 1934, powered by a 225-hp Lycoming R-680-4 engine. Three special order aircraft, each with a gross weight of 3,475 pounds. NC13837, s/n 9202, s/n 9205, and NC13843 s/n 9210 were manufactured with small tail surfaces.

SR-5 Reliant Special 4PCHWM ATC 2-492 approved November 4, 1934. This aircraft, s/n

9211, was identical to the SR-5 except it was fitted with wing flaps and redesigned with small tail surfaces.

SR-1 Reliant Special 4PCHWM ATC 2-496 approved December 31, 1934 with a 225-hp Lycoming R-680-B4 engine. Built for Lucius B. Manning, president of Stinson. Only s/n 8900 eligible. This aircraft was equipped with a Lear T-30 radio transmitter and a Lycoming-Smith controllable metal propeller.

SR-5X 1934 245-hp Lycoming R-680 engine experimental aircraft, project abandoned, no ATC approval. It may have been the SR-6 prototype.

1935

SR Reliant Special 4PCHWM ATC 2-499 approved March 6, 1935, powered by a 215-hp Lycoming R-680 engine. A special order aircraft, NC13802, s/n 8756.

SR-5A Reliant Special 4PCHWM ATC 2-511 approved July 25, 1935, powered by a 245-hp Lycoming R-680-6 engine. One aircraft, s/n 9349 at 3,550 pounds gross weight.

SR-6 Reliant 4-5PCHWM ACT 580 approved July 23, 1935. Standard equipment was a 245-hp Lycoming R-680-6 engine. The SR-6 retained many of the innovations of the SR-5 but was considerably refined. The interior of the cabin was enlarged, offering more passenger comfort, the fuselage was given a more rounded appearance and the wing tip design was improved to give better control at low speeds. With 75 gallons of fuel on board, a cruising speed of 128 mph and with a fuel consumption of 13.5 gallons per hour gave the SR-6 a 695-mile range. The SR-6 was equipped with a Lycoming–Smith controllable propeller. It used a modified Clark Y airfoil with a wing chord of 80 inches, a wing span of 43'3", empty weight listed as 2,315 pounds, a gross weight of 3,550 pounds, and a landing speed listed as 52 mph. The landing flaps were vacuum operated and could be lowered to any desired setting from a control marked "Selective-Guide" in the cabin.

CAA approved the following extra equipment: wheel streamliners, flares, fog light, landing lights, provisions for a camera hole in the cabin floor, fire extinguisher, parachute pilot seat, releasable cabin door, and 100 gallons of fuel carried in 50-gallon tanks in each wing. The aircraft could also be ordered with a metal lining in the baggage compartment and a spring rear seat. No baggage was allowed under the rear seat. The following placard had to be displayed in full view of the pilot: "Always check fuel flow at strainer drain before takeoff. Never fly on one tank when fuel is low." A representative sampling of registration numbers assigned to the Model SR-6 was NC15111, NC15121, NC15145, and NC15170 and serial numbers 9601 and up.

SR-6A Reliant 4PCHWM ATC 580 approved July 23, 1935, powered by a 225-hp Lycoming R-680-4 engine. Fitted with the 225-hp power plant, it was approved as a four-place aircraft. This model was equipped with a fixed-pitch metal propeller.

SR-6B Reliant 4-5PCHWM ATC 580 approved July 23, 1935, powered by a 260-hp Lycoming R-680-5 engine. This aircraft offered a cruising speed of 130 mph, a ceiling of 15,200 ft, and using 14 gallons of fuel per hour, offered a maximum range of 660 miles. A Lycoming–Smith controllable propeller was offered as standard equipment.

SR-6C Reliant 4-5PCHWM ATC 580 approved July 23, 1935 fitted with a 240-hp Lycoming R-680-2 engine. One aircraft built, perhaps a special order.

SR-6X experimental gull-wing, no ATC approval, 1 built.

1936

SR-7 Reliant gull-wing 4PCLM ATC 594 approved February 13, 1936 powered by a 225-hp Lycoming R-680-4 engine. This model was equipped with a fixed-pitch metal propeller and was approved as a four place aircraft. The SR-7 cannot be fitted with floats.

SR-7A Five built with the 225-hp Lycoming.

SR-7B Reliant gull-wing 5PCLM ATC 594 approved February 13, 1936 equipped with a 245-hp Lycoming R-680-6 engine. Following the tradition of manufacturing elegant aircraft, this was the most beautiful Stinson to enter production. Based on the tri-motor Model A design, Stinson's engineers adapted the wing to the SR-6 fuselage. With the maximum thickness at the strut attach point, there was a graceful taper inward to the fuselage and outward to the wing tip. Utilizing a single-wing strut, the double taper wing gave the SR-7 the appearance of a totally new aircraft. The landing flaps were vacuum operated and could be lowered to any desired setting. With 70 gallons of fuel on board, using 14.5 gallons per hour with a cruising speed of 138 mph, the aircraft offered a maximum range of 645 miles. Using a modified Clark Y airfoil, the wing had a maximum chord length of 96 inches at the strut attach point and 38 inches at the tip. The SR-7B displayed a wingspan of 41'7", overall length 27 ft, and an overall height of 8'6". The SR-7B was approved to carry five passengers and was equipped with the Lycoming-Smith controllable propeller. Serial number 9650 and up eligible. The SR-7B was eligible for export to all countries except Australia. A representative sampling of registration numbers assigned to the Model SR-7B was NC16100, NC16107, NC16123 and NC16135.

SR-7C Reliant gull-wing 5PCLM ATC 594 approved February 13, 1936, powered by a 260-hp Lycoming R-680-5 engine. With a cruising speed of 140 mph burning 15 gallon per hour, it offered the pilot a maximum range of 640 miles. Empty weight was listed as 2,335 pounds and a gross weight of 3,600 pounds. It was equipped with the Lycoming-Smith controllable propeller.

SR-8A Reliant gull-wing 4PCLM ATC 608 approved May 28, 1936, powered by a 225-hp Lycoming R-680-4 engine. The Model SR-8A was equipped with a fixed-pitch metal propeller and was approved as a four-place aircraft. The SR-8A cannot be fitted with floats.

SR-8B Reliant gull-wing 5PCLM ATC 608 approved May 28, 1936, powered by a 245-hp Lycoming R-680-B6 engine. The SR-8B fuselage was widened with inside measurements of the rear seat 52 inches. The new wing was not a true gull, but had that appearance. As the SR-7 and the SR-8 gained wide acceptance, they became known as the Gull-wing Stinsons. The small cross-section of the wing at the fuselage attach point gave the pilot substantially improved visibility. The SR-8 was offered as a deluxe aircraft with leather covered seats offered as standard equipment. Data for the SR-8B is as follows: wingspan 41'7", the maximum wing chord at the strut attach point 96 inches, and used modified Clark Y airfoil. It had an empty weight of 2,262 pounds and a gross weight of 3,375 pounds with four passengers. This aircraft was approved for 100 pounds of baggage. A cruising speed of 136 mph while carrying 50 gallons of fuel and burning 14 gallons per hour, gave the aircraft a 475 mile range. To offer a 52 inch wide cabin, the fuselage was totally redesigned displaying a wider entrance door. This was the first application of the new and improved Lycoming R-680-B6 power plant. Fitted with a new engine and a redesigned fuselage, from a marketing standpoint, Stinson offered the SR-8B as a new model. Serial numbers 9702 and up manufactured prior to September 30, 1939 were eligible. This aircraft was equipped with a Lycoming-Smith propeller with Curtis blades. The SR-8BM was offered as a multipurpose type designated by the letter M. This type could have an auxiliary door aft of the main door on the right side, large doorframe for the main and auxiliary doors, removable back on copilot's chair, stretcher door in the back wall, ski type fuselage, provisions for ambulance litter, and installation of metal lined cabin. A representative sampling of registration numbers assigned to the Model SR-8B was NC16138, NC16186, NC17105, NC17119, and serial numbers 9702 and up.

SR-8C Reliant gull-wing 5PCLM ATC 608 approved May 28, 1936 powered by a 260-hp Lycoming R-680-B5 engine. The interior cabin width was increased to 52 inches. The SR-8C was approved for maximum fuel of 70 gallons and with increased horsepower using 75% power, could cruise that 140 mph. This aircraft was approved as a seaplane mounted on Edo 39–4000 twin floats. Lycoming incorporated many improvements into the R-680-B5 engine, and when fitted with a controllable propeller, gave the SR-8C spectacular performance.

SR-8D Reliant gull-wing 5PCLM ATC 609 approved June 3, 1936, powered by a 285-hp Wright R-760-E2 engine. Data for the SR-8D is as follows: utilizing the same dimensions as the C model, the fuselage was strengthened to support the heavier engine. The Model D was approved for an empty weight of 2,395 pounds, gross weight of 3,800 pounds, and a cruising speed with 75% power of 140 mph. This aircraft was approved for a surface ceiling of 14,000 feet and could be fitted with Edo 39-4000 twin floats.

SR-8E Reliant gull-wing 5PCLM ATC 609 approved June 3, 1936, powered by a 320-hp Wright R-760-E2 engine. Data for the SR-8E is as follows. The exterior dimensions and interior construction on all gull-wings were identical. The Model E used the same structural integrity as the Model D. Landing speed with flaps was 58 mph, cruising speed with 75% power 148 mph, and a ceiling of 15,000 feet. The empty weight was listed as 2,502 pounds and a gross weight of 3,800 pounds.

Model B, a twin-engine executive based on Model A, mock-up only.

Model PT experimental low wing with retractable landing gear designed as a military trainer, project abandoned.

1937

SR-9A not assigned to an aircraft

SR-9B Reliant gull-wing 5PCLM ATC 621 approved December 30-1936, powered by a 245-hp R-680-B6 Lycoming engine. Stinson engineers totally redesigned the SR-8B fuselage from the back of the passenger compartment forward. This was the first use by Stinson of a molded windshield, which was curved to fit the expanded forward fuselage. For center of gravity consideration, the engine was moved slightly forward, and the Model 9 was fitted with a deeper engine cowl. The cabin walls were increased in thickness to allow for greater insulation and provided a much quieter interior. The interior was totally redesigned using a wider door. The curved windshield gave the pilot better visibility. The redesign of the forward fuselage gave the SR-9B the appearance of a totally new aircraft. Data for the SR-9B is as follows: empty weight was listed as 2,457 pounds and gross weight as 3,700 pounds. With a cruising speed of 136 mph, carrying 70 gallons of fuel and burning 15 gallons per hour, the aircraft had a 610-mile range. The aircraft had a wingspan of 41'11", and the maximum wing chord at the strut attach point was 96 inches. The aircraft used modified Clark Y airfoil. The wing span grew slightly longer because of increased fuselage dimensions. The SR-9B was equipped with the Lycoming-Smith controllable propeller fitted with Curtis blades. Serial numbers 5100 and up were eligible manufactured prior to October 25, 1940. A representative sampling of registration numbers assigned to the Model SR-9B was NC17110, NC18401, NC18438 and NC18452.

SR-9C Reliant gull-wing 5PCLM ATC 621 approved December 30, 1936 powered by a 260-hp R-680-B5 Lycoming engine. The 9C was the most popular model in 1937, with a production run of 65 aircraft. Stinson engineers totally redesigned the SR-9B and SR-9C fuselage from the back of the passenger compartment forward. This was the first use by Stinson of a molded windshield, which was curved to fit the expanded forward fuselage. For center of gravity considerations, the engine was moved slightly forward, and the Model 9 was fitted with a deeper engine cowl. The cabin walls were increased in thickness to allow for greater insulation and provided a much quieter interior. The interior was totally redesigned using a wider door, and the curved windshield gave the pilot better visibility. The redesign of the forward fuselage gave the SR-9C the appearance of a totally new aircraft. Data for the SR-9C is as follows: empty weight was listed as 2,515 pounds and the gross weight was 3,750 pounds. With a cruising speed of 140 mph while carrying 70 gallons of fuel and burning 14 gallons per hour, the aircraft had a 690 mile range. The aircraft was built with a wingspan of 41'11", the maximum, and the wing chord at the strut attach point was 96 inches using modified Clark Y airfoil. The wing span grew slightly longer because of increased fuselage dimensions. The exterior dimensions and interior construction on gull-wings were identical in all gull-wing aircraft. The SR-9B was equipped with the Lycoming-Smith controllable propeller. When made with a ski-type fuselage, the letter "S" was added to serial number.

Baggage in the compartment behind the cabin must be limited to a maximum of 50 pounds when three passengers occupy the rear seat. A representative sampling of registration numbers assigned to the Model SR-9C was NC17150, NC17159, NC17180, and NC18453.

SR-9D Reliant gull-wing 5PCLM ATC 625 approved February 2, 1937 powered by a 285-hp Wright R-760-E2 engine. Responding to customer requests starting in 1936, Stinson offered aircraft powered by Wright engines. Because of increased horsepower, these aircraft offered spectacular performance and had a higher retail price point. Data for the SR-9D is as follows: empty weight was listed as 2,260 pounds and a gross weight of 4,050 pounds. With a cruising speed of 152 mph while carrying 78 gallons of fuel and burning 17 gallons per hour, the aircraft had a 630 mile range. The aircraft was built with a wingspan of 41'11", the maximum, and the wing chord at the strut attach point was 96 inches using modified Clark Y airfoil. The wing span grew slightly longer because of increased fuselage dimensions. Overall length was listed as 28'1" and the height was 8'6". The exterior dimensions and interior construction on gull-wings was identical in all gull-wing aircraft. The SR-9D was equipped with either the Lycoming-Smith or Hamilton-Standard controllable propeller. Serial numbers 5200 and up were eligible manufactured prior to October 25, 1940. Balanced maximum 40 pounds required amount is noted in the actual weight and balance report and should be marked on installation with the notation "Do not remove." The SR-9DM was offered as a multipurpose type designated by the letter M. This type may have an auxiliary door aft of the main door on the right side, large doorframe for the main and auxiliary doors, removable back on copilot's chair, stretcher door in the back wall, ski-type fuselage, provisions for ambulance litter, and installation of metal-lined cabin. A representative sampling of registration numbers assigned to the Model SR-9D was NC17130, NC17132, NC17186, and NC17420.

SR-9E Reliant gull-wing 5PCLM ATC 625 approved February 2, 1937 powered by a 320-hp Wright R-760-E2 engine. Interior design and exterior appearance was identical in all Model 9 aircraft. Responding to customer requests starting in 1936, Stinson offered aircraft powered by Wright engines. Because of increased horsepower, these aircraft offered spectacular performance and had a higher retail price point. Data for the SR-9D is as follows: empty weight was listed as 2,640 pounds with a gross weight of 4,050 pounds. With a cruising speed of 152 mph while carrying 78 gallons of fuel and burning 19 gallons, the aircraft had a 600 mile range. The SR-9E was equipped with either the Lycoming-Smith or Hamilton-Standard controllable propeller.

SR-9F Reliant gull-wing 5PCLM ATC 640 approved May 26, 1937 powered by a 400-hp P&W Wasp Jr. SB engine. The exterior dimensions and interior construction on all gull-wings were identical. Responding to customer requests, Stinson offered aircraft powered by Pratt & Whitney Wasp Jr. engines. Because of increased horsepower, these aircraft offered spectacular performance and had a higher retail price point. Data for the SR-9F is as follows: empty weight was listed as 2,990 pounds with a gross weight of 4,500 pounds. With a cruising speed of 165 mph while carrying 102 gallons of fuel and burning 24 gallons per hour, the aircraft had a 500 mile range. The SR-9F was equipped with the Hamilton-Standard controllable propeller. The Model F could be ordered with the maximum fuel capacity of 102 gallons. Serial numbers 5700 and up were eligible manufactured prior to October 25, 1940. The SR-9F could be ordered from the manufacturer with a special, long cabin that provided a compartment aft of the baggage compartment with a 200 pound maximum capacity. The Model F differed structurally from other models of the SR-9 series. The SR-9FM was offered as a multipurpose-type designated by the letter M. A representative sampling of registration numbers assigned to the Model SR-9F was NC17191, NC18414, NC18450, and SR-9FM NC18451.

1938

The SR-10 line of aircraft was produced from 1938 to 1941 virtually unchanged. The 1938 SR-10 line of aircraft was designated the 5800 series, and the 1939 through 1941 SR-10 production was designated the 5900 series.

SR-10A was not assigned to an aircraft

SR-10B gull-wing Reliant 5PCLM ATC 678 approved April 29, 1938 powered by a 245-hp R-680-6 Lycoming Engine. Interior design and exterior appearance was identical in all Model 10 aircraft. The Model B did not gain wide acceptance with only two manufactured in four years. Serial numbers 5801 and up were eligible manufactured prior to February 28, 1941.

SR-10C gull-wing Reliant 5PCLM ATC 678 approved April 29, 1938, powered by a 260-hp R-680-D5 Lycoming engine. The 10C was the most popular model with a four-year production run of 53 aircraft. Stinson engineers totally redesigned the SR-10B, SR-10C, SR-10G, and SR-10J fuselage from the back of the passenger compartment forward. The landing flaps were vacuum-operated and could be lowered to any desired setting. The SR-10C used five flat panels, which fit the expanded forward fuselage. For center of gravity consideration, the engine was moved slightly forward, and the Model 10 was fitted with a deeper, smooth engine cowling. The cabin walls were increased in thickness to allow for greater insulation and provided a much quieter interior. The interior was totally redesigned using flush-fitted doors, and the new windshield gave the pilot better visibility. The redesign of the forward fuselage gave the SR-10C the appearance of a totally new aircraft. Data for the SR-10C is as follows: empty weight was listed as 2,530 pounds with a gross weight of 3,875 pounds. With a cruising speed of 147 mph while carrying 76 gallons of fuel and burning 16 gallons per hour, the aircraft had a 660-mile range. The aircraft was built with a wingspan of 41'11", the maximum, and the wing chord at the strut attach was point 96 inches using modified Clark Y airfoil. The wing span grew slightly longer because of increased fuselage dimensions. The exterior dimensions and interior construction on gull-wings were identical in all gull-wing aircraft. The SR-10C was equipped with the Lycoming - Smith controllable propeller fitted with Curtis Blades. Standard equipment included an electric engine starter, battery, generator, fuel gauges, carburetor heater, compass, clock, dual controls, navigation lights, hydraulic wheel brakes, parking brake, cabin heater, cabin vents, vacuum-operated wing flaps, bonding and shielding, a full-swivel tail wheel, map pockets, ashtrays, nickel hardware, and a first-aid kit. Optional equipment available for the SR-10C included the Hamilton-Standard controllable propeller, wheel pants, landing lights, paraflares, pressure-type fire extinguisher, extra fuel tanks, radial gear, Edo pontoons, custom interiors, custom colors, and a trailing antenna. Corrosion proofing for both saltwater and freshwater was also available as options. Serial numbers 5801 and up were eligible manufactured prior to February 28, 1941. A representative sampling of registration numbers assigned to the Model SR-10C was NC18487, NC21103, NC21132 and NC22583. All-American AAS-3 mail pickup and delivery equipment (All-American Aviation Inc.) was installed on the SR-10C. The equipment included a pickup unit, hydraulic reeling system, pickup rope and hook, reinforced floor, reverse cabin structure, and removal of rear seat.

SR-10G gull-wing Reliant 5PCLM ATC 678

approved April 29, 1938, powered by a 290-hp R-680-E1 Lycoming engine. Interior design and exterior appearance were identical in all Model 10 aircraft. Data for the SR-10G is as follows: empty weight was listed as 2605 pounds with a gross weight of 3900 pounds. With a cruising speed of 150mph while carrying 76-gallon of fuel and burning 18 gallons per hour, the aircraft had a 600-mile range. The SR-10G was equipped with the Lycoming-Smith controllable propeller. The Hamilton-Standard controllable propeller was offered as optional equipment. Model SR-10G serial numbers 5943 and up were eligible at 4,000 pounds when equipped with six-ply tires.

SR-10G3 gull-wing Reliant 5PCLM ATC 678, the same as the SR-10G, but with a more deluxe interior and minor structural changes.

SR-10J gull-wing Reliant 5PCLM ATC 678 approved April 29, 1938, powered by a 300-hp R-680-E3 Lycoming engine. Interior design and exterior appearance were identical in all Model 10 aircraft. Data for the SR-10J is as follows: empty weight was listed as 2,610 pounds with a gross weight of 4,000 pounds. With a cruising speed of 152 mph while carrying 100 gallons of fuel and burning 18 gallons per hour, the aircraft had an 800-mile range. The SR-10J was equipped with the Lycoming-Smith controllable propeller. The Hamilton-Standard controllable propeller was offered as optional equipment. All-American AAS-3 mail pickup and delivery equipment (All-American Aviation, Inc.) was installed on the SR-10J. The equipment included a pickup unit, a hydraulic reeling system, pickup rope and hook, a reinforced floor, reverse cabin structure, and removal of rear seat.

SR-10J3 gull-wing Reliant 5PCLM ATC 678, the same as the SR-10J, but with a more deluxe interior and minor structural changes.

SR-10D gull-wing Reliant 5PCLM ATC 679 approved May 12, 1938, powered by a 300-hp Wright R-760-E1 engine. They were built for export only. Three were manufactured and shipped to Brazil.

SR-10E gull-wing Reliant 5PCLM ATC 679 approved May 12, 1938, powered by a 350-hp Wright R-760-E2 engine. Interior design and exterior appearance were identical in all Model 10 aircraft. Data for the SR-10E is as follows: empty weight was listed as 2,730 pounds with a gross weight of 4,150 pounds. With a cruising speed of 155 mph while carrying 76 gallons of fuel and burning 19 gallons per hour, the aircraft had a 620-mile range. The SR-10E was equipped with the Lycoming–Smith controllable propeller fitted with Lycoming blades. Standard equipment included an electric engine starter, battery, generator, fuel gauges, carburetor heater, compass, clock, dual controls, navigation lights, hydraulic wheel brakes, parking brake, cabin heater, cabin vents, vacuum-operated wing flaps, bonding and shielding, full-swivel tail wheel, map pockets, ashtrays, nickel hardware, and a first-aid kit. Optional equipment available for the SR-10E included wheel pants, landing lights, paraflares, pressure-type fire extinguisher, extra fuel tanks, radial gear, Edo pontoons, custom interiors, custom colors, and a Hamilton-Standard controllable propeller. Corrosion proofing for both saltwater and freshwater was also available as an option. Model C RCA radio equipment was available for the SR-10E including a compass with a rotatable loop, a compass with a fixed loop, a receiver, and a transmitter. Five types of antennas were available: exterior mounted T-type and V-type, interior mounted with remote reel (Aero radio) and two types with hand reels (Air Associates and Lear). A representative sampling of registration numbers assigned to the Model SR-10E was NC18478, NC22526 and NC23787. Serial numbers 5802 and up.

SR-10K gull-wing Reliant 5PCLM ATC 679 approved May 12, 1938, powered by a 420-hp Wright R-975-E engine. Two high-performance aircraft specifically designed for the New York Police Department: NC21147, s/n 5905 and NC21148, s/n 5906. The SR-10K was equipped with the Hamilton-Standard controllable propeller.

SR-10F gull-wing Reliant 5PCLM ATC 685 approved June 22, 1938, powered by a 450-hp P&W Wasp SB engine. Responding to customer requests, Stinson offered aircraft powered by Pratt & Whitney engines. Because of increased horsepower, these aircraft offered spectacular performance and had a higher retail price point. To accommodate the higher horsepower, the structural integrity of the fuselage was redesigned. From the firewall forward, it was totally new and included an increase in cowl length to aerodynamically cover the larger power plant. The Model F was approved for 150 pounds of baggage. 50 pounds could be placed under the rear seat and 100 pounds in a separate compartment behind the passenger compartment. A hat shelf was built into the rear of the passenger compartment. Data for the SR-10F is as follows: empty weight was listed as 3,045 pounds with a gross weight of 4,650 pounds. With a cruising speed of 177 mph while carrying 100 gallons of fuel and burning 25 gallons per hour, the aircraft had a 680-mile range. The SR-10F was equipped with the Hamilton-Standard controllable propeller. A 124-gallon fuel tank was offered as an option. Other optional equipment available for the SR-10F included wheel pants, landing lights, paraflares, pressure-type fire extinguisher, extra fuel tanks, radial gear, Edo pontoons, custom interiors, and custom colors. Corrosion proofing for both saltwater and freshwater was also available as an option. Model C RCA radio equipment was available for the SR-10F including a compass with a rotatable loop, a compass with a fixed loop, a receiver, and a transmitter. Five types of antennas were available: exterior mounted T-type and V-type, interior mounted with remote reel (Aero radio) and two types with hand reels (Air Associates and Lear). Additional optional equipment included a hinged engine cowl, drift indicator, a paint polish of 14-16 coats, removable right-hander copilot window, and three types of doors: emergency quick release, emergency top-hinged, and camera. Serial numbers 5800 and up were eligible manufactured prior to February 28, 1941. A representative sampling of registration numbers assigned to the Model SR-10F was NC18479, NC18495, NC21116 and NC21112. The Adams mail pickup and delivery device was installed on the Model SR-10F only (Kirkham Engineering Corporation). The equipment included a pickup unit that replaced the rear seat, a delivery unit, cable and hook, rope and basket, a reel unit and controls, structural modifications, metal skin on belly, and an extra set of rear controls.

1939

HW-75 3PCLM ATC 709 approved May 20, 1939, powered by a 75-hp Continental A-75-3 engine. This was a totally new aircraft. The HW-75 was a small aircraft with a wingspan of 34'0", length 22'2", height 6'6", a wing chord of 60 in. and a wing area of 155 sq. ft. The HW-75 used a NACA-4412 airfoil. It had an empty weight of 923 pounds, a useful load of 675 pounds, and a payload with 20 gallons of fuel of 360 pounds. The new design offered a cruising speed of 100 mph, a landing speed with flaps of 43 mph, and a ceiling of 10,500 feet. At its cruising speed fuel consumption was 4.8 gallons per hour, giving the aircraft a 350-mile range. The landing gear was totally redesigned with this type of landing gear fitted to all 3 and 4-place Stinson aircraft throughout their production run. The gear consisted of one-piece cantilever legs, and the gear attach points were flush-mounted on either side of the fuselage. Each landing gear leg hinged and was attached to a shock-absorbing strut completely enclosed in the fuselage. Each gear operated independently and was designed to absorb landing loads, giving the passengers a comfortable ride over uneven terrain. To provide the pilot with light control pressures, ball bearings were used throughout the control system. This was the first use by Stinson of built-in leading edge wing slots positioned forward of the ailerons. The HW-75 was designed as a three-place aircraft with the pilot and front passenger facing forward, seated side-by-side. To stay within the center of gravity limits, a third seat was mounted sideways. A Sensenich wood propeller was standard equipment. Airspeed limits were as follows: Level flight: 120 mph. Dive: 144 mph. Flaps extended: 85 mph. Serial numbers 7000 and up were eligible manufactured prior to February 28, 1941.

1940

Model 10 3PCLM ATC 709 approved April 22, 1940, powered by an 80-hp Continental A-80-6 engine. This aircraft was often identified as the Model 105. The Specifications for the HW-75 and the Model 10 were identical with three exceptions. The 10 was powered by a different engine, the inside width of fuselage was increased from 39 to 42 inches, and one 20-gallon wing fuel tank was standard equipment with a second one offered as optional equipment. Serial numbers 7501 and up were eligible manufactured prior to February 28, 1941.

L-1 Vigilant 2PCLM ATC LTC-26-2 retroactively approved November 17, 1947, powered by a 300-hp R-680-90 Lycoming engine. The aircraft was designed by Stinson in Wayne, Michigan and produced under the Stinson name in Nashville, Tennessee.

1941

Model 10-A 3PCLM ATC 738 approved March 3, 1941 powered by a 90-hp Franklin 4AC-199-E3 engine. Data for the 10-A is as follows: it had a wingspan of 34'0", length 21'8", height 6'6", a wing chord of 60 in., and a wing area of 155 sq. ft. Compared to the Reliant series, this was a small aircraft. The 10-A used NACA-4412 airfoil. It had an empty weight of 948 pounds, a useful load of 677 pounds, and a payload with 20 gallons of fuel of 317 pounds. The gross weight was listed as 1,625 pounds. The new design offered a cruising speed of 108 mph, a landing speed with flaps of 47 mph, and a ceiling of 13,000 feet. At cruising speed the fuel consumption was 6 gallons per hour, giving the aircraft a 320-mile range. The engine cowling was shortened for better visibility. Wheel pants were standard equipment, and the cantilever landing gear tread measured 84 inches.

1943-1944

V-77 [AT-19] gull-wing 5PCLM ATC 774 approved November 26, 1946, powered by a 290-hp R-680-E3B Lycoming engine. Listed below are the specification and performance data for the V-77: the empty weight was listed as 2,634 pounds with a gross weight of 4,000 pounds. With a cruising speed of 145 mph while carrying 76 gallons of fuel and burning 14 gallons per hour, the aircraft had a 575-mile range. It had a wingspan of 41'11", the maximum, and the wing chord at the strut attach point was 96 inches using modified Clark Y airfoil. Overall length was listed as 28'3" and height as 8'7". The V-77 was equipped with a Hamilton-Standard controllable propeller. The majority of all V-77 aircraft were given as Lend-Lease to the British Navy Fleet Air Arm.

1945

L-5 2PCLM ATC 764 approved December 17, 1945, powered by a 185-hp Lycoming O-435-A engine. Data for the L-5 is as follows: it had wingspan of 34'0", a length of 24'1", a height of 7'1", a wing chord of 60 in, and a wing area of 155 sq. ft. The L-5 used NACA-4412 airfoil. The aircraft had an empty weight of 1,495 pounds, a useful load of 686 pounds, and the gross weight was listed as 2,158 pounds. In an effort to conserve critical war material, the L-5 was designed with maximum use of wood construction. The fin and stabilizer were of wood construction similar to the 10A. The wing spar was spruce, and wing ribs were mahogany.

L-13A and **L-13B** 2PCLM ATC AR-10, powered by a 245-hp Franklin 0-425-9 engine. Two prototypes were built in Michigan as XL-13. A total of 298 L-13A and L-13B aircraft were manufactured by Consolidated Vultee in San Diego under the Stinson name.

108 Voyager 4PCLM ATC 767 temporary approval was granted on January 17, 1945. It was powered by a 150-hp 6A4-150-B3 Franklin engine. Formal approval for the 108 aircraft was granted July 19, 1946.

The huge increase in civilian aircraft production in 1946 exhausted the CAA pool of unassigned numbers, and a new numbering system was developed with a letter on the end of the NC number. Stinson's first block of numbers was NC8130K. When that group was exhausted, Stinson was assigned a new block beginning with NC150C. The CAA assigned unused blocks of numbers to the surplus aircraft running from NC30000 through NC99999. All Army Air Force surplus aircraft were given five digit numbers. There were no exceptions.

Registration Number Blocks	Year CAA Assigned Numbers
NC1 to 4999	1927
NC5000 to 7999	1928
NC8000 to 9999	1929
NC1 through 999 with ending letter E, H, K, M, N	1929
NC1 through 999 with ending letter V, W, Y	1930
NC10000 to 12999	1931
NC13000 to 13999	1932/33
NC14000 to 14999	1934
NC15000 to 15999	1935
NC16000 to 17999	1936
NC18000 to 18999	1937
NC19000 to 19999	1938
NC20000 to 28999	1939
NC29000 to 36999	1940
NC37000 to 44999	1941
NC45000 to 99999	1946

This is a general overview of Stinson aircraft specifications and cannot be used in aircraft certification, aircraft restoration, or flight operations. Current type certificate data is available from the FAA.

1934 SR-5A Special (NC13840, s/n 9349-A) 4PCHWM, with a 245-hp Lycoming R-680-6 engine. ATC 2-511 approved July 25, 1935 allowing for weight adjustment at 3,550 pounds gross weight. One built, original owner New York News Syndicate

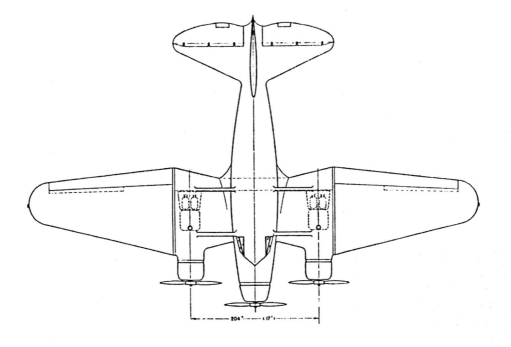
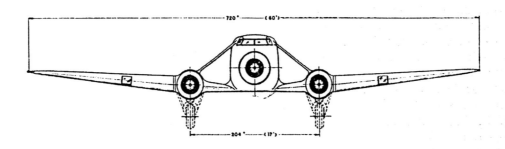
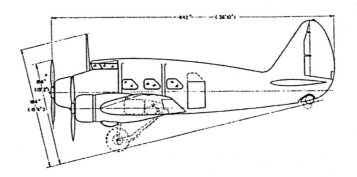

STINSON AIRCRAFT CORPORATION
Wayne, Mich.
Model A ———— 10 Place
Engines: Three Lycoming R-680-5

1935 Stinson Model A, tri-motor, ATC 556

Top: 1935 Stinson SR-6B Reliant powered by a 260-hp Lycoming R-680-5 engine, ATC 580

Middle: SR-5A Reliant ATC 536 sold to US Coast Guard as Coast Guard Model GQ-1

Bottom: 1935 Stinson Model A, CAA approved on September 25, 1934, ATC 556

CHAPTER 16

Top: The famous adventurer Aloha Wanderwell was known as "The Amelia Earhart of the Automobile" for being the first women to drive herself around the world, in a Model T Ford. She repeated this feat many times until proposing to do it by airplane. She is pictured here at Roosevelt Field on Long Island posing with her 1934 Stinson SR-5A, ATC 536.

Middle: 1936 SR-8EM (CF-AZI, s/n 9725) shown as-built from factory. The SR-8 was awarded ATC 609 The letter 'E' designation signifies its power was a 320-hp Wright R-760-E2 radial piston engine. The letter 'M' denotes a "Multi-Purpose" function build which, according to Jane's All the World Aircraft included "metal floors and side walls to the window sills, resulting in a strong, durable compartment for the transport of supplies, equipment, machinery, and merchandise, and for ready sterilization when used for Ambulance or Emergency Relief work. The 'Multi-Purpose' door, operating in conjunction with the regular cabin doors, permits the loading and unloading of large bulky packages or stretcher and patient." Standard 'M' equipment included "metal reinforced lending-edge, special exterior steps and hand grips for refueling with small capacity containers where modern pump and service facilities are not available."

Bottom: CF-AZI as delivered to McIntyre-Porcupine Mines late June 1936, shown with McIntyre chief pilot C. A. "Duke" Schiller, a famous bush pilot with experience in the Stinson Detroiter Royal Windsor (see Chapter 24). A later owner leased CF-AZI to the Royal Norwegian Naval Air Force, in Toronto where, in November 1940 a terrific gale ripped the craft from its mooring, causing it to sink. Although raised the next day and said to be easily repairable, as of this writing no evidence has been found to indicate that it ever flew again.

1938 advertisement for a float-equipped Stinson SR-10F, ATC 685

1940 advertisement for a Stinson SR-10E, ATC 679, and a Stinson 105, ATC 709

Chapter 17
The Stinson Greyhound

The Stinson Greyhound *at Curtis Field, Long Island after testing by* Aerial Age Weekly.
*The aircraft was next headed to Philadelphia. This original photograph was sent
by Eddie to his sister Katherine, on the back he wrote: "Curtiss Field Rarin' t' go."*

In late 1919 Eddie Stinson decided to design, build, and market his own airplane. Rather than a stunt plane such as he used in his aerial act, he envisioned an aerial jitney—a two-place pleasure and commercial aircraft that would also be used for "observation work." What was not included in the description was the word "exhibition." This aircraft would not be designed for stunting, but instead to provide something akin to basic transportation in the air, as the Model-T Ford did on the ground.

The motivation behind that decision was a front-page opinion piece in the January 19, 1919 edition of *The Philadelphia Inquirer* which announced, and lamented, the news that Henry Ford had declined to build a small plane that would appeal to the several thousand Army and Navy aviators who were on their way home from the Great War. The article—ghost written by a former instructor colleague of Eddie's from Kelly Field—took manufacturers to task over the lack of initiative that they were exhibiting. The author, wrongly believing that the supply of used airplanes would soon be depleted, laid out the material list and construction sequence for the building of a simple, inexpensive airplane, noting that it would be an easy task for nearly any producer of manufactured goods. Additionally, he observed that with military contracts on the wane, there were more than enough experienced aircraft workers hoping to remain in the industry. The author went on to describe seeing an airplane built at a "ridiculously low cost" and called out Eddie Stinson—by name—as someone who could build such an aircraft from scratch.

Separating from the Army after the end of the war, Stinson set up briefly at Newport News, Virginia as an instructor and offering passenger trips while he planned and trained for his appearance at the Second Annual Pan-American Aeronautical Convention at Atlantic City during the month of May (Chapter 13). By mid-June he and two other pilots were preforming together in what the newspapers were calling a "Flying Circus." Those same papers were also calling Eddie "Lieutenant Colonel Stinson" due to his newly acquired rank in the New York City Police Reserve Aviation Section. Ever since *The Philadelphia Inquirer* article, Stinson had been mulling over the idea of building an airplane. Eventually the idea turned to planning, then to actual construction.

With his wife and her son, his mother and his brother Jack, he moved to Dayton, Ohio. He found a suitable workshop at 44 South Canal Street in a 35'x65' two-story building that had gas, electricity, and an elevator. This was Stinson's first attempt at creating an aircraft manufacturing company. He moved into the newly formed Stinson Aeroplane Company and began building. The resulting *Greyhound* is recognized as the first offering from a Stinson company. The 1920 first flight of the *Greyhound* was commemorated in 2020, rightfully celebrating the 100th anniversary of Stinson's first product available to the public.

In the Army Stinson had scavenged wrecked planes for free or low-cost parts, and now did the same in Dayton. He switched from experimenting with rotary-style engines to installing a 90-hp Curtis OX-5 V-8 water-cooled engine for the *Greyhound*. As noted in the first chapter, hardware, gauges, control cables, hinges, bracing, pulleys, and more were taken from surplus or wrecked Curtiss Jennys. Wood from the wings and fuselages of the wrecks was redesigned and reworked into a new and unique airframe.

In anticipation of future orders, the assets and property of the Stone Propeller Company at 815 East Fifth Street in Dayton were purchased by the Stinson family members involved in the Stinson Aeroplane Company. Just the year before Stone Propeller had been heavily advertising for dozens of woodworkers on airplane propellers, cabinet makers, woodworking glue men, expert band sawyers, and woodworking machine men—promising all the best of wages. This was to fulfill a contract with the Bureau of Airplane Production for 500 aircraft propellers. When the war ended the government cancelled the order in mid-run and paid the Stone Propeller Company only $7,290 out of the $18,576 that had been contracted, pushing them into receivership. With Jack acting as the front man, the Stinsons spent $1,125 for the building and woodworking machinery. The goal was to move the expected volume production of the *Greyhound* out of the rented building on South Canal Street, and into their new property on East Fifth Street.

Eddie had set up a travelling air show where he and the two other pilots would put on exhibitions and offer the public rides for $15 (and an extra $10 for stunt flying) usually spending three-to-five days at a location. This is how he made money to finance the building of his new aircraft. In-between shows he would return to his Dayton headquarters to plan his next trip, and to continue work on the *Greyhound*. While he was on his way to Chattanooga to perform at Marr Field, his mother, Emma B. Stinson, and brother Jack incorporated the Stinson Aeroplane Company in Columbus, Ohio on November 26, 1919 with a capital stock of $25,000. (Some period accounts called it the Stinson 'Airplane' Company, but the Stinsons always used 'Aeroplane' in the name of this company.)

Having the family matriarch and siblings involved together in business was nothing new for the Stinson clan. In May 1913 Katherine, her mother Emma, and a man named Abner H. Cook incorporated the Stinson Aviation Company in Hot Springs Arkansas for the purpose of "buying, manufacturing, selling, owning, and renting flying machines." Nothing came of that venture and just over two years later Emma, Katherine, Marjorie, and Eddie worked collectively to establish what would eventually come to be called the Stinson Municipal Airport in San Antonio—now the second oldest general aviation airport in continuous operation in the country. Today it is part of the San Antonio International Airport system, acting as a reliever field. The Stinson Municipal Airport stills uses its original three-letter identifier: SSF, which reveals the airfield's original purpose, the **S**tinson **S**chool of **F**lying. In 1916 Katherine recycled the name Stinson Aviation Company when attempting to establish an aviation school in Ottawa as an offshoot of the San Antonio school.

Taking a break from the 1919 air show circuit, Eddie returned to Dayton by train, arriving Christmas day. He checked on the progress of the *Greyhound* and decided to try for a first flight on January 1, 1920. On the 27th he ferried an old

The Greyhound *being transported from the workshop on South Canal Street to Wilbur Wright Field, where final assembly took place. Note the bump-out for the rocker arms on the engine hood.*

The Greyhound, *with more parts attached, is towed through the streets of Dayton. Note the nickel plated landing gear.*

Curtiss that he had been storing at Wilbur Wright Field for some time back to Chattanooga, where he was attempting to start a flying school. As of this writing the exact date of that first flight remains unknown, but there is evidence that it did not occur until late February or early March. However, enough progress had been made by the third week of February that the company was advertising for cabinet makers and sheet metal workers who were experienced "in making airplane fittings" as well as hiring "general airplane men." In the expectation of orders to be generated at the New York Aeronautical Exposition in March 1920, the Stinson Aeroplane Company was gearing up to do big business.

The prototype *Greyhound*, as built, revealed the need for specialty craftsmen. Although any "general airplane men" could build wings and a fuselage, skilled cabinet makers would be used to craft the mahogany cowls, while experienced airplane sheet metal workers would hand-form the aluminum engine hoods.

The two-place aircraft had a novel arrangement, in that instead of the usual tandem layout for the pilot and passenger, the cockpit featured side-by-side seating on deep green velour upholstery, with a vanity box provided for lady passengers. Dedicated compartments for tools now occupied the rear-seat space. The color of the paint on the *Greyhound* was, of course, gray. The steel tubing of the landing gear, as well as all wires and fittings, were nickel-plated and highly polished. Along with the three-place Curtiss K-1 Oriole, the *Greyhound* was one of the first civilian aircraft to have an electric starter.

On March 10, 1920 at 8:30 a.m. Eddie Stinson, with his mechanic Harry Kioebge—who had served at Kelly Field with him—sitting next to him, lifted off from Wilbur Wright Field. They were already four days late for the New York Aeronautical Exposition (more commonly known as the New York Aero Show), which had started on the 6th and would run through the 13th, leaving a scant three days to exhibit the *Greyhound*. Eddie's mother Emma and wife Estelle witnessed the take off. Stinson predicted a five-hour flight, including a refueling stop in Winchester, Virginia. His sister Katherine was waiting for him when he landed in New York on time, where he promptly fired off a telegram back home to Dayton to inform the family of his safe arrival.

Held in the Seventy-First Regiment Armory building, the 1920 New York Aero Show differed from the 1919 exposition—which highlighted military aircraft—by featuring post-war commercial planes. Including the Stinson Aeroplane Company's "two passenger Stinson airplane," there were eleven manufacturers displaying some seventeen different models, although the Glenn L. Martin Company from Cleveland elected to show only scale models of their transports and mail planes, and to show motion pictures of the operations of the "Martin factory and various Martin planes in construction and in flight." Still, Martin concluded

Eddie Stinson in the two-seat cockpit of the Greyhound. *Note the mahogany woodwork.*

CHAPTER 17

Original photograph of the Greyhound *taken by* Aerial Age Weekly *and used in the April 5, 1920 issue*

several sales. Curtiss had the most numerous offerings with four different models including their standard JN-4-D, while Stinson and five other manufacturers submitted only one offering each.

Seven different engine manufacturers displayed twelve motors, while dozens of other companies hawked such accessories as varnishes, spark plugs, wires, instruments, starters, propellers, aerial cameras, life insurance, and magazines, along with displays by the American Flying Club, the Bureau of Standards, and one featuring the Army and Navy Radio Telephone. It is interesting to note that, while the Liberty Starters Corporation was displaying as-yet-uninstalled electric starters for airplanes, one only had to walk to the Stinson display to see a non-Liberty starter fitted on the *Greyhound*, which had already flown some 540 miles from Dayton to New York City. Also exhibiting at the show was the much-reduced Stone Propeller Company of Dayton, Ohio.

The only other two-place aircraft at the show besides the *Greyhound*, and thus its main competition, was the Curtiss JN-4-D. All the other airplanes, except for the diminutive single-seat LWF Model L Butterfly, were three-place or greater capacity. Although the *Greyhound* used the same engine as the larger Jenny, the Stinson airplane was not built for aerobatics, making it the less desirable choice. Not a single *Greyhound* was ordered. By contrast, on the third day of the show—the day before Eddie even took off for New York—Curtiss sold one 'Curtiss-Standard' biplane, one twelve-passenger Eagle, six new JN-4s, 35 three-passenger Orioles, and an additional 200 JN-4s that had been repurchased from the government after the war. The 235 Orioles and repurchased JN-4s that were ordered constituted the largest single sale of commercial airplanes in history.

After the show Eddie flew to Curtiss Field at Garden City on Long Island to allow a crew from the magazine *Aerial Age Weekly* test-fly the *Greyhound*.

Aerial Age Weekly April 5, 1920

The new Stinson "Greyhound" biplane, which Eddie Stinson recently flew from Dayton, Ohio to the New York Aeronautical Exposition in March is a very interesting design. The fuselage has two-place, side-by-side seating that is streamlined, offering less resistance than the ordinary type. In the rear of the cockpit are compartments for tools. The fuselage is finished in grey, the cowling is mahogany, and the engine hood, which is bumped out for the rocker arms to ensure effective streamlining, is natural aluminum. Seats are upholstered in deep green velour, making a striking contrast with the mahogany finish of the cockpit. The U.S.A.-4 wing section is of the five-panel type, and the ribs are three-ply veneer. The aircraft has box-type compression ribs; the other ribs are cut out for lightness.

Stick control is used, which operates ailerons by means of a rocker arm and adjustable spacers working on bell cranks that are fastened to a tube running through

Halftone of the Stinson Greyhound *as it appeared in the April 5, 1920 issue of* Aerial Age Weekly

the lower wing forming the leading edge of the lower aileron. The lower aileron is connected to the upper aileron by an adjustable steel tubing spacer. This ensures control in case the wings' ailerons are disabled.

The elevators are controlled by a single mast; the top arm is in the vertical stabilizer and the lower in the fuselage. The landing gear is of V–type and made of steel tubing, giving it a high safety rating. It is nickel plated and polished, adding greatly to the appearance of the aircraft. Shock absorption is carried out in the usual manner using rubber cord.

The power plant consists of a 90-hp Curtis OX-5 engine equipped with an electric starter. The aircraft is finished excellently with all wires and fittings nickel-plated and buffed. A Hartzell Walnut propeller is used with very good results. The performance of the aircraft exceeds all expectations in speed and climb.

When *Aerial Age* was finished with their test flights, Stinson flew to Pennsylvania to display the *Greyhound* in Philadelphia, but again was met with no interest and no sales. Eddie and his mechanic departed Philadelphia early Sunday, March 21 to return to Dayton. As they were nearing Pittsburg—about the half-way point of the trip—the control stick broke off at the weld on its attached point on the floor—a weld that Stinson himself had made. He was forced to use the rudder and throttle to maintain some semblance of control over the aircraft and make a somewhat controlled crash landing. This was the incident that led to the famous sign in Eddie's later factory in Detroit which read:

"The Pilot Depends on You."

The Pittsburg Press
Monday Evening, March 22, 1920
Page 9

Airplane Falls 3,500 Feet; Two Flyers Bruised

Special to the press

Johnstown, Pa., March 22.—An aviator, said to have been Eddie Stinson, and his mechanic, miraculously escaped death yesterday at noon when an airplane in which they were riding crashed through space 3,500 feet and landed in a field at Ehrenfeld, nine miles east of Johnstown. Both men suffered bruises and scratches.

The airplane was seen passing over several towns east of here and residents of Summer Hill, one mile east of Ehrenfeld, while watching the plane, were astounded when the machine suddenly darted towards the ground at a terrific speed. They ran towards where the airplane fell and discovered the two men crawling from the wreckage. The machine had fallen in a field owned by the Pennsylvania Coal & Coke Corp.

Dr. Ray Parker of Ehrenfeld, attended both men. The physician asserted the mechanic said that Eddie Stinson was the driver of the machine and that the lever controlling the elevator broke, causing the airplane to crash to the ground. Neither man would discuss the accident. The driver asked the physician how far they were from Johnstown and this led many people here to believe that Stinson was the driver of the plane, as he has appeared here in many daring exhibition flights. Where the airplane came from or where it was going could not be learned.

After their injuries had been dressed, the driver and mechanic returned to the scene of the accident and took the machine apart and shipped it away.

The two men, it is said, boarded a Pennsylvania railroad train, westbound. Efforts to locate either in the vicinity of Johnstown proved futile.

The driver of the machine was described as being a tall, dark, thin man, and answered a description of the daring aviator.

According to an employee of the Pennsylvania Coal & Coke corporation, the airplane was bound from New York to Dayton, O. He said that the machine fell into a pile of rocks and that he was told the driver was Eddie Stinson. The employee also stated that the two men left on the 4 o'clock train for New York City.

Stinson had the *Greyhound* shipped by train back to Dayton and by the middle of May it was back in the air, sporting sheet metal repairs around the cockpit. However, with the disappointing lack of interest in the aircraft, Eddie handed it completely over to Jack. He gathered his acrobatic team, and they made their way to the 1920 Pan-American Aeronautical Congress in Atlantic City, where he observed Bert Acosta give passenger-carrying demonstration flights with the Junkers-Larsen JL-6. After performing in the Aeronautical Congress, Eddie temporarily relocated to Chattanooga, where he went to work as a flying salesman for the Chattanooga Automobile Company's Aerial Division. The Chattanooga Automobile Company was the biggest Curtiss distributor in the South, and they had been one of the two distributors who had placed the huge order at the New York Aero Show, and now Eddie was selling those very airplanes. On July 14 Stinson bought a new Curtiss JN-4-D for his flying circus. He shelved any plans of being a manufacturer for the time being and at the end of the year the Stinson factory on South Canal Street was abandoned—the move to East Fifth Street having never been made. In fact, after mid-October, while Eddie was still in Tennessee, the Stinson Aeroplane Company was never mentioned again.

Now in sole possession of the rebuilt *Greyhound*, Jack started his own ride-for-hire and air taxi service operation and began looking for customers further afield. His flying season extended well into fall. On October 8 he was in Bucyrus, a little over 100 miles from Dayton, to set up *Greyhound* rides over the weekend flying out of Bittikofer Field, with a Colonel F. D. Henderson acting as pilot. On Saturday October 16 Jack flew over Norwalk and dropped leaflets announcing that he would be offering rides there on Monday the 18th and Tuesday the 19th. He was flying at Monroeville on Wednesday, Bellevue on Thursday, and at Clyde on Friday.

For the 1921 season Jack teamed up with Wilbur Wright Field pilot Richard Lees to open a flying field along the Mad River outside of Dayton, and once again his mother provided assistance. Emma, who was said to be of Scotch/Irish ancestry but with a Cherokee mother (Eddie's maternal grandmother), had leased the old war-time Red Cross building at 24 West Second Street and at great cost and effort turned it into a first-class establishment called the Hotel Dayton. Here Jack not only lived, but maintained his flying business office.

Jack Stinson, now the sole owner of the rebuilt Greyhound, *poses with new partner Richard Lees at the Mad River field near Dayton. Note replaced lower engine panel, and the sheet metal repair around the cockpit.*

In mid-May Jack Stinson and Richard Lees began offering rides above Dayton with Lees as the aerial chauffeur. In June, Jack himself took an entire Knights of Pythias convention aerial sightseeing—one Knight at a time. In July he announced a new flying field on thirty-seven acres east of Harshmanville (Harries, Ohio), which would serve as a new base of operations for the *Greyhound*. However, the 1921 season, as well as the entire venture, came to an early and abrupt halt on Friday, August 19, 1921, when the *Greyhound* crashed into a store.

Jack had been selling rides at Buckeye Lake when the engine died over the water. He banked back over land and brought the aircraft down but could not stop and crashed into the front of a grocery. While neither Jack nor the passenger were injured, the store owner had a writ of attachment issued against the *Greyhound*. Ultimately Jack retained ownership of the *Greyhound*, but as of this writing no report has been found to indicate that it ever flew again, even though the aircraft appears to have survived until at least 1933.

At nine o'clock in the morning on Friday June 4, 1926, with one-month advance notice, Jack had the *Greyhound* auctioned off with extra propellers included. In December 1927, the new owner of the Stinson *Greyhound* was issued the registration number NC2554 (s/n 1) during the first year such numbers became available. In 1930 the *Greyhound* was sold to Ted Eisan, a Shell Oil mechanic in Sacramento. He re-registered it as NC352V (s/n 10) [sic], and began learning to fly in March 1932. It appeared that Eisan hoped to complete flying school by the time he finished restoring the 12-year-old airplane. However, he was suddenly transferred to the Shell plant in Reno, and on February 8, 1933 the *Greyhound* was deregistered. No further records have come to light, and with that, that one single *Greyhound*—the only airplane ever built by the Stinson Aeroplane Company, and for that matter the only plane built by Eddie Stinson in Dayton—ceased to exist. The Stinson Aeroplane Company itself, which had devolved from being an aircraft manufacturer (pop. 1), into a ride-for-hire concern, likewise faded from history. The Stinson Aircraft Syndicate—which was established in Detroit in 1925; built the SM-1 Detroiter, and became the Stinson Aircraft Corporation—was a completely different company with a completely different vision and product. In fact, the only thing the old company and the new Syndicate had in common was Eddie Stinson.

Specifications of the Stinson biplane:	**Performance (actual test):**
Span.....................................34' 2 ¼"	High-speed...................................96 mph
Overall length........................22' 4"	Low landing speed......................25 mph
Height.....................................9' 0"	Economical speed......................55 mph
Gap..5' 0"	Fuel capacity, full speed............3 ¼ hrs
Cord.......................................5' 0"	Fuel capacity, economical speed......5 ½ hrs
Total wing area....................320 sq. ft	Climb, first minute......................1150 ft
Weight, empty.....................947 lbs	Power Plant.......Curtis OX -5 90 H.P. at 1400 rpm
Weight with pilot, passenger, & 26 gals....1492 lbs	
Weight per square foot..........4.66 lbs	
Weight per horsepower........16.57 lbs	

Specifications and performance figures for the Greyhound *as tested by* Aerial Age Weekly *in March 1920*

WANTED
At once, Cabinet Makers, Sheet Metal Workers, experienced in making airplane fittings and general airplane men. Apply at once
THE STINSON AEROPLANE CO.
44 South Canal

The Steven P. Bogdan Collection

Left: This February 21, 1920 classified ad from The Dayton Herald *was placed when the Stinson Aeroplane Company was anticipating volume sales from the upcoming New York Aero Show in March.*

Top: The first ad for rides for hire in the post-rebuild Greyhound *appeared in the May 14, 1921 issue of* The Dayton Herald. *The Hotel Dayton was owned and operated by Emma Stinson, the matriarch of the extended family.*

Middle: From the October 8, 1920 edition of The Bucyrus Evening Telegraph, *Bucyrus, Ohio with original first word misspelling*

Bottom: The last ad mentioning the Greyhound *by name, placed in the July 23, 1921 issue of* The Dayton Herald. *The plane crashed for a second (and last) time 27 days later over 100 miles away at Buckeye Lake near Hebron, Ohio.*

All images above from The Steven P. Bogdan Collection.

Chapter 18
The Early Airplanes

Eddie Stinson and Major General William Crozier with the Humming Bird *at Kelly Field in 1918. This photo, reproduced in the official history of Kelly Field (see top photo on page 155), was sent to Katherine by Eddie.*

On November 23, 1919, an article appeared on the front page of the *Coshocton Tribune* (Coshocton, Ohio) announcing that all four Stinson siblings and their mother were incorporating a $25,000 company to build airplanes in Dayton. The newspaper noted that the airplane currently nearing completion was not the first airplane that Eddie Stinson ever built, nor was it even his second. The airplane that would be known as the *Greyhound*, was in fact, the third successful airplane to be built and flown by Eddie. There were, however, some failures and growing pains along the way.

Eddie was ten years old when the Wright brothers made their first flight, while 'Kate' and 'Madge' were twelve and eight respectively, and Jack was eight days short of his third birthday. The flying feat was announced in early January 1904. Marjorie remembered that not long after Eddie, using magazine illustrations of gliders as a guide, built his first airplane out of sticks, nails, and his mother's bedsheets. Not having an engine, Eddie decided to roll it downhill to get it airborne. To this end he removed the wheels from his toy wagon and attached them to the bespoke aircraft. Luckily, it grew too dark for an attempt that day, and that night a storm came in and wrecked the little plane.

In 1908 the three older Stinson children, using for guidance clear photos of the original Wright aircraft—published for the first time in the September issue of *The Century Magazine*—reportedly managed to build and fly a glider, gaining nearly 100 yards at an altitude of ten to fifteen feet. In both Canton and Jackson, Mississippi, the Stinson children were collectively, albeit fondly, known as "those crazy kids" because of the risks they took "in wheezing, clanking contrivances which were the predecessors of the modern airplane."

Around 1909 Eddie left Jackson for his first away from home job, travelling to St. Louis, where he found work as a mechanic. Sometime later he also took a second, part-time job at the Fauna Flora Roadhouse owned by the notorious gambler Mark Gumbert. Working for tips only, this job consisted of hand-cranking cars to start them for departing customers. The experience likely contributed to his early adoption of electric starters in aircraft.

During Eddie's stint at the roadhouse, two men approached the owner with a proposition: if Gumbert would finance an airplane project, one of the men would design and build an engine while the other would do the same for fuselage and wings—all that was needed was someone to fly it. Eddie, the erstwhile glider pilot, volunteered, his lack of actual motorized flying experience notwithstanding. When the aircraft was completed, the fledging test pilot attempted to take it aloft. The only altitude that could be gained came from the bumps and rocks on the field which caused the plane to hop. Reworking the craft allowed for some longer hops, but eventually as the hopping and bouncing took a toll, the airframe began to disintegrate. Ultimately the aircraft was abandoned in an East St. Louis field. As payment for his piloting services, Eddie was allowed to keep the engine. When the Wright Model B Flyer was introduced in 1910, Eddie decided to build a duplicate of it, again without the benefit of any plans. He could not get that one off the ground either.

In October 1911 Eddie's mother and siblings travelled to St. Louis to visit him and together they attended the aviation meet being held at Kinloch Field (now the Lambert-St. Louis International Airport). Katherine had developed a deep attraction to aviation the previous December when she watched John Moisant preform in Memphis. Just two weeks before arriving in St. Louis, she had taken her first flight in a balloon at the International Balloon Race in Kansas City. Now she and Eddie were examining actual Wright Model B Flyers—not just magazine photos. Then Katherine took her very first ride in a motorized aircraft—one made there in St. Louis by the Benoist Aircraft Company—and made the life changing decision to move to St. Louis and attend an aviation school. The actual flight training did not go well, and she would later finish her education in Chicago where she earned her pilot's license just nine months after that first balloon ride and subsequent Wright Flyer inspection. She returned to Kinloch Field in St. Louis in October 1912, not as a spectator, but rather as a performer in the aviation meet. After the event was over, she stayed in St. Louis practice her flying and to learn 'trick' flying. While she was there, she taught Eddie the assembly/disassembly procedures of the Wright Flyer for shipping and receiving by train. More importantly for Eddie—and contrary to popular myth—she also gave him his first flying lesson.

During 1913, while Katherine was performing with her Wright Model B Flyer on the State Fair circuit, Eddie remained in St. Louis. He too purchased a Model B that he carefully assembled after it was shipped to him in knocked-down form—in essence a Wright Brothers designed and built kit.

In the fall of 1914, after his sister Marjorie received her pilot's license, the three of them joined to perform their own air show, travelling by rail from town to town. When the train arrived at a destination, Katherine went about the business of the show. As their mechanician, Eddie arranged to have the Wright Flyer unloaded from the ac-

As with the earlier Wright Model B Flyer, later planes were also disassembled and shipped on to the next stop on the tour to be reassembled and tested by the ground crew. Years later Katherine would remark, "We used to express our plane then. Now the express goes by plane."

From left to right: Jack, Marjorie, Eddie, and Kathrine Stinson. Marjorie is at the wheel of her Overland, while Eddie is at the controls of the Wright Model B Flyer. These are the vehicles that Katherine, Marjorie, and Eddie used in their 1914 airshow.

companying boxcar and uncrated. After he assembled the aircraft, it would be taken through the streets to the fairgrounds, where he would prepare it for flight. Meanwhile Marjorie would go to the local Overland dealer to pick up her prepared racecar (an otherwise stock vehicle that had fenders, windshield, lights, etc. removed for racing). The exhibition consisted of Katherine performing her usual aeronautical show, followed by a race around the track between Katherine in the Wright Flyer and Marjorie in the Overland. After the event was over, Eddie would transport the airplane back to the depot, disassemble it, repack it in its crate and load it back onto the boxcar. With the boxcar attached to the passenger train, the three siblings would settle in for the trip to the next performance. Eddie now had a thorough hands-on education in assembling and operating the Wright Model B Flyer. It was time to graduate to the next level of airplane.

By April 1916 Walter L. Brock, the famous racer and aeroplane builder, was in San Antonio working with the Stinsons. He had recently built an aircraft in Chicago for Katherine, and modified Marjorie's Wright Flyer, as the *Aerial Age Weekly* magazine wrote it, "from a 'warper' to one with 'flappers'" to supplement the Stinson School of Flying's standard Model B. Now Brock was building a French Caudron/Wright hybrid. Next, he would begin construction on two Bristol type tractors powered by 50-hp Gnome engines for Marjorie and Eddie. In addition to being their personal air show rides, the planes would be used at the school as advanced trainers. However, the main benefit of Brock's employment was that he took Stinson under his wing and taught him the aircraft design and construction capability that served him in building his next two airplanes—airplanes

Open house day at the Stinson School of Flying, where they are displaying the Walter L. Brock designed airplanes Eddie helped build. The man in the derby is Col. George Washington Brackenridge, a prominent banker in San Antonio.

that flew beyond all expectations.

The Bug

The January 19, 1919 article in *The Philadelphia Inquirer* that had inspired the *Greyhound* had explained:

> There is liable to be a wide variance between actually building an airplane and building one on paper. I have seen an airplane built at a ridiculously low cost—an airplane by Eddie Stinson, at San Antonio, Tex., last summer. Stinson, who is a brother of the noted girl flier, Katherine Stinson, was a civilian instructor at Kelly Field, the army training station at San Antonio. He has been a flier for years. For a small sum Stinson laid hold of a secondhand rotary motor of the type used in single seater scout planes. He got some scraps of fabric from the engineering and repairing shops at the airdrome. He picked up old pieces of wood work, patched them together, and stitched the canvas over a skeleton work that resembled more the chassis of a chicken coop than of an airship.
>
> It was a baby airplane, if ever there was such a thing-a weird combination of tin, canvas, baling wire, scantlings, and a rotary motor. It sat in front, and the exposed cylinders had the appearance of a succession of railroad lanterns attached by their handles to a disk. The airplane was so small that it could have been inserted in the cockpit of a Handley-Paige bomber. It looked rickety, ramshackle, suicidal. But how Ed could flip around in it! Down at Kelley they called it the "*Bug*," and that describes its looks. But there was no other craft around the airdome in which a pilot could perform so many hide-rippling maneuvers and acrobatics—not even the speedy single seaters.
>
> At an outlay of a few hundred dollars and a few spare hours of labor, Stinson had built himself a "tin Lizzie" of the air. And if Stinson can do it with his bare hands and odd fragments what about the fellows who own the factories?

No photos of the *Bug* are known to exist, but the achievement of building and flying the tiny, chicken-coop looking plane, made of scavenged and reworked parts, impressed the command staff at Kelly Field so much that they gave Eddie their blessing—and three sergeants from the maintenance department—to design and build from scratch a second, more graceful aircraft.

Eddie posing with one of the two airplanes that he helped Walter L. Brock design and build at SSF

The *Humming Bird*

On June 20, 1918, the camp newspaper *Kelly Field Eagle* reported a 'record-breaking' first flight of a Stinson-built airplane that the airfield personal took to calling it the *Humming Bird*. The article is transcribed below.

Stinson Flies Humming-Bird Airplane Here

Little High-Powered Plane Shoots "Straight up" from Ground

Relic of Other Days Makes Climbing Mark

Instructor in Knock-Down Ship Does Stunt Flying

"Look at Eddie's flivver fly."

Nearly everyone—officers and enlisted men at the Kelly Field Flying Department watched Instructor Edward Stinson's new small ship with eager interest and curiosity as he sailed it Saturday for the first time.

It appeared to be traveling higher all the time, and with its little frame and low hanging wheels, it presented a peculiar picture as it pranced overhead. Its wings dipped almost vertically as it banked around the curves, and in climbing, its nose appeared to be headed straight upward.

Other machines looked slow in comparison to the manner in which it climbed, circled and sped through the air. Instead of the gradual elevation and the wide swinging spirals, the machine darted up and down and around in a manner that astonished even experienced flyers. "Looks like a dash blank humming bird, one mechanic said.

Built on the style of a Bristol Scotch [Scout], with a Gnome seven-cylinder rotary engine weighing only 165 pounds, and bicycle wheels like the Wright Brothers' early models, the dainty plane looks more like a toy than an airship.

It is a circus plane, a knock-me-down affair, which can be taken apart and folded together in 35 minutes.

So maneuverable was the aircraft, that one stunt that Eddie used to perform was still being talked about well into World War II. With wheels barely off the ground, he would fly the craft straight at the base of the tall water tower that served the camp. Just as it appeared that he would slam into it, Eddie would pull up into a vertical climb with his wheels scant inches from the wall of the tank. He then cut the power until he came to a stall barely clear of the top of the tower. There he would gently nose over the top and power vertically down the other side of the tank, pulling back into level flight at the last possible second—his wheels once again just off the ground.

The *Humming Bird* so impressed the officials at Kelly Field, that a photo of was included in the official history of Kelly Field, *Kelly Field in the Great World War*, edited by Lt. H. D. Kroll (Press of San Antonio Printing Company, 1919).

The disposition of the *Bug* is not known, but the *Humming Bird* stayed with Eddie during the war. He was able to use it as his personal plane.

One story reported in the *Kelly Field Eagle* was picked up by *Aerial Age Weekly* magazine. It told of Eddie's mother, who farmed on Alamo Heights in San Antonio, calling Eddie at work to tell him that his sister Katherine had sent him a telegram. Eddie said he would hurry there to get the wire. His mother waited patiently but didn't see him driving down the road. His younger brother Jack spotted him first, pointing to the sky. Eddie was arriving in the *Humming Bird*. He circled around until he spotted a suitable landing site on a neighbor's farm. Once down, the whole neighborhood turned out to greet him. After the war he was able to keep it. He held on to it until June 1920, then offered it for sale through the Stinson Aeroplane Company in the ad pages of *Aerial Age Weekly*. Ironically, the *Humming Bird*—the second plane built by Eddie—was the only aircraft that the Stinson Aeroplane Company of Dayton, Ohio ever sold, and not the single airplane that the Stinson Aeroplane Company had built.

Opposite page: Article about the Humming Bird *printed in the June 20, 1918 newspaper* Kelly Field Eagle

Above: The water tank that Eddie "climbed" was located behind the Flying Department Headquarters.

Inset: The photograph from page 150 as it appeared in the 1919 book Kelly Field in the Great World War

Chapter 19
Edward Stinson: More Than a Pilot

"Miss Wayco" SM-1 NX1524, s/n M210, flown by Eddie Stinson to victory 1927 Ford Reliability Air Tour

Little has been written about the life of Edward (Eddie) Anderson Stinson Jr. before 1918, and while it is not the purpose of this book to offer an extensive accounting of the life of Eddie Stinson or the Stinson family of flyers, it is entirely appropriate to provide a brief biographical look into his early years before his success in Michigan. Although some items have been covered in other chapters, they have been included here in chronological order.

Eddie was born on July 11, **1893**, in Fort Payne, Alabama. He was the second child born to Edward A. Stinson, Sr. (a city engineer) and Emma A. Beavers. Eddie had three siblings: Katherine (Kate), Marjorie (Madge), who were also born in Fort Payne, and Jack (his given name) who was born in Canton, Mississippi. The family settled in Jackson, Mississippi but Edward Sr. and Emma would separate not long after Jack was born, leaving Emma to raise the four children. Eddie was ten years old when the Wright brothers made their first flight, while Kate and Madge were twelve and eight, respectively, and Jack was eight days short of his third birthday. Marjorie remembered that not long after Eddie, using a magazine illustration of the Wright brothers craft as a guide, built his first airplane out of sticks, nails, and his mother's bedsheets. Not having an engine, Eddie decided to roll downhill to get airborne, so he removed the wheels from his toy wagon and attached them to the bespoke aircraft. Luckily, it grew too dark for an attempt that day, and that night a storm came in and wrecked the little plane.

At the age of thirteen Eddie completed his formal education in **1906** as he finished the eighth grade. In **1908** the three older Stinson children—again using a photo of a Wright aircraft for guidance—reportedly managed to build and fly a glider, gaining nearly 100 yards at an altitude of ten to fifteen feet. In both Canton and Jackson, the Stinson children were collectively, albeit fondly known as "those crazy kids" because of the risks they took "in wheezing, clanking contrivances which were the predecessors of the modern airplane."

CHAPTER 19

Around **1909** Eddie left Jackson for his first away from home job, travelling to St. Louis, where he found work as a mechanic. Sometime later he also took a second, part-time job at the Fauna Flora Roadhouse owned by the notorious gambler Mark Gumbert. Working for tips only, this job consisted of hand-cranking cars to start them for departing customers. The experience likely contributed to his early adoption of electric starters in aircraft.

Between **1909 and 1911**, during Eddie's stint at the roadhouse, two men approached the owner with a proposition: if Gumbert would finance an airplane project, one of the men would design and build an engine while the other would do the same for fuselage and wings—all that was needed was someone to fly it. Eddie volunteered—lack of actual motorized flying experience notwithstanding. When the aircraft was completed, the fledging test pilot attempted to take it aloft. The only altitude that could be gained came from the bumps and rocks on the field which caused the plane to hop. Reworking the craft allowed for some fairly longer hops—long enough that Eddie considered it 'flying' and dated his debut as a pilot from this point. Eventually, as the hopping and bouncing took a toll, the airframe began to disintegrate. Ultimately the aircraft was abandoned in an East St. Louis field. As payment for his piloting services, Eddie was allowed to keep the engine. Sometime after the Wright Model B flyer was introduced in 1910, Eddie decided to build a duplicate of it—again without the benefit of any plans—and used the engine from the abandoned plane. He could not get this one off the ground either.

In October Eddie's mother and siblings travelled to St. Louis to visit him and together they attended the aviation meet being held at Kinloch Field (now the Lambert-St. Louis International Airport). Katherine had developed a deeper attraction to aviation the previous December when she watched John Moisant preform in Memphis. Just two weeks before arriving in St. Louis, she had taken her first flight in a balloon at the International Balloon Race in Kansas City. Now she and Eddie were examining actual Wright Model B Flyers—not just magazine photos. Then Katherine took her very first ride in a motorized aircraft—one made there in St. Louis by the Benoist Aircraft Company, and she made the life changing decision to move to St. Louis and attend an aviation school. The actual flight training did not go well, and she would later finish her education in Chicago where she earned her pilot's license just nine months after that first balloon ride and subsequent Wright Flyer inspection. She returned to Kinloch Field in St. Louis in October **1912**, not as a spectator, but rather as a performer in the aviation meet. After the event was over, she stayed in St. Louis to practice her flying and to learn 'trick' flying. While she was there, she taught Eddie the assembly/disassembly procedures of the Wright Flyer for shipping and receiving by train. More importantly for Eddie—and contrary to the popular myth that his sisters tried to prevent him from learning to fly—Katherine gave Eddie his first flying lesson.

During **1913**, while Katherine was performing with her own Wright Model B Flyer on the county fair circuit, Eddie remained in St. Louis. He also bought a Model B that he carefully assembled after it was shipped to him in knocked-down form, in essence a Wright Brothers designed and built kit.

In the fall of **1914**, after sister Marjorie received her pilot's license, the three of them joined to perform their own aerial exhibitions. For some of the shows they were aligned with the local chapters of the Equal Suffrage League. The chapter would sponsor the Stinson exhibition, which would be followed by band concert, then speeches on equal suffrage by some of the movement's most noted leaders.

The trio would travel from city to city by rail. When the train arrived in a town, Katherine went about minding the business end of the show. As their mechanician, Eddie arranged to have the Wright Flyer unloaded from the accompanying boxcar and uncrated. After he assembled the aircraft, it would be taken through the streets to the fairgrounds, where he would prepare it for flight. Meanwhile Marjorie would go to the local Overland dealer to pick up her car, which had also been shipped by rail. The dealer took the stock vehicle and removed the fenders, windshield, lights, etc. removed for racing. The exhibition consisted of Katherine performing her usual aeronautical show, followed by a race around the track between Katherine in the Wright Flyer and Marjorie in the Overland. After the event was over, Eddie would transport the airplane back to the depot, disassemble it, repack it in its crate and load it back onto the boxcar. With the boxcar attached to the passenger train, the three siblings would settle in for the trip to the next performance.

The airplane versus automobile exhibition race had been around for a few years. All three Stinson siblings used a variation of it in their individual show over the years, which has led to a persistent myth being told of Eddie—that being he used to race Barney Oldfield. In reality none of the Stinsons ever raced Oldfield, although Katherine came close. She and Oldfield often appeared on

This photo is from Eddie Stinson's pilot's license as reproduced in the January 24, 1916 edition of Aerial Age Weekly.

The Steven P. Bogdan Collection

the same bill in their own separate acts because they had the same manager/promoter, William H. Pickens. It is true that Pickens arranged for Oldfield to pit his "Golden Submarine" race car against Katherine's Curtiss "Speed Scout" in an "Air-and-Earth" match at the Sheepshead Bay Speedway in Brooklyn, New York on August 18, 1917. She had beat the champion driver Dario Resta in a similar race in 1916. Leaving Albany, New York at an early hour in order to make it to Brooklyn in plenty of time for the race, a fuel line broke and sprayed gasoline in her face at 84 mph. She landed, made the necessary repairs, and resumed her trip, but arrived too late for the race. Most of the crowd had gone home by the time she landed.

For most of **1915** the three Stinson siblings went their separate ways, while staying in touch to plan for their upcoming shared venture, the Stinson School of Flying in San Antonio. Katherine and Marjorie already lived there, having contracted with the army to use their airshow downtime over the 1914-1915 winter to instruct army aviators at Fort Sam Houston. Eddie concentrated on improving his flying skills, and to this end applied to the Wright Flying School in Dayton, Ohio. His first instructor, Roderick M. Wright, remembered Eddie as being one of only three students to enter the school with any pre-existing knowledge of the aircraft and its operation. That Eddie knew how to fly before he entered the school was no surprise since at the time a pilot's license was not required by law. While it was important if you wished to be an instructor, many pilots never attended a school or got a license. Even Eddie's own brother Jack, who was flying Eddie's *Greyhound* in 1920, did not bother to get a license until 1927 when a new law made it a requirement for flying.

In 1915 tuition for the Wright school was around four-hundred dollars and Eddie was a bit short. To make up the shortfall, he agreed to perform chores such as cleaning, sweeping, and being a general gofer. The problem with the Wright school, however, was that it was overflowing with Canadian students trying to jumpstart their wartime flying careers. The school had just one aircraft at that point, and flying time was next to impossible to come by. Having squeezed as much instruction and flying time as he could—and anxious to get to San Antonio to help his sisters at the new Stinson school—Eddie left Dayton before earning his pilot's license. Instead, the Stinson School of Flying's head mechanician became part of the school's first class, graduating with his license in December, having qualified on a Wright Model B.

At the beginning of **1916**, Katherine was north of the border in Ottawa, Canada trying to set up a new Stinson School of flying. The crush of Canadians wanting flying lessons had not lessened and she was attempting to set up several schools. Eddie however, had temporarily left the Stinson School of Flying in San Antonio and was said to be south of the border in Mexico. According to friends who got together after Eddie died, he had taken his Wright Model B to Chihuahua to fly for the "Mexican Government."

He got the idea from Howard M. Rinehart, the head instructor of the Wright Flying School in Dayton. When Eddie attended there Rinehart had just returned from a stint flying a Wright Model HS for Pancho Villa. He had quit because he was not getting paid, and no number of promises, commissions, or any amount of bribery could entice him to return. Another former Wright student, Farnum T. Fish took his place. Fish was soon wounded while aerial scouting for Villa.

It was never said for whom he flew, but while in Mexico promises and promotions were given to him that were very similar to those give to Rinehart and Fish. Eddie was made the head of the army's air forces with the rank of general (an air force that consisted of only one pilot and only one plane—Eddie and his Wright Flyer). He was also made the minister of Aeronautics and put in charge of airports (any level field where he could land his plane). Whomever he worked for, he was back in the United States before Villa attacked Columbus, New Mexico in early March.

Even while Walter L. Brock was teaching Eddie the theory and application of airplane design and construction, Stinson was participating in aerial exhibitions. April 28 was San Antonio's annual Flower Day, wherein street battles of flower throwing traditionally took place. This year Eddie added an element of surprise as he flew over the crowd and dropped "flower bombs" on the combatants. In July he was in Houston helping establish the Houston Aviation School, later renamed the National School of Flying, in a field next to the Rice Institute (now Rice University). By August his Bristol type tractor was completed and within a month Eddie was appearing with it at the Boone County Fair in Omaha, Nebraska. In October he was in Arizona—first at the Northern Arizona Fair in Prescott, then at the Southern Arizona Fair in Tucson (Katherine had been the flying attraction at the Fair in Tucson the year before).

Throughout most of **1917** Eddie was instructing at various flying schools, and even took the time to establish one at Bartlesville, Oklahoma. At the end of April tragedy struck at the National School of Flying in Houston as one of Eddie's star pupils crashed during his first solo. It was the first fatality among the more than 400 students that Eddie was said to have taught. Stinson was an honorary pallbearer at the funeral. By July he was instructing at the Atlantic Coast Aeronautical Station (Curtiss Aviation School) in Newport News, Virginia. On August 3 he was testing a Curtiss two-ton, twin-motor, double pontoon combination land and water hydroaeroplane. Looping such a large aircraft was generally considered impossible. Eddie did the impossible twice in succession. Four days later he set a new looping-the-loop record while carrying a passenger, with 22 loops counted. Five days after that, he upped the record to 58.

Eddie eventually made his way back to San Antonio, where he too, went to work for the army as a civilian instructor. Much has been written about certain escapades Stinson supposedly performed in **1918** while at Kelly Field, but careful research has revealed that no less than three other people named Edward Stinson were stationed at the camp at various times while our subject was there. The only antics that can accurately be attributed to Edward Anderson Stinson, Jr. have to do with flying, such as his habit of repeatedly popping the bulbs of the obstruction lights on the top of flagpole and the water tank with his wingtip.

There were numerous flying demonstrations put on for visiting dignitaries, or for benefits such as for the Red Cross. Eddie would demonstrate basic army flying, including bombing maneuvers by leading nine ship bombing formations (for a time he was the instructor for advanced cross county flying). Later he would perform solo, described by on witness as "almost unbelievable, but he nose-dived, tail-spinned, looped, Immelmann-turned, flew upside-down, fell like a leaf and everything else in the category of aerial gyrations, and all with perfect ease." At the end of the show, he would haul Rodman Law—who was at Kelly Field to do parachute experiments—thousands of feet into the air so that Law could jump out and float back to earth.

Eddie tried to enlist as an officer numerous times. One of his students was a friend of the clerk who handled such requests. The student was told that each time the request was denied because of suspected tuberculosis. It does not make sense that the army would keep an instructor around who was suspected of having TB. What does make sense, however, is the army wanting to keep him where he was—this is, after all, the man who figured out how to recover from the deadly tailspin after falling four thousand feet. (He would go on to attribute a patch of grey hair to that incident.) Eddie then threw himself into spin after spin un-

Lieut. Edward A. Stinson, army aviator and brother of Katherine Stinson, since the most recent Mexican border troubles has been an instructor in aviation for army flyers. He is waiting for orders now to receive machine gun instruction, and as soon as he is proficient with this weapon he will get his chance in warfare.

This wire copy photo of Lieutenant Edward A. Stinson was sent to newspapers in late September 1918. However, most did not publish it until after the November 11 armistice. This example is from the November 14, 1918 edition of The Grand Rapids Tribune.

til he perfected the recovery technique. The technique that was then taught to every pilot, thus saving countless lives. However, his employment status was about to change dramatically.

It was late spring when Eddie decided to experiment with the broken bits of airplanes laying about in the scrapyard. That was when he built the ugly little "*Bug*" (see Chapter 18 The *Early Airplanes*). The army took notice and assigned him help to design and build a plane from the ground up. That plane, similar in look and feel to the Brock designed Bristol type, was completed in time to appear in another show. This exposition was in honor of a visit by the newly promoted Major General William Crozier, who was thrilled by the spectacle—and Eddie's performance in particular. Crozier was so enthralled that he insisted on be photographed posing with Eddie and his new airplane. That same photo made it into Kelly Field's official history book. Within two weeks Edward Stinson was commissioned as a second lieutenant in the United States Army. Thanks to the Major General, it seems that he did not have tuberculosis after all. To celebrate, he set a new record at 143 loops.

At last Eddie was getting to go "Over There" as he had wanted since the war began. First, however, he had to finish training his current class, and then take a crash course in being an officer. By early November all that he lacked was machine gun training—as soon as he mastered that he would ship out. Because he was semi-famous for being the brother of Katherine Stinson, a headshot photo of him in his uniform was provided to the wire services, along with copy written in such a way that it could be easily edited it make the story fit in available space. Many of the newspapers that ran the photo and blurb did so on November 13, 1918—two days after the armistice. Eddie never went overseas. Instead, he was given an Honorable Discharge in early **1919**.

Figuring to take advantage of the great number of returning veterans who may wish to take up flying, his immediate plan was to return to Newport News to establish his own flying school with five airplanes. The government was already surplusing thousands of now unneeded aircraft. In order to pay for the five airplanes he needed, Eddie requested twenty. The extra 15 were brokered to buyers in Central and South America for just enough money to cover all costs.

Now established in Newport News, he began to venture out with a partner to perform air shows and offer rides. Mid-February found him in Pittsburgh, where he met Estelle Claire Judy. Estelle and Eddie married on Tuesday, October 21, 1919. A few months after the wedding, Eddie adopted Raymond Judy, Estelle's son from a previous marriage.

By early April 1919 Eddie was advertising advanced instruction if you wanted to learn to fly, or if you just want to observe, he offered passenger trips for ten dollars from his base in Newport News. In addition to the passenger-carrying Curtiss two-seat aircraft, for strictly exhibition work Eddie had also purchased a single-seat Ace made the Aircraft Engineering Corporation of New York. Later that month, when the first of the returning troops marched under the newly constructed Arch of Triumph in Newport News, Eddie preceded the parade in his plane, dropping miniature flags along the line of march.

In May he was involved in the Second Annual Pan-American Aeronautical Convention in Atlantic City (see story on page 89). One act had him landing on the fifth fairway at the Atlantic City Country Club Tourney at Northfield during the medal round. June found him in Miami, testing the Sperry gyroscopic turn indicator that would be used the Navy's NC seaplanes during their upcoming trans-Atlantic flight. In July he took the youngest ever passenger to fly in a plane—eight month old Mitzi May Kuntz of York, Pennsylvania (and her father William)—on a cross-country flight from York to Cly.

By now Eddie had estab-

Stinson used Curtiss JN-4s in his Flying Circus and as training planes from 1919 through 1921. This Flying Circus example was photographed between venues, and carries an early example of a registration number, C-1379. The C stood for 'Commercial'.

lished a sophisticated air show routine with his troupe known as the Stinson Flyers. Upon landing in the town in which they would perform, the three flyers would pick up bundles of the local sponsoring newspaper and fly off to deliver them to towns that did not normally receive that publication. Sometimes their name would temporarily change for the event, such as when they were performing under the sponsorship of the *New Castle Herald* newspaper, they were known as the "Herald-Stinson Flyers." Naturally the large ads promoting the Stinson exhibition drew in larger crowds that would have normally attended. For his chief mechanic, Eddie brought along Theodore Lovington, who had been his chief mechanic at Kelly Field. Lovington had been one of the three men assigned to help Stinson carry out the physical construction of the *Humming Bird*.

In August the Stinson Flyers were sponsored entirely by the Akron, Ohio realtor J. L. Smith, who wanted them to perform during his huge land sale of his Wooster Avenue allotment. Instead of having the bold name STINSON painted on the top and bottom of their wings, the Curtiss machines now sported JLSWA (J. L. Smith Wooster Allotment) for the crowd to see. It was also in Akron that Eddie began picking up other sponsorships—one of the first being Quick-Start Gasolene made by the Akron Oil Refining Company.

For the time being, having abandoned the idea of maintaining a flight school for the far more lucrative business of aerial exhibitions, Eddie and the Stinson Flyers spent the rest of the year on a circuit that covered Tennessee, Kentucky, Ohio, Pennsylvania and beyond. Near the end of the year, it was announced that the Stinson family intended to manufacture airplanes in Dayton, Ohio.

After the *Greyhound* experiment Eddie flew at the Third Annual Pan-American Aeronautical Convention in Atlantic City, then continued his exhibition flying throughout **1920**, pausing only briefly for a time to work in Chattanooga as related in Chapter 19. In the fall he performed exhibitions in eight different states under the auspices of the T L X Ranch in Oklahoma, drumming up business for their resort, and so the Stinson outfit was known as the "T L X Flying Circus." After the season was over Eddie removed to Birmingham, Alabama and opened the Stinson Aero Service at the Dixie Flying Field, where he operated a flying school and established a Curtiss dealership.

The start of **1921** found Eddie training mechanic Jack Irwin to 'wing walk' through a loop. Two weeks later Eddie had two wing walkers holding on with their feet as he looped-the-loop fourteen times. He was aiming for twenty loops. In

Photo for dual passport awarded to Estelle and Eddie Stinson for the El Paso-Chihuahua-Mexico City airline venture in 1921

February Eddie took a break to go hunting near Greenville, Mississippi. Flying back to Birmingham in a Curtiss Oriole with a friend, he stopped in at Aberdeen to see his father, E. A. Stinson, Sr. The elder Stinson was revered in Aberdeen as "The Father of Aviation" because of his famous flying children. That reverence was later extended to the late Eddie Jr. when in 1945 the city bought an auxiliary army airfield and named it the Stinson Field Municipal Airport in honor of Eddie A. Stinson, Jr. Today air operations are no longer in service, and it is now known as the Stinson Industrial Park.

The Curtiss Oriole, which was capable of carrying two passengers in addition to the pilot, had become the airshow mainstay for Eddie, whose loop-the-loop record now stood at 187 consecutive loops. He also held the record for the longest flight while upside down. By now the Flying Circus no longer needed a single large entity to underwrite their shows. More frequently the businessmen and merchants of smaller towns were banding together to bring the famous flyers to their venue.

The summer of 1921 brought another Mexican adventure when Eddie attempted to establish an airline serving El Paso and Chihuahua, shortening the day-long rail journey down to a two-hour air excursion. Service could later be expanded to Mexico City. Using a large Italian Ansaldo A.300C six-seat biplane (aptly named the *Chihuahua*), Eddie intended to provide regular service.

However, after initial sponsoring from within the Mexican government, all official interest in the project dried up when Stinson indicated to a planeload of generals that he was not willing to bomb some rebel positions. As the governor of Chihuahua had facilitated the purchase of the plane, Eddie left it in Mexico, where it remained in government service until at least 1926.

Returning to the United States and moving his operation to New York, Eddie was soon scheduled to fly an exhibition in a smaller Ansaldo SVA.9 airplane at the annual American Legion convention in Kansas City in the fall. However, he arrived there flying a salmon-colored Junkers-Larsen JL-6 (a rebadged, Americanized version of the Junkers F13) in formation with two others. While at the convention Eddie racked up another first, as he was the pilot of the JL-6 when the first wedding aloft took place. Stinson had been introduced to both the Ansaldo and the JL-6 at the 1920 Pan-American Aeronautical Convention. Leaving both the Ansaldo and Curtiss behind, Stinson eventually purchased two surplus Junkers-Larsen JL-6s, and this became his airplane of choice for the next several years.

Even with the business of work, Eddie still found time to humor his dare-devil side. In late 1921, Lloyd Bertraud of New York approached him concerning an endurance flight. On December 30 Bertraud and Eddie set a flying record of 24 hours 50 minutes and 7 seconds flying the Junkers-Larsen JL-6 monoplane. A wire-copy had newspapers across the country reporting that the pilots were "a sorry looking pair" when they got out of their aircraft, noting their bloodshot eyes and that Bertraud's ears had been temporarily deafened from the constant sound of the engine.

In **1922**, the Stinson family moved to Detroit and operated a charter service from Packard Field. The charter business connected Eddie to Detroit businessman, William A. Mara, and Mara joined him in building the operation.

Early January saw Eddie and Lloyd Bertraud break the endurance record. The next month saw that particular airplane sold, and in May Stinson announced his charter service.

In June Eddie Rickenbacker hired Stinson and his other JL-6 to fly him to 64 cities—travelling some 15,000 miles by air in order to make a survey of the aeronautical conditions in relation to national defense. The name 'Rickenbacker' was painted in bold letters on the side of the fuselage, and below that was the famous 'Hat in the Ring' emblem that Rickenbacker during the Great War. Leaving Long Island on the seventh, headed for San Francisco. After a lightening strike fused engine parts together and knocked three mechanics unconscious while on the ground in Detroit, the trip was plagued with mechanical problems. A leaking water line forced them down at Ypsilanti, and a seized piston caused a delay for new parts at Dexter, Iowa. Taking off from Omaha, the engine suddenly quit when the aircraft was only a few feet off the ground. At that point Rickenbacker decided to continue on to San Francisco by train while the airplane's BMW engine was repaired. The two Eddies remained close friends and Rickenbacker served as a pallbearer at Stinson's funeral.

The engine kept giving trouble throughout the summer. While on his way to South Bend to do aerial mapping, the engine quit again, forcing him to make a tricky landing in Hammond, Indiana. A reporter interviewed him and noted that Eddie was one of the very few pre-war pilots still active—even his sisters had quit flying.

In late July **1923**, averaging 110 mph, Eddie inaugurated the first non-stop night flight from Chicago to New York, taking 8 1/2 hours compared to an 18 hour train trip. The feat made headlines across the country and helped lead to the acceptance of night flying for the Airmail Service.

August found him flying the Pathe movie film of President Harding's funeral train from Chicago to New York, only to have heavy fog force him to land in Pennsylvania and pass the film off to an automobile. Later that month Stinson's 3-plane Flying Circus (including his yellow Junkers-Larsen) was inaugurating the new Coney Island Airdrome in Cincinnati. This was perhaps the last performance of the Stinson Flying Circus. To date

Edward A. Stinson in 1921

the author has found no other appearance on record.

In late September he was in a cross-country race between two film companies—one starting from Seattle and one from San Francisco—to rush the first movies of the great Japanese earthquake to New York. Eddie, flying for the Seattle relay, took the handoff at Great Falls, Montana at 5:30 in the afternoon on Monday the 24th. Wednesday afternoon he touched down at Curtiss Field in Mineola, New York.

He was due to participate in the Pulitzer Trophy race in October, but the airplane he had been testing—the Dare Variable Camber monoplane—was disqualified due to the manufacturer not supplying required technical data. Some of the pilots in the Selfridge Field event didn't think that the odd airplane could even fly, let alone survive the rigors of the race. Criticism ended after Eddie gave a demonstration flight.

After the race Stinson was scheduled to fly visiting former British Prime Minister Lloyd George from Cleveland to Toledo, then on to Detroit. However, multiple changes cut the airplane portion out of the official itinerary.

Instead, he flew the Detroit Board of Commerce to their annual national meeting in Cincinnati. Among the passengers was their President, Harold H. Emmons, who also happened to be the President of the Detroit Aviation Society. During the Great War the Liberty engine was developed under his direction. Other Board of Commerce members aboard were also members of the , while attendee William A. Mara served as Secretary of the Detroit Air Board, an organization dedicated to making Detroit the aviation center of the nation. Both the Detroit Air Board, created in June, and the Detroit Aviation Society would go on to sponsor the National Air Tours.

1924 was a quiet year for Eddie once he had retired from exhibition flying. Now he was fully engaged with his charter flights. It was said

Having acquired two former Air Mail Junkers-Larsen JL-6s, Eddie used one for his endurance record flight, then sold it off. The second one he kept longer than any other aircraft he ever owned—from late 1921 to early 1926—using it for his Flying Circus, his charter service, and as his personal aircraft. Here that airplane appears in three different liveries.

Top - *As purchased in 1921 from the Post Office*

Middle - *As it appeared during the 1922 Rickenbacker charter, with Rickenbacker's name and 'Hat In The Ring' logo on the fuselage, and "New York To San Francisco' on the nose*

Bottom - *While sporting the 'Stinson Flyers' logo and Eddie's initials on the fuselage, this 1923 photo actually commemorated the first charter flight between Detroit and Pittsburgh. 'Stella' and Eddie Stinson are on the right.*

that his plane was "the largest in the country engaged in passenger service."

One such charter in early August was for repeat customers, sexagenarians Mr. and Mrs. Robert Butler, who had flown with Eddie the previous year. On both occasions they had been visiting their sons in Detroit and hired Stinson to fly them home to McKeesport, Pennsylvania. This type of service was still such a novelty that a number of Pennsylvania newspapers carried the story—with a few of those noting that Eddie was "the husband of Estelle Judy-Stinson, a former McKeesport girl."

In late August he visited his mother in Dayton, where a reporter found him looking over airplane engines offered for sale at the Fairfield airport.

As an example of how profitable his charter service was, in September he flew seven delegates of the Redford Exchange Club from Redford, Michigan to the National Convention in Nashville with a stop in Cincinnati for fuel and lunch. It took seven hours and 40 minutes, with over an hour spent on the ground for lunch and refueling in Cincinnati. The non-stop return trip of 600 miles took six hours. Each conventioneer paid $1,000 for round trip, earning Eddie over three times the average yearly income—for just two days work.

In November he entertained the Lansing Lions Club with free airplane rides.

In early February **1925** Eddie began to talk about an attempt to take back the endurance record held by the French. April found Eddie flying to Aberdeen, Mississippi where father was was seriously ill with pneumonia. His wife Estelle and brother Jack accompanied him on the trip.

In mid-May Horace E. Dodge, Jr. of the Dodge Brothers Motor Car Company, hired Stinson to fly him to New York where he was divesting the family business. Dodge later became a Stinson aircraft enthusiast, buying several Stinson-Detroiters over the years.

On May 23 he was flying a Curtiss plane over Detroit while a representative of that city's largest clothiers dropped fifty 'Georges Meyer nonbreakable Swiss Straw Hats' over the city, and then the ballpark after the conclusion of the game there.

In July he flew his LJ-6—now sponsored by Cyclogas—to an aviation meet in Cheboygan. Due to mechanical problems, he flew another plane for his stunt show.

In mid-September Eddie was occupied with his duties as the official Pathfinder for the Edsel B. Ford Reliability Tour, while the end of the month saw frustrating delays for his endurance record attempt.

November saw the first announcement of 25-person syndicate forming to back Eddie Stinson's plan to build a four-place biplane as a demonstrator to gauge public interest. From then to early 1926, they raised $25,000 to fund a new aircraft manufacturing enterprise.

The Stinson-Detroiter debuted on Sunday, February 21, **1926** at Packard Field at 2:00 p.m., and was an instant hit.

The Stinson Aircraft Corporation was officially formed on May 4, 1926. It was the dawn of the Golden Age of Stinson.

As his company grew, Eddie remained deeply invested. He was one of its two salesmen in **1927**, selling the SM-1. Eddie also participated in air tours to gain publicity for Stinson aircraft. He placed third in the **1926** Ford Reliability Air Tour, first in **1927**, and fifth in **1928**. When Cord bought the Stinson Aircraft Corporation in November **1929**, Eddie became the company president. In this capacity, he worked hard to strengthen the Stinson dealer organization, often giving flight demonstrations at dealerships. In **1931**, Eddie proposed the Model R to the Stinson Board of Directors and was influential in establishing a marketing strategy of planned obsolescence. This strategy increased production and sales, and the company followed it for many years.

January 25, **1932** was a sad day for the Stinson Aircraft Corporation. That day, Eddie flew the new Model R to Chicago's municipal airport to give demonstrations flights with a local Stinson dealer. Flying out of Clark Field at dusk, he neglected to refuel his aircraft, confident he had sufficient fuel for one more demonstration flight. Flying over the Lake Michigan shoreline, the engine suddenly stopped from fuel starvation. Rather than landing on the beach, Eddie attempted to land on a golf course. He successfully landed the Model R on the Jackson Park golf course, but soon after touchdown, the right wing struck a sturdy flagpole. A large, male passenger riding in the back seat had neglected to secure his seat belt, and when the aircraft struck the flagpole, he flew forward into his pilot, crashing Eddie's chest into the control column. Sustaining some broken ribs and other injuries, Eddie was pulled from the aircraft by a caddie and driven to Illinois Central Hospital, where he collapsed in the admitting room. He never regained consciousness and passed away early the next morning. By the time of death at age 38, Edward Stinson had acquired more than 16,000 hours of flying time.

Edward Anderson Stinson, Jr.
July 11, 1893–January 26, 1932.

Chapter 20
Estelle: The Aviator's Wife

Estelle Stinson presents the Stinson Memorial Cup to Neil R. McCray, who won it by taking first place in the Edward A. Stinson Memorial Cup race at the National Air Races on September 4. 1932. McCray flew a Lycoming powered Stinson Junior, as did the 2nd and 3rd place winners.

Movie actress, beauty contest winner, supervisor of a major telephone switchboard complex, aircraft saleswoman, chairman of a factory war bond drive, notary public, wife and mother—Estelle Lorene Rose Claire Judy was a remarkable woman.

Stella, as she was affectionately known throughout her life, was born February 2, 1889 in McKeesport, Pennsylvania. She graduated from eighth grade in 1902 at the age of 13. She married newspaper editor Robert Green Ingersoll Geeting on September 10, 1907. Her son, Raymond, was born in 1911. Robert and Stella divorced on July 9, 1912, and she went to work as a clerk in the F. O. Reed Shoe Store on Main Street in McKeesport. Within three years she had changed jobs and worked her way up to be the chief operator for the Bell Telephone Company in McKeesport. On the first day of September 1915, the October issue of *Photoplay Magazine* hit the newsstands. In it was a six-page spread detailing the rules and requirements of the "great *Photoplay*

Magazine—World Film 'Beauty *and* Brains' contest," which had been teased in the previous issue.

"Beauty *and* Brains" Contest

Any girl or woman who has had no professional stage or picture experience is eligible to enter. Age, height, weight or marriage is no bar."

To enter the contest send two good photographs to The Judges, "Beauty *and* Brains" Contest, *Photoplay Magazine*, 350 North Clark Street, Chicago. Send a profile and full face study.

Contestants must also write a letter of not more than 150 words to the judges telling: "Why I would like to be a photoplay actress.'" The letter must accompany the pictures.

Merely to aid the Judges in determining their selection, contestants should state their age, weight, height, complexion and color of hair and eyes.

The eleven fortunate contestants will be taken to New York in first-class trains and lodged in one of Manhattan's most celebrated hotels without any expense to them. They will be properly chaperoned.

Within two weeks after their arrival in New York they will be given photographic and dramatic trials at the Fort Lee, New Jersey, studios of the World Film Corporation.

Contestants who pass final photographic and acting requirements under the tutelage of the world's greatest directors, will be given contracts for a period of not less than one year at a regular salary.

Those who do not pass the final trials will be returned to their homes in a first-class manner and without any expense to them whatsoever.

The United States was divided into five divisions, with Canada serving as a sixth. Two contestants from each division—plus one from Canada—would make up the eleven winners.

Co-sponsored by the World Film Corporation, the contest ended at midnight on February 29 and the winners named in July 1916 issue of *Photoplay Magazine*. Out of over 10,000 entries (ranging from 3 years old to 65), the six judges—headed by Lillian Russell—picked Estelle Claire Judy as one of the two Eastern Central Division winners. She was described as having dark brown hair, gray-brown eyes, perfect teeth and a medium slender figure. Her age was listed as 23, but she was actually 27 years old.

Stella was no stranger when it came to beauty contests, as she had recently entered and won a competition arranged by a newspaper in her town, and before that her photograph took first prize for a McKeesport exhibitor at a national convention of photographers. As for the "no professional stage or picture experience" requirement, the contest judges broke their own rule when they acknowledged that Stella had "played the leading female part in a local photo-drama some time ago, and played it well." By September 14 the winners were in the film studios in Ft. Lee, New Jersey, beginning their screen tests. Stella promised to "certainly do all that is possible to make good when the time comes for the try-out."

Out of the eleven chosen from the 10,000, only five signed contracts. One of those never made

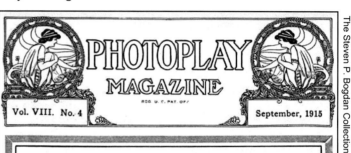

The September 1915 issue of Photoplay Magazine *reached newsstands on August 1, teasing the upcoming "Beauty* and *Brains" contest, which ran from September 1, 1915 to February 29, 1916.*

a movie, and three of the others had modest to moderate success in the movies. The final contract winner became quite accomplished in vaudeville and garnered 25 film credits to her name.

Of the remaining six young women, one was offered a contract but declined and accepted the expense money and train ticket home. One of those who had not been offered a contract travelled home as well, but went on to have some success on the stage.

Of the remaining four, there was some confusion and disgruntlement concerning the lack of offers for movie contracts after the screen tests, and there was talk of filing suit against the World Film Corporation. Ultimately, they rejected the expense money and train tickets due them and decided to try and make it on their own. *Photoplay Magazine* said it was characteristic of their "pluck and grit." That pluck and grit got them all into the movies. Two of them had some limited success, while the third went on to a stellar career with more movie shorts to her credit (under two different names) than all of the contracted actresses put together. Stella however, elected to go different direction.

She hired Robert Gordon as her manager, and after two years of acting lessons, financial considerations, and some work with the World Film Corporation, Stella believed she was ready. She signed a contract with Filmgraphs, Inc. and was immediately cast as the leading actress in a five-reel, full-length, black and white, silent movie filmed in Pittsburgh, Pennsylvania. On-set filming and editing ran from January to June 1919. With the success of her first project behind her, Stella was positioned to take the same path as had eight other alumni of the "Beauty and Brains" Contest. However, something happened in the second month of filming that would cause her to turn her back on the movie industry forever. She had met Eddie Stinson.

At this time, Lieutenant Edward Stinson and Lieutenant Maurice Murphy were barnstorming through the East Coast of the United States spending several days at every major city. Eddie

Estelle Claire Judy's official portrait in the July 1916 issue of Photoplay Magazine *announcing the winners of the "Beauty and Brains" contest*

would obtain permission to fly from a grassy field or cow pasture that was very close to the city. He would set up his signs, which he carried in the aircraft, announcing rides. His rate was whatever the traffic would bear. If his customer looked affluent, it would be more expensive, and less if not. In larger cities he often teamed up with the local newspaper, and had his expenses underwritten by that entity. Eddie was headquartered out of Columbus, Ohio where he rented a small apartment.

He flew into Pittsburgh one day, set up his

sign and was ready for business the second week of February 1919. Business was starting off slow, and in midmorning a very attractive young woman, Stella, approached Eddie concerning her first flight in an aircraft. The air was calm, and the flight was uneventful. Stella thanked Eddie for the opportunity to fly with him and departed the field.

Early Tuesday morning, Stella arrived at the airfield and approached Eddie asking for a second flight in his aircraft. After the flight, Stella and Eddie talked for some time until the next paying customer arrived.

If the weather was fine, Eddie would sleep under the wing of his aircraft, and would ask whoever might have been at the airfield for a ride to town for an evening meal. By Wednesday, the news had spread that someone was taking passengers in an aircraft, and business was booming. Paying passengers were standing in line for the opportunity to fly with Stinson for their first flight. Stella arrived at the field at noon with a nice sandwich and a bottle of water, which Eddie ate between flights. From a nearby fence Stella watched him fly. Thursday was slow, and over lunch Stella suggested that tomorrow being Valentine's Day, perhaps they could double date with two of their friends. Eddie agreed this would be an excellent idea and suggested they pick him up at dusk on Friday. Stella delivered lunch on Friday and in between flights, they had an opportunity to chat. The foursome had a good time that night. Eddie wrote down Stella's home address and promised to write. He departed for Dayton, Ohio early Saturday morning.

Eddie's letter writing consisted of postcards from the various cities where he was barnstorming. He was able to manage his schedule and visit Pittsburgh for a day or so in March, April, May, and June. On Friday, July 18 Eddie and his partner Murphy were in Pittsburgh giving a two-day Aeronautic Exhibition under the auspices the *Pittsburgh Post* and *Sun*. With The name *'Post'* painted on the bottom of the lower starboard wing, and *'Sun'* on the port side, the flyers put on a different show than usual, as they picked different sections of Allegheny County from each other in which to perform. The idea was to fly over the different boroughs and put on small-scale airshows for the town before moving on to the next. The route Eddie took led up the Monongahela Valley to McKeesport, where he certainly put on a special show for Stella.

The next day Stinson and Murphy performed together until engine trouble on Murphy's plane had them both land. When Eddie took off again, he was carrying Stella with him. She stayed aboard for an afternoon of stunt flying over various locations, all the while being filmed from the ground. On Friday, July 25 Stinson and Murphy arrived in Canton, Ohio for a six-day exhibition. Stella rode down with Eddie from Pittsburgh in order to take lessons from him. She had just been offered a new movie about smuggling by aircraft and wanted to do her own flying on film. According to the July 28, 1919 edition of *The Canton Daily News*, the day before—with Eddie in the back seat and she at the controls—Stella made her first flight with the aircraft solely at her command. Shortly after, Eddie proposed to Stella and they became engaged. Years later she told a reporter from the *Detroit Mirror* exactly how it happened:

> It was a forced landing that hastened her marriage to Stinson nearly thirteen years ago, [Estelle] revealed. She was living then at McKeesport, Pa., 200 miles from where he was working, and he hopped off in an old Curtis-Jenny one day to call on her. "On the way he ran out of gas and was forced to land in a field fifteen miles from our home," she said. "He stopped a bread truck on the road and asked the driver to take him into town. "When the driver demurred because of deliveries, Eddie bought the bread and dumped it into the road. After that experience he decided to marry me—I had cost him enough so he thought I should belong to him."

The wedding was set for October 1, 1919, but Estelle had some contractual obligations to fulfill first. On Tuesday, August 5, 1919, her movie—temporarily titled *"Shooting a Romantic"*—was shown as a sneak preview in Cleveland at the Strand Theatre. Starting on Tuesday, September 23, an official two-day premiere was held at the Strand Theatre in Sharpsburg, Pennsylvania where the movie was filmed. Estelle was scheduled to appear there in person on July 24.

Miss Estelle Claire Judy and Lieutenant Edward Stinson were indeed married on October 1, 1919, in a small private ceremony. Only close family and acquaintances were invited. Her wedding outfit was described as a peacock blue two-piece suit that featured a fully lined jacket with the telling 3/4 length, full sleeves. The skirt, lightly tucked on the waistband, fell fairly straight down to ankle-length. Both the jacket and the skirt were embellished with ivory trim. Her jacket covered a white blouse with gathered puff sleeves. A black silhouette brooch with a silver tone setting attached it to the blouse.

At the time of their wedding, Edward was 26 and Stella was 30. She seemed to have passed on the movie offer because Eddie rented a small house in Dayton and after a short honeymoon, Stella and her son, Raymond, accompanied Eddie to their new home. A few months following the wedding, Eddie adopted Raymond.

Although he was an excellent pilot, Eddie had a history of wasting money, and there are written accounts that he had a binge drinking problem. It came as a surprise to Stella that Eddie's banking system consisted of a leather pouch containing his total cash assets, which was stowed in the back of his aircraft. After their marriage, Stella placed a steady hand on Eddie's shoulder. She managed the household expenses and assisted in structuring the new aircraft company's cash flow. Eddie loved Stella, yet his binge drinking problem continued several years into their marriage.

Eddie's dream was to manufacture aircraft, and in 1919 he formed the Stinson Airplane Company. 18 months later, he designed and manufactured a small, two-place biplane named the *Greyhound*. Stella worked every day in the construction hangar sewing together fabric, rib stitching and applying dope to shrink the fabric.

In the summer of 1922, Stinson moved his family and his aircraft to Detroit and established the headquarters for his charter business at Packard Field. Estelle was the business manager for the charter business and was able to maintain a comfortable cash reserve. Eddie's binge drinking problem persisted and he gained a reputation as that "happy drinking pilot." With tough love though, Stella was able to have a positive effect on him and point him in the right direction. Through the next four years, 1922-1925, Eddie ran a very successful aircraft charter business.

In 1924, Eddie decided to design another aircraft that would be an improvement over current production aircraft. The basic design was laid out on brown paper on the Stinson's kitchen table. Stella was very supportive. She assisted in weight and balance calculations, maintained a supply of sharp pencils, and carefully rolled each drawing after its completion. Stella also had the opportunity to meet Bill Mara that year, and this was the start of a lifelong friendship.

The Stinsons moved from Detroit to Northville, Michigan in 1926 to be closer to the new factory. The beginning of the Stinson company was an exciting time for their family. Stella was quite proud of what her husband had accomplished. Through the next few years, the Stinson Aircraft Company grew steadily, and Estelle continued her help and support.

When the Stinson Aircraft Company was organized, Bill Mara and Eddie Stinson were given a considerable block of stock for their contribution in forming the company. After the stock market crashed on October 29, 1929, Eddie sold 100% of his holdings for cash. Before finishing the sale, E.L. Cord (mentioned in earlier chapters) suggested that because of their contribution to the company and their minimal salaries, an extensive block of stock would be issued to Eddie and Bill Mara. Cord consulted Stella soon afterwards, suggesting she supervise the small fortune they had just received since Eddie had a poor reputation for handling his personal finances. Eddie was accustomed to Stella handling their finances and in their personal investments, she was always prudent. After considering several options, she decided that

1928 publicity photo of Mrs. Estelle Claire Stinson

an investment in a family home was one of the safest ways to go. She purchased a home that was listed in the U.S. Census dated March 12, 1930 with a value of $54,000. Stella bought new furniture, and she and Eddie purchased a new car. The Stinsons also hired two servants. The remainder of the funds were invested in secure financial instruments and not in the stock market.

After the factory was moved to Wayne, Cord had some concern about the business practices of the company. He hired an accounting firm and recruited Stella to step in as office manager. In April 1929 at the age of 40, Estelle Stinson became a paid employee of the Stinson Aircraft Corporation. Stella had an understanding of aircraft operations and a pleasant personality, making her an excellent customer-relations person. With Cord's approval, she reorganized the company's office procedures.

In 1931 Stella and Eddie's son, Raymond, eloped at 19. After returning to Wayne with his new wife, the former Ann Nichols, Raymond went to work for the Stinson company. They lived with Eddie and Stella.

Occasionally, Stella would fly with Eddie when demonstrating and selling new aircraft. She would marvel at his transformation in the years she had known him. A devil-may-care barnstorming pilot was now the president of a company named after him, and instead of his pilot apparel, he now wore an expensive three-piece suit and spats. Stella was proud of her husband and her contributions to

For those who have never had the opportunity to view a period Stinson Bill of Sale, this one for a 1946 Stinson 108-1, signed by Estelle Stinson acting as Notary Public, should be quite informative.

his success.

Tragedy struck the Stinson home, however, on January 25, 1932. Eddie was killed in an aircraft accident flying the new Model R. A few days after the funeral, Cord made a call on Stella. He was concerned about her finances and asked about the money from the sale of their Stinson company stock. Stella reported how she had handled their finances, and that the remainder of the funds were invested in certificates of deposit and other secure investments. Cord assured Stella that her job was safe at the company and told her he would direct the treasurer to draw a check for Eddie's 1932 salary.

Feeling something should be done to recognize Eddie Stinson's contribution to aviation, Mara organized an event. The 1932 National Air Races were held in Cleveland, Ohio from August 27 through September 5. There were 21 closed course races in the event, and the Stinson Memorial Cup was one of them. Aircraft participating in this race were limited to SM-1 through SM-8s powered by engines not exceeding 230-hp. Eight aircraft registered, and the race was conducted in two events with four aircraft participating in each race. Neil R. McCray of Fairview, Pennsylvania, won first place flying a SM-8B.

Mara accompanied Stella, flying a Model S fresh off the assembly line. She was treated like royalty and had an opportunity to meet many of the pilots. Mary Haizlip, Gladys O'Donnell, Roscoe Turner, Bennie Howard, Jimmy Doolittle, and Amelia Earhart were just a few of the many famous aviators Stella had an opportunity to associate with there. Granted VIP seating, Stella witnessed several very important races. In the Men's Shell 3 km Speed Dash, Jimmy Doolittle became the first person to push an aircraft in level flight past 300 mph. Doolittle also won the Thompson Trophy race flying a 800-hp GB R-1 with a speed of 252.6 mph. Mary Haizlip won the Women's 3 km Speed Dash, and Gladys O'Donnell won the Woman's Aerial Trophy race flying a Howard "Mike" with the winning speed of 185.5 mph.

In 1933 Robert W. Ayer came to Stinson from the Grangeville Brothers Aircraft Company, and Stinson began building the tri-motor Model A. The sales strategy for the Model A was to present it to airlines at their corporate headquarters as an operational airliner. Mara became the lead salesman and Jack Kelly, Jr. worked as pilot, transport engineer, and technical representative. Mara suggested Estelle Stinson be selected for the sales team as well, pointing out that she was very attractive, very knowledgeable, and had met many of the airline executives in previous tri-motor presentations. Mara made his point well and Estelle was chosen for the sales team, and they immediately began making presentations to the airlines.

Their first presentation was to American Airlines. American Airlines liked the aircraft and signed a contract for 15 Model A airliners. Mara later reported they could not have closed the sale without Estelle's help. This was an exciting time for her. It reminded her of 1926-27 when Eddie and Mara were selling SB-1 aircraft to the airlines. She wondered what life would be like if Eddie was still president of Stinson.

Stella continued to work for the Stinson Aircraft Corporation in the same capacity from 1932 until the fall of 1934. Aviation Manufacturing Corporation acquired the Stinson Aircraft Corporation from Cord in August of that year, and Victor Emmanuel became a director and visited the factory in September. Victor was very impressed with Estelle and suggested she be given considerably more responsibility in dealing with accounts receivable from the Stinson dealerships and payments from the dealerships for aircraft and parts. With this new responsibility, came a corresponding increase in salary.

Aviation Manufacturing Corporation gave the Stinson Aircraft Company a great deal of autonomy, and Stinson management saw the opportunity for sales outside of the traditional civilian dealer organization. All branches of the U.S. military, foreign embassies, major corporations and airlines maintained offices in Washington D.C., and it seemed logical that the company should have an agent centered in the nation's capital. Based on her performance on the Model A sales team, Mara suggested Stella would be a natural. Aviation Manufacturing Corporation's management team agreed and approved the appointment of Stella as a Washington D.C. sales representative. She was given a desk and a telephone line in their Washington D.C. office.

Stella moved to Washington D.C. in the summer of 1935 and continued working there until November 1939. Her primary responsibility was to research and develop sales opportunities. Once these were developed and an appointment set up, Mara would fly in, and they would make the sales presentation. Although the total extent of her activities is unknown, the following is a list of sales presentations made through the Washington D.C. office. Three Reliant aircraft were sold to a Brazilian airline in 1935. One SR-5A was sold to the U.S. Navy and one to the U.S. Coast Guard. Nine Model O aircraft were sold in 1935 to foreign governments from 1934 production, and sales presentations were given to the Argentine Navy, Royal Australian Air Force and Uruguay Air Force.

In November 1939, Vultee Aircraft Division of Aviation Corporation was recognized as an independent company, and Richard Millar, general manager of Vultee, assumed management responsibilities for the Stinson division. Estelle was immediately ordered to return to the Wayne factory. Before Millar left San Diego, Victor Emmanuel briefed him concerning the excellent contribution to the Stinson Company that Estelle had made since it was founded and advised that she continue as receptionist and office manager. Millar visited the Stinson factory in December and took the opportunity to meet with her. He explained to her that she had friends in very high places and asked if she would continue her present responsibilities, which she did. In the June 1940 census, Estella was recorded as a receptionist with her 1939 salary listed as $840—several hundred dollars above the average for a woman in her position. Considering inflation and the dramatic rise in the cost of living, her annual salary had the equivalent spending power of over $58,000 in 2022.

When Millar arrived in Wayne in December, he announced that the Stinson Division would move to Nashville, Tennessee. The employees were informed that the move would be permanent, and the Michigan plant would be sold. Because this was to be a permanent relocation, the Stinson employees put their houses on the market and were given paid leave to find and purchase new ones in Nashville. Once they had found permanent residences, the company provided moving vans to transport their possessions there. Stella sold her house and purchased a more modest one in Nashville. Raymond and Ann were living in the family home in Michigan and moved with Stella to Nashville in April 1940.

The move to Nashville did not go as expected. After producing 138 aircraft, the factory was ordered to be moved back to Wayne. A few employees were offered positions in Nashville, but the majority were offered employment at the same pay grade if they moved back to Michigan. Stella, Raymond, and Ann saw little opportunity in Nashville and elected to move back to Wayne. In 1940, there was a seller's market in Michigan and a buyer's market in Tennessee. In moving back, Stella took a financial loss. Factory management was unable to find sufficient moving vans and many employees' furniture were moved in open trucks covered by loose tarpaulins. The Stinsons returned to Wayne in September, and their furniture was damaged by rain and rough handling.

As a contribution to the war effort, Stella organized and chaired the factory war bond drive. 100% of Stinson employees subscribed to the payroll deduction plan for the purchase of war bonds. On May 6, 1942, representing the Stinson factory personnel, Estelle accepted the U.S. Treasury Department's Minuteman flag in Washington D.C. to honor their support.

Estelle also named the Stinson L-5, a new aircraft produced in 1942, the "Sentinel."

Wichita Evening Eagle
Wichita , Kansas
Friday, November 13, 1942

STINSON BUILDS "FLYING JEEP"

WAYNE, MICH., Nov. 13.—(UP)—The Stinson division of Vultee Aircraft Inc. yesterday unveiled two new airplanes—a "flying jeep" for the United States army and a navigation trainer for British naval pilots.

The planes, both of which are in production, were christened at an employees' rally by Mrs. Eddie Stinson, widow of the famous flyer who was one of the founders of the Stinson plant, and Mrs. Richard M. Smeeton, wife of the assistant naval attaché for air at the British embassy, Washington, D. C.

Carries Two

The L-5 "Sentinel" or "flying jeep" is a small highly maneuverable plane designed to be the "eyes upstairs" of the artillery, tank corps, cavalry and infantry. The L-5, carrying a pilot and observer, can land with ease on a cow pasture or a highway. In many operations it replaces the "sausage" observation balloons used in the last war.

The "flying jeep's" fuselage is made of welded steel tubing. Its wings and tail surfaces are wood. Overall weight is 2,100 pounds.

The other plane, the navigation trainer AT-19, is essentially the peacetime Stinson "Reliant" used extensively by business executives and sportsmen. Extent of the design changes is a military secret. The new "Reliant" has seating capacity for four persons

William Mara, director of private sales and service for Consolidated Vultee, resigned effective September 30, 1944. The company that Eddie Stinson and Bill Mara organized in 1927 did not exist in 1944, and both Bill and Stella were disgusted with the dictatorial attitude of the San Diego general office. Ending 18 years of service with the Stinson division, Mara became an officer of the Bendix Corporation. Mara discussed Stella with senior Bendix management, and they authorized him to offer her a position in the Bendix Aviation corporate office in Chicago. The offer included an increase in pay, and moving expenses, if she would come to work for Bendix. After much consideration, Stella decided to continue working for Stinson. Her house was paid for, she had numerous friends both in and outside of the factory staff and wasn't ready to start over in a new company.

Stinson was the last unit of Consolidated Vultee to operate as a freestanding division. When the San Diego general office decided to strip Stinson of all management decisions in August 1945, it sent shockwaves through the staff and management. The engineering and research department would be moved to San Diego, leaving only sufficient staff to complete the certification of the new 108. Once again production was moved to Nashville, and employment at the Wayne plant was reduced from 900 to 200 employees. Only key management and production personnel were transferred to Nashville. At this time, eight key Stinson employees, including Albert Schramm, left Stinson for employment with Bendix Aircraft Corporation. Stella was again invited to work for Bendix and again she declined. Stella felt fortunate she still had employment and decided to continue on and see how the future unfolded. This proved to be a wise decision as only ten aircraft were produced in Nashville before production was moved back to Wayne.

At this time, Stella's responsibilities were reduced to being a secretary. She was asked to obtain a notary license, and her primary responsibilities were to notarize aircraft bills of sale and related documents. At one time, the author owned a 108-1 Stinson, and Stella Stinson signed the bill of sale on October 31, 1946. She had a beautiful signature with a distinctive flair.

Stella notarized signatures on the bills of sale of these aircraft in preparation for delivery to Stinson dealers:

Serial number 10, NC87608 on 01-24-46
Serial number 1516, NC2643 on 01-26-47

When the announcement was made that the Stinson production line would move to San Diego, those employees who had continued in Wayne until the plant was closed were offered employment in San Diego. Consolidated Vultee offered them a job at same pay grade but did not provide moving expenses. Records do not indicate that Stella accepted the move to San Diego, but she holds a record for the longest tenure with Stinson, totaling over 19 years. She eventually relocated to Los Angeles, and passed away there in 1981 at age 92. Her remains were cremated and interred next to her beloved Eddie

Estelle Claire Stinson: February 2, 1889-1981

Baptized Estelle Lorene Rose Claire Judy, she was born February 2, 1889 in McKeesport, Pennsylvania. Little is known of Stella's early life. She attended her eighth-grade graduation in June 1902 at the age of 13. Estelle was united in marriage with Robert Green Ingersoll Getting on September 10, 1907. To this marriage one son was born, Raymond Getting, on June 2, 1911. After her divorce in 1912, while maintaining custody of Raymond, she worked at the F. O. Reed Shoe Store in McKeesport, then moved to the Bell Telephone Company as a switchboard operator, where by 1915 she was the chief operator. On October 1, 1919, she married Edward Anderson Stinson Jr. who adopted Raymond soon after the wedding. Estelle helped her husband realize his dream of manufacturing aircraft. In 1929 Estelle started her work at the Stinson Aircraft Corporation. During her 19 years with the company, she worked as office manager, member of the Model A sales team, sales representative in Washington D.C., receptionist, and Notary Public. She was even known to pitch in at the mail room when help was needed. She holds the longest tenure at the Stinson company. Estelle passed away in Los Angeles in 1981 at age 92. She was preceded by her husband, Edward Stinson, who passed away in 1932, and followed by her son Raymond in 1984.

Chapter 21
The 1928 Ford Reliability Tour

Eddie Stinson's SM-1DA, NC5900 (c/n M300-1DA) at Mahoney Field (old Ryan Field) in San Diego, where the Tour overnighted July 11-12, 1928. NC5900 was owned by the Tulsa Junior Chamber of Commerce and sponsored by them and the Barnsdall Oil Corporation, who was promoting a new airplane engine oil. John Day of the Barnsdall Oil and Lloyd Stone of the Chamber of Commerce flew with Eddie on the Tour as two of his four passengers.

The National Air Tour for the Edsel B. Ford Reliability Trophy" was sponsored by the Ford Motor Company to convince the public that air travel was safe. Ford sponsored tours from 1925 to 1931. They were designed to generate public interest and promote aviation as something more than a military and county fair show activity. In this account we will be following five aircraft in the 1928 tour, three Stinson and two Monocoupes, as they travel 6,300 miles across the Western United States.

Planning for the 1928 Reliability Tour began months in advance. The Stinson line of aircraft had gained a reputation of performing well in competition. Flying a SB-1, Eddie Stinson placed third in the 1926 tour, and flying a SM-1, finished first in the 1927 tour. The success of Stinson aircraft in previous tours prompted two flyers, Randolph G. Page and George C. Lower, to ask the factory to manufacture specialty aircraft for 1928. A preproduction SM-2 Junior was prepared for Page, a former airmail pilot. This aircraft NC5889, s/n 1002, was powered by a 110-hp Warner Scarab 7-cylinder, air-cooled, radial engine and received ATC 194 approval in August 1928. A SM-1DB Stinson Detroiter was built for Lower. His aircraft NC6580, s/n M301-1DB, received ATC approval in October and was powered by a 220-hp Wright J-5C 9-cylinder, air-cooled, radial engine.

Eddie Stinson selected a production SM-1DA, s/n M300-1DA, powered by a 220-hp Wright J-5C 9-cylinder, air-cooled, radial engine for the tour. It received ATC 74 in October. Eddie reviewed the pool of license numbers the factory had received from the CAA and chose NC5900. It is interesting to note that Eddie, Page and Lower's aircraft flew with NC numbers painted on them but did not receive ATC approval until after the tour.

Phoebe Fairgrave Omlie, a petite woman, with closely cropped hair lived in Memphis where she and her husband operated a flying school. Phoebe became acquainted with Estelle when she and her husband visited the Stinson factory. Phoebe purchased a Monocoupe 70 NC5878, s/n 58, powered by a 55-hp Velie M-5 five-cylinder air-cooled radial engine. After picking up her aircraft at the Moline, Illinois factory she flew to the Stinson factory and suggested Estelle accompany her on a great adventure flying as a passenger in the 1928 air tour. Eddie pointed out the 6,000-mile tour would be a long and grueling event, but Estelle replied that she was ready for adventure. Phoebe was the only woman pilot flying in the 1928 tour.

The Monocoupe was a very small aircraft with very limited baggage compartment space, so Phoebe and Estelle had to put all of their luggage and accessories in NC5900, the Detroiter that Eddie was flying. With aircraft arriving at different times and the variability of available parking spaces, the aircraft could be parked anywhere around the landing field. This made finding and retrieving their luggage a challenge throughout the tour, although occasionally Estelle would fly a leg with Eddie.

The last person of interest to this story, L. H. "Jack" Atkinson, the head of an aviation school in Gary, Indiana, purchased a Monocoupe 70 NC5877, s/n 77, powered by a 55-hp Velie M-5 five-cylinder air-cooled radial engine for the tour. It was the same model as Pheobe's aircraft.

Twenty-eight aircraft gathered at Dearborn airport on June 28th and 29th in preparation for Edsel Ford to wave the starting flag the next day. The official timers examined each aircraft, and they were assigned Entry Numbers for takeoff positions. Entry No. 1 was William S. Brock's Bellanca monoplane, and he graciously gave his starting position to Entry No. 26—the Monocoupe flown by Phoebe F. Omlie.

On the morning of Thursday, June 30th, three non-competing aircraft, including an army Fokker trimotor carrying newspaper reporters and race officials, took off ahead of the competitors. Then, at 10:15 a.m., Edsel Ford waved the flag and the race began as Phoebe Omlie lifted off, followed in one-minute intervals by the remaining 24 aircraft.

The following is a selected list of pilots and passengers flying out of Dearborn on the first leg of the tour.

Edward A. Stinson flying NC5900 with four passengers: Soule, Stone, Porter, and Day.
George C. Lowers flying NC6580 carrying no passengers.
Randolph G. Page flying NC5889 with two passengers, Clausen and Carlson.
Phoebe F. Omlie flying NC5878 with one passenger, Estelle Stinson.
L. H. "Jack" Atkinson flying NC5877 with one passenger, Bennett Phelps.

Immediately after the aircraft departed, 12 balloons participating in the 22nd Annual James Gordon Bennett Balloon Race—representing seven different nations—were inflated and lifted off in a wherever-the-wind-took-them race. These were not hot air balloons but were filled with either hydrogen or helium.

Finishing their first leg of the race, the aircraft landed at the Indianapolis Speedway. After being showered with rose petals and greeted by celebrities, the aircraft departed for St. Louis Lambert airfield. Despite her starting first, Phoebe's slow aircraft was the last to reach St. Louis.

After a short presentation by St. Louis dignitaries the aircraft flew on to and spent the night at the Springfield municipal airport. Everyone soon discovered the routine at all the overnight stops. Once the aircraft were tied down, the pilots and passengers were escorted to their hotels and attended banquets and receptions that sometimes lasted late into the evening. The next morning, the sleepy group would return to the airport to supervise the refueling and preflight inspections of each aircraft and take off once again.

The weather was uncooperative during the next leg of the tour. All aircraft were flying by visual flight rules, and the tour continued on to Tulsa, stopping once in Wichita, Kansas to refuel. Because of poor flying conditions and many social events, the tour did not reach Fort Worth until July 6th. The small Monocoupes' pilots and passengers experienced a very bumpy ride across the Kansas and Texas plains.

The tour settled down to its routine of evening social events with tired pilots and crew arriving at the airport each morning. Particularly helpful to the small aircraft, the morning air was smooth, and many made the effort to have their aircraft serviced and ready to depart by 7 am. This routine

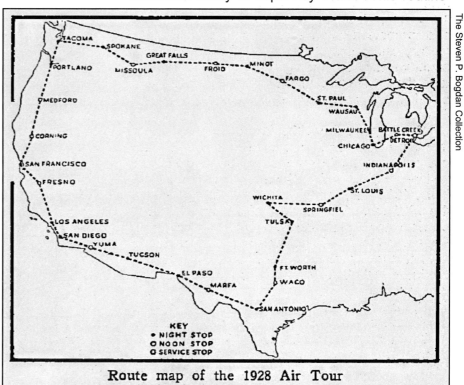

Route map of the 1928 Air Tour

Map of the route of the 1928 National Air Tour for the Edsel B. Ford Reliability Trophy, as printed in the August 1928 issue of Aero Digest *magazine*

Stinson SM-2, NC5889 (s/n 1002) in Stewart Aircraft Company livery. Flown to 3rd place by Randolph Page, shown here taking on fuel

continued with overnight stops at Waco, Texas, July 7th, San Antonio, July 8th and Marfa Army base, July 9th.

With an altitude of 4,800 feet and the temperature running 90 °F, the density altitude at Marfa Army base was 7,500 feet. As Phoebe made the let down into the hot turbulent air, she came in over the end of the runway a little hot and landed past the halfway mark. Carrying excessive speed, she turned to sharply off the runway and rolled the plane over, damaging a wheel and one wing. This was Estelle's first experience hanging upside down in an aircraft and asked Phoebe "What do we do now?" Phoebe explained she should not pop her seatbelt until she had pulled her legs up close to the seat and had one hand on the ceiling to catch her fall. With some giggling and a few choice words, they exited the aircraft tearing holes in the underside of the wing in the process

Eddie's aircraft had landed earlier, and he missed the excitement. L. H. "Jack" Atkinson's Monocoupe, NC5877, followed Phoebe in and witnessed the incident. Jack parked his aircraft nearby and ran to where the women were standing to check on their condition. Finding them okay, he put his arm around Phoebe and offered his aircraft for the two women to continue the tour. After some initial hesitation, she accepted Atkinson's offer and continued the tour while he would repair Phoebe's damaged Monocoupe at Marfa and try to catch up and continue the race himself. From the Marfa Army Airfield the tour travelled on to El Paso, leaving there the next day. After a quick stop at Fort Bliss, the Tour arrived and spent the night in Tucson on July 10th. The next day, they continued to Yuma for a quick fuel stop, then on to San Diego for lunch. The tour then flew to Los Angeles stopping there July 12th.

Refueling stops were always chaotic with each pilot trying to spend the minimum amount of time on the field. San Diego was no exception, and when the fuel truck reached Phoebe's aircraft there were only a few gallons remaining. Phoebe made a decision that with the fuel on board and a small amount added, she could reach Los Angeles. Rather than flying a straight line to Los Angeles, however, she flew up the coast for a beautiful view of the Pacific Ocean. A few miles south of Laguna Beach, they ran out of fuel and landed on the beach very close to the water line in about two feet of salt water. Wading ashore, Phoebe and Estelle summoned a team of horses to retrieve the plane, and a fuel truck to fill it. The two women then continued on to Los Angeles.

For publicity purposes, the tour did not leave Los Angeles until July 14th. July 16th was the longest day's flight of the tour. With a fuel stop at Fresno, Phoebe continued on to San Francisco where she was reunited with her own Monocoupe NC5878, as Jack Atkinson had finally caught up with the tour. From there it was on to Corning and Medford, Oregon.

Page and Eddie Stinson had previously flown through the mountains in the Western United

Stinson SM-1DB, NC6580 (s/n M301-1DB). This green and yellow Stinson-Detroiter, owned by Milo Hilton, was flown to 6th place by George C. Lowers, shown here taking off at the start of the Tour.

States and saw this as an opportunity to improve their times. After the fuel stop in Corning, the suggested route was to fly a northeasterly direction and then turn north flying between North Fork Mountain and Soldier Mountain. Going through that pass they would fly west past Mount Shasta and then turn north and continue on to Medford. The route reasoning was correct. This was the only leg of the trip that Page came in first and Eddie second.

Weather-related issues held up the tour and gave the women some time to do laundry and minor maintenance on the aircraft. The women were in fine form and planned to continue the tour.

The tour got underway again with the next night stay at Tacoma. They flew 418 miles on July 19 with fuel stops in Vancouver and Pascoe. The tour arrived in Spokane experiencing very poor visibility conditions. Because of the height of the Cascades and severe turbulence, the tour doubled back to Vancouver. Turning east, the aircraft followed the Columbia River to Pascoe and then turned northeast to Spokane. Eddie had hoped the prevailing winds from the West could be used to his advantage, but the big WACO and Ford trimotor were just too fast.

July 20th and 21st were exhausting days with overnight stops at Missoula, Montana, and Great Falls. Departing Missoula, they flew due east across the Rocky Mountains through a pass with a floor of at least 6,000 feet. Once through the pass, they turned northeast to reach Great Falls, Montana. Many pilots had navigational problems on this leg

With an altitude of 2,300 feet, the airport at Glasgow, Montana was located directly north of the city. In an effort to save a few minutes off the day's flight, Eddie made a straight-in approach and a wheel landing. Just as he touched down, a car pulled on the runway near the halfway point. Eddie applied full power regaining flying speed, flew straight toward the car, and pulled up just before impact. He climbed out to pattern altitude and followed in behind a Ryan. The overnight stay at Glasgow was uneventful with a refueling stop at Minot, Montana. The tour reached Fargo North, Dakota, on July 23rd.

The national air tour organization had selected officials to establish the arrival and departure of each aircraft at every stop. Arriving at Minot, Phoebe and Estelle were hot and tired and forgot to check in. The delay and confusion concerning their check-in time caused them to be late to the flyers' reception. Because of minor problems, they were the last plane off on July 23rd on the 228-mile hop to Fargo, North Dakota. Eddie's aircraft was one of the first in and he had locked his aircraft and left the airfield. When the Monocoupe arrived, the women found their luggage in a locked aircraft. Phoebe borrowed a large screwdriver and pried the door open on the Stinson to retrieve their luggage. When Eddie complained the next morn-

Top: Phoebe F. Omlie's Monocoupe NC5878 (s/n 58) warming up at Ford Airport in Dearborn at the start of the Tour. Despite being Entry No. 26, Entry No. 1 gave her the honor of taking off first.

Bottom: George C. Lowers' Monocoupe NC5877 (s/n 77) on its takeoff roll at Ford Airport at the beginning of the Tour

ing concerning the minimal damage to his aircraft, the women told him he should feel lucky because they had thought of just cutting a hole in the fabric and pulling out their suitcases.

The tour stopped overnight at St. Paul on July 24th and Wausau on July 26th. With a fuel stop at Milwaukee, the tour reached Chicago municipal airport on July 27th. The last leg of the race was to Dearborn, Michigan with an overnight stay at Battle Creek. 22 aircraft completed the last 250 miles, arriving in Dearborn Monday, July 29th. Only four aircraft dropped out of the 6,300 mile, 23-day air tour.

After the times were tabulated, the tour committee announced the 1928 winners:

1st Place, John P. Wood...........WACO NC5633
2nd Place, Frank M. Hawks..........Ford NC3443
3rd Place, Randolph G. Page....Stinson NC5889
4th Place, Charles W. Myers......WACO NC6528
5th Place, Edward A. Stinson.....Stinson NC5900
6th Place, George C. Lowers.....Stinson NC6580
19th Place, Jack Atkinson.....Monocoupe NC5877
24th Place, Phoebe Omlie....Monocoupe NC5878

Phoebe earned $200 for finishing, albeit in last place.

The recorded times between takeoff and landing at each official stop were the only criteria in the tour. Fuel consumption and efficiency were not considered. Randolph G. Page was very proud that he flew Stinson NC5889 to third-place in a field of 22 aircraft. His SM-2 had been fitted with a full-cruise propeller and the carburetor and carburetor linkage were fine-tuned to produce maximum performance. One of Page's passengers had served as the navigator, and his point A to point B navigation had been excellent. Page continued on with a career in aviation. George C. Lowers was also proud of his sixth-place finish in his Stinson NC6580. He flew away from Dearborn and disappeared into history. In 1929, sponsored by the Monocoupe Aircraft Company, Phoebe participated in the world's first all-women air race, which became known as the "First Women's National Air Derby." Flying from Santa Monica, California, to Cleveland, Ohio, she placed first in the small aircraft division. When questioned concerning women aviators Pheobe replied, "The airplanes don't know the difference."

After the July 30th award ceremonies, Estelle boarded NC5900 and flew home to Northville, Michigan. With many sales leads on his office desk, Eddie immediately transitioned into the company's foremost salesman. He was very proud of the showing Stinson aircraft had made on the tour, placing three in the top six. He was especially pleased that the Stinson aircraft posted better times than the Ryan Brougham and Bellanca aircraft that were competing for Stinson sales.

In the first Ford Reliability Tour in 1925, Edward Stinson flew the advanced Pathfinder aircraft. The aircraft was a Junkers Larson JL-6 powered by a BMW engine. Stinson received $2,250 expense allowance.

The second Ford Reliability Tour departed Dearborn, Michigan August 7, 1926. Edward Stinson flying a Stinson Detroiter SB-1 aircraft powered by a Wright J4 engine rated at 200-hp. For finishing third in a field of 13 aircraft, Stinson received $2,000

If their navigation was accurate the aircraft were scheduled to fly 2,585 miles. The 1926 schedule included 11 overnight stops and 12 days to finish.

NC license numbers and ATC certification were not required until 1927.

Tulsa Junior Chamber of Commerce/Barnsdall Corporation Stinson Detroiter SM-1DA, NC5900 at the Missuola Municipal Airport in Montana on Saturday, July 21, 1928 during the Tour's noon service stop. A Barnsdall oil can is seen below the step. Aircraft to the left is the eventual Tour winner—the WACO-10 NC5533 sponsored by Baby Ruth Candy.

Rexie Shaw Photo/Pat Shaw Collection

Two Stinson's were entered in the 1927 Ford Reliability Tour.

Departing Dearborn, Michigan Monday, June 27, 1927 Edward Stinson flying a Stinson SM-1 NC4307, s/n M201, ATC 16 powered by a Wright J5 rated at 225-hp. Stinson placed first in a field of 13 aircraft in the 1927 Ford Reliability Tour and received $2,500 for finishing first place.

Leonard Flo flying a Stinson SB-1 NC3027, most likely s/n 105, ATC 24 powered by a Wright J5 rated at 225-hp. Flo finished sixth in a field of 13 and received $1,250.

If their navigation was accurate the aircraft were scheduled to fly 4,121 miles. The 1927 schedule included 15 overnight stops and 16 days to finish.

Three Stinson aircraft flew in the 1928 Ford Reliability Tour, departing Dearborn, June 30. There are two other aircraft of interest.

Randolph Page flying Stinson Jr. SM-2 NC5889, s/n 1002, ATC 48 powered by a Warner Scarab engine rated at 110-hp, placed third in the competition. Page received $1,750 for finishing. third place in a field of 24 aircraft.

Edward Stinson flying a Stinson SM-1DA NC5900, ATC 74 powered by a Wright J5 rated at 225-hp. Stinson placed fifth. He received $1250 for fifth place out of a field of 24.

George Lowers flying a Stinson SM-1 DB NC6580 ATC 76 powered by a Wright J5 engine rated at 225-hp. Lowers placed sixth in and received $1.000.

L. H. Jack Atkinson flying a Monocoupe 70 NC5877 ATC 70 powered by a Velie M5 engine rated at 55-hp. Atkinson flew the aircraft to Marfa Army Airfield, Texas. Phoebe Omlie and Estelle Stinson then flew NC58077 to San Francisco where Jack changed back into NC5877, continuing on to a 19th place finish, earning $200.

Phoebe Omlie and Estelle Stinson flying Monocoupe 70 NC5878 ATC 70 powered by a Velie M5 engine rated at 55-hp. Omlie damaged her aircraft at Marfa Army Airfield, Texas. Jack Atkinson repaired NC5878 and flew the aircraft to San Francisco, where Phoebe Omlie changed back into NC5878 and proceeded to Dearborn and a 24th place finish.

If their navigation was accurate the aircraft were scheduled to fly 6,304 miles. The 1928 schedule included 21 overnight stops and 22 days to finish.

No Stinsons were entered in the 1929 and 1930 Ford Reliability Tour.

Departing Dearborn, Michigan July 4, 1931 Edward Stinson flew in the 1931 Ford Reliability Tour. Flying a 1930 Stinson SM-8A NC242W, s/n 4028, ATC 295 powered by a Lycoming R580 rated at 215-hp. Stinson received $550 for finishing eighth place in a field of 14 aircraft.

If their navigation was accurate, the aircraft were scheduled to fly 816 miles. The 1931 schedule included 20 overnight stops and 21 days to finish.

Upper half photo: Onlookers gather around Monocoupe NC5878 at the Fort Worth Municipal Airport on Friday, July 7 as it was about to undergo a christening ceremony

Lower half photo :(left to right) Mrs. Ray Cooper (wife of Tour manager travelling on the Buhl Airster Entry No. 7) and Phoebe Omlie watch as Estelle Stinson breaks a bottle of sour lemon soda on Mrs. Omlie's plane, christening it "Chiggers" as Phoebe had never experienced the tiny bug before landing at Fort Worth. She decided to have the name painted in gold on the tail, as she had the tiniest aircraft in the competition. Image from the Saturday, July 7, 1928 issue of the Fort Worth Record-Telegram

Chapter 22
Record Attempts

The "Pride of Detroit" Stinson SM-1, NC857 (s/n M201) at Harbour Grace, Newfoundland on Thursday, August 25, 1927. The around-the-world attempt began the next day.

Within the decade of 1927 through 1937, there were more then twenty recorded attempts to set records flying the SM-1 Stinson Detroiter. With the exception of the SM-4 *Sally Sovereign/K of New Haven*, and the New York-to-Bermuda aircraft *Pilot Radio*, which both used a 300-hp Wright Whirlwind engine, all the aircraft were powered by a 220-hp 9-cylinder Wright Whirlwind J-5 engine. Many of the Stinson aircraft were given creative names because of the fame of *The Spirit of St. Louis*. Of more than 20 attempts, only two records of significance were achieved. Six were abandoned because of engine failure, and in four, the crew and aircraft never reached their destination and were recorded as lost at sea. A few examples are given here in no particular order.

—

Pilots: Edward S. Schlee and William S. Brock
Goal: To fly around the world in 15 days
Aircraft: *Pride of Detroit* (painted yellow)
Model: SM-1 NC857, s/n 201
Date: August 26, 1927-September 14, 1927
Accomplishment: Flew to Tokyo, Japan

Aero Digest
December, 1931

Edward S. Schlee, Detroit businessman, and William S. Brock, former airmail pilot, successfully completed the first leg of their flight around the world when they landed safely at the airdrome in Croydon, England at 5:30 a.m. (New York Time) on Sunday, August 28, after a 23 hour and 21 minute nonstop flight from Harbour Grace, N.F. The plane they piloted was the Stinson Detroiter monoplane (Wright Whirlwind) that recently won the 1927 National Reliability Tour and later named the *"Pride of Detroit."*

Ideal weather conditions prevailed at Harbour Grace as the flyers climbed into their plane, which had been placed at the head of the 4000-foot runway. The plane carried a total load of more than 5000 lbs of which 2000 lbs weighed as fuel. After a 20-minute tuning test of the engine, chocks were pulled from in front of the wheels, and the yellow painted monoplane started down the runway. The takeoff was perfect and in a short time the plane had gained altitude and was heading out over the North Atlantic.

According to statements made by the flyers, the good weather held until after sunset, but then it began to rain. A storm increased in velocity during the last three hours of darkness. The pilots were flying in a terrific downpour that sloshed at the windows and seeped in over the windshield. In an effort to get above the storm, the distressed pilots climbed the plane to a 10,000-foot altitude, but when the thermometer registered 20 °F they descended to a lower-level for fear that ice might form on the wings.

The *Pride of Detroit* was first reported during the night as being about 400 miles west of Ireland, and at 8 a.m. (London time), it was sighted over Plymouth, England. Half an hour later, the Coast Guard station at Padleigh Saltern, Devonshire reported that the flyers had passed over and dropped a message requesting that the name of the location be written in the sand. The request was fulfilled, and at 10:35 the plane was guided to earth on the Croydon airdrome.

The plane had been fueled with 385 gallons of gasoline and 15 gallons of oil when it took off at Harbour Grace, and when it landed in Croydon, about 85 gallon of gasoline remained in the tanks. Only 2 gallons of oil had been used during the flight. An inspection revealed the plane and its Wright Whirlwind engine to be in excellent condition.

The route and the number of miles to be flown by Schlee and Brock in the around-the-world flight follows:

City	Miles
Harbour Grace, Newfoundland	Start
London, England	2,350
Stuttgart, Germany	460
Belgrade, Yugoslavia	610
Constantinople, Turkey	500
Aleppo, Syria	590
Baghdad, Iraq	485
Bender Abbas, Persia	710
Allahabad, India	925
Calcutta, India	485
Rangoon, Burma	665
Tourane, French Indochina	600
Hong Kong	890
Tokyo, Japan (radio beacon)	1,820
Sand Island of Midway Islands, U.S. (radio beacon)	1,440
San Francisco, U.S	2,400
Cheyenne, Wyoming U.S	925
Chicago, Illinois, U.S	865
Detroit, Michigan, U.S	257
Harbour Grace, Canada	1,550
Total mileage	18,527
Estimated Number of Flying Hours	240

During the course of flight planning, they requested support from the U.S. Navy for their Pacific crossing. The U.S. Navy refused any assistance to the flyers, but Schlee and Brock decided with the publicity of their flight around the world, the Navy would change its mind and offer support when they reached Tokyo. While in Tokyo, the flyers requested the Navy to supply navigation, and if necessary, rescue ships to support their Pacific Ocean crossing. The Navy again refused, so the flyers abandoned their flight, disassembled their aircraft, and booked passage for themselves and their aircraft on the next available ship. *The "Pride of Detroit"* is on display in the Henry Ford Museum in Detroit, Michigan.

Stinson NC857, the second production SM-1 aircraft, was purchased by Edward F Schlee, president of Wayco Oil Company. It was named *Miss Wayco*. This aircraft was flown by Eddie Stinson to victory in the 1927 Ford

Edward S. Schlee (center) and William S. Brock (right), with unidentified man in front of the "Pride of Detroit"

The "Pride of Detroit" being lifted aboard ship at Tokyo, Japan

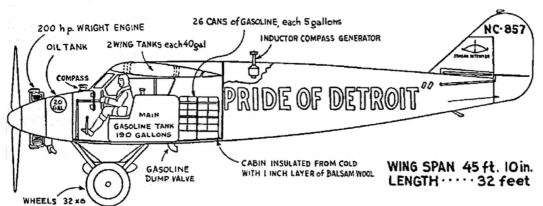

Diagram of the "Pride of Detroit" from the December 1931 issue of Aero Digest magazine, which featured a review of the 63 successful Atlantic crossings to that date, out of 118 attempts

Reliability Air Tour. Edward Schlee and William Brock obtained NC857 and with slight modifications, a new engine and a new name, took off from Harbour Grace, Newfoundland on August 26. On September 14, they landed at Tokyo, Japan after flying 11,090 miles across the Atlantic, Europe, and Asia.

—

Pilot: Paul Redfern
Goal: To fly nonstop from Brunswick, Georgia, to Rio de Janeiro, Brazil
Aircraft: *Port of Brunswick* (painted green and yellow—Brazil's national colors)
Model: SM-1 NX773, s/n 200
Date: August 25–September 5, 1927
Accomplishment: Departed Brunswick, Georgia in the morning of August 25, 1927

After the notoriety in the press and attention given to Lindbergh and his *Spirit of St. Louis*, Paul Redfern saw the opportunity for comparable fame and fortune. The Stinson SM-1 was very comparable in size and load carrying ability of the *Spirit of St. Louis*, and both were powered by the same model 220-hp Wright J-5C engine.

The first production SM-1 was licensed as experimental. License number 773 was from the first block of numbers assigned to Stinson and was the smallest number Stinson ever received. Since the company did not receive ATC 16 until November 1927, theoretically all aircraft manufactured prior to that date were licensed as experimental. The factory at Northville did not have the facilities to convert NX773 into a flying gas can. Bill Mara supervised the modification of the aircraft in a Canadian location.

A 428-gallon gas tank was assembled inside the aircraft and was designed to keep the maximum weight near the center of gravity of the aircraft. The aircraft was equipped with a 45-gallon fuel tank in each wing giving the aircraft a maximum fuel capacity of 518 gallons. Redfern estimated he would be able to stay in the air for about 52 hours.

The completed aircraft was ferried to Brunswick, Georgia by Redfern and Eddie Stinson, and the departure date was set for August 2, 1927. With a 12:46 p.m. departure from Glenn Isle beach, Redfern estimated his time of arrival in the Brazilian capitol about 11:00 p.m. August 4. If he could maintain 105 mph it would take 44 hours to cover the 4600 mile route, and if he could maintain his fuel consumption at 10 gallons per hour, he would consume 440 gallons.

If he did not encounter headwinds; was not required to fly around storms; maintain at least 105 mph; hold fuel consumption to no more than 10 gallons an hour; and his navigation was perfect, Redfern would have sufficient fuel to reach Rio de Janeiro.

When the Stinson did not arrive in at the capitol at the estimated time of arrival, the Brazilian authorities waited until August 5 to declare the aircraft lost. The only report of the plane, having been seen during its flight, was received on the first night August 3 from a cargo ship that gave its position as being east of the Bahamas.

There was considerable speculation covering the location of the downed aircraft. Prevailing winds could have blown it off course. Three scenarios were advanced: it was forced to land on one of the islands near Trinidad; a power failure could force a landing in the open water; or it crashed on the northern coast of South America. Emergency equipment Redfern carried with him included a rubber life raft and food supplies that will last him for ten days.

United States Coast Guard cutters operating in the waters of the Bahamas had been ordered to watch for the aircraft. Shipping in the vicinity of his proposed course was advised of the potential of a downed aircraft. Aircraft based in Miami retraced his first day's flight without picking up a radio signal or finding a downed aircraft.

Paul Redfern with Paul Varner at Glenn Isle beach, where Redfern would begin his flight to Brazil. Varner was the chairman of the flight committee.

Paul Redfern and his Stinson *Port of Brunswick* SM-1 NX773 vanished without any record of a land crash site ever being discovered.

—

Pilots: Ruth Elder and George Haldeman.
Goal: To fly from Roosevelt Field, New York to Paris, France
Aircraft: *American Girl* (painted orange)
Model: SM-1 NX1384, s/n M207
Date: October 11, 1927

Associated Press
Tampa, Florida
September 15, 1927

The Stinson Detroiter monoplane American Girl *is the aircraft in which daring flyer, Ms. Ruth Elder, plans to fly across the Atlantic in a nonstop flight to Paris. Ms. Elder departed Tampa this morning. Wheeling, West Virginia is the first stop in her proposed flight to New York where she will begin her flight across the ocean with George Haldeman as copilot.*

Ruth Elder and George Haldeman departed in the *American Girl* on Tuesday, October 11, 1927 for a flight from Roosevelt Field, New York to Paris, France. They had engine trouble and landed in the sea alongside a vessel 350 miles from the Azores. The American Girl was abandoned, but the crew recorded the longest flight over water: a distance of about 2,620 miles.

Top left: On Tuesday morning, September 20, Ruth Elder was issued her official pilot's license after taking her written test, followed by a flying test in her personal WACO airplane. Seen here later that afternoon, she is at the controls of her Stinson SM-1 NX1384 American Girl *for a series of instrument test flights.*

Bottom left: Tuesday, October 11, 1927 - the American Girl *is being maneuvered into position for its takeoff roll at Curtiss Field, Long Island, New York at the start of Ruth Elder and George Haldeman's New York-to-Paris attempt.*

Right: Ruth Elder and George Haldeman pose with the American Girl *at Curtiss Field, Long Island, New York on Sunday, September 18, 1927. Earlier that morning Ruth had passed her physical exam in preparation for taking her pilot's test. After a post-exam test flight, she and George answered questions from the reporters gathered here.*

All photos The Able Collection

—

Pilots: Eddie Stinson and Fred Kohler
Goal: To race from New York City to Spokane nonstop and set a speed record
Model: SM-1 NX1524, s/n 210
Date: September 1927
Accomplishment: The record attempt was abandoned because of engine problems, and the aircraft made an non-eventful landing at Missoula, Montana.

—

Pilot: Eddie Stinson
Goal: A flight around the rim of United States to promote the SM-1.
Aircraft: *The Eddie Stinson - Veedol* (painted yellow)
Model: SM-1 NC1524, s/n 210
Date: October 1927

After repairs were made in Missoula, Stinson continued on to Spokane. The fuselage tanks were removed and the aircraft was converted back to a standard SM-1. The registration number became NC1524. Veedol Motor Oil Company sponsored the aircraft and Veedol was painted on each side of the fuselage. The aircraft was named *The Eddie Stinson* with that name prominently on the forward fuselage just behind the engine.

Now acting as official Pathfinder for the upcoming 1928 Ford Reliability Tour, Eddie was joined by Tour General Manager Ray Cooper. They flew to Portland and scouted down the Pacific Coast, examining every potential airfield that could be used for the Tour.

Turning inland at San Diego, they inspected airfields in Arizona and Texas. Stinson made a detour to visit his sister Katherine in Santa Fe before returning to Texas. Then they followed a zig zag route that took them to Kansas Indiana, Ohio, Pennsylvania, New York and Boston before turning for home.

The United States tour was completed in 62 days and covered over 18,000 miles. Eddie made many contacts and sold five aircraft. At least two other record attempts in Stinson Detroiters took place during this time.

—

Pilots: Eddie Stinson and George Handelman
Goal: To set a non-refueling endurance record flying from Jacksonville, Florida
Aircraft: *The Stinson Detroiter*
Model: SM-1 NC1524, s/n 210
Date: March 28, 1928
Accomplishment: Non-refueling endurance record: 53 hours, 36 minutes and 5 seconds.

In the early morning hours of Monday, March 26, Eddie Stinson and George Handelman lifted off of the Jacksonville, Florida airport in an aircraft named *The Stinson Detroiter*. Setting a world endurance record of 53 hours, 36 minutes, and 5 seconds, they touched down in Jacksonville on March 28. The Stinson Aircraft Company owned the aircraft and financed the flight for publicity purposes. This aircraft was the 10th SM-1 manufactured, s/n 210.

Jack T. Whitaker, aeronautical engineer for sponsor Tidewater Oil Company (Veedol engine oils and Flying A gasoline), and Eddie Stinson pose at San Diego October 6, 1927. Other passengers included Estelle Stinson and Ray Cooper general manager of the Ford Reliability Tour. In addition to promoting his Stinson Detroiter, Eddie was acting as the official Pathfinder for the 1928 Tour, scouting the route in reverse.

—

Pilots: The Hon. Elsie Mackay and Capt. Walter G. R. Hinchecliffe
Goal: To fly from Cranwell Airdrome in Lincolnshire, England to the North American continent.
Aircraft: *The Endeavor* (painted black and gold)
Model: SM-1 NX4183, s/n 223.
Date: March 13, 1928.

The Endeavor had been disassembled for its shipment to England. When it arrived, it was reassembled and made several test flights over the Cranwell Airdrome. The aircraft was fueled and departed Lincolnshire, England in the early morning of March 13, 1928. There was no press coverage of the actual departure.

The Endeavor made a low pass over a westbound freighter and was reported about 170 miles off the west coast of Ireland. The aircraft went down in the Atlantic, and the crew did not survive.

Eddie Stinson lands at East Boston Airport on October 19, 1927, nearing the end of his flight around the United States to promote the SM-1 and scout the route of the 1928 National Air Tour

The Greater Rockford *preparing for the flight from Rockford, Illinois to Stockholm, Sweden, with stops at Cochrane, Ontario and the Mount Evans Observatory in Greenland*

—

Pilots: Bert Hassell and Parker D. Cramer
Goal: Fly to the Swedish capital by way of Greenland and Iceland
Aircraft: *Greater Rockford* (painted blue and yellow
Model: SM-1 NX5408, s/n 235
Date: March 1928

Bert Hassell and Parker D. Cramer departed Rockford, Illinois on July 26, 1928 in the *Greater Rockford* and crash-landed about 15 minutes after takeoff when they struck the top of a low hill. The aircraft was repaired, and they flew to Cochrane, Ontario for the planned flight to Stockholm, Sweden. They departed August 16th with a planned route to Scandinavia via Greenland and Iceland. Flying over unexplored territory, they planned to make several stops, including one at an airstrip prepared by a Michigan University scientific expedition located at Stromfjord, Greenland. After flying some 24 hours, they experienced strong headwinds and crash landed about 80 miles short of Stromfjord on August 19th. They remained stranded for two weeks, but were eventually spotted and rescued.

In 1968, the *Greater Rockford* was found and airlifted by helicopter off of the Greenland ice cap. The aircraft was in amazingly good condition after spending 40 years exposed to the harsh weather of Greenland. It was restored and is on display at the Rockford Museum in Rockford, Illinois.

—

Bert R. J. "Fish" Hassell and Parker B. "Shorty" Cramer at the moment of their rescue from the Greenland ice cap

Pilots: Glenn L. Loomis and Joseph Glass
Goal: Endurance Record
Aircraft: *Houston - Billion-Dollar City*
Model: SM-1
Date: July 1929

In competition with two other simultaneous endurance record attempts, Loomis and Glass flew 233 hours and 12 seconds over Houston before engine failure caused them to land on July 27.

Eddie Stinson lifting off from the ice runway on Saginaw Bay in the Sally Sovereign*, February 28, 1929*

—

Pilots: Eddie Stinson and R. G. Page
Goal: World Endurance Record
Aircraft: *Sally Sovereign*
Model: SM-4 NX9696, s/n X10
Date: February 1929

The Stinson SM-4 was powered by a 300-hp Wright Whirlwind J-6 engine. This aircraft, the *Sally Sovereign*, was designed specifically to break the world endurance record. It had a retractable landing gear and special nose cowl to reduce head resistance. Theoretically, the *Sally Sovereign* was capable of sustaining 200 hours of flight without refueling. It was equipped to carry about 1,000 gallons of fuel.

Flight tests were conducted at Saginaw Bay in February 1929. The landing gear collapsed in a takeoff attempt, and the retractable landing gear was removed from the aircraft. The aircraft was sent back to the factory and rebuilt with fixed landing gear and aerial refueling capability, and rechristened *K of New Haven*. (See next entry)

—

Pilots: Herbert C. Partridge and George A. Pond
Goal: A non-stop refueled endurance flight from Hartford, Connecticut to Buenos Aires, Argentina
Aircraft: *K of New Haven* (painted white and gold)
Model: SM-4 NX9696, s/n X10
Date: May 30, 1930

The *K of New Haven* departed from Connecticut on May 30, but experienced a leak and landed at Roosevelt Field, Long Island. The sponsors, Kolynos Toothpaste, withdrew their support, ending the attempt. (See next entry)

*The ex-*Sally Sovereign *rebuilt with fixed landing gear and rechristened the* K of New Haven

—

Pilots: Garland Peed, Randy Enslow and Jimmy Garrigan
Goal: A non-stop refueled endurance flight from New York to Buenos Aires
Aircraft: *K of New Haven* (painted white and gold)
Model: SM-4 NX9696, s/n X10
Date: July 15, 19230

A new non-stop refueling flight, again backed by Kolynos Toothpaste but with different pilots, was planned. Leaving New York in on July 15, the crew became lost in dense fog and ran out of fuel, forcing them to bail out over Georgia. The *K of New Haven* crashed and was totally destroyed.

—

Pilots: Brian K. Newcomb and Roy L. Mitchell
Goal: World Endurance Record
Aircraft: *City of Cleveland*
Model: SM-1 NR5485, s/n 239
Date: June 28, 1929

Brian K. Newcomb and Roy L. Mitchell chose

The City of Cleveland *fueling at the Cleveland Municipal Airport before the record attempt. Eddie Stinson was on hand to observe.*

a Stinson Detroiter for their record attempt and named it *City of Cleveland*. On June 28, 1929, the pilots took off from the municipal airport in Cleveland. Remaining aloft for eight days, it came down with a new world endurance record of 174 hours. After further review, however, it was not recognized as an official record by FAI because it did not exceed the previous record by at least 1%.

—

Pilots: Russell C. Mossman, C. E. Steel, and Wilson Herren
Aircraft: *Chicago We Will*
Date: August 6, 1929

On Monday, August 6, 1929 the three flyers took off from Chicago Municipal Airport in an attempt to break the endurance record of 17.5 days made by the Curtiss-Robertson built *St. Louis Robin* airplane. Because of engine problems and difficulties refueling, the record attempt was abandoned.

The Chicago We Will *in hangar three days before flight*

—

Pilots: William H. Alexander, pilot, Zeh Bouck, radio operator and Lewis A. Yancey, navigator.
Goal: To fry from New York to Bermuda
Aircraft: *Pilot Radio*, Stinson SM-1 Detroiter powered by a 300-hp Wright Whirlwind engine
Model: SM-1 NC487H, s/n 519
Date: April 2, 1930
Accomplishment: Completed a nonstop flight to Bermuda

This was the first nonstop flight from New York City to the Bermuda Islands. While the distance was only 759 miles, the flight was unusually hazardous because of small size of the island group and the necessity of exact calculations. The pilots made it to Bermuda, and they intended to continue on to South America, but because of several hard landings in the open sea, the pontoon structure connected to the fuselage was damaged. Lacking facilities to repair the aircraft in Bermuda, it was disassembled and returned to New York City. The aircraft was owned by the Pilot Tube Company, a major manufacturer of vacuum tubes for radios.

Stinson Detroiter Pilot Radio *at Bermuda after successful crossing. Pilot and navigator stand on pontoon, while the radio operator sits on the strut*

—

Pilots: Kenneth Hunter and John Hunter
Aircraft: *City of Chicago* (painted orange and blue)
Model: SM-1 NC5189, s/n 233
Date: June 1930
Accomplishment: Set endurance record: 553 hours, 44 minutes

John and Kenneth developed a unique aircraft-to-aircraft refueling system for their record attempt. The refueling aircraft would fly over and slightly in front of the *City of Chicago* and a crew

Kenneth Hunter stands on engine service catwalk as brother John pilots the City of Chicago. *Two other brothers flew the refueling plane, also a Stinson Detroiter.*

member would reel out the refueling hose. Then, one of the crew members in the *City of Chicago* would depart the cabin, stand on the steel tube scaffolding, and service the engine. The *City of Chicago* departed from and returned to Sky Harbor Airport near Chicago.

—

Pilots: Eddie Stinson and George Handelman
Goal: To set a non-refueling endurance record flying from Mount Clemens, Michigan.
Aircraft: *The Stinson Detroiter*
Model: SM-1 NX 1524, s/n 210
Date: October 17, 1930

In midday Friday, October 17, Eddie Stinson and George Handelman lifted off of the Mount Clemens, Michigan airport in an aircraft named *The Stinson Detroiter*. This was an attempt to break their own endurance record set in 1928. The fuel capacity was increased and the engine was fine-tuned for maximum efficiency. After 20 hours in the air, the record attempt was abandoned because of engine problems.

—

Pilots: Edwin L. Pearson and Robert H. Colignon
Goal: To fry from Detroit to Copenhagen, Denmark
Aircraft: Stinson SM-1 Detroiter
Date: August 18, 1931

The flyers departed on August 18, 1931, on a flight to Copenhagen, Denmark, over the same route followed by Hassell and Cramer in 1928. The purpose of the flight was to determine the feasibility of an airmail route over the northern Atlantic Ocean. After four stops in Canada and layovers due to weather, the flyers landed at Port Harrison on the edge of Hudson Bay. Because of fog, they were grounded until September 6. With their emergency rations exhausted and fuel running low, they decided to fly back to Detroit. Because of the many difficulties they experienced, any further North Atlantic flights were canceled. This aircraft may have been NC445H, s/n 516.

The Sir John Carling *before its ill-fated attempt to cross the Atlantic west-to-east, while the* Royal Windsor *would attempt a simultaneous crossing*

—

Pilots: Clyde A. Lee and John Bochkon
Goal: To fly nonstop from Harbour Grace, Newfoundland to Oslo, Norway
Aircraft: *The Green Mountain Boy* (painted red)
Model: SM-1 NR7576, s/n 261
Date: August 25. 1932

Lee and Bochkon took off from the airport at Harbour Grace on August 25, 1932 to set a nonstop record by flying to Oslo. Somewhere over the North Atlantic, *The Green Mountain Boy* and its crew were lost at sea.

—

Pilots: Terrance B. Tully and James V. Metcalf
Goal: To fly from London, Ontario to London, England
Aircraft: *Sir John Carling* (painted dark green with burnt yellow wings)
Model: SM-1, s/n 202
Date: September 1, 1927

As a public relations event, two aircraft, the *Sir John Carling* and the *Royal Windsor*, were to depart their respective airports simultaneously. The departure date of each aircraft was September 1, 1927, and that morning the *Sir John Carling* took off from the Carling brewery airdrome near London, Ontario at 5:35 a.m. Bad weather and

Pontoon equipped Stinson Detroiter attempted to follow the route of Bert Hassell and Parker D. Cramer to establish an airmail route

The Royal Windsor *before the attempt to cross the Atlantic was cancelled after the* Sir John Carling *went missing. Note Stinson SB-1 Detroiter NC881 (s/n 30) behind the SM-1. Built in March 1927, the NC881 was ten and a half years-old in this photograph. The original owner was Horace Dodge.*

heavy fog caused them to land near Caribou, Maine, around 680 miles short of their refueling stop at Harbour Grace, Newfoundland. Clear weather allowed them to continue four days later. On Friday morning, September 7, the *Sir John Carling* lifted off from Harbour Grace. Somewhere over the Atlantic, the aircraft and crew were lost at sea.

—

Pilots: Phil Wood and C.A. "Duke" Schiller
Goal: To fly nonstop from Windsor Ontario, to Windsor, England
Aircraft: *Royal Windsor*
Model: SM-1 NC1100, s/n 203
Date: September 1, 1927

The *Royal Windsor* departed Windsor, Ontario at 9:18 a.m. Bad weather forced the aircraft to land at Old Orchard, Maine. They were not able to leave until the morning of September 7, heading to Harbour Grace where the *Sir John Carling* had left hours before. There they learned that a non-Stinson plane attempting a New York-to-Rome crossing had gone missing. A gas tank leak kept the *Royal Windsor* grounded for another day. On September 9, with the *Sir John Carling* now also missing, the official Windsor Flight Committee canceled the attempt and told the pilots to return home to their families.

The committee decided instead to enter the New York-to-Spokane air race later that month.

—

Pilots: Jack Little and Merle "Mope" Moltrup
Goal: Endurance Record
Aircraft: *Buffalo Evening News* (painted blue and yellow)
Model: SM-1
Date: September 1929

In an attempt to capture the endurance record set over the summer by the *St. Louis Robin*, Little and Moltrup flew 197 hours and 30 minutes over Buffalo, New York before a refueling accident caused them to land on September 20.

Earlier Moltrup had tried to repair a stream-lined cable brace on the right side of the stabilizer which had parted for some unknown reason, but was doubtful that the fix would hold in rough weather.

A long rope ladder was delivered to the *Buffalo Evening News* by the refueling plane, and at 5:00 p.m. mechanic Dale Dryer ascended in an open cockpit biplane with an airmail pilot at the controls. Dryer caught the rope ladder and climbed up into the Detroiter. Coming out of the refueling hatch Dryer, an experienced wingwalker, maneuvered down the fuselage and secured a new stabilizer brace in about ten minutes. He then parachuted back to the ground.

Just two hours later, as the support plane approached to refuel, an anxious reported accidently kicked out the hose, which swung down and damaged the tail fin beyond repair, forcing an end to the flight.

The Detroiter Buffalo Evening News *which in July 1929 attempted to break endurance record set in the summer*

Chapter 23
The V-77 (AT-19)

Royal Navy AT-19 FK887 (s/n 74) later carried U.S. number 42-46713, then civilian number NC69996

In mid-1941 Stinson approached the Army Air Force training command concerning the possible use of the SR-10 series as an advanced trainer. The production and engineering department Materiel Command reviewed an SR-10 aircraft and found it to be a fine aircraft but lacked the structural integrity the Air Force required in an advanced trainer. Stinson requested the opportunity to submit a redesigned aircraft.

Specifications for Model 77 (Vultee sequence number 77) were completed by November 21, 1941. At this time the aircraft was assigned its military designation (Advanced Training Airplane Air Corps model number AT-19). Basic stress analysis engineering data was complete by March 9, 1942.

The Stinson AT-19 had the outward appearance of an SR-10 Reliant series aircraft. Stinson engineers completely reengineered the aircraft to all-metal construction with fabric covering. The SR-10 series used a great deal of wood in their construction and the only wood found in the AT-19 was the floorboard. The design was totally new and there were no interchangeable parts with the SR-10 series. As the aircraft was redesigned the structural strength of the aircraft was increased to meet military specifications. The first prototype began a test flight program in July 1942

At this time all training aircraft were required to be built with tandem seating where the student and the instructor are seated one behind the other. Side-by-side seating was not used in training aircraft until the student transitioned into a multi engine advanced trainer. The most popular training aircraft at this time was the Stearman PT-17 Kaydet, Consolidated Vultee BT-13 Valiant, and the North American AT-6 Texan. After further evaluation by the Army Air Force, the need for the AT-19 type trainer did not exist.

By this time Stinson had transitioned from a Division of Vultee Corporation to the Stinson Division of Consolidated Vultee Corporation with the general office in San Diego, CA. Stinson had invested a massive amount of resources into an aircraft the Air Force did not want. San Diego immediately contacted the British purchasing agent in Washington D. C. and presented the AT-19 as a candidate for a Lend-Lease contract. A lend lease contract was approved by the Air Force and the Royal Navy's "Fleet Air Arm" accepted the AT-19.

History does not tell us if in 1943 the Royal Navy's "Fleet Air Arm" requested 250 additional AT-19 Reliant aircraft. The 1943 contract does not say direct Lend-Lease but supplemental number 10. There is the possibility that Consolidated Vultee San Diego lobbied the Materiel Command for a follow-on contract. Consolidated Vultee was a major contractor with a strong lobbying organization and could influence a contract whether or not the Army Air Force had a need for that type of aircraft. These aircraft were delivered to England under the Lend-Lease program with the last aircraft leaving the factory November 18, 1944.

First Stinson AT-19 Reliant Contract (Covering 250 aircraft) Contract DA-1072 DA 2-14-42 direct Lend-Lease (USAAF 42-46640 through 42-46889)	
Fleet Air Arm Serial Number FK814 through FK999:	186 aircraft
Fleet Air Arm Serial Number FL100 through FL163:	64 aircraft
Stinson retained:	1 aircraft NC13325 (s/n 164) 42-46802
Fleet Air Arm received:	**249 aircraft**

Second Stinson AT-19 Reliant Contract (Covering 250 aircraft) Contract DA-1072 PR 10-14-43 Supplemental 10 (USAAF 43-43964 through 43-44213)	
Fleet Air Arm Serial Number FB523 through FB772:	250 aircraft
The US Navy received:	10 aircraft
Canada received:	10 aircraft
Stinson received:	1 aircraft
Fleet Air Arm received:	**229 aircraft**

The Lycoming engine was not Stinson's engine of choice to power the new aircraft. Lycoming was a division of Consolidated Vultee and a great deal to pressure was applied to Stinson to use their engine. Stinson had offered a 245-hp R-680-D5 Lycoming (2,100 rpm at sea level) powered Reliant. This aircraft was underpowered and very few examples were sold. The V-77 was a heavy aircraft and Stinson engineers felt that a minimum of 300 horses would be required.

With minimal modifications Lycoming rerated the R-680-D5 engine to 285-hp. The new version ran at 2,200 rpm at sea level (and rated at 285-hp at 2,300 rpm for takeoff.) The Lycoming division overcame Stinson's resistance and delivered the R-680-E3B to Stinson to power the V-77. This engine was rated 285-hp at 2,300 rpm at sea level. The AT-19 was underpowered and experienced many service problems in the effort to push more horsepower from the 245-hp Lycoming engine.

The contract specified the U.S. government would furnish the propeller and power plant fully funded and at no cost to Stinson. In the first contract for 250 aircraft the USAAF paid Stinson $22,496 per aircraft. The AT-19 Reliant 1 was delivered as a five-place airplane used to ferry personnel. The AT-19A Reliant 2 was equipped with radios and used to train navigators. The AT-19B Reliant 3 was used for observation and photo-work and the AT-19C Reliant 4 was used mostly for hauling cargo and air express throughout England.

All radios were furnished by the United Kingdom Royal Navy and installed by Stinson at the factory. In a 2007 interview with Harry W. Smith he described the British radios. Because of the shortage of aluminum in Great Britain, the structural cases of their radios were made of Formica. The Lucas electrical company manufactured many of the components and they probably assembled the radios. The shielding was very poor and by American standards for noise level was too high for operational use. The Royal Navy dispatched a technician from Great Britain to diagnose and help resolve the problems. All aircraft were held at the factory while Harry W. Smith supervised the replacement of all British tubes with American tubes. With the problem solved the aircraft were released for delivery to the Royal Navy Air Arm.

Each aircraft was completed as a flyable airplane and then test flown to certify that all mechanical, electrical, and communication equipment were operating perfectly. Harry W. Smith participated in the flight-testing of each aircraft and remembers having numerous propeller problems. In one incident they were forced to land at Willow Run where Consolidated Vultee B-24 bombers were being produced.

Each aircraft was equipped with a real antenna. In order to transmit the radio operator must extend and adjust the antenna in order to tune the radios. Occasionally, a pilot would forget to rewind the antenna. If the weight on the end of the antenna snagged the airport boundary fence the internal real mechanism would be instantly destroyed.

AT-19 Cockpit

Royal Air Force and Fleet Air Arm serial numbers were broken into odd and even batches to confuse the German intelligence. English military aircraft serial numbers were broken into what was known as the shadow-number fashion and successfully confused the German intelligence and contemporary historians.

Each aircraft was ferried to Newark, New Jersey before being disassembled and crated for shipment to England. The crated aircraft were then held for available space as deck cargo. All aircraft bound for England were usually placed as top cargo on freighters when space was available. Some tankers were modified to carry many crated aircraft as deck cargo and their normal cargos of oil.

Not all of the aircraft were shipped to England. Quite a large, but identified, batch went to Piarco, Trinidad, where they were used as navigational trainers. Another consignment went to the East Indies where they were employed on communication and miscellaneous training duties in India and Ceylon.

By late 1944, 49 Fleet Air Arm stations throughout the world had been issued a few AT-19 aircraft. No aircraft were ever officially fitted with armament

German U-boat strength reached 212 and sank 37 ships in January 1943. With 100 German U-boats operating in the Atlantic through February 1943, 63 Allied ships were lost to submarine attacks. The highest number of ships lost to submarine attacks occurred in March 1943 with 72 ships lost from North Atlantic convoys.

The AT-19 aircraft were loaded as deck cargo on North Atlantic convoy ships bound for England. A cargo ship or tanker may carry one aircraft or several depending upon space availability. 47 AT-19 were lost at sea while being shipped as deck cargo.

Disposition of Fleet Air Arm AT-19 aircraft	
Total Fleet Air Arm aircraft (249 + 229)	478
Lost at sea	47
Lost to accidents	79
Inventory of AT-19 aircraft at war's end	352
Returned to the U.S. in 1946	352

As a military production aircraft it was not necessary for Stinson to apply for type certificate approval. Stinson requested an Approved Type Certificate (ATC) approval for the AT-19 as the V-77 in January 1946. Temporary approval was granted in April 1946 and ATC 774 was issued November 26, 1946, for the Stinson V-77. Stinson announced in June that if the new owners would ferry their aircraft to the Stinson plant in Wayne, Michigan, Stinson would convert them to five place executive transports. With a liberal application of time and money Stinson would convert the aircraft to nearly new condition.

***

Western Flying
June 1946

Stinson AT-19's On Surplus List

More than 350 surplus Stinson AT-19 cabin monoplanes, former lend lease aircraft, which have been returned by the British will be offered for sale beginning June 3 at $1500, $2000, and $2500, each depending on condition. Terms of the sale: cash only with no discount.

The AT-19 is similar to the commercial Stinson Reliant, but parts are not interchangeable. It is a high "gull" wing type. The cabin now has three seats but can be modified to carry five. The plane is powered with a 295 horsepower Lycoming engine. Type testing for the AT-19 has been completed, and it has been declared to be eligible for certification by the Civil Aeronautics Administration for civil flight use. Wings of the planes were removed prior to shipment back to the United States, and they have not been reassembled. The purchase price, however, includes wings of identical serial numbers.

The planes are located at Chambers Field, Naval Air Station, Norfolk Virginia, and may be inspected there until May 20. Since there are no facilities on the field for putting them into flyable condition, shipping arrangements must be made. Buyers will be given 15 days after purchase to remove their planes.

For a period of 15 days after June 3, 1946, sales will be made to priority claimants only on a first come, first served basis. After June 17, 1946, these airplanes will be available for sale to the general public.

The successful buyer must contact the CAA who issues an NC license number. Once the new owner has assembled the aircraft and if the airplane can pass line check, a permit to fly it to the new owner's home base will be issued. After that one flight, the owner must ground his airplane until a permanent airworthiness certificate is granted.

The 352 surplus Stinson AT-19 were former lend lease aircraft to the United Kingdom Royal Navy Fleet Air Arm. These aircraft carried both Army Air Force and Fleet Air Arm logbooks and the War Assets Administration required all paperwork be destroyed. All new engine and airframe logbooks do not begin at the time of manufacture but start in 1946.

As part of the lead lease agreement the Fleet Air Arm was to establish the next color trim and markings for the AT-19 aircraft. Before the start of production, the Fleet Air Arm furnished the Stinson factory at Wayne, Michigan, blocks of serial numbers to be assigned to individual aircraft.

Stinson was required to finish all aircraft to be operationally ready. The Fleet Air Arm would not accept aircraft that required modification, repainting or refinishing once assigned to a fleet air station. USAAF numbers were assigned but did not appear on the exterior of the aircraft. Each aircraft left the Stinson factory with exactly the same exterior paint trim; there were no exceptions.

In the 80-plus years since these aircraft entered service, the lack of precise color information have allowed erroneous paint trims to be presented. The majority of incorrect color schemes have been published in model airplane magazines and unfortunately contemporary restorers have applied non-authentic paint trims to their aircraft.

It was the CAA's policy in 1946 to assign five-digit NC numbers to surplus aircraft. In the 76 years since 1946 many aircraft have received new N numbers. The following list of 105 aircraft is included to give the reader a better understanding of the numbering system in 1946.

The material that Steve Sevier obtained from the Imperial War Museum, Air Britain Historians and Fleet Air Arm Museum was invaluable in solving the mystery surrounding the assignment of Fleet Air Arm serial numbers. My thanks go to Steve Sevier as he has been a fantastic resource in my AT-19 research.

It is the accepted practice that serial numbers are assigned to aircraft in a sequential order. In assigning the U.S. serial numbers and Fleet Air Arm serial numbers to the individual aircraft, the author assumed this is correct. If the factory deviated in sequential order in assigning numbers small numerical errors could occur. This is a general overview and the author could not authenticate the application of every number.

CHAPTER 23

Stinson Model AT-19 & Model V-77				Stinson Model AT-19 & Model V-77			
Aircraft Serial Number	NC Number 1946	USAAF Numbers	Fleet Air Arm Numbers	Aircraft Serial Number	NC Number 1946	USAAF Numbers	Fleet Air Arm Numbers
1	NC74656	42-46640	FK814	151	NC70090	42-46789	FK962
2	NC53547	42-46642	FK815	152	NC69721	42-46790	FK963
10	NC49252	42-46648	FK823	154	NC64271	42-46792	FK965
11	NC69565	42-46649	FK824	156	NC69510	42-46794	FK966
13	NC67070	42-46652	FK826	160	NC70066	42-46798	FK970
20	NC69443	42-46659	FK833	164	NC13325	42-46802	FK974
23	NC67025	42-46662	FK836	165	NC70064	42-46803	FK975
28	NC69981	42-46667	FK841	169	NC69416	42-46807	FK979
30	NC69986	42-46669	FK843	174	NC69141	42-46812	FK984
36	NC79458	42-46675	FK849	178	NC70094	42-46816	FK988
37	NC61545	42-46676	FK850	185	NC66139	42-46823	FK994
38	NC88793	42-46677	FK851	199	NC67453	42-46837	FL113
41	NC69159	42-46680	FK854	211	NC69993	42-46839	FL125
45	NC58571	42-46684	FK858	227	NC69775	42-46865	FL141
57	NC69724	42-46696	FK870	229	NC52028	42-46867	FL143
61	NC29767	42-46700	FK874	231	NC69441	42-46869	FL145
64	NC69745	42-46703	FK877	248	NC50238	42-46887	FL161
74	NC69996	42-46713	FK887	254	NC36921	43-43967	FB526
76	NC55943	42-46715	FK888	256	NC69442	43-43969	FB528
77	NC73373	42-46716	FK889	257	NC55939	43-43970	FB529
103	NC58285	42-46742	FK915	271	NC64365	43-43984	FB543
107	NC69440	42-46746	FK919	272	NC65442	43-43985	FB544
109	NC69893	42-46748	FK921	274	NC60890	43-43987	FB546
122	NC64313	42-46761	FK934	275	NC69418	43-43988	FB547
124	NC69711	42-46763	FK936	276	NC73393	43-43989	FB548
127	NC70057	42-46766	FK938	283	NC69989	43-43996	FB555
131	NC79496	42-46770	FK942	284	NC70012	43-43997	FB556
141	NC60079	42-46779	FK952	286	NC67617	43-43999	FB558
143	NC50227	42-46781	FK954	291	NC63654	43-44004	FB563

Stinson Model AT-19 & Model V-77

Aircraft Serial Number	NC Number 1946	USAAF Numbers	Fleet Air Arm Numbers
293	NC69398	43-44006	FB565
310	NC69726	43-44023	FB582
329	NC69548	43-44042	FB601
332	NC69386	43-44045	FB604
333	NC60634	43-44046	FB605
336	NC52904	43-44049	FB608
340	NC73589	43-44053	FB612
348	NC65977	43-44061	FB620
351	NC65019	43-44064	FB623
361	NC65345	43-44074	FB633
363	NC60843	43-44076	FB635
366	NC55775	43-44079	FB638
368	NC69990	43-44081	FB640
372	NC87675	43-44085	FB644
373	NC33543	43-44086	FB645
379	NC91037	43-44092	FB651
380	NC79556	43-44093	FB652
385	NC69984	43-44098	FB657
387	NC73340	43-44100	FB659
390	NC69985	43-44103	FB662
394	NC70092	43-44107	FB666
395	NC69984	43-44108	FB667
406	NC65826	43-44119	FB678
411	NC88026	43-44124	FB682
413	NC64444	43-44126	FB685
417	NC69874	43-44130	FB689
418	NC79158	43-44131	FB690
419	NC69876	43-44132	FB691
420	NC55638	43-44133	FB692
426	NC70056	43-44139	FB698
442	NC59121	43-44155	FB714
443	NC66274	43-44156	FB715
445	NC66096	43-44158	FB717
448	NC69357	43-44161	FB720
453	NC69394	43-44166	FB725
454	NC65814	43-44167	FB726
457	NC91015	43-44170	FB729
458	NC50226	43-44171	FB730
461	NC40053	43-44174	FB733
468	NC69886	43-44182	FB740
475	NC75417	43-44188	FB748
477	NC69395	43-44190	FB750
480	NC69128	43-44193	FB753
486	NC79132	43-44199	FB758
487	NC69794	43-44200	FB759
490	NC69747	43-44203	FB762
492	NC64640	43-44205	FB764
496	NC67227	43-44209	FB768
499	NC64435	43-44212	FB771

Chapter 24
Airmail Stinsons

This composite picture shows a Stinson SR-10C operated by All-American Aviation preparing to hook a mailbag container, having just dropped one off. The real photo (left) inspired the painting by an unknown artist that was commissioned by Allegheny Airlines, the successor to All-American Aviation (now US Airways/American Airlines).

Entrepreneur and inventor, Dr. Lionel Adams, a dentist practicing in Seattle, developed a plan to bring airmail service to rural America. He proposed a system where an aircraft could leave and pick up cargo without landing. Utilizing his own capital, Dr. Adams began to develop his unique operation. He shared his design with William E. Boeing of Boeing Aircraft, and with the help of Boeing's engineers and pilots, his system was tested successfully in 1928. In that same year, Dr. Adams moved to New York to obtain capital for the design. All-American Aviation (AAA) was founded in 1929 and Richard du Pont, a young aviation enthusiast, purchased controlling interest in the firm.

From 1929 to 1937, with an infusion of new capital, new investors and new engineers perfected the system. The ground equipment consisted of two upright, steel poles with small V-shaped extensions at the top. Each pole was 33 ft. long with 5 ft. below the surface embedded in concrete, which allowed them to be 28 ft. above ground level. A loop of manila rope was strung across the top of the polls and then connected to the item to be picked up. A grappling hook attached to a long cable that trailed from the aircraft caught the manila rope, and an electric reel inside the aircraft retrieved the object.

The pickup system was presented to the post office as a means of serving small rural communities without rail service. This began a long and frustrating approval process with the post office and the struggle to obtain funding for this revolutionary service. Based on provisions in the Airmail Act of 1934, the Postmaster General created a one-year experimental airmail service and accepted bids from All-American Aviation for two routes. Route one ran from Philadelphia to Pittsburgh and served 24 small cities. Route two began in Pittsburgh, serving 28 locations in Appalachian Mountain territory and ending back in Pittsburgh.

All-American Aviation purchased its first Stinson, the SR-10C NC21107, and began installing the pickup equipment. To facilitate CAA approval, the aircraft was relicensed in the experimental category, NX21107. Once approved, four more SR-10C Stinson aircraft, the NC18499, NC18489, NC18488 and NC18496 were purchased.

Before the first flight could be launched, an enormous amount of logistical planning and expense was needed. Pilots had to be hired and trained in the pickup procedures, and a second crew member had to become proficient in dropping and recovering the mail. The reel mechanism for pick up also needed to be manufactured and flight-tested in each aircraft. Each Stinson interior was modified with a hole approximately 18 inches in diameter cut through the rear cabin compartment. Mailbags were ordered from the post office department with sufficient strength to be dropped through the hole of the fuselage and to handle the stress of being picked up and pulled through the hole. Also, each of the 52 communities to be served had to be contacted and approval obtained for locations to place the pickup equipment. Many of the cities did not have airports, forcing the placing of pick-up sites in some quite creative places, including cemeteries. Lastly, employees had to be hired in each of the 52 communities to pick up the outgoing mail for the post office, rig the pickup lines, and deliver the incoming mail back to the post office.

Pick-up poles were manufactured and transported to each community and installed in the proper manner along with several hundred manila rope loops. Each pole was spaced 54 feet apart, and to help the pilots locate the pickup point, they were painted white and international orange.

The procedure started with the mailbags being carefully loaded into the aircraft in the order in which they would be dropped. As the aircraft approached each community, the pickup point would be recognized with the pilot making a slow gliding approach 50 to 75 ft. above ground level. As the aircraft approached the pick-up point, the incoming mail was dropped, and the line with the grappling hook was extended through the hole in the cabin floor to snag the rope with the outgoing mail attached. In this manner, the incoming mail would be dropped and outgoing mail snagged in one operation.

Pilot training and site selection was well underway by March 1939. As pick-up equipment was installed, demonstration flights were conducted in selected cities through May. Nearly half of the pickup points were completed by June and airmail service began in these communities, and full service to both route one and route two started the first week of July. Dr. Adams' dream of airmail service to rural communities had been achieved.

The winter of 1939-1940 was extremely harsh, but the Stinson pilots flew through snow, rain, fog, and aircraft icing with an almost 100% on-time record and zero aircraft accidents. On the downside however, the revenues for the post office did not cover the costs of operation and All-American Aviation was running in the red. The post office had signed contracts for 12 months of experimental airmail service, but after a review of the company's operations, the contracts were not renewed. Airmail service stopped on May 13, 1940.

Through legislative change, the Civil Aeronautics Board (CAB) now controlled the fate of the airmail service. The company applied to the CAB for a permanent certification and additional routes. On July 22, 1940 the CAB issued the necessary authorization for All-American Aviation to fly over five routes, and service began to the new routes in early August. Once approval was received, four more Stinson SR-10C aircraft, the NC21109, NC21130, NC21131 and NC21182, were purchased.

As new routes were established, the pickup poles were reengineered. They were no longer designed as permanent equipment and were delivered to the site in three pieces: a base, two 20 foot poles, and a bamboo extension. This gave much more flexibility in the ground pick-up procedures. Engineers had also worked hard to improve the reel mechanism that pulled the mail bag into the aircraft. From an operational standpoint, the flight personnel, ground staff, air and ground

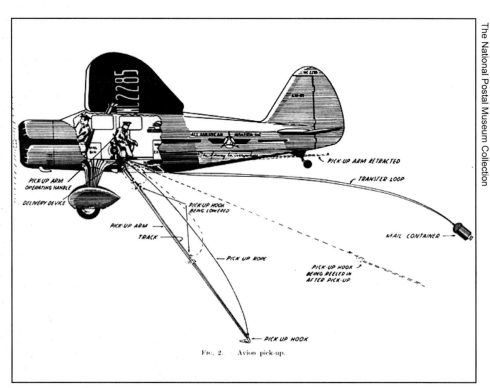

Cutaway showing mailbag handling equipment

equipment had been perfected—the All-American Aviation airmail delivery system was now operational.

The year 1942 brought many changes to All-American Aviation, including the need for additional aircraft. The SR-9 NC17158 and SR-10C NC21182 were purchased from private owners to expand flight operations, and the SR-6 NC15131 was purchased for pilot training. By 1943, the volume of airmail from all routes had increased substantially, and the SR-10J NC23757 and SR-10J NC47303 were purchased as used aircraft. When these aircraft were serviced in 1943 and 1944, they were repainted in silver and blue with red trim.

Through 1942 to 1945, All-American Aviation was involved in many activities in support of the war effort. This created sufficient funds to subsidize the airmail activities, but as World War II was winding down in late 1945 and early 1946, the airmail portion of the company's income declined substantially, so they looked at the possibility of carrying passengers in the airmail aircraft as one way to generate additional cash flow. A Noorduyn Norseman V and two Beechcraft D-18C were purchased in an effort to convince the CAB that airmail and passenger service could be combined. This proposal was rejected. In the fall of 1947, the CAB had no sympathy for increasing the rates for the airmail pickup and delivery operation, but the board began to look favorably on All-American Aviation for short haul airline service. The Washington bureaucracy moved very slowly, but the announcement was made in February 1948 that All-American Aviation could start regular feeder airline service in selected areas. The company began to purchase Army surplus DC-3 aircraft, and in March 1948, airmail pickup and delivery was terminated. Over the next several months, AAA liquidated its fleet of Stinson aircraft. In January 1953, All-American Aviation was changed to Allegheny Airlines, and in October 1979 it became US Air.

From 1938 through 1948, All-American Aviation owned 15 Stinson aircraft. Four were lost in accidents: two in 1943, one in 1944, and one in 1945—leaving 11 operational until airmail service was suspended. A complete list of the Stinson aircraft with serial number is included here:

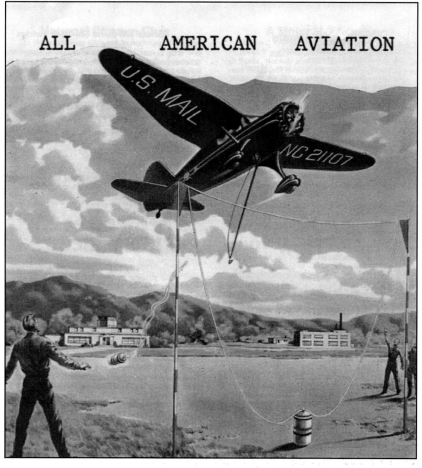

On March 5, 1939, the pick-up method of Air Mail was demonstrated at Coatesville, Pennsylvania by pilots Norman Rintoul and Victor Yesulantes, using a Stinson Reliant operated by All-American Aviation. During 1940 and 1941 this company developed and operated its Air Mail pick-up systems on five routes radiating from Pittsburgh to 108 cities and towns in the six states of Pennsylvania, West Virginia, Kentucky, Delaware, New York and Ohio. Route average 275 miles in length and each served about 20 communities an average of 18 miles apart. This painting is dedicated to the memory of Don Fyock, who owned and was restoring a Stinson SR-10J, N-47303, used by All-American Aviation in this service (original APM Bulletin caption).

SR-10C	NC21107	s/n 3-5828
SR-10C	NC18499	s/n 3-5808
SR-10C	NC18489	s/n 3-5816
SR-10C	NC18488	s/n 3-5817
SR-10C	NC18496	s/n 3-5829
SR-10C	NC21109	s/n 3-5844
SR-10C	NC21130	s/n 3-5855
SR-10C	NC21131	s/n 3-8856
SR-10C	NC21182	s/n 3-5908
SR-10F	NC23110	s/n 5910
SR-10E	NC22526	s/n 5914
SR-10J	NC23757	s/n 5923
SR-10J	NC47303	s/n 5942
SR-9C	NC17185	s/n 5303
SR-6	NC15131	s/n 9624

Left: Article from the June 1939 issue of Popular Aviation about the just introduced Air Mail service
Right: A Stinson generated advertisement announcing the sale of the fleet of Sr-10Cs to All-American Aviation

Both items The John C. Swick Collection

Chapter 25
Northwest Airlines' Stinsons

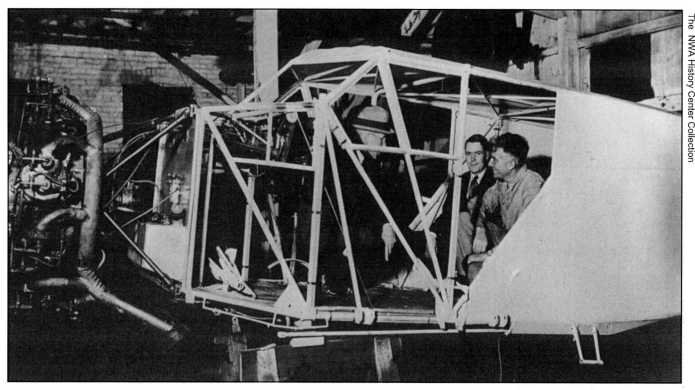

Edward A. Stinson (right) and Northwest founder Lewis H. Brittin (left, in hat) in the Stinson Detroiter SB-1 NC881 (s/n 30) in late 1926. This particular aircraft was sold to Horace Dodge and registered on March 3, 1927. See upper-left photo on page 190.

Northwest Airways sold their first passenger airline ticket July 5, 1927—just 49 days after Charles Lindbergh departed New York to Paris on May 20. A group of investors, headed by Col. Lewis H. Brittin, had organized Northwest Airways on September 1, 1926 to fly airmail for the United States post office. The company's first aircraft were a Thomas Morse Scout and a Curtis Oriole. Both were open cockpit biplanes.

Bill Mara, representing the Stinson Aircraft Company, demonstrated the new SB-1 aircraft to Brittin. Mara presented the SB-1 as an ideal aircraft for the start-up airline. As he examined the SB-1, Brittin agreed that passengers would be attracted to an airline that offered closed-cabin aircraft as well as an excellent cabin heater for winter operations in Minnesota and Wisconsin. Northwest Airways management negotiated the purchase of production aircraft four, five, and six. In order to close the sale, Bill Mara agreed to start the Northwest Airways aircraft with serial number 1: s/n 1, CAA license number C872; s/n 2 C873; and s/n 3 C874 were delivered in October 1926. (NC was not used on early production aircraft—the C stood for commercial.). Northwest Airways purchased their fourth SB-1 in 1927, s/n 90, NC2707.

Northwest Airways began airline service with four SB-1 Stinsons. In 1934, the company name was changed to Northwest Airlines. Through the years, the airline offered passenger service throughout Canada, Alaska and the Western Pacific. In 1950, the company became Northwest Orient Airlines. The opportunity for further expansion was realized when Republic Airlines merged with Northwest Orient on October 1, 1986, becoming Northwest Airlines once more. It was now the sixth largest United States airline and served more Canadian cities than any other airline. In 2008, Northwest Airlines was purchased by Delta Airlines, losing its identity as an independent airline.

On Sunday October 30, 1926 the first flyaway of SB-1 Stinson Detroiters: C872, s/n 1; C873, s/n 2; and C874, s/n 3, took off from the Ford airfield in Detroit, heading for St. Paul, Minnesota. There, they went into service for Northwest Airways on the route between St. Paul and Chicago. These Stinsons were sold OFF Detroit, which means On Flying Field at Detroit—then the aviation equivalent of Freight On Board (FOB). The purchaser takes possession of the planes at the airfield, and his insurance starts when his pilots take off.
These first 3 Detroiters received their C (NC) numbers on March 28, 1927.

Northwest Airways Inc. Stinson Detroiter C872, s/n 1. Registration was canceled on September 16, 1931, and was said to have been presented to Historical Society of Minnesota.

Chapter 26
Diesel-Powered Stinsons

1930 Stinson SM-8D, NC200W, s/n 4036 powered by a 225-hp Packard diesel engine—the first diesel-powered airplane sold in America

In the early years of the Stinson Aircraft Corporation, diesel engines were just beginning development. Two companies, Packard Motor Car Company and the Guiberson Corporation, began designing diesel aircraft engines. The following are accounts of their engine manufacturing and their involvement with Stinson.

Packard Motor Car Company

In 1927 Packard Motor Car Company's chief aeronautical engineer, Captain Lionel M. Woolson, came across a new patent for a diesel injection system that had been issued to Dr. Hermann Dorner of Germany. Woolson had Packard acquire both an air-cooled and a water-cooled Dorner diesel for testing. Those tests convinced him to persuade the corporate management of Packard that there was an opportunity to develop and sell an air-cooled, radial, diesel aircraft engine. On August 18, 1927, a license agreement for the Dorner injection system was signed between Alvan Macauley, President of Packard, and Dr. Dorner.

Captain Woolson, his assistant engineer Marvin Steele, and the Packard engineering department began designing a lighter-weight engine, while Dr. Dorner and his assistant Adolph A. Widmann started work on the combustion system. Within a year they had a working prototype with a displacement of 982 cu. in. Eventually six handbuilt prototype engines would be made and tested. This radial engine was a 4-stroke cycle diesel of nine cylinders with a single valve per cylinder. It produced 225-hp at 1,950 rpm utilizing a 16 to 1 compression ratio, although after some redesigning to get idle speeds down, most production engines would have a compression ratio of 14:1. To handle the high compression ratios, Packard engineers made the moving parts (such as pistons, connecting rods and crankshafts) stronger and heavier than in gasoline engines. Production engines would use a conventional starter and generator electrical system.

When it was time for operational tests, Packard purchased a new 1928 Stinson Detroiter SM-1D, NC7654, s/n M262. After removing the factory installed 220-hp Wright J-5 Whirlwind engine, the 225-hp Packard diesel was mounted, and the Detroiter was reregistered as SM-1DX, NX7654, s/n M262.

Just 13 months after the project was started, the diesel-powered Stinson was scheduled to be officially tested for the first time at the Packard Proving Grounds on September 19, 1928. However, Packard's chief test pilot Walter E. Lees took it up the day before to check for any problems and found a high idle complication that a quick workaround temporarily solved. This marked the first flight of a diesel-powered aircraft. The next day the official test proved so successful that Packard approved the engine for production and broke ground for a new factory.

Production engine development continued, as did the airborne testing of the prototype powerplant. On May 13, 1929, Lees and Woolson flew the Stinson SM-1DX Detroiter from Detroit to Langley Field in Virginia—a 700-mile trip that took six-and-a-half flying hours. Fuel cost was an astonishing 20 percent of that of a gasoline engine. The first production engine (s/n 100) passed its 50-hour certification test in February 1930, and on March 6 the Department of Commerce awarded Packard engine type certificate number 43. On March 9, 1930, Lees and Woolson made an 1,100-mile flight from Detroit to Miami in 10 hours and 15 minutes, with fuel costs being eight dollars and fifty cents. While designed to as a diesel burner, the engine could actually use almost any distillate fuel oil, and Packard used simple furnace oil for all of its testing and endurance flights.

The production engine, called the RD-980—much improved over the prototype and priced to various aircraft manufacturers at $7,500—was shown for the first time at the All-American Aircraft Show in Detroit starting on April 5, 1930. Packard had a small number of diesel-engined airplanes at the show, including the Stinson NX7654, which now had over 1,500 hours of testing on the engine. There was also a second Packard diesel-powered Stinson in attendance.

On April 8, 1930, Stinson was granted ATC 312 for the Model SM-8D, which was powered by the RD-980 Packard diesel. Except for the engine difference, this aircraft was basically the same as the SM-8B Junior. The author could identify two SM-8D aircraft: NC200W, s/n 4036; and NC227W, s/n 4100. NC200W was one of 75 Stinson sold between February 15 and April 1, with 68 of those airplanes being Stinson Juniors. It was the first sale of a diesel-powered airplane, and although sold to Charles T. Stork of New York, NC200W was at the Detroit show as part of the Stinson lineup. For the New York Air Show beginning on May 3, Packard honored Stinson by clearing out their showrooms at Sixty-first and Broadway, leaving just one car. They filled the empty space with the NC200W, which had the world's fastest speedboat, Miss America VIII, which was powered by two 1,100-hp Packard gas engines, tucked under its right wing. The remaining space was taken up by various other Packard-built engines.

Alvan Macauley (left), President of the Packard Motor Car Co. and Charles A. Lindbergh with SM-1DX, NX7654—the first airplane to fly using a diesel engine. Photo taken on August 16, 1929, when Lindbergh visited the Packard Proving Grounds, test-flying the Stinson for approximately 40 minutes.

The Smithsonian Institution Collection

Stinson SM-8D, NC200W, s/n 4036 being set up in Packard's New York City their showrooms at Sixty-first and Broadway, where it was displayed during the New York Air Show week May 3rd - 11th 1930

As a result of the demonstrations at the air shows, Thompson Aeronautical Corporation, which had Air Mail contracts, had the 220-hp Wright J-5 Whirlwind on their 1928 Stinson Detroiter SM-1DA, NC9600, s/n M303 replaced with the RD-980 Packard diesel, making it a SM-1DX. Stinson NC9600 became the first diesel powered aircraft to fly an Air Mail route. Also due to the New York show, Elmer Jones, the sales manager for the Scranton Packard dealer, changed the work order for his Stinson SM-8A Junior, NC227W, s/n 4100 that was under construction, having it instead built as a SM-8D.

Packard continued to refine its engine, producing various horsepower ratings, even winning the Collier Trophy in 1931 for its contribution to aviation with this engine. However, a combination of factors—the death of Capt. L. M. Woolson on April 23, 1930, just after the public debut of the RD-980, and the lack of sales to aviation manufacturers both at home and abroad at the start of the depression—caused the diesel program to be discontinued in 1933 with just around 100 engines produced.

Of the four Stinson RD-980 Packard diesel-powered airplanes that have been identified here, the registration for the SM-8D, NC200W was canceled on June 8, 1931, while the Thompson Aeronautical Corporation sold their SM-1DX, NC9600 to Transamerica AW, which had it converted to a SM-1D300 with the installation of a 300-hp Wright J-6 engine. The SM-8A, NC227W was in service longer that any of the others, not relinquishing its registration until November 22, 1939. Packard continued to use SM-1DX, NX7654 as a testbed, replacing the original prototype RD-980 with production engine number 134. The original engine was donated to the Smithsonian, where it is on display today. In 1935 Packard donated NX7654 to the Henry Ford Museum where it was displayed for many years until it was sold to the Golden Wings Flying Museum in Minnesota, where it is on display in its original condition. However, as of this writing it has been offered for sale.

The Guiberson Corporation

Through the 1920s and early 1930s, the Guiberson Corporation of Dallas was the world's largest builder of oil well drilling equipment. Allen Guiberson used aircraft in his day-to-day business operations. Being in the oil business, he knew that in the refining process, diesel fuel was cheaper to "crack." Diesel fuel was slower burning than gasoline but produced roughly the same amount of power, and in commercial operations, it proved to be more fuel-efficient. Guiberson also knew that diesel fuel could be refined and sold to the retail market at a cheaper price than aviation gasoline, and that the Guiberson Corporation's engineering and development departments had the ability to build almost anything, including an air-cooled, diesel aircraft engine.

With this idea in mind, Guiberson flew to California and met with Fred Thaheld, who was working on his own diesel engine design. Guiberson hired Thaheld as chief of the new aircraft engineering department. Research and development began in 1929, and progress continued until a 125-hp five-cylinder, air-cooled, radial aircraft engine was running on a test stand. The 125-hp engine was only suitable for trainer aircraft, making the engineering department switch to a larger engine for the executive and small airliner market. The new engine, the Guiberson, was a 14-cylinder, air-cooled radial with a 14 to 1 compression ratio producing 330-hp. It was started with the use of a Breez "shotgun" starter. The Guiberson engine burned 7 gph while a comparable gasoline powered version would have burned more than 20 gph.

Under the direction of Fred Thaheld, the engineering department began the development of a diesel aircraft engine designed for volume production in late 1939. In April 1940, Guiberson Corporation was granted ATC 220 for a nine-cylinder, air-cooled, radial, diesel aircraft engine. The Guiberson A–1020 was rated at 310-hp at 2,150 rpm at sea level. Number One Diesel as we know it today was not available in the 1930s, so the A–1020 was designed to run on kerosene or the slightly cheaper distillate.

The Wright radial 350-hp R760-E2 engine was removed from Stinson Reliant SR-9D NC17132, s/n 5210, and a Guiberson A–1020 diesel engine was installed on the aircraft. This aircraft made an extensive sales tour through North and South America. Every aircraft manufacturer was given an opportunity to examine and fly the Guiberson-powered Stinson Reliant. At every airport, the Stinson received favorable comments from aircraft owners and pilots, yet there was a lack of interest from aircraft manufacturers. The A–1020 passed 1,600 hours of operation without overhaul and was then removed and replaced with a Wright R760-E2. During WWII thousands of modified versions of the engine, the 250-hp T-1020 and the 350-hp T-1400, were produced by the Buda Engine Company of Harvey, Illinois as light tank engines. In the early 1980s, there was an unsubstantiated rumor of a restoration project in California, where a Stinson Reliant owner was planning to install an A–1020 engine in his aircraft.

Fred Thaheld left Guiberson in 1944 to carry on his development of a diesel engine for the light three- and four-place aircraft. The 125-hp, four-cylinder Thaheld engine was eventually mounted on a Stinson 10A. The complete account of the Thaheld diesel is presented in *Stinson's Golden Age, Volume 1*.

In the mid 1950s, Dresser Corporation purchased Guiberson in an effort to expand its oilfield service business. Dresser Tools, acquired by GE Capital in 2011, continues to hold the design rights to the Guiberson diesel aircraft engine.

Stinson SR-9D NC17132, s/n 5210 had the original 285-hp Wright R-760-E1 engine replaced by a 310-hp Guiberson A–1020 diesel engine and reregistered as NX17132, making it the first airplane to fly using a Guiberson engine.

This converted Stinson SM-1DX NC9600, s/n M303 belonging to the Thompson Aeronautical Corporation, became the first diesel engine-powered airplane to fly the Air Mail.

Chapter 27
Albert H. Schramm: Pioneer Aviator and Stinson Test Pilot

Stinson test pilot Albert H. Schramm with the red and white 1944 Stinson 108-1, NX31519, s/n Experimental 1, created from the 1941 Stinson 10A, NC31519, s/n 7769

With Eddie's love for flying and an engineer's mind, Albert Schramm proved to be an excellent resource for the Stinson company. As a corporate pilot, he flew a Stinson Model R 2,272 hours from 1932 to 1935. After becoming the chief test pilot for Stinson in 1935, Schramm collaborated in the development of Stinson aircraft, specifically the Model 105 and SR-8. His innovative engineering modifications contributed to the certification of the 105 and its successor models.

Albert was born to German immigrant parents who settled in South Dakota in the early 1890s. At an early age, Albert decided farming was not for him. He saw his first airplane at age 16 in 1925 and chose to pursue a career in aviation. His father furnished the facilities on the farm to raise and sell hogs to cover tuition and living expenses so that Albert could attend aviation school.

Albert enrolled at the Auto Electrical and Aviation School located in Aberdeen, South Dakota for the fall term of 1927. The school year ran for eight months—September 1, 1927 to May 1, 1928. Near the end of the school year, aviation flight hours were available at $250 per hour. The student was expected to solo after two hours of flight instruction, making satisfactory takeoffs, level flight, do turns and make satisfactory landings. Albert paid $500 in advance for two hours of flight instruction, and he soloed on March 10, 1928. After graduating with honors in May, he began a search for employment in the aviation field.

Two men from eastern South Dakota were planning to form a flying circus, which would consist of two airplanes and a woman who would do wire walking and exhibition parachute jumps. They approached Albert and asked if he would fly the aircraft carrying the parachute jumper, explaining that besides the aerial acts, his primary source of income would be from carrying passengers on short flights. His salary would be a percentage of the revenue his aircraft generated. Albert accepted the job and began a summer-long adventure. The parachutist would pack her parachute in a large bag, securely fasten the parachute harness around her, climb into the aircraft, and tie the bottom of the bag securely to the floor. When the aircraft was positioned sufficiently upwind, she would climb over the side of the aircraft. As she fell free, the parachute would be pulled from the canvas bag and deployed, and she would glide to the landing zone in front of a crowd of spectators. The jumps were made from 2,000 to 3,000 feet AGL (Above Ground Level). On occasion, the parachutist would make two to three jumps a day.

Over the next several years he had an opportunity to fly a variety of interesting aircraft. The first was a World War I surplus Curtiss Jenny powered by a V-8 engine, followed by a WACO-9, and later a WACO-10. One of his favorite aircraft was the Kari-Keen Coupe, a petite two-place aircraft manufactured in Sioux City, Iowa. The next aircraft was a six-place Travel Air 10-B monoplane powered by a 300-hp 9-cylinder Wright J-6 radial engine. He was very unimpressed with the small, two-place side-by-side Monocoupe because he found it had a tendency to ground loop. It was very unstable and would not fly hands-off and level flight. The next two aircraft were an American Eagle open-cockpit, 3-place biplane, and a Curtiss Wright Junior, a two-place, tandem high-wing monoplane powered by an air-cooled, 3-cylinder Szekely pusher engine that was mounted back and above the wing.

In early 1932, Albert became chief pilot for a company that owned Silver Fox Ranches across the western United States. Technically, he was employed by The Silver Fox Ranch at Hackensack, Minnesota, the headquarters for the American Division of the Mascot International, AG, with their main office located in Zürich, Switzerland. They planned to purchase a new aircraft and based on their needs, Albert suggested a Stinson. Working with a Stinson dealer, they reviewed specifications and performance data for the Model S and the Model R. The Model R was a deluxe aircraft powered by a 215-hp R-680 Lycoming engine with a base price of $5,595. It was special ordered with larger fuel tanks, landing lights, modern instruments, and a top-of-the-line compass, which pushed the price to over $7,000. On April 3, 1932, Albert took possession of the Stinson Model R NC10874, s/n 8514, at the factory. This was the first of many trips to the Stinson factory in Wayne, Michigan. The Stinson company maintained an extensive maintenance facility, and except for the most minor issues, all inspections and repair were completed in Wayne.

The Model R was a very reliable aircraft, and Albert flew from New York City to the West Coast across the upper tier of states many times, including several trips to Alaska. In his first year of employment for Silver Fox Ranch, Albert flew over 1,100 hours. The winters in Minnesota were very cold, and he had a canvas cover designed to cover the engine and developed a gasoline heater to warm it. When the aircraft was away from his home base and tied down out in the cold, he would drain the oil before it had an opportunity to cool and take out the battery. By keeping the oil in a warm room, he could pour it back into the engine, and was always amazed to watch the engine start with warm oil on a fresh battery.

In the mid-thirties, aircraft used for IFR flight had the following instruments: a good compass, a vacuum-powered turn and bank, a rate of climb indicator, and a sensitive altimeter. Radios were not available for light aircraft and the airlines were just beginning to use radios near their landing fields. Pilots used roadmaps, railroad tracks, highways, and the names of towns painted on the top of buildings as their primary navigation aids. Some communities painted the town name on the water tower and a large arrow marking magnetic North for the benefit of the pilots.

In his autobiography, *My Life's Journey*, Albert covered many exciting flying adventures while flying for the management of the Silver Fox Ranches. One of his accounts is presented here. In this story, he was flying the Stinson Model R NC8514.

> On one of my flights during the dust storms of the thirties, was with a lady passenger. I left Casper, Wyoming for Backus, Minnesota with a fuel stop scheduled in Rapid City, South Dakota and Huron, South Dakota. About one hour into the flight, I observed a big black dust cloud covering the entire horizon in front of me as far as I could see. I was flying about 3,000 feet and began to climb to see if I could see the top of the dust storm. Flying blind in the dust storm for any length of time could ruin the engine. On reaching my altitude of 12,000 feet, I was on top of the dust storm, and continued to Rapid City. My only means of navigation was my compass, since I could not see the ground for checkpoints. I hoped that when I reached Rapid City, the storm would be over.
>
> When I reached my expected arrival time for my first fuel stop, I was concerned for all I could see below me, now and in the distance ahead, flying above the storm, was dust. Rapid City is located about halfway between Casper and Hu-

ron. My fuel gauges were starting to show half empty. I was somewhere in the vicinity of Rapid City now, and no way could I make an emergency blind landing for fuel in this mountainous Black Hills area. Returning back to Casper was out for I would be out of fuel before I arrived there with a headwind to contend with, and no suitable place to make an emergency landing. My only choice now was Huron, South Dakota.

As I continued on flying above all of the dirt in the sky below me, my feelings were that the dust storm would still be blowing when I reached my next scheduled stop, and this time I would be making an emergency landing because of lack of fuel. My landing in some cow pasture or at the Huron airport would depend on how my navigation by compass under these extreme conditions turned out and how well I allowed for wind drift in not being able to see the ground below me.

After four hours in the air since I left Casper, my fuel gauges were showing near the empty mark. It was now the time to start down while I still had some fuel left. I informed my lady passenger sitting up front with me not to become alarmed for we are low on fuel, and we are going down to the land. Also, I told her it would be dark inside the cabin as we glided down. I assured her my instrument lights would be on, and I will be watching them very closely for I will be flying by using the instruments the rest of the way.

We were still at 12,000 feet when we began our descent. I started down with the engine at idle at 500 feet per minute rate of descent. My sensitive altimeter was set for sea level because the intended landing was 1,275 feet above at Huron. In other words, when my altimeter showed a reading of 1275 feet, we should be on the ground. It certainly was pitch dark inside the dust storm, and when the altimeter showed 3,000 feet, I reduced my dissent to 200 feet per minute and eased down to 2,000 feet. I was now 725 feet above the ground. I used engine power to maintain level flight for a few minutes and eased down to 500 feet above the ground. Now I could just make out the ground appearing below me now and then. I lowered my altitude some more and visibility improved some. The dust was sure blowing along the ground below. I was very much relieved now for the ground below me was farmland and level. If I was way off on my navigation and could not locate the Huron airport, I could make an emergency landing most anyplace. I came to a small town as we were flying along at 150 to 200 feet altitude. I recognized this small town as Wosley, South Dakota located west and a few miles northwest of Huron for a distance of 15 miles.

I headed straight for the Huron airport north of town, using the appropriate compass heading. Visibility was extremely limited. My fuel gauges were now showing empty. From my past experience, I knew there was still a small amount of fuel left, but it was a critical position for me to be in, and I certainly needed to land soon. The sky was dark; it was just like flying at night. It was noon time as we approached the city of Huron on the north side and the airport was close by to my left. The lights were on downtown and the cars were driving with their lights on. I made my left turn, approached the airport, turned on my landing lights, and landed. I taxied to the hangar, parked, and covered the engine with the canvas cover to keep the blowing dust from entering the engine compartment. The two of us went inside the office to wait out the storm, which blew itself out at about three in the afternoon. During our waiting period for the storm to let up, I visited with my passenger. She showed no effects from the flight and was anxious to fly again. I had the airplane refueled according to the amount of gas required to fill the tanks; there was about 2 gallons left when we landed. We then left for our very relaxing and pleasant three hour, nonstop flight to Backus airport. My passenger helped me put the airplane in the hangar, and in our drive to Hackensack, she told me how much she enjoyed her Western trip by air. Even today, I still am amazed at how calm she remained during that dark, blind flight down to the Huron airport.

In his second-year flying for The Silver Fox Ranch, Albert met a very beautiful young woman, Miss Mary Marie Smerke. On his first date, he learned she preferred the name Marie. Just three months after they met, they parked at their favorite spot by a beautiful lake with reflection of the full moon shining over the waters, and Marie gladly accepted an engagement ring. Mary Marie Smerke was united in marriage with Albert Schramm on February 3, 1934. Their wedding vows were exchanged in the Crosier Monastery at Hastings, Nebraska. After a memorable honeymoon, the newlyweds arrived back in Hackensack on February 8, 1934. The Lycoming engine on the Model R NC10874 required its second overall before the flying season started again. His boss suggested he take Marie with him to the Stinson factory in Wayne while this work was being done. This trip turned out to be a real honeymoon trip for the Schramms. They stayed in a hotel near the Stinson plant from February 15 to March 10 with no business problems or flying to do.

The Chinchilla-Silver Fox bubble was collapsing and the need for a corporate pilot had passed. On May 29, 1935, Albert was told to retire the airplane and put it up for sale. Although the airplane was in good condition, it had many hours and the price was set at $2,500. Because of financial hardships, the company was behind on his salary, and to make up for back pay and severance pay, he would receive one half of the sale price of the aircraft. Working through the Stinson dealer that sold him the aircraft, the sale was completed. Albert received his $1,250 and became officially unemployed. Total time on the Model R at the time of the sale was 2,272 hours.

As Albert inquired about the availability of flying jobs, the Stinson dealer suggested he should contact the Stinson factory service manager because he had had a work relationship with the service department there. An interview was soon arranged, and Stinson management was impressed with Albert's total flight time of 3,466 hours. Albert was hired as a mechanic and a corporate pilot for Stinson. He immediately began flying, and by November 1935, he was flying full-time. Demonstration flights for prospective customers and sales trips with the service manager became routine. Stinson aircraft owners were having serious problems with the Smith electric controllable pitch propeller. Lycoming motors of Williamsport, Pennsylvania, was in the process of certifying the Hamilton Standard two-position propeller, and Albert was asked to pick up a SR-6 at the Newark airport that was ex-

Cover of the Albert H. Schramm's very rare autobiography, My Life's Journey, which Schramm self-published and gave out copies to friends and family and is a collector's item today

periencing high fuel consumption and ferry it to Williamsport for in-flight fuel flow tests. While there, he was also to start flight tests for CAA approval of the Hamilton Standard propeller. A Stinson SM-8A was fitted with the new propeller for the certification flight tests. The Smith electric propeller was also modified, and Albert flight tested it. By January 17, 1936, both the SR-6 fuel test and the Hamilton Standard propeller test were completed, and he returned to the Stinson factory.

About mid-year 1938, rumors began that Stinson was to build a small, three-place aircraft. The pilot and a passenger would be side-by-side up front with dual controls and a third passenger would sit crosswise in the back seat. Albert was very involved with the flight testing and development of this aircraft, the HW-75. He describes his input further in his autobiography:

On February 3, 1939, I made the initial flight with our new HW-75. To my amazement, the trim was perfect, and the HW-75 flew straight and level with my hands and feet off the controls. Stinson management, and the sales and engineering departments wanted a spin-resistant or virtually spin-proof airplane in the HW-75. I knew from the very beginning this would be a very big order to accomplish for an airplane of this size—to haul three passengers without spinning. As predicted, the spin test program continued for three months before the problem was solved. That little airplane would spin like nobody's business and did it well.

Engineering kept on making changes after each flight, but it did not help. It kept on spinning. I was approaching the end of the second month in the spin test program with no solution in sight. I went home and spent the day with my family, and they were pleased I was able to do so. We all went for a nice long drive and stopped at a few ice cream stores. That evening when I retired for the night, I must have had the spin problem on my mind when I fell asleep. I woke around midnight from a dream, and during the dream, I figured out what could be the solution to our spin problem on the HW-75.

The next morning at work, I went over my dream with my engineering friend, Chief Engineer R. W. Middlewood, to see what he thought about the idea. He remained silent for a few minutes, and then with a big smile, he said I believe it will work. In my dream, I installed a device that would limit the up travel of the elevator to the very minimum with the flaps up and still execute a three-point landing at the maximum forward CG loading. That device would then disengage to allow the full increase up elevator travel required with the flaps down under the same forward CG loading. Most airplanes require considerably more up elevator travel with the flaps down than with the flaps up, and the HW-75 was one of them.

The next day, the shop mechanics attached a fixed stop on the elevator tube.

1932 Stinson Model R, NC10874, s/n 8514 purchased by Clement A. Pepin of St. Paul, Minnesota

The next morning with the chief engineer as an observer, we climbed to 10,000 feet to check the stall conditions at idle power. With the elevator control all the way against the stop and flaps up, it continued to ride along below the minimum landing speed. I went for the full power spin to the left first as I would have the benefit of the engine torque pulling us to the left, and when the airplane stopped climbing, I applied all controls rapidly for a left spin. I found out immediately that I did not have enough up elevator to throw the airplane into a spin. All we did was to nose down into a half turn and pick up flying speed again. We next tried for a full power spin to the right. We did not even get a half turn to the right on this one.

I continued with the HW 75 spin program. Engineering policy was to move the CG back in increments of one half percentage point for each spin. With the maximum rear CG location, I tried the right spin first, and the aircraft made one turn to stop rotation on its own with the controls still held for the right spin. On the attempt to the left, it made almost two turns before rotation stopped on its own with the controls held for the spin. After nearly three months of spin testing with over 1500 spin rotations during this period, a spin proof on a conventional-type aircraft was achieved. The CAA certified the capital HW-75 during the first week of May 1939, and delivery to Stinson dealers began one week later.

Test flying the HW-75 was not Albert's last experience with spin difficulties. He nearly crashed when the prototype for the L-5 went into a spin. The following is his hair-raising account of the flight:

The first military airplane I flight-tested was a military version of the three-place Model 10A Voyager. This airplane carried the model number L-5 known to the military as the "Flying Jeep". The fuselage was reworked into a tandem, two-place seating arrangement with extensive use of Plexiglas for good visibility in all directions.

My first spin to the left was with maximum rear CG. It wanted to keep on rotating, and I was receiving a very unsatisfactory reaction to the spin. On the second flight, I decided to fly higher than usual to 10,500 feet. I made my first attempt on a spin to the left. It went right into the spin with the nose well down on the first turn. On the next one half turn the L-5 started to shake and the nose started to come up. This I knew from past experience was a start of a flat spin. I immediately applied controls for spin recovery, but it was already too late, and the nose kept coming up. The elevator control stick back pressure was so great, it overcame my physical strength and continued to move all the way back and was locked in this position. The engine stopped running as they all do in a true flat spin with a gravity fed fuel system. After a loss of 3,000 feet and some 30 turns, there was no change in the attitude of the flat spin nor could I produce a change in attitude by use of the controls. The rudder was useless; there was no effect or feel.

I checked the fuel tank gauges, and I was losing fuel as it was being sucked out of the gasoline tank vents. I was also losing my engine oil as it was being sucked out through the engine breather vent. My altitude was now showing 6,000 feet and I went for the emergency spin recovery. I dumped the ballast first knowing from past experience this would not help recovery, but since this spin was more violent, it might help some to get rid of the weight. The ripcord on the left spin chute was pulled first; no change in the spin. Then I pulled the right spin chute; still no change, I looked back to see if the spin chutes had opened, but the canopies were being torn to shreds and twisting themselves into pieces as if in extreme turbine air. They soon twisted the flexible steel cables apart and left the airplane.

My only hope for spin recovery was gone. This was first time the spin chute did not get me out of a spin problem. There was no question in my part now—I would have to leave the airplane. I was down to 5000 feet with no change in the spin. Complications soon began to appear for me. The only exit was the right side door. I pulled the door release and the door stayed in place. None of my emergency equipment was working for me. I now realized how great the forces were on the right side of the airplane caused by the rapid rotation of the left flat spin and the rapid movement going to the right. With great effort, I finally got the door to leave. As it left, it followed the right side of the airplane all the way back to the tail services, tearing the fabric off the fuselage as it went back. It hung on the vertical tail for a moment, then came loose and tore a hole in the vertical fin and rudder as it left the airplane.

I tried to move out of the seat to jump, but I was locked in by the extreme back pressure on the elevator control stick. I could not move myself up out of the seat to even get close to the door. I lost a lot of altitude getting the door released, and there was not a whole lot of altitude left. The feeling came over me that I was on my last ride and not going to make it this time. With nothing to lose knowing what was going to happen, I moved aileron fully in the direction of the spin. As I expected it would do, the rotation increased rapidly and tightened up extremely. I was now experiencing high G forces. The L-5 was not spinning flat now, but still rotating in its fast, crazy hard way, giving me my first change in spin condition since I left my altitude at 10,500 feet. I felt the back pressure starting to ease up on the elevator control stick and was able to move the control to the full-forward position. I could recover now if I had enough altitude left. The left wing and nose went down into a near vertical position. Rotation ceased in an inverted dive and the L-5 really picked up air speed that was fast enough to start the propeller rotating. I rolled the L-5 out of its inverted dive and did an extremely rapid high G pull out—far in excess of the 6G's, because I did not know if I had enough altitude left to complete the pull out. I came out close to the ground. The engine started, and I pulled up and flew back to the Stinson field. From the altitude I had lost during the spin, I knew I had gone in excess of 100 turns during my ride down.

It was decided the next morning to have a meeting with Peter Altman, Stinson's consultant aeronautical engineer and a professor at the University of Detroit, for ideas to save the L-5 project. Peter Altman suggested three items during this meeting. The first was to remove one half of the fixed-in board and half of the wing leading edge slot. The most efficient way to achieve this would be to replace the existing wing with a standard 10-A wing. Secondly, increase the horizontal and vertical tail areas by at least 30%, and thirdly, rig the up travel of the elevator to the minimum to satisfy the three-point landing condition at the most forward CG location. The changes took about a week to accomplish. The less up elevator travel was responsible in solving the past spin problems. I did my first spin test with the tail changed, and the L-5 was now spin-less.

There was a great sense of relief at Stinson knowing the L-5 program would be moving forward. I continued the spin test, moving the CG rearward until we reached the maximum rear CG loading. The L-5 went from spin-less at normal CG to a spin resistant at maximum rear CG. At maximum rear CG, I could induce a few spin rotations using full power, and then the rotating would cease. If the controls were still held for spin, the L-5 would go into a spiral turn. The worst of the experimental flights were over for this model, and the design changes were now being incorporated into the production models.

Albert Schramm worked for Stinson from 1935-1945, contributing much to the company and increasing the performance of its aircraft. He also experienced the company's many ownership transfers and changes, and in 1945, he was not pleased with the way Vultee was managing Stinson. That year, Albert ended his career with Stinson and began working for the Bendix Aircraft Corporation, where he foresaw a happier future. He writes:

> I had wanted to wind down my career as an experimental test pilot. I now have flown a total of 8,554 hours. From this total, I have flown a total of 5,118 hours for Stinson during the last 10 years. I did not like what I saw in the future for the Stinson division, and I went for a visit to the Bendix Corporation. I liked what I saw and was offered a job as director of experimental flight operations. I accepted their offer and gave Stinson 30-days notice. On November 1, 1945, I began my first day with Bendix.

Material for this chapter was taken with permission from *My Life's Journey*, an autobiography by Albert H. Schramm.

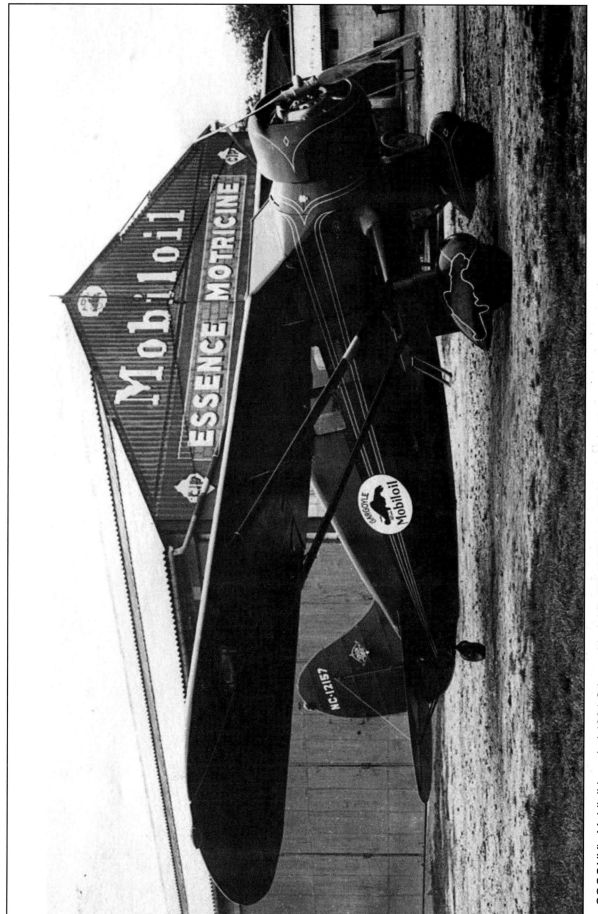

SOCONY's Mobiloil branded 1931 Stinson Model R, NC12157, s/n 8510, powered by a 215-hp Lycoming R-680, was exported to Belgium and later sold to the Aviators Club of Brussels and registered January 6, 1933 as OO-HVS. On May 19, 1939 it was sold to Southern Aircraft Ltd. at Gatwick Airport in England and registered as G-AFUW. On February 10, 1940 it was impressed into service with the Royal Air Force and assigned to the Air Transport Auxiliary at White Waltham Airfield in Berkshire as X8522 where it was later withdrawn from use. Photograph by Harry White

The San Diego Air and Space Museum Collection

Chapter 28
Stinson Personnel

October 1925

Edward A. Stinson, President
William A. Mara, Secretary, Treasurer
Professor Peter Altman, Chief Engineer
William C. Naylor, Engineer
Ben B. Jacobson, Crew Chief for the Junkers-
  Larsen JL-6 (Junkers F.13)

May 1926 - October 1929

Edward A. Stinson, President
Henry E. Hund, Vice President
William A. Mara, Secretary
Richard Fitz-Gerald, Treasurer
Kenneth M. Roman, Chief Engineer in 1928
J. K. Livingston, Chairman, Board of Directors

Board of Directors

Frank W. Blair, President, Union Trust Company
George E. Bachmann, President, Bachman and
  Huff Coal Company
Edward S. Evans, President, E. S. Evans and
  Company, Inc.
Richard Fitz-Gerald, Partner, Lybrand Ross
  Brothers and Montgomery
Richard R. Graham, President, Owen and Graham
George M. Holley, President, Holley Carburetor
  Company
Henry E. Hund, Vice President, Stinson Aircraft
  Corporation
J. K. Livingston, President, McNaughton, Living-
  ston and Griffin
William A. Mara, Secretary, Stinson Aircraft
  Corporation.
Wm. E. Metzgre, Capitalist
Luther D. Thomas, President, Fidelity Trust
  Company
Harold H. Emmons, General Counsel

November 1929—Stinson becomes part of the Cord Holding Company

E. L. Cord, Chairman, Board of Directors
Edward A. Stinson, President
Harvey J. Campbell, Vice President
William A. Mara, Secretary
Kenneth M. Roman, Chief Engineer
William C. Naylor, Engineer

Bruce A. Raun, Factory Superintendent
Randolph G. Page, Chief Test Pilot
Professor Peter Altman, Consulting Engineer
Estelle Stinson, Office Manager

May 1930—Cord Corporation

E. L. Cord, Chairman, Board of Directors
Edward A. Stinson, President and Director
William. A. Mara, Vice President and Director
R. S. Pruitt, Secretary and Director
W. R. Deerfield, Treasurer
Estelle Stinson, Office Manager

1931—Cord Corporation

E. L. Cord Chairman, Board of Directors
Edward A. Stinson, President and Director
William A. Mara, Vice President and Director
R. S. Pruitt, Secretary and Director
Bernard D. DeWeese, General Manager
A. H. Saxon, Chief Engineer
Bruce A. Raun, Factory Superintendent
Estelle Stinson, Office Manager
John C. Kelly, Traveling Sales Manager
Raymond Stinson, Employee

February 1932-August 1934—Cord Corporation

E. L. Cord, Chairman, Board of Directors
L. B. Manning, President and Director
William A. Mara, Vice President
Bernard D. De Weese, General Manager
O. R. Stocke, Treasurer
R. S. Pruitt, Secretary
Robert L. Hall, Chief Engineer (former engineer for
  Grangeville Brothers Aircraft Company. He
  was responsible for designing the famous GB
  racers).
Robert W. Ayer, Chief Transport Engineer (a Har-
  vard graduate also from Grangeville Brothers
  and responsible for designing the GB racers)
J. C. "Jack" Kelly Jr., Transport Engineer and
  Sales Manager (SM)
C. R. "Jack" Irvine, Chief Engineer of Reliant
  Division
Lloyd Skinner, Artist and Industrial Stylist
Professor Peter Altman, Consulting Engineer
Estelle Stinson, Office Manager
Raymond Stinson, Employee

1934—Stinson becomes a subsidiary of Aviation Manufacturing Corp

September 1, 1934 Stinson Management Team:
Bernard D. De Weese, President
William A. Mara, Vice President and General Mgr.
R. S. Pruitt, Secretary
O. R. Stocke, Treasurer
Robert L. Hall, Chief Engineer
Robert W. Ayer, Chief Transport Engineer (designed the Model A Gull Wing)
J. C. "Jack" Kelly Jr., Transport Engineer and SM
C. R. "Jack" Irvine, Chief Engineer of Reliant Div.
Lloyd Skinner, Artist and Industrial Stylist
Professor Peter Altman, Consulting Engineer
Estelle Stinson, Member of Model A Sales Team
Raymond Stinson, Employee
Victor Emmanuel, Director
Henry Lockhart, Director
Tom Gridler, Director

Aviation Manufacturing Corporation Personnel

W. H. Beal, President
Albert L. Lodwick, Executive Vice President from Curtiss Wright Corporation
(Duties included general supervision of the corporation's several manufacturing subsidiaries.)

1935—Subsidiary of Aviation Manufacturing Corp

Bernard D. De Weese, President
William A. Mara, Vice President and Director
John M. Rogers, Secretary
Robert L. Hall, Chief Engineer
Robert W. Ayer, Chief Transport Engineer
J. C. "Jack" Kelly Jr., Transport Engineer and SM
C. R. "Jack" Irvine, Chief Engineer of Reliant Div.
Lloyd Skinner, Artist and Industrial Stylist
Estelle Stinson, Member of Model A Sales Team
Raymond Stinson, Foreman (Frmn)
Albert H. Schramm, Test Pilot

January 1936-August 1938—Subsidiary of Aviation Manufacturing Corp

B. D. De Weese, President (left to become president of Howard Aircraft Corp in July 1936)
William E. Valk, Vice President
John A. Sunborn, Secretary
O. R. Stocke, Treasurer
John M. Rogers, Director
William A. Mara, SM
Robert L. Hall, Chief Engineer
Robert W. Ayer, Chief Transport Engineer
C. R. "Jack" Irvine, Chief Engineer of Reliant Division (designed Gull Wing)
E. H. Huff, Factory Manager
Lloyd Skinner, Artist and Industrial Stylist
Cy Younglove, Test Pilot
Albert H. Schramm, Test Pilot
Estelle Stinson, Export and Military Sales Representative in Washington, D.C.
Walter J. Carr, delivered Model A to China
Raymond Stinson, Foreman

Aviation Manufacturing Corporation Personnel

W. H. Beal, President
O. R. Stocke, Treasurer
William A. Mara, Vice President

Aviation Manufacturing Corporation Divisions

Vultee Aircraft Division Downey, California
Lycoming Division Williamsport, Pennsylvania
Stinson Division Wayne, Michigan

August 1938—Stinson Aircraft Division of Aviation Manufacturing Corporation

W. H. Beal, President
William A. Mara, Vice President
R. S. Pruitt, Secretary
O. R. Stocke, Treasurer
Robert L. Hall, Chief Engineer
Robert W. Ayer, Chief Transport Engineer (went to Grumman Aircraft Co. late 1938)
J. C. "Jack" Kelly Jr., Transport Engineer and SM
C. R. "Jack" Irvine, Chief Engineer of Reliant Div.
Professor Peter Altman, Consulting Engineer
B. D. De Weese Jr., SM
F. O. Johnson, Asst. SM
Cy Younglove, Roving SM
Arthur Thompson, Service Manager
E. H. Huff, Factory Manager
Estelle Stinson, Export and Military Sales Representative in Washington D.C.
Raymond Stinson, Subassembly Production Frmn
Albert H. Schramm, Chief Test Pilot
Victor Emmanuel, Director
Henry Lockhart, Director
Tom Gridler, Director

1939—Stinson Aircraft Division of Aviation Manufacturing Corporation

W. H. Beal, President
William A. Mara, Vice President and SM
O. R. Stocke, Vice President
E. H. Huff, Factory Superintendent
R. W. Middlewood, Chief Engineer
Robert R. Osborne, Chief Engineer (ex-chief engineer for Curtis Wright and a contributor to aviation magazine, appointed chief engineer in May 1939.)
Lewis E. Reisner, (former vice president of Kreider

-Reisner, and Fairchild Hagerstown) becomes Factory Manager.
Estelle Stinson, Export and Military Sales Representative in Washington D.C.
L. H. Wright, Export Manager
A. C. Schwalm, Purchasing Agent
Raymond Stinson, Subassembly Production Foreman
Albert H. Schramm, Chief Test Pilot
Victor Emmanuel, Director
Henry Lockhart, Director
Tom Gridler, Director

November 1939—Stinson becomes a division of Vultee Aircraft Inc

Richard W. Millar, President

June 1940—Vultee Aircraft Inc, Vultee Field: Downey, California

Richard W. Millar, President
Victor Emmanuel, Director
Henry Lockhart, Director
Tom Gridler, Director

Stinson Aircraft Division of Vultee Inc:

William A. Mara, Sales Manager
Lewis E. Reisner, General Manager
Robert R. Osborne, Chief Engineer
P.A. Hewlett, Export Manager
E. H. Huff, Factory Superintendent
A.C. Schwalm, Purchasing Agent
B.A. Rrupert, Production Manager
F.X. Mara, Sales
Dan Thomas, Welding Supervisor
Estelle Stinson, Receptionist
Albert H. Schramm, Chief Test Pilot
Harry W. Smith, Pilot
Russell W. Padgett, Time Keeper
Howard Miller, Sr. Foreman
Raymond Stinson, Subassembly Production Frmn
John Abner, Accountant

1941—Vultee Aircraft Inc.

Richard W. Millar, President
Harry Woodhead, Chairman of Board
Victor Emmanuel, Director

Divisions

Vultee Aircraft Division
Stinson Aircraft Division
Nashville Division

Stinson Division of Vultee Aircraft Inc

C.M. Kaltwassor, Factory Superintendent

William A. Mara, Sales, Advertising and Publicity Manager
A.P. Fontaine, Chief Engineer
L.E. Waggoner, Chief Accountant
A.C. Schwalm, Purchasing Agent
L.M. Challis, Employment Manager
Dan Thomas, Welding Supervisor
Estelle Stinson, Secretary and Notary Public
Raymond Stinson, Final Assembly Production Foreman
Albert H. Schramm, Chief Test Pilot
Harry W. Smith, Pilot

January 1944—Consolidated Vultee Aircraft Corporation: San Diego

Tom M. Girdler, President
Harry Woodhead, Executive Vice President
C.W. Perelle, Vice President of Finance
F.A. Calorie, Secretary and Treasurer
H.A. Sutton, General Sales Manager
Arthur Foristall, Washington Representative

Vultee Divisions

Allentown Division
Elizabeth City Divisiion
Fort Worth Division
Louisville Division
Miami Division
Nashville Division
New Orleans Division
San Diego Division
Stinson Division
Tucson Division
Vultee Field Division
Stout Research Division

Stinson Division of Consolidated Vultee Aircraft Corporation

A. E. Shelton, Division manager
W. A. Mara, Contract Coordinator (left for Bendix Aircraft Corporation in September 1944)
P.A. Hewlett, Washington Representative
D.M. Trask, Industrial Relations Director
C.H. Pace Jr., Production Manager
W. L. Lawson, Factory Manager
A. C. Schwalm, Purchasing Agent
A. G, Tsongas, Chief Engineer
W. C. Lilley, Plant Engineer
Dan Thomas, Welding Supervisor
Estelle Stinson, Secretary and Notary Public
Raymond Stinson, Final-Assembly Production Foreman
Albert H. Schramm, Chief Test Pilot (Left for Bendix Aircraft Corporation in August 1945)
Harry W. Smith, Pilot

Chapter 29
W. A. Wylam Technical Drawings

William Austin "Bill" Wylam was born in Chicago on March 9, 1915. His father worked for the U.S. Signal Corps as a civilian flight instructor, teaching aviation cadets at Chanute Field. By his own admission Bill was heavily into modelling before he turned ten years old. In 1930 he learned mechanical drawing and switched from building models to drawing airplanes. While in college he helped support himself as a part-time designer for various model kit manufacturers, including the Cleveland Model & Supply Company.

From 1932 to 1940, and then again from 1946 to 1970, Bill produced hundreds of technical aviation drawings for *Model Airplane News*. Soon hobbyists were carefully removing these diagrams from the magazine and preserving them in folders and filing cabinets for future scrutiny—this author being among those hobbyists. Of particular interest to this work are the series of 31 drawings of Stinson aircraft that he produced between December 1958 and December 1961.

Due to an increasing workload at NASA, where he was Senior Electrical Engineer for the Space Program, Bill Wylam left *Model Airplane News* in 1970. However, even before his departure, the magazine began producing a series of books containing his drawings, starting in 1964 with *Model Airplane News Presents the Best of Wylam, Book 1*. The fourth volume, published in 1971, contained all the Stinson drawings that had been produced in the late 1950s and early 1960s.

W. A. Wylam passed away in 2015, and as a tribute to his extraordinary talent, *Model Airplane News* has graciously allowed the entirety of his Stinson collection to be reproduced in this volume.

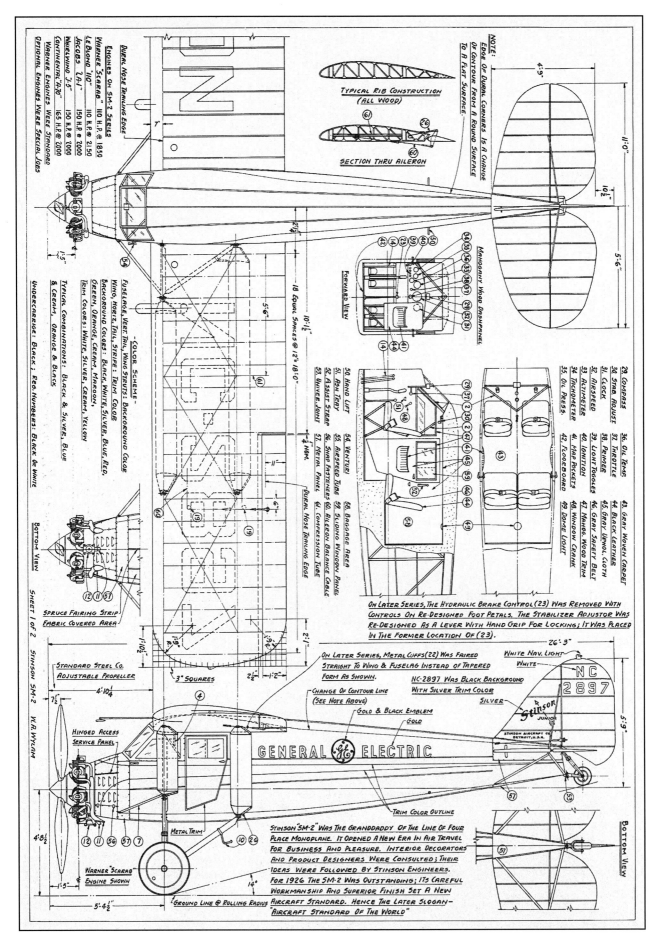

CHAPTER 29

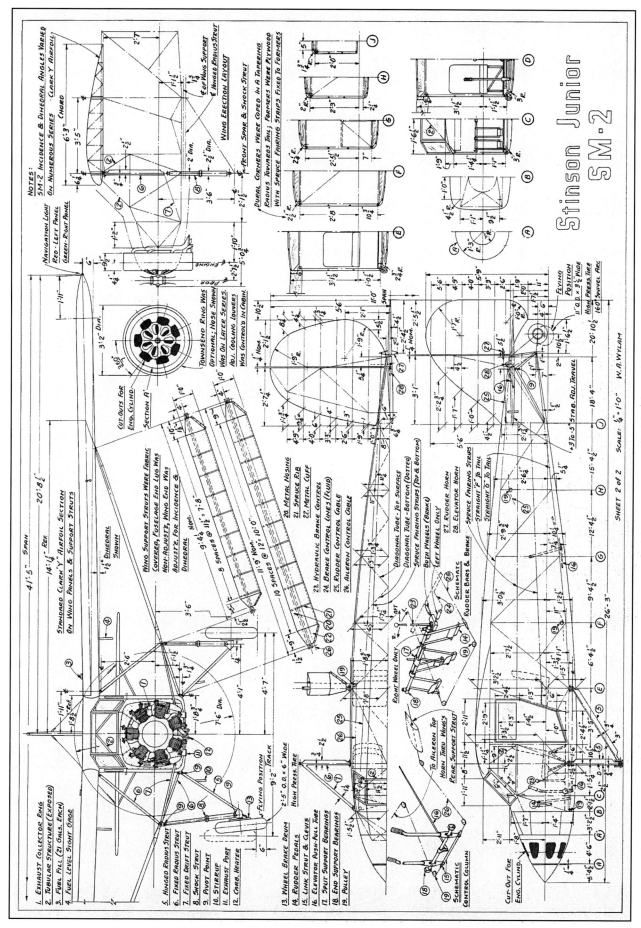

Stinson Junior Model SM-2 - Sheet 2 of 2. Originally published January, 1959

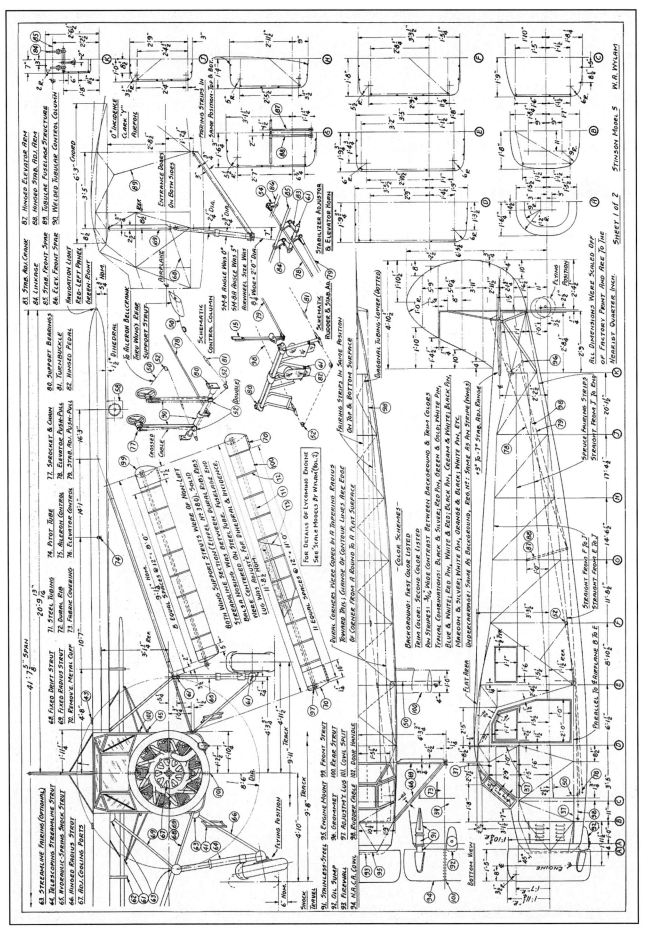

CHAPTER 29

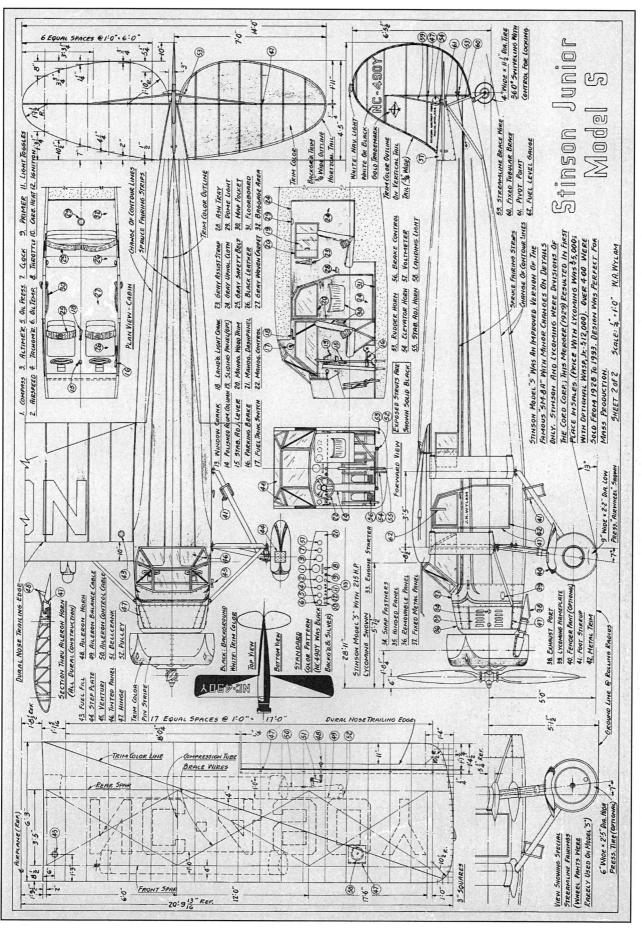

Stinson Junior Model S - Sheet 2 of 2. Originally published December, 1958

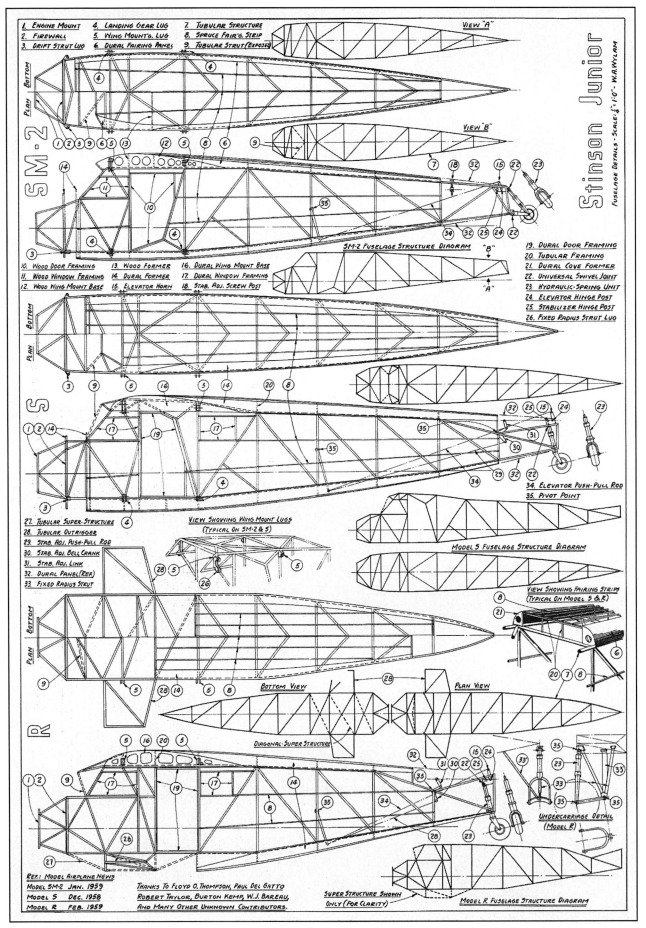

CHAPTER 29

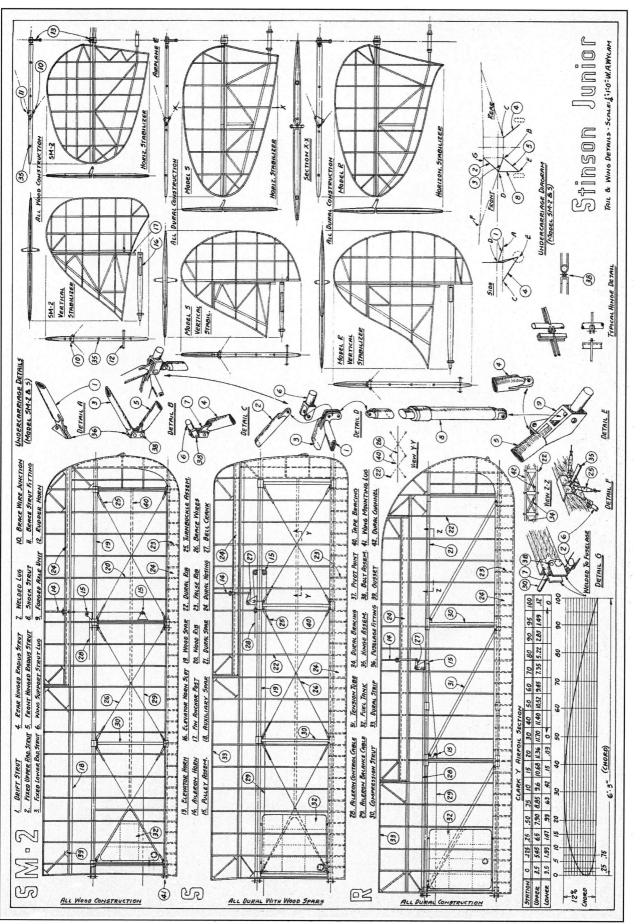

Stinson Junior Tail & Wing Details - Sheet 1 of 1. Originally published November, 1959

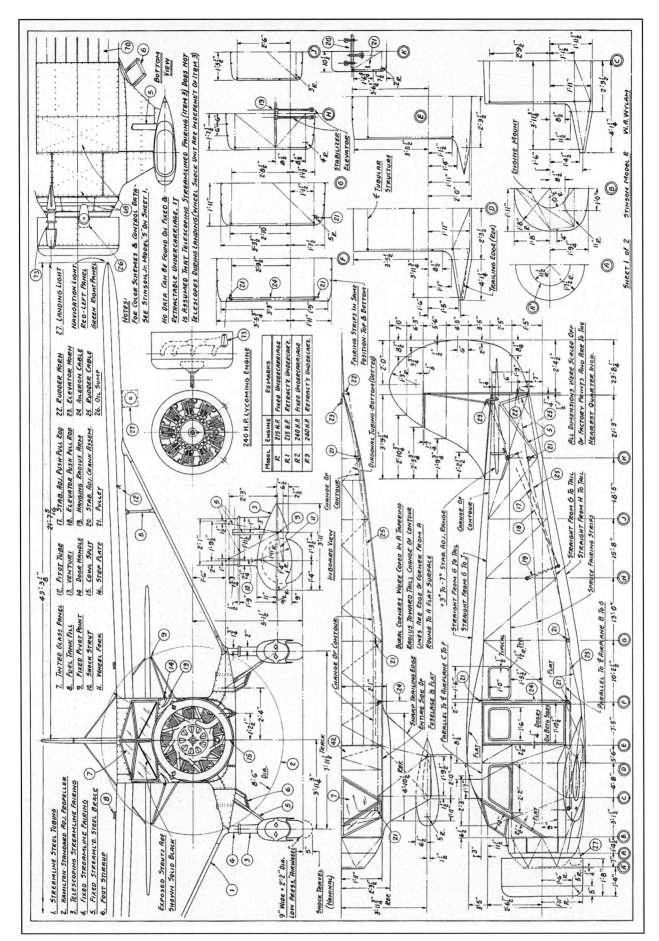

Stinson Junior Model R - Sheet 1 of 2. Originally published February, 1959

CHAPTER 29

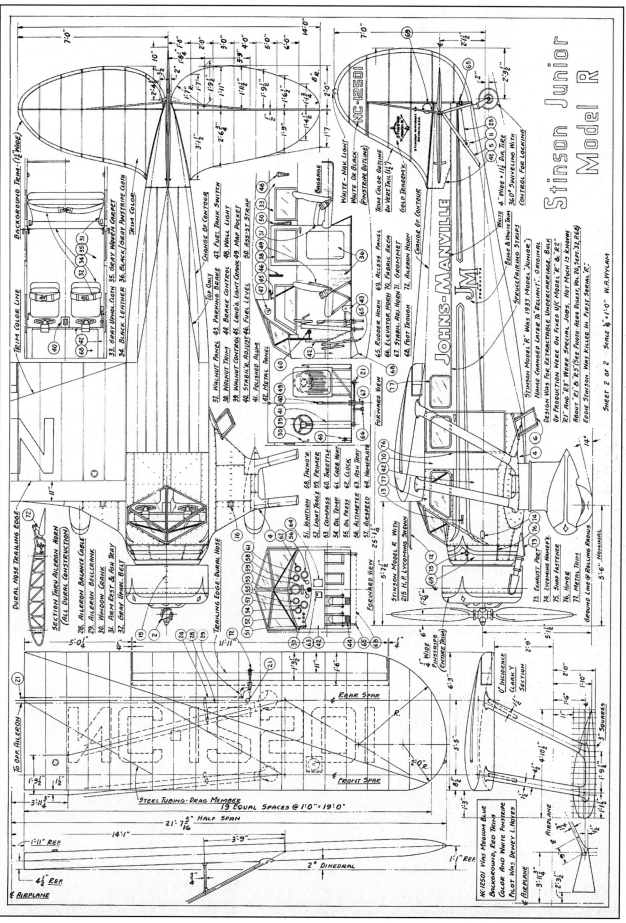

Stinson Junior Model R - Sheet 2 of 2. Originally published February, 1959

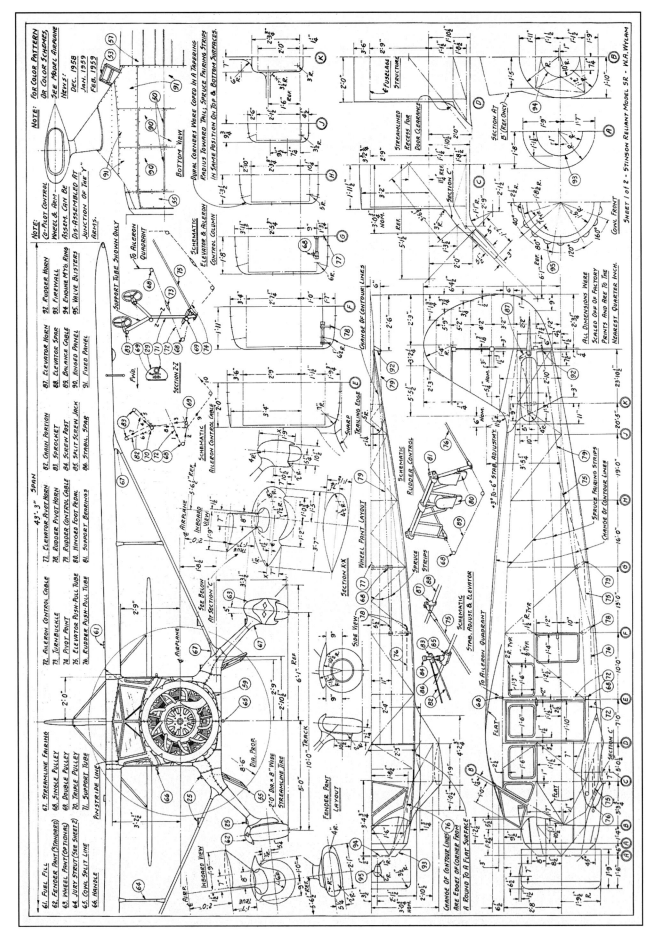

CHAPTER 29

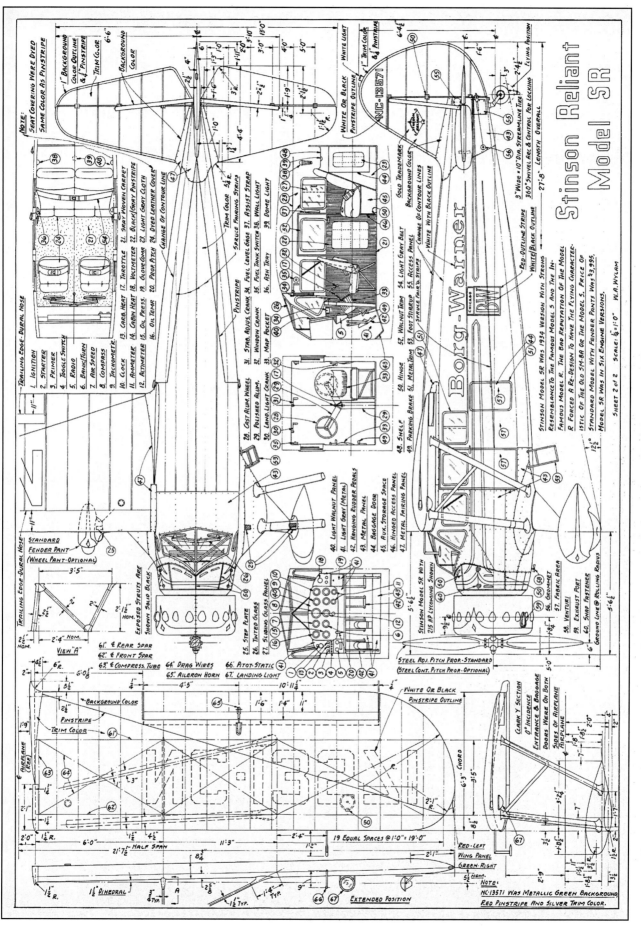

Stinson Reliant Model SR - Sheet 2 of 2. Originally published December, 1959

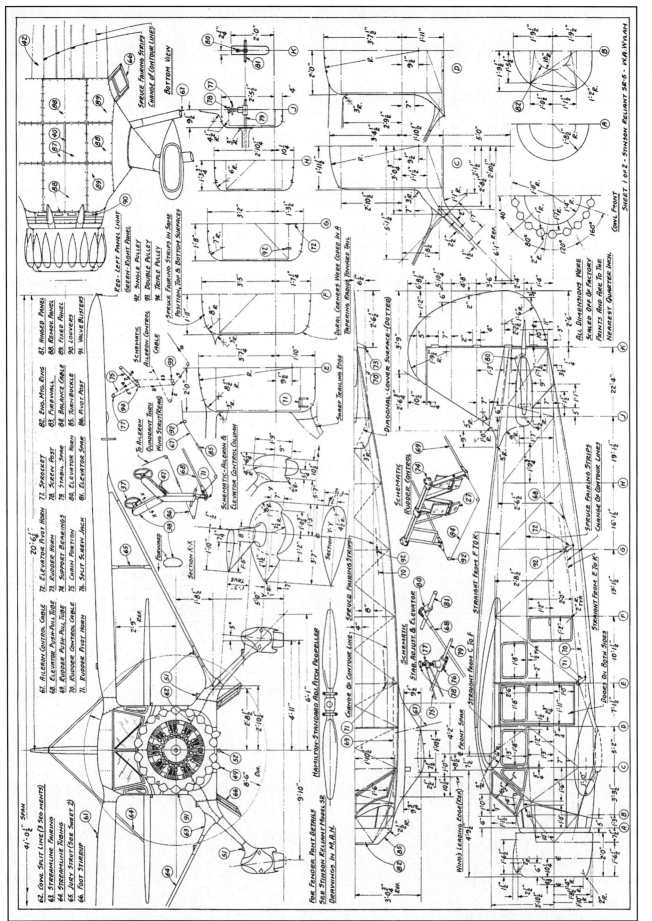

CHAPTER 29

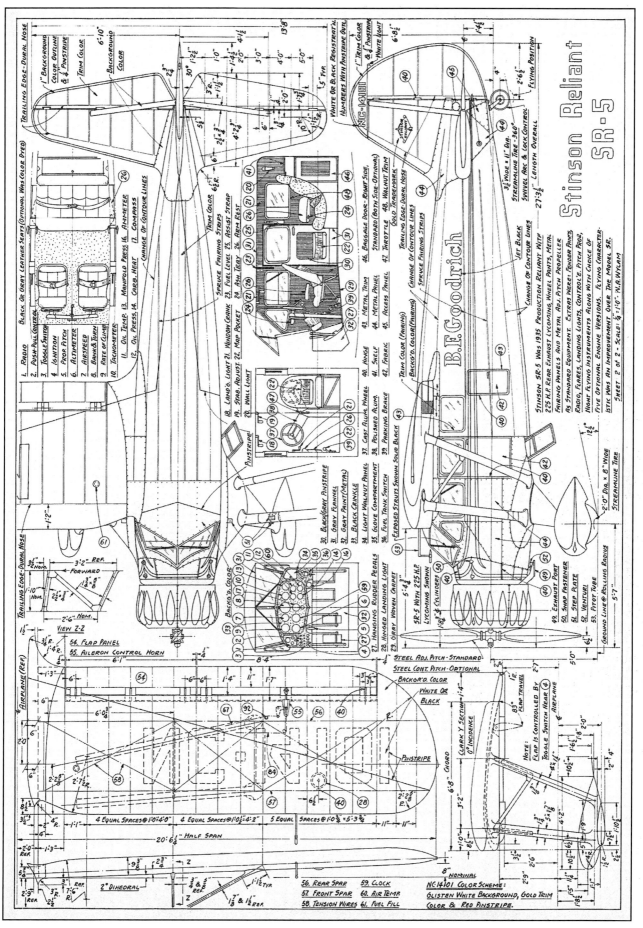

Stinson Reliant Model SR-5 – Sheet 2 of 2. Originally published February, 1960

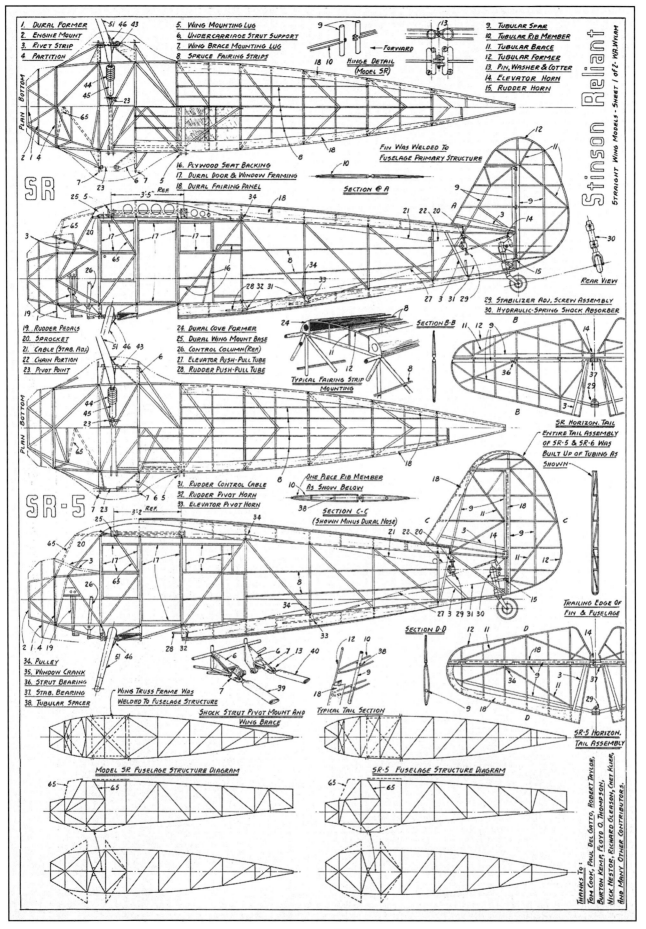

CHAPTER 29

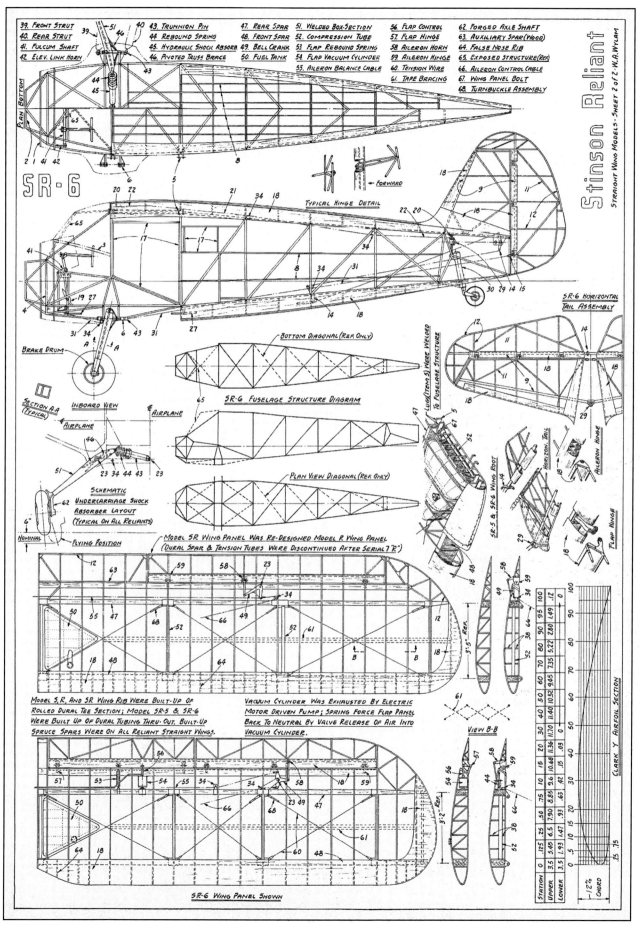

Stinson Reliant Straight Wing Models—Sheet 2 of 2. Originally published May 1960

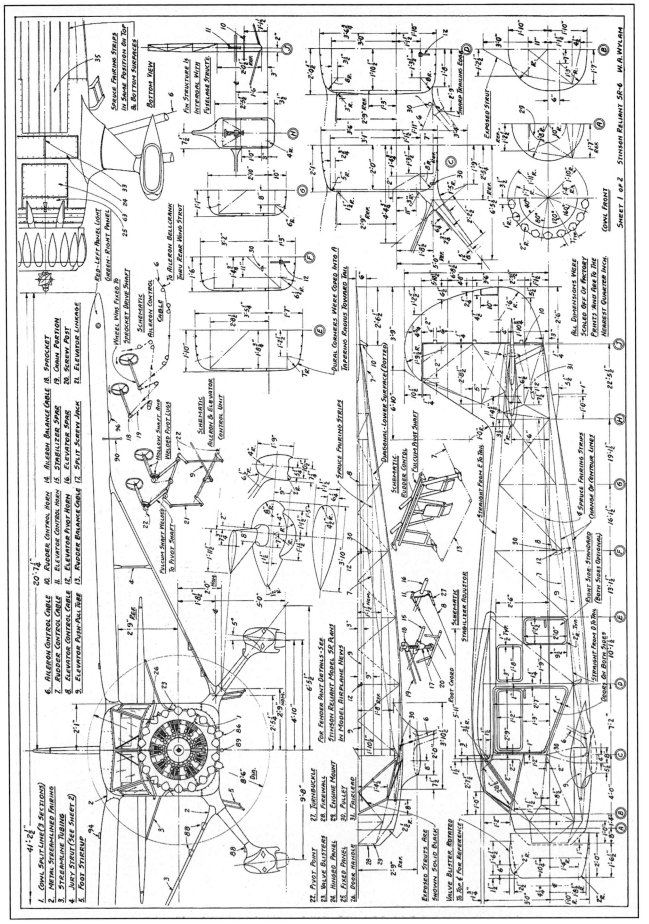

Stinson Reliant Model SR-6 - Sheet 1 of 2. Originally published June, 1960

CHAPTER 29

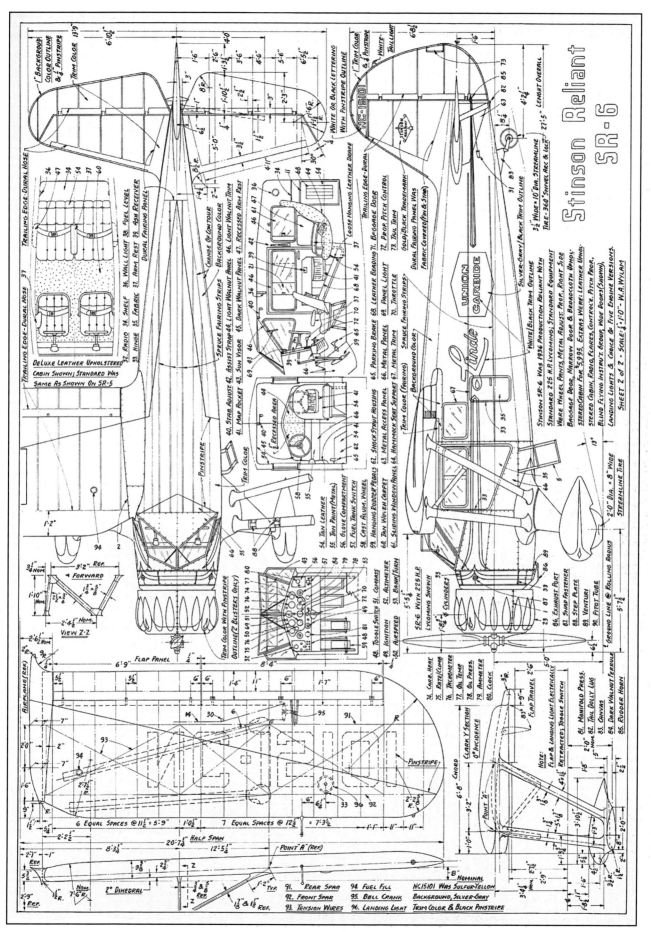

Stinson Reliant Model SR-6 - Sheet 2 of 2. Originally published June, 1960

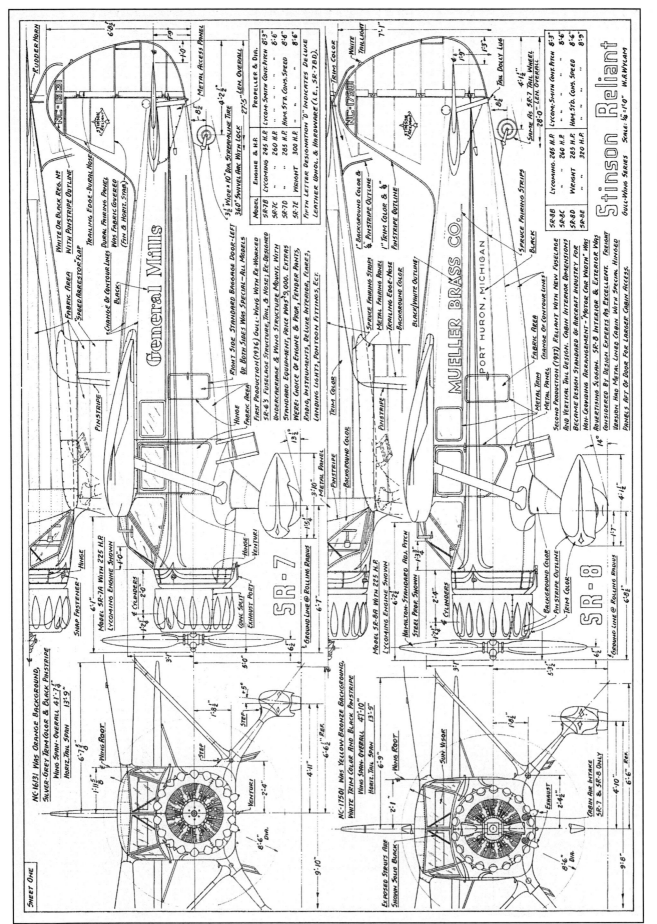

Stinson Reliant Gull-Wing Series Models 7 & 8 - Sheet One (of 10). Originally published December, 1960

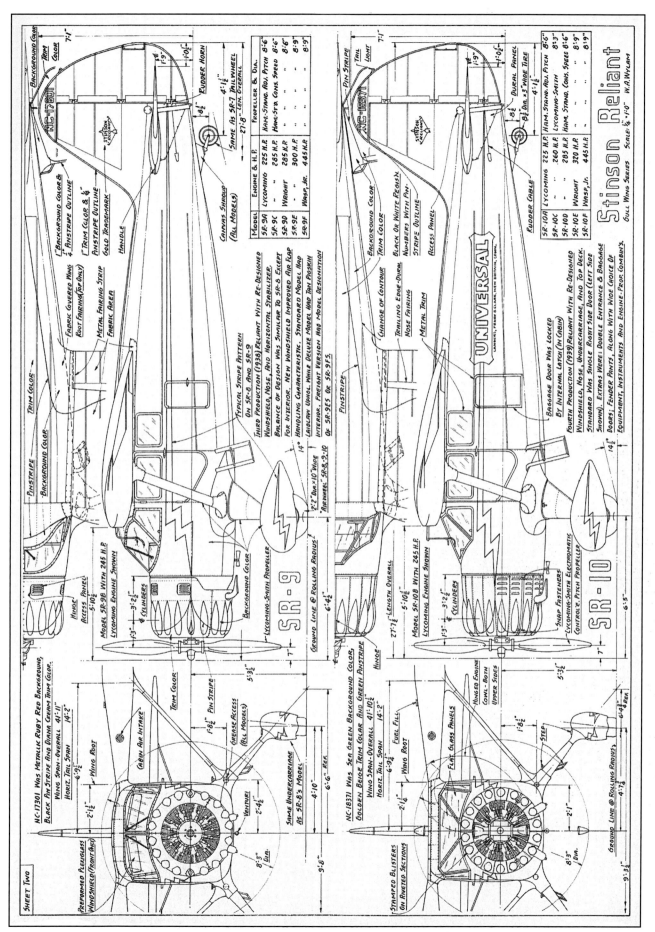

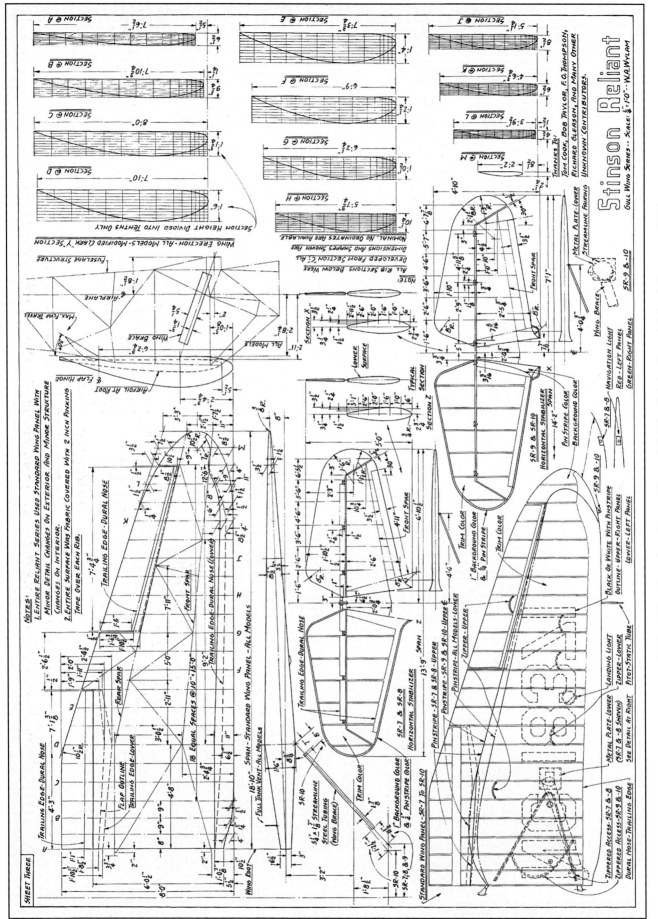

Stinson Reliant Gull-Wing Series Wing Details - Sheet Three (of 10). Originally published January, 1961

CHAPTER 29

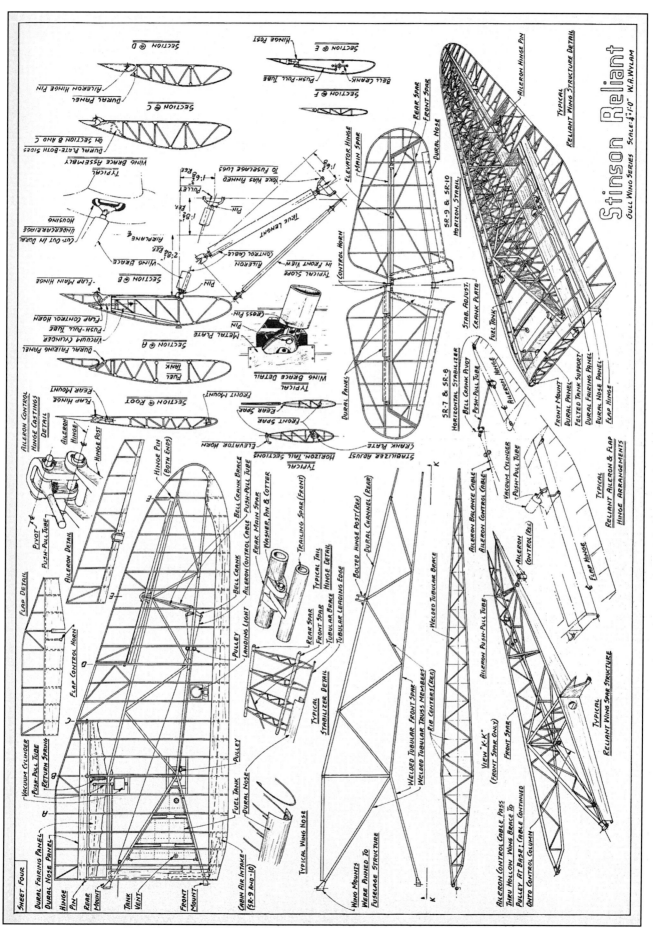

Stinson Reliant Gull-Wing Series Wing Details - Sheet Four (of 10). Originally published January, 1961

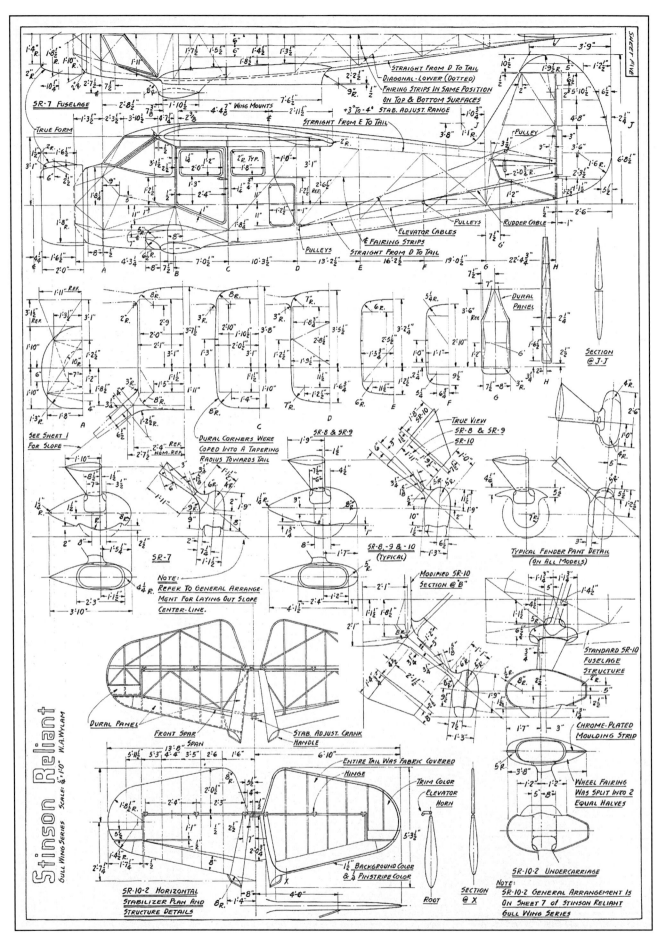

Stinson Reliant Gull-Wing Series Fuselage Details - Sheet Five (of 10). Originally published March, 1961

CHAPTER 29

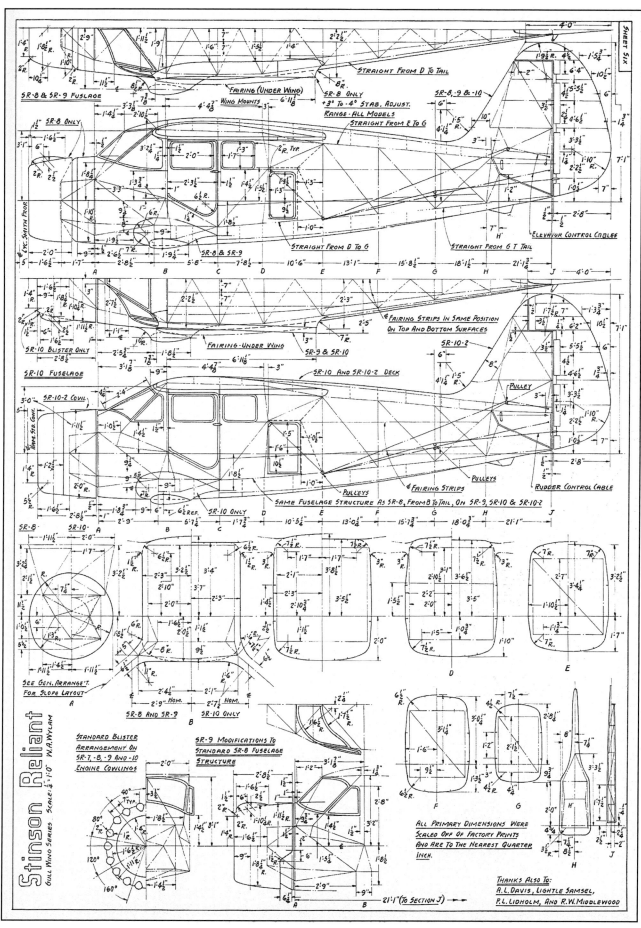

Stinson Reliant Gull-Wing Series Fuselage Details - Sheet Six (of 10). Originally published March, 1961.

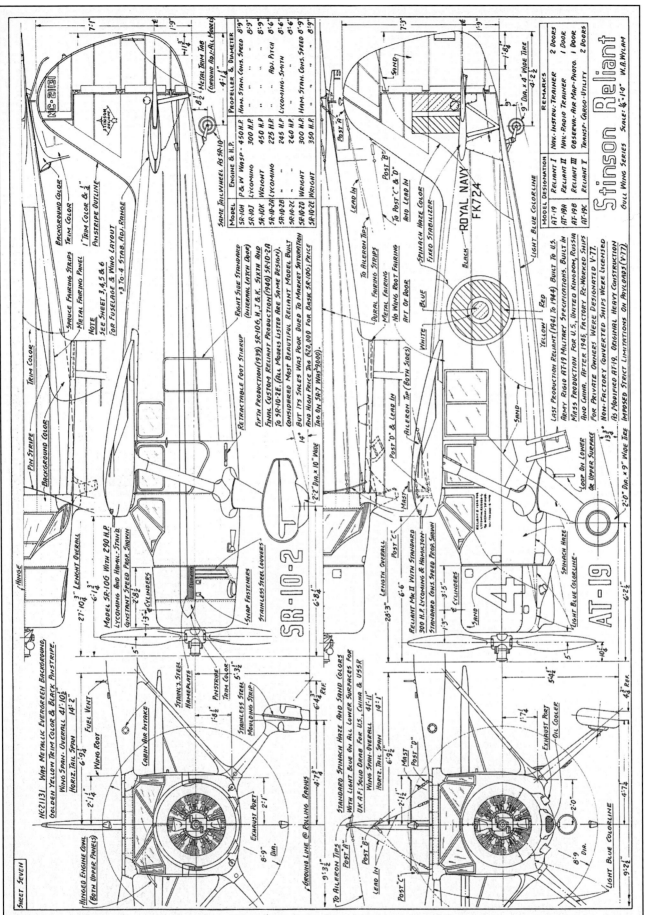

Stinson Reliant Gull-Wing Series Models SR-10-2 & AT-19 - Sheet Seven (of 10). Originally published June, 1961

CHAPTER 29

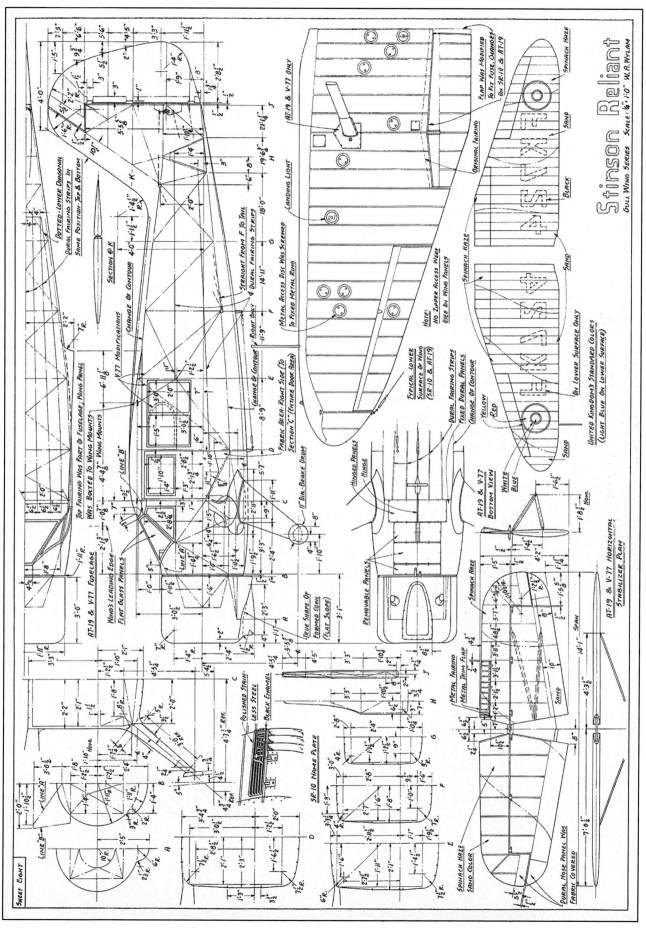

Stinson Reliant Gull-Wing Series Models At-19 & V-77 - Sheet Eight (of 10). Originally published June, 1961. Model Airplane News

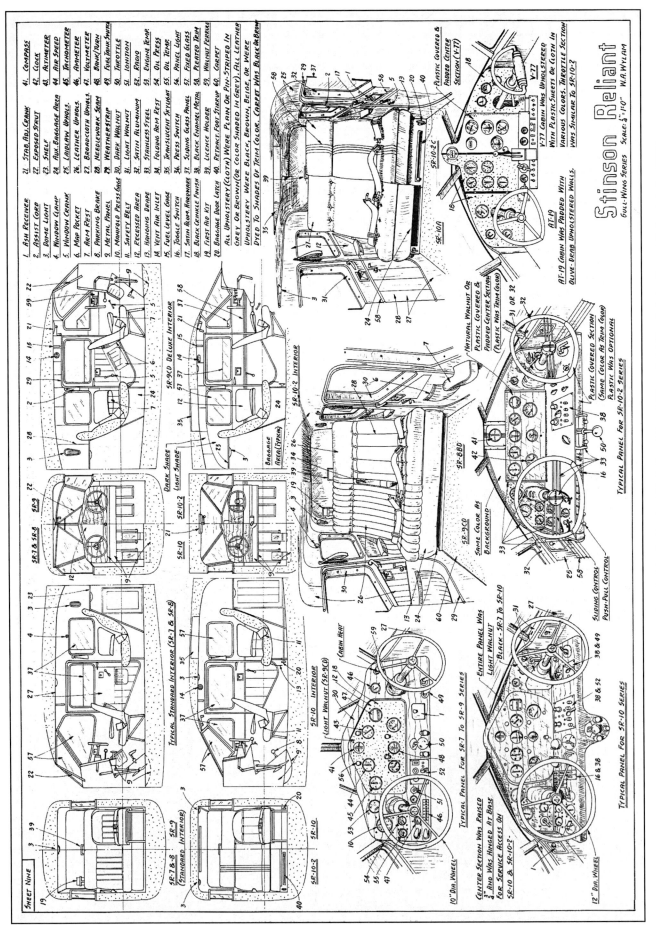

CHAPTER 29

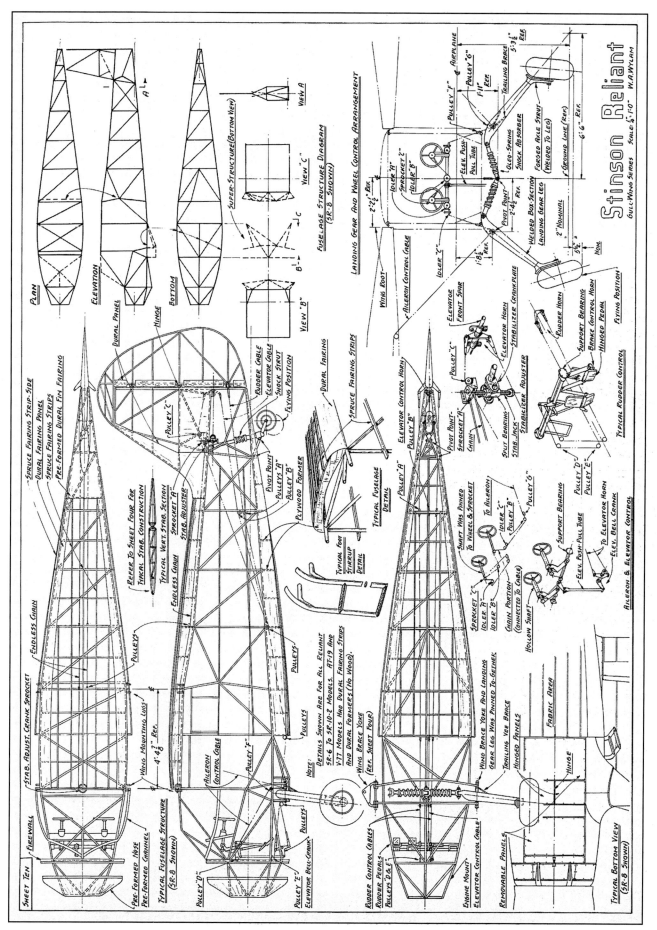

Stinson Reliant Gull-Wing Series Cabin & Control Details - Sheet Ten (of 10). Originally published July, 1961

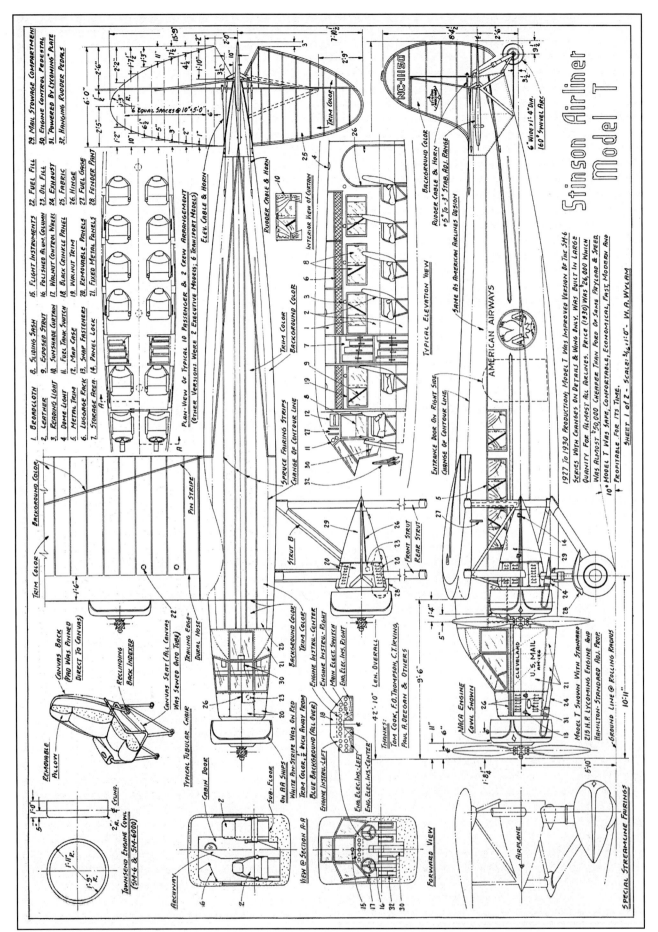

Stinson Airliner Model T - Sheet 1 of 2. Originally published October, 1961

CHAPTER 29

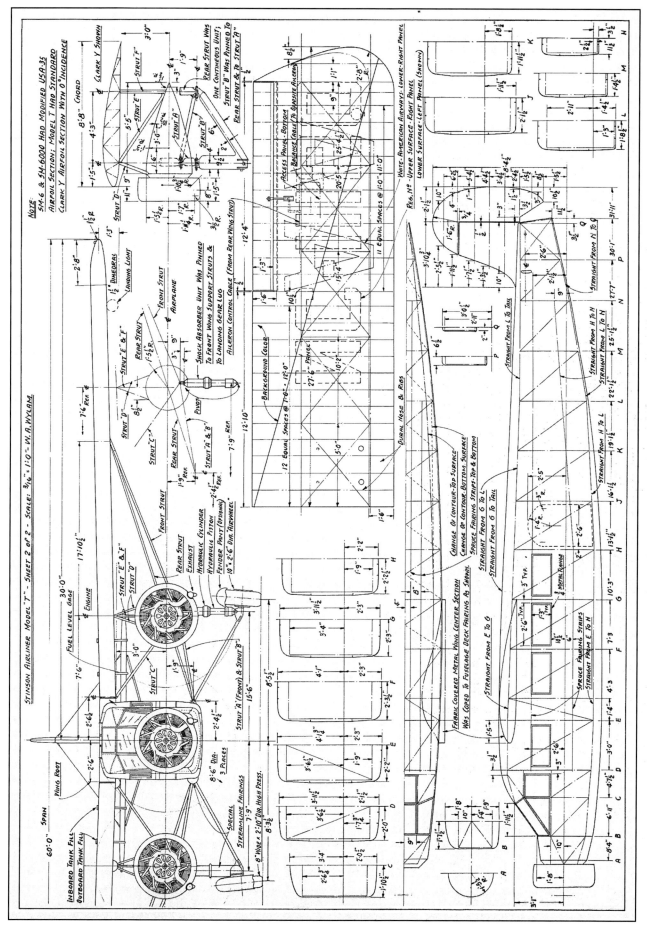

Stinson Airliner Model T - Sheet 2 of 2. Originally published October, 1961

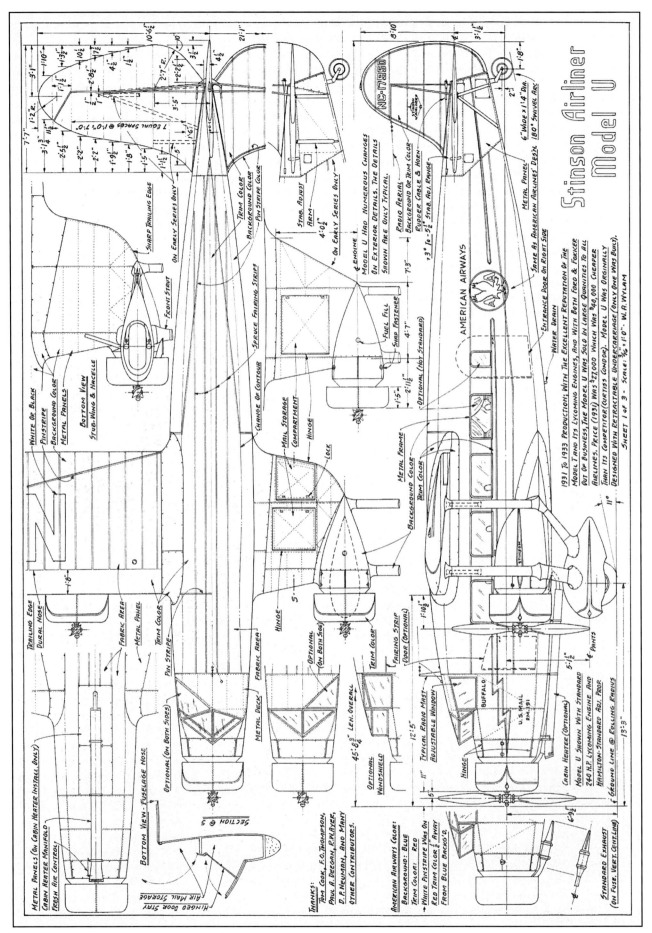

CHAPTER 29

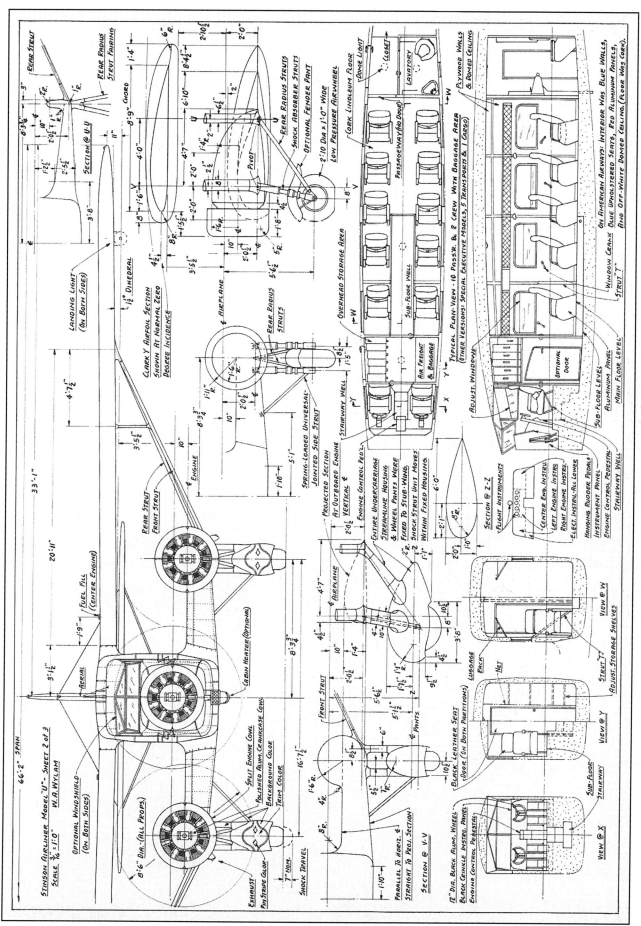

Stinson Airliner Model T - Sheet 2 of 3. Originally published December, 1961

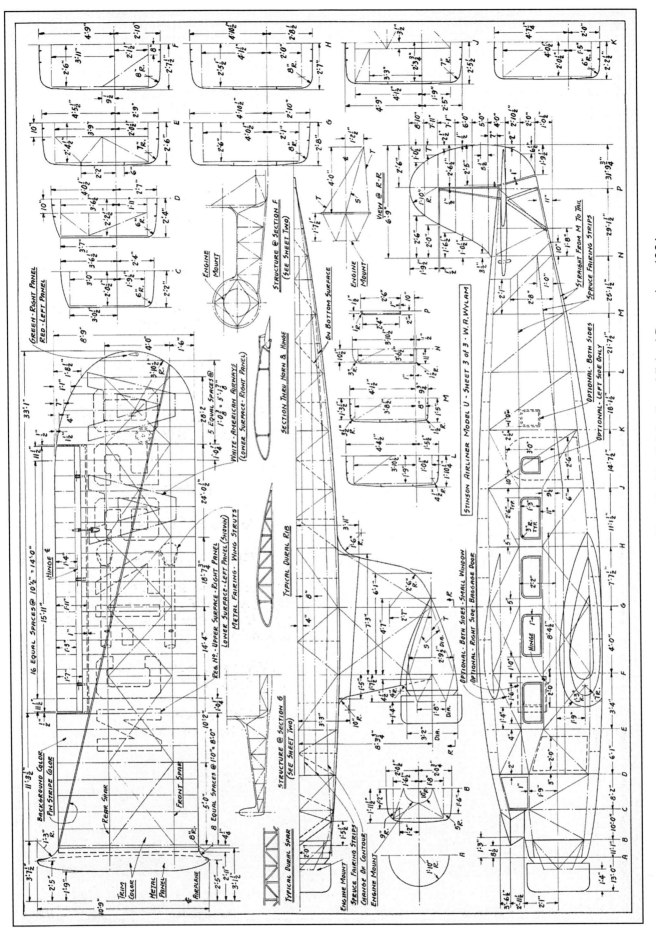

Bibliography

Books

Antique Aircraft Association: *Antique Aircraft Directory*, 1966

Bluth, John A: *Stinson Aircraft Company*
Arcadia Publishing, 2002

Department of Commerce, Aeronautics Branch: *Air commerce Regulations*, United States Government Printing Office, 1927

Department of Transportation: *Aircraft Specifications, Federal Aviation Administration, Type Certificate Data*, April 1967

Federal Aviation Agency, *United States Civil Aircraft Register*, U.S. Government Printing Office, 1964-1970

Juptner, Joseph P: *U. S. Civil Aircraft*
McGraw-Hill, Volume 1-9

Kobernuss, Fred O. : *WACO: Symbol of Courage and Excellence*, Mystic Bay Publishers, 1999

Lewis, W. David & Trimble, William F: *The Airway to Everywhere*, University of Pittsburg Press, 1988
Peek, Chet with Goodhead, George: *The Spartan Story*, Three Peeks Publishing, 1994

Matt, Paul: *Historical Aviation Album, Volume XIII*, Historical Aviation Album, 1974

Ruble, Kenneth D.: *Flight to the Top*
Viking Press, 1968

Schramm, Albert H: *My Life's Journey*
Albert H. Schramm, Publisher, 1988

Smith, Herschel: *Aircraft Piston Engines*
Sunflower University Press, 1986

Stinson Aircraft Division: *Manual of Inspection and Instruction for Stinson Reliant Model "SR-9" Airplane*, Vultee Aircraft Inc., Wayne, Michigan

Thompson, Jonathan: *Vultee Aircraft 1932-1947*
Jonathan Thompson, Publisher, 1992
John W. Underwood: *The Vantage and Veteran Aircraft Guide*, Heritage Press, 1968

Underwood, John W.: *The Stinsons*
Heritage Press, 1969

Wegg, John: *General Dynamics Aircraft and Their Predecessors*, Naval Institute Press, 1990

Wood, Derek & Dempster, Derek: *The Narrow Margin*, McGraw-Hill Book Company, 1961

Journals

American Aviation Historical Society Journal
Volume 19, Number 3: Fall 1974

American Aviation Historical Society Journal
Volume 24, Number 3: Fall 1979

American Aviation Historical Society Journal
Volume 51, Number 1: Spring 2006

Periodicals

Pilot News, Volume 10, Number 4, September 1981.
Pilot News, Volume 10, Number 9, February 1982.

A Court Case: Corman Aircraft Corporation V. Weihmiller July 3, 1935 of Appeal from the District Court of the United States of Northern District Illinois, Eastern Division.

En Route, Volume 9, Issue 1
January-March 2000

The Stinson Factory Newsletter: *"The Stinsonair"*
Courtesy of the Harry W. Smith Collection

Aerial Age
January 26, 1920

Aerial Age
April 5, 1920

Aero Digest
1934-1945

Air Progress
October-November 1963

Popular Aviation
1939-1940

Southern Flight
1940-1945

Interviews

Hammond, Jim
Stinson Restorer

Phillips, Randy
Stinson Historian

Sevier, Steve
AT-19 Historian

Shemwell, Carl
Aviation Historian

Smith, Harry W.
Stinson Employee: 1939-1948

Swick, Kelly Strait
Genealogist
Greeley, Colorado

Taylor, Robert L.
Founder, Antique Airplane Association

Index

Page number in *italics* = photo
Page number in **bold** = chart

Aircraft Development Corporation, 112
All American Aviation, 133-134, 197, 199, 197-200
Altman, Peter, 3, 9-10, 18, 39, 79, 87, 214, 216-217
American Girl, 183, 184
Approved Type Certificate (ATC), 4, 10, 14, 109, 121-136, 193
Atkinson, L. H. (Jack), 175-176, 178-179
Aviation Corporation (AVCO), 21, 40-41, 43, 49-50, 63, 88, 104, 110, 113, 116, 117, 172,
Ayer, Robert W., 39, 48, 129, 171, 216, 217
Beavers, Emma A., (see Stinson, Emma B.)
Bendix Aviation, 13, 21, 173, 214, 218
Brittin, Lewis H., 201, 201
Buffalo Evening News, 190, 190
Chicago We Will, 188, 188
City of Chicago, 188, 188-189
City of Cleveland, 187, 187-188
Cord Corporation, 11-12, 15, 35, 40-44, 50, 111, 116, 216
Cord, E. L. (Errett Lobbman), 11, 13-15, 18-23, 29, 35, 39-41, 43-44, 49-50, 63, 113, 116, 125, 129, 164, 169-172, 216
Cord Holding Company, 15, 22, 23, 35, 50, 110, 125, 216,
Consolidated Vultee, 104, 118, 136, 172-173, 191-193, 218
Corman Aircraft Corporation, 13-15
Corman Aircraft Model Designations:
    Corman 3000, 13, 13-15, 17, 19, 20, 18-22, 35, 110, 124, 125
Crozier, Major General William, 150, 160
Detroit Athletic Club, 2-3, 12
Detroit Board of Commerce, 2, 3, 163
Detroit Wayne Industrial Airport, 12, 26
Edwards, Katherine, 73, 73-75
Emmanuel, Victor, 49, 50, 171, 172, 217, 218
Fleet Air Arm, 104, 118, 136, 192, 192, 193, 193, 194, 195, 196,
Greater Rockford, 186, 186
Greyhound, vii, 1-2, 142-147, 142-149, 150, 153, 158, 161, 169
Guiberson Corporation, 203, 205-206
Gull-Wing, 62, 79, 87. 114-117, 130-134, 136, 236-245
Hall, Robert L., 39-40, 48, 72, 216-218
Houston – Billion-Dollar City, 186
Hughes, Howard, 89-93

Irvine, Jack, 39, 48-49, 54, 62, 216-217
Judy, Estelle Claire (see Stinson, Estelle)
Junkers Larson JL-6 (Junkers F.13), 2-3, 4, 147, 162, 163, 178, 216
K of New Haven (also see *Sally Sovereign*), 180, 187, 187
Kelly Jr., John C. (Jack), 13-15, 19-20, 29, 39, 171, 216, 217
Lycoming Manufacturing Company, 15, 41, 42, 43
Mara, William A. (Bill), 2-4, 9-10, 11-13, 15, 18, 22-23, 26, 29-30, 34-35, 39-40, 48-50, 79, 109, 122, 162, 163, 169, 171, 172-173, 182, 201, 216-218
Nashville plant, 88, 99, 99, 117
Naylor, William C., 3, 9-10, 12, 15, 18, 29, 216
Northfield, 3-4, 12, 23, 121, 123, 160
Northwest Airways, viii, 2, 4, 5, 46-47, 122, 201, 202
Omlie, Phoebe F., 174-179, 177, 179
Packard diesel engine, 22, 111, 203, 203-205, 125
Packard Field, 2, 162, 164, 169
Packard Motor Car Company, 22, 54, 203-205, 204, 205,
Page, Randolph Gilham (Dizzy), 10, 18, 174-179, 176, 187, 216
Pilot Radio, 10, 180, 188, 188
Reliability Tour, 156, 164, 174-179, 180, 181-182, 184, 185
Rezabek, Rick, viii, 72, 75
Rockefeller, Schroder, 49, 87
Royal Windsor, 139, 189, 189-190, 190
Sally Sovereign (also see *K of New Haven*), 10, 110, 124, 180, 187, 187
Schramm, Albert H., vii, 173, 208, 208-214, 211, 217, 218
Selective-Guide, 50, 129, 130
Sir John Carling, 189, 189-190, 190
Skinner, Lloyd, 39, 48, 54, 216-217
Stinson Aircraft Corporation, 3, 10, 12, 15, 21, 23, 26, 29-30, 35-36, 41, 43, 49, 55, 58, 79, 109, 111, 116, 148, 164, 170-171, 173, 203, 216
Stinson Aircraft Model Designations:
    Model A, 44, 48-49, 54, 55, 56, 57, 58, 59, 54-58, 62, 71, 78, 113-15, 129, 130, 137, 138, 171, 173, 217
    Model R, 30, 34, 34-35, 36, 38, 39, 44, 112, 113, 126-127, 164, 171, 208-209, 211, 212, 215,
    Model S, viii, 30, 32, 35, 39, 44, 47, 111-112, 122, 126, 171, 209

Model SB-1 Detroiter, 4, *5*, *6*, *8*, 109, 111, 121-122, 126, 171, 174, 178-179, *190*, *201*, 201, *202*
Model SM-2 Junior, 10, *11*, *12*, 12, 21, *27*, 30, *47*, 110-112, 123-126, 174, *176*, 178, 179,
Model SM-6000, 18, 19, 21, 22, 22-23, 25, 29-30, 32, 33, 35, 111, 124, 125-126, 127
Model U, 35, 40, 41, 44, 48, 111-112, 127
Model V-77 (AT-19), 101, 103, 103-104, 118-120, 136, 172, 191-196, 193, **192**, **193**, **195**, **196**, 243
Model 74 (O-49 Vigilante), 79, 87-88, 99, 117, 120
Model 105, 87, 100, 100-102, 116, 117, 135, 208
Stinson Jr., Edward Anderson (Edward, Eddie), vii, 2-5, 5, 12, 14-15, 23, 26, 29-30, 34, 34-35, 36, 89-90, 109, 112, 142, 144, 144-148, 150, 150, 153-154, 156, 156, 156-164, 158, 159, 161, 163, 165, 167-169, 171-173, 174, 174-176, 178-179, 181, 183-185, 185, 187, 187, 189, 201, 216
Stinson Sr., Edward Anderson, 156, 161
Stinson, Emma B. (Emma A. Beavers), 143-144, 147, 149, 156
Stinson, Estelle (Estelle Judy, Stella), vii, viii, 1, 18, 35, 39, 73, 144, 160, 161, 163, 164, 165, 167, 169, 165-173, 173, 174-179, 179, 185, 216-218
Stinson, Jack, 1, 142-143, 147, 147-148, 150, 152, 155, 156, 158, 164
Stinson, Katherine, 142, 142-144, 150, 151, 152, 151-152, 153, 155, 156-160, 184
Stinson, Marjorie, 143, 150-152, 152, 156-158
Stinson, Stella, (see Stinson, Estelle)
The Bug, 153, 155
The Endeavor, 185
The Green Mountain Boy, 189
The Humming Bird, 150, 154-155, 155
The Stinson Detroiter, 185, 189
Vultee Aircraft Division, 172, 217-218
Vultee Aircraft, Inc., 88, 99, 104, 112-115, 117-118
Vultee, Gerald F. (Jerry), 43, 50, 79, 112
Vultee monoplane, 43, 49
Warner Scarab, 10, 12, 110, 123, 174, 179
Wylam, W. A., vii, 219

Cover Captions and Credits

Front cover: A 1935 Stinson SR-5E owned by David Jackson, NC14585, s/n 9322-A, originally powered by a 225-hp Lycoming R-680-4 engine, now fitted with a 300-hp Lycoming. See notes at bottom of page ii. Photo courtesy The Sparky Barnes Collection.

Back cover: First row, left to right: Detail of a watercolor by Jerome Biederman featuring a 1927 Stinson SM-1 Detroiter 6PCLM powered by a 220-hp Wright J-5C engine. See Chapter 2. The Steven P. Bogdan Collection.

Promotional collector card featuring the 1939 Stinson SR-10K NC21147 of the New York Police Department. In 1940 the promotional cards were in packs of Wings Cigarettes from the Brown and Williamson Tobacco corporation. See Chapter 13. The Steven P. Bogdan Collection.

The NC21147 today with Canadian registration C-FFBB. See page 96. The Mike Ody Collection, photo by George Trusssell.

Second row, left to right: Period postcard of 1937 Stinson SR-9E Reliant with Canadian registration CF-OAZ, s/n 5258. Still in service. The Able Collection.

1931 Stinson Junior S NC443G, s/n 8069 in Northwest Airways livery. See pages 46 and 47. The John C. Swick Collection.

1937 Stinson SR-9C NC18407, s/n 5313. Still in service. The Able Collection.

Third row, left to right: Detail of painting presented to Northwest Airlines, Inc. by the Pittsburgh Institute of Aeronautics. See bottom photo on page 5. Northwest Airlines History Center Collection.

1936 Vultee V-1AD Special, NC16099, s/n 25. See page 49. The John C. Swick Collection.

Detail from painting of an All-American Aviation Stinson SR-10C preparing to hook a mailbag. See Chapter 24. The Steven P. Bogdan Collection.

Fourth row, left to right: 1935 advertisement featuring the new Stinson Model A. See Chapter 9. The Steven P. Bogdan Collection.

Stinson Aircraft Corporation insignia donated by Miss Katherine M. Smart to the National Air and Space Museum Collection.

A 1929 Berryloid advertisement featuring a Stinson SM Detroiter painted to resemble a Redstart bird. The Steven P. Bogdan Collection.

Fifth row, left to right: A 1934 chewing gum trading card from the National Chicle Company Sky Birds Series, featuring the late Eddie Stinson. Although depicted in a fighter plane, Eddie never got the chance to attend machine gun school. See Chapter 18. The Steven P. Bogdan Collection.

A Berry Brothers Berryloid paint chip chart with Stinson Green in the left column. The Steven P. Bogdan Collection.

Stinson factory brochure detailing approved outdoor displays for retail Stinson dealers. Detroit Historical Society Collection.